The Judgment of Love

DISTINGUISHED DISSERTATIONS
IN CHRISTIAN THEOLOGY

Series Foreword

We are living in a vibrant season for academic Christian theology. After a hiatus of some decades, a real flowering of excellent systematic and moral theology has emerged. This situation calls for a series that showcases the contributions of newcomers to this ongoing and lively conversation. The journal *Word & World: Theology for Christian Ministry* and the academic society Christian Theological Research Fellowship (CTRF) are happy to cosponsor this series together with our publisher Pickwick Publications (an imprint of Wipf and Stock Publishers). Both the CTRF and *Word & World* are interested in excellence in academics but also in scholarship oriented toward Christ and the Church. The volumes in this series are distinguished for their combination of academic excellence with sensitivity to the primary context of Christian learning. We are happy to present the work of these young scholars to the wider world and are grateful to Luther Seminary for the support that helped make it possible.

Alan G. Padgett
Professor of Systematic Theology
Luther Seminary

Beth Felker Jones
Assistant Professor of Theology
Wheaton College

www.ctrf.info
www.luthersem.edu/word&world

The Judgment of Love

An Investigation of Salvific Judgment in Christian Eschatology

JAMES M. MATARAZZO JR.

◆PICKWICK *Publications* · Eugene, Oregon

THE JUDGMENT OF LOVE
An Investigation of Salvific Judgment in Christian Eschatology

Distinguished Dissertations in Christian Theology 15

Copyright © 2018 James M. Matarazzo, Jr. All rights reserved. Except for brief quotations in critical publications or reviews, no part of this book may be reproduced in any manner without prior written permission from the publisher. Write: Permissions, Wipf and Stock Publishers, 199 W. 8th Ave., Suite 3, Eugene, OR 97401.

Pickwick Publications
An Imprint of Wipf and Stock Publishers
199 W. 8th Ave., Suite 3
Eugene, OR 97401

www.wipfandstock.com

PAPERBACK ISBN: 978-1-5326-4462-7
HARDCOVER ISBN: 978-1-5326-4463-4
EBOOK ISBN: 978-1-5326-4464-1

Cataloguing-in-Publication data:

Names: Matarazzo, James M., Jr. (1968–), author. | Jackelén, Antje, foreword writer
Title: The judgment of love : an investigation of salvific judgment in Christian eschatology / James M. Matarazzo, Jr. ; foreword by Archbishop Antje Jackelén.
Description: Eugene, OR : Pickwick Publications, 2018 | Series: Distinguished Dissertations in Christian Theology 15 | Includes bibliographical references.
Identifiers: ISBN 978-1-5326-4462-7 (paperback) | ISBN 978-1-5326-4463-4 (hardcover) | ISBN 978-1-5326-4464-1 (ebook)
Subjects: LCSH: Universalism. | Judgment of God. | Salvation—Christianity. | Salvation after death. | Hell—Christianity.
Classification: LCC BX9941.3 M17 2018 (print) | LCC BX9941.3 (ebook)

Manufactured in the U.S.A.

In memory of my father
Dr. James M. Matarazzo (1941–2018)
A Dean, a Professor, and a well-loved Man
αἰωνία ἡ μνήμη

Contents

Foreword by Archbishop Antje Jackelén ix

Preface xi

Acknowledgments xviii

Abbreviations xxi

1. Introduction 1
    1. Eschatology as an Exercise of Hope 7
    2. The Task 12
    3. The Methodological Approach 12
    4. Argument for Disposition and Exclusions 14
2. The Symbols and Problems of Judgment 17
    1. Introduction 17
    2. The Symbol and Problem of Death 18
    3. Discarnation: The Problem of Intermediate Eschatology 52
    4. Pessimistic Eschatology and the Problem of Hell 89
    5. Conclusion 139
3. The Larger Hope: Divine Judgment in Optimistic Soteriology 142
    1. Introduction 142
    2. Sergei Bulgakov: The Judgment of Love 143
    3. Hans Urs von Balthasar: The Judgment of Hope 155
    4. John A. T. Robinson: Defending the Doctrine of God 172
    5. Marilyn McCord Adams: Horrors and Therapeutic Eschatology 185
    6. Conclusion 199

4. The Purpose of Divine Judgment 203
   1. Introduction 203
   2. Judgment's Purpose as Dualistically Retributive 205
   3. Judgment's Purpose as Salvific Retribution: Sergei Bulgakov 209
   4. Judgment's Purpose as Non-retributive and Rectifying: Jürgen Moltmann 220
   5. Judgment's Purpose as the Transformation and Constitution of Personhood: Markus Mühling 229
   6. Conclusion 236
5. Towards a Christian Eschatology of Absolute Recognition 238
   1. Absolute Recognition: Eschatic Recognition Theory 239
   2. The Problem of Eschatic Libertarian Free Will 251
   3. Christ as the Recognizer of Human Beings: The Christological Dilemma 261
   4. The (Im)Possibility of Eschatic Non-Recognition 266
   5. *Semper Novum*: The Outcome of the Judgment of Absolute Recognition 268
   6. Conclusion: *Ut sit Deus omnia in omnibus* 281
6. Conclusion 285

Bibliography 295

Foreword

ABOUT TWO DECADES AGO, when I was doing research on time and eternity from a science-and-theology perspective, I had the opportunity of discussing eschatology with two distinguished scholars in religion and science. One of them said something like: "Why would you deal with eschatology? There is nothing we can say about it." The other one referred to one of his books: "Read chapter 9. It's all there." These two responses represent fairly well the two major challenges that a book on eschatology has to face: On the one hand, eschatological thought requires a fair amount of agnosticism; no one can know the future for sure. In that sense, there is indeed very little we can say. On the other hand, eschatological claims are a reality. They influence strategies and actions of individuals and communities. Hence, they have both political and existential consequences, which makes the call for critical analysis in theological thought and writing ever so urgent.

From an existential point of view, eschatology actualizes the question "what may we hope for?" It is precisely the question we find at the bottom of the major challenges of our time. Whether we are talking about the greatest meta-narrative humankind may ever have been exposed to, climate change, or about migration or artificial intelligence, sooner or later we will have to face the question of hope. This also applies to the four dangerous "P"s of our time: polarization, populism, protectionism, and post-truth: in their own particular ways, all four are an expression of a lack of hope.

Thus, the need for theological work on eschatology stands clear. And yet, it takes courage to delve into its intricacies. The necessity of accommodating both the apophatic and the kataphatic aspects of eschatology always entails the risk of being accused of mere speculation.

The author of this book has taken this risk and embarked on a journey that has rendered a novel contribution to this field of study. The pivotal argument is that God's judgment and justice are issuant from God's love and therefore are salvific. Accordingly, judgment is not denunciatory. Rather, it is the eschatological event of absolute recognition: the absolute recognition of human beings by God in Jesus Christ who is described as the eschatic judge.

With death understood as the moment of salvific judgment and concepts of the intermediate state following death as well as hell revisited, the author is convinced that Christian theology is above all an exercise of hope for the future of creation. He acknowledges that dualistic soteriology is and has been a powerful strand in Christian tradition. Nevertheless, Matarazzo sees good reasons to reject this strand, since this dualism destroys the coherence of the doctrine of God as omnibenevolent, as well as the ontological ascription of God as that of love itself.

At the end of the book, and maybe even at the end of the day, what may stay with the reader is the desire to hold on to the enticing tune of *iudicandus est salvandus*. On the one hand, this is a reassuring equation, capable of inspiring boldness in trust and hope. On the other hand, the grammatical form of Latin gerundive always is slightly unsettling, pointing us to that which is not yet achieved and beneficially reminding us of our relational dependence. Taken together, this makes for an encouraging reading of the eschatological tension between the "already" and the "not yet." It certainly is a tune worth exploring: *iudicandus est salvandus*!

The Most Reverend Dr. Antje Jackelén
Archbishop of Uppsala, Church of Sweden

Preface

This book offers a constructive exploration of divine judgment as salvific rather than destructive which I describe aphoristically as *iudicandus est salvandus* ("to be judged is to be saved"). My provocation to Christian eschatology is that human beings are not saved *from* judgment, but are saved *within* it. I thus propose a reversal of an Augustinian predestination which understands the majority of humanity as non-elect and thus *massa damnata*. While this inheritance has been reformulated and challenged, its theological legacy remains palpable. My proposed reversal is to deem humanity universally as a *massa amata*, the object of divine love. I therefore argue against salvific dualism on the grounds that it severely damages the coherence of the doctrine of God and eternalizes evil in the eschatic realm.

In chapter 1, I introduce the context of the study, the problems of divine judgment, and the concept of salvific judgment as solution. My proposal that divine judgment is salvific and creative does not yield to the traditional understanding of universal salvation. Rather, I argue that no human being is "lost" but that the post-eschatic constituted person is by no means a glorified version of the *same* individual as instantiated on earth. The creative judgment yields both continuity and discontinuity as far as earthly human lives and *excludes* sameness. We are not now what we shall be.

In chapter 2, I engage in an exploration of the symbols and problems of judgment through a reappraisal of *De novissimis* ("concerning the last things"), the last section found in traditional works of dogmatics, by exploring death, the discarnate intermediate state, and hell.

Death—Human beings are mortal and Heidegger's assertion that "as soon as man comes to life, he is at once old enough to die" (i.e.,

Sein-zum-Tode) is self-evident. However, in atheist existentialist terms, death is absurd and it is an absurdity without solution. Protestant neo-orthodox existentialism counsels a stoic hope in the face of death, but offers no remedy to human depersonalization that is part of death. I argue that the solution to personal dissolution in death is trust—trust that God will preserve our created personhood. In other words, human beings die *in Deo*—and it is "in God" that we are preserved from oblivion. I do not argue for *anima separata*, nor do I argue for a variant of Eberhard Jüngel's *Ganztodtheorie*. The dead are no longer beings-in-time, but are eschatic. Thus, the moment of death is the moment of eschaton. In this sense, *Ganztodtheorie* is refuted without denying death's radical finality as it relates to earthly existence. Death itself is therefore a state of *eschatic being*, even if the process of dying is a process of dissolution that separates human beings from earthly existence and relationships.

The Discarnate Intermediate State—I argue against an intermediate state whether in the form of purgatory or the less formally defined intermediacy in Eastern Orthodoxy and among certain Protestant theologians. Since I do not hold to the scholastic concept of *anima separata*, I argue that the intermediate state is a purgative, atemporal, and eschatic event *within* the divine judgment. In this sense, all human beings "go to purgatory" for "we must all appear before the judgment seat of Christ" (2 Cor 5:10). There is thus no intermediate or purgatorial *state* apart from divine judgment.

Hell—The doctrine of hell is the most problematic symbol of judgment. The very concept that human sin—which is finite, no matter its gravity—is deserving of infinite punishment makes the traditional understanding of hell a problem of evil with God as the author. For example, William Lane Craig defends the traditional doctrine in the form of transworld damnation. Craig argues that in an infinite number of possible worlds that God could create, there are persons who will always reject Christ. Thus, an eternal hell is compatible with a loving God who desires the salvation of all. However, this example illustrates the extraordinary lengths required to square the consignment of persons to everlasting torment by a God who is omniscient, omnipotent, and omnibenevolent. I argue that this and all arguments that seek to defend the doctrine of God as amenable to everlasting punishment fail. Thus, hell must be redefined, but not discarded. The symbol of hell is part of the Christian tradition. It is also part of human experience on earth in the form of horrendous evils. I provocatively redefine hell not as punishment or damnation, but rather as a *post mortem* eschatic experience issuant from the love of God in which all that is non-love in persons and humanity as a whole is purged.

In chapter 3, I critically engage with the soteriological optimism posited by four twentieth- and twenty-first-century theologians: Sergei Bulgakov, Hans Urs von Balthasar, J. A. T. Robinson, and Marilyn McCord Adams. While these theologians do not define divine judgment itself as salvific, I argue that their investigations in soteriology and eschatology lead to this ultimate conclusion.

Sergei Bulgakov develops an eschatology that demands universal salvation. Human salvation occurs *within* the judgment at the eschaton and the judgment is one of divine love. I argue that Bulgakov implicitly accepts the concept of salvific judgment, but that his eschatology fails to take appropriate account of the horrors of human history and the problem of human free will in his overall universalist scheme.

Hans Urs von Balthasar embraces a hopeful soteriology, but I argue that Balthasar fails to deal adequately with divine judgment in terms of a dual outcome of salvation and damnation. For Balthasar, damnation is a problem of evil (with God as perpetrator), but he never follows through on this dilemma and simply recommends that one should hope that all are saved and remain agnostic about damnation.

J. A. T. Robinson overtly advocates for universal salvation in his early work *In the End God*. He arrives at this position through a defense of the doctrine of God, dialoguing with Emil Brunner and Thomas Aquinas and asserting his universalist project in biblical terms, giving overriding weight to those passages that support his hypothesis. Robinson fails, however, to square the place of judgment with salvation. He simply writes that judgment "can never be God's last word, because if it were, it would be the word that would speak his failure." Thus, divine judgment for Robinson is one of love, but it is separated from salvation and rendered into a sort of pre-salvific stocktake of human responsibility for sin. Therefore, for Robinson, human beings are saved *from* the judgment rather than within it. Robinson, like Bulgakov, also fails to deal with the problem of human free will and its possible resistance to God's salvific will.

Marilyn McCord Adam's eschatology is set within her christological project that engages the problem of evil. Adams specifically denies that God as creator has any obligations to creatures, thus there is no theodicy involved with a God who by creating a vulnerable, material universe is the ultimate cause of earthly evil. Adams embraces universal salvation, however her reasoning for it is unique. For Adams, the horrendous evils of human this-worldly existence mean that human freedom and human responsibility are attenuated. "Salvation" is, in effect, divine contrition: God who has allowed material evils will latterly grant human beings, by way of compensation, fully meaningful existence in the eschaton. While I find Adams' idea that human beings on earth are not truly free compelling, her universalist scheme does not explain why eschatically healed human beings would uniformly desire reconciliation with God. I argue that in this Adam's fails not because of her universalism, but because she does not deal with the eschatic transformation of the human will.

In chapter 4, I explore the four versions of the purpose of judgment: (1) as retributive with a dual outcome, engaging the works of Matthias Scheeben and Paul O'Callaghan; (2) as retributive and universalist, in conversation with Sergei Bulgakov; (3) as non-retributive, rectifying, and universalist, exploring the oeuvre of Jürgen Moltmann; and (4), as non-retributive, constitutive of personhood; and quasi-universalist, investigating the eschatological thought of Markus Mühling.

In view of my thesis that divine judgment is the judgment of divine love and is salvific, I reject the retributive judgment with a dual outcome as represented by Scheeben and O'Callaghan as well as the idea that God's offer of mercy ends at death. This stance would seem to contradict God's ontic love and Christ's victory over evil. God would not be "all in all" if there is a place of eternal torment in the eschatic reality.

Bulgakov's concept of judgment is ultimately salvific and is grounded in God's love, although the hellish fire of this love in its wrath against sin that effects an intrapersonal separation, splitting the sinful element away and destroying it, contains a seemingly barbarous element of metaphysical amputation. The other aspect that seems at odds with the synergistic system that Bulgakov advocates is that, in the end, God's grace is irresistible. Human will, though free, conforms to that of Christ's *ex opere operato*. The demands of Bulgakov's sophiology and its unstoppable divinization of the cosmos trump questions of whether human beings are forced to accede to God's love or rather are set free to do so.

Moltmann's approach is to insist on a gracious universalism that heals the victims of evil and transforms the evildoers into saints. Demands for recompense or justice are rejected as functionally idolatrous because human justice is never the equivalent of divine justice. Moltmann cannot allow for an eschatic judgment where any human will would resist divine reconciliation. The justifying judgment will rectify the 'bound' human will, freeing it from its earthly bondage. This does mean that Moltmann's universalism is achieved through irresistible grace, but this is not problematic. Moltmann denies that human beings are masters of their own destinies. God alone is Lord of human destiny. However, if God desires relationality with human beings and that relationality is based on love, must it not be freely given by the creature to the Creator? For Moltmann, human beings are meant to be freely loving, but this is not realizable on earth. The eschatic judgment is the event that instantiates this love in freedom by divine fiat.

Mühling tries to resolve the apparent conflict between grace and freedom that is passed over by Moltmann. Those who are judged will also be self-judges. By the illumination of the Spirit, human beings in the judgment will be compelled by the truth set before them. They will not only accept any divine verdict, but will plead that the "sentence" be carried out upon them. Instead of irresistible grace, Mühling posits irresistible truth. However, will the eschatically constituted person, regardless of aesthetic differences, freely love the God who has re-created them? Mühling would answer yes because it is only in the eschaton that human beings attain the fullness of personhood which entails an orthonomous agency that is freely loving.

In chapter 5, I propose that divine judgment is the event of absolute recognition: the event of absolute recognition of God, the self, and the other. It is this recognition, which may be harrowing, that initiates the process of transformation and glorification. This event is not bound by earthly timespace or locality. The outcome of absolute recognition would not be a verdict on persons, but on their earthly identity claims (taking a page from Markus Mühling). Not all identity claims will endure the judgment. It can thus be presumed that there is a universal discontinuity between the earthly person and the eschatic person constituted by the judgment. The eschatic person will be changed and only that which was loving will be "saved" while all non-loving identity claims will be rejected and destroyed. Thus, there is both continuity and discontinuity between earthly and eschatic instantiations. This renders traditional ideas about universal salvation false, but maintains that no person is ever totally lost in the life to come.

I address the issue of human free will, but I reject the idea that human libertarian free will as experienced on earth (and thus is a "bound" will) is not transformed at the judgment. Rather, I propose that the divine judgment is an event of the creation and constitution of the fullness of human personhood, inclusive of a human will that accords with the eschatic reality as totally good. The human will only becomes truly free in and through divine judgment.

I investigate the issue of christology in terms of the requirements of absolute recognition of the Judge who is Jesus Christ. My argument is that the recognition of Christ as the God-Human who alone can judge human beings takes precedence over earthly claims about the nature of Jesus Christ. In this recognition, Christ is revealed as the incarnation of the Son of God in Jesus of Nazareth, but this revelation has no punitive or triumphal import. I reject the idea that eschatic indifference could result in non-recognition, which would be a type of hell, as this allows for an eschatic dual outcome. However, I do retain "hell" within the context of judgment. "Hell" is not a place, but *a process*. It is the stripping away of all that is non-loving. The outcome of this purgation is not known for any one person or humanity as a whole, but we can *trust* that whatever it is, it will be entirely good.

The problems with earthly and anthropomorphic ideas of eternal life ("heaven") are explored. The idea of "heaven" as some sort of perfected, earth-like paradise with immortal denizens is rejected as a "bad infinity." Rather, I propose that the new creation of the eschaton is not the Last Thing, but the New Thing that comprises the *semper novum* of eschatic novelty that allows for an infinite and creative participation in God's goodness. Eschatic boredom, which would also be hell, is avoided.

Within the concept of *semper novum*, I explore the concept of Boethius that eternal life is the possession of simultaneous, unlimited life. This led to a discussion of the problem of the "timing" of the judgment. I recover and affirm Gisbert Greshake's idea of immediate resurrection-in-death. Thus, the eschaton happens *in hora mortis* for every person and all of humanity in a divine timespace that is not bound by linearity. I also explore what the implications of this type of eschatology means for the communion of saints. I suggest that there is a connection (communion) between those in earthly timespace and eternal life, but this connection is, as Karl Rahner asserts, based in faith, hope, and love.

In chapter 6, I conclude this book by arguing that divine judgment is the judgment of love: salvific, non-dualistic, in which nothing is lost except that which is non-love. The process of judgment is the event of absolute recognition where everything is revealed, the chaff is burned away, the will is freed, and that which remains is glorified and experiences the *semper novum* of the realm of God to which no limits can be ascribed. We may therefore approach this judgment with faith, hope, and love—not only for ourselves, but for the whole human race, past, present, and future, and humanity's interrelationship with God's creative and reconciling project.

Acknowledgements

THE INSPIRATION FOR THIS book came from my field work in the international development sector on faith-based responses to the HIV pandemic; in particular, work done with Christian Aid, London, and INERELA+ (the International Network of Religious Leaders Living with or Affected by HIV and AIDS). The aim of this work was to enable religious communities in developing countries to use their ample resources to respond to the pandemic with evidence-based approaches to counteract stigma and discrimination and to promote prevention, treatment, and empowerment for affected persons. The chief obstacle for this work across the spectrum of faiths was one of stigma for persons living with HIV. Many religious leaders and communities approached the HIV pandemic with an attitude that accorded with the Pauline dictum "the wages of sin is death" (cf. Rom 6:23). This association with HIV disease and divine judgment led me to reflect on eschatology and eventually to pursue doctoral studies.

    I opted to undertake doctoral work and write a dissertation on the subject of salvific judgment. I needed to find an academic willing to take on my project. I found this in Werner G. Jeanrond whom I first met at the University of Glasgow. Soon after matriculating at Glasgow, I followed him to Oxford when he was appointed Master of St Benet's Hall. As a doctoral supervisor, he has, with extraordinary patience, enabled me to give shape to my topic in ways I could not have imagined. His theological commitments have been deeply formative—"Don't argue denominationally, argue theologically"—and this stance is witnessed throughout this book. I am deeply grateful to him for his superb counsel, mentoring, and strong belief in the value of my doctoral dissertation which has become this book.

I thank my college advisor, Brian Klug. He has been my academic pastor and confidant since I arrived at Oxford. Our many conversations over meals, wine, or coffee have been feasts for my intellectual soul. I have been engaged with Judaism as a Christian outsider since my youth and this gave our conversations an inner depth that would not be possible otherwise. I am grateful for his wisdom, friendship, and, above all, his *mentshhayt*.

Special thanks are due to my examiners at my doctoral defense: Philip Kennedy (Campion Hall, Oxford) and Antje Jackelén (Archbishop of Uppsala, Sweden). I am grateful to Gillian Paterson, who introduced me to Werner G. Jeanrond, and to Julie Clague, my onetime co-supervisor during my brief time in Glasgow. I also thank Richard R. Crocker and Roger Feldman whose counsel I always value.

I am grateful to my peer reviewers: Ulrich Schmiedel, Panayiotis Christoforou, Martin Ritchie, and Sarah Lane Ritchie. They worked through my dissertation with precision, providing invaluable edits, comments, and queries. It has been essential to have their insights. I also thank my proof-reader, Philippa Nuttall, whose eagle-eyed editing provided the crucial final review to ensure my dissertation was fit for submission.

I also thank Ulrich Schmiedel (once again) and Rens Krijgsman, friends and former housemates in Oxford, for accompanying me along the way to the completion of my dissertation. Without their jolly company, my experience as a doctoral student at Oxford would have been much diminished. Other friends within the academy who made my experience all the richer include Justin S. E. Smith, Lee Johnston, Samuel Shearn, Marijn de Jong, and Elmarie van Heerden.

I am also grateful to St Benet's Hall, a place of growth and transformation within the University of Oxford. St Benet's enabled me to be part of an extraordinarily close college community that greatly enriched my university experience . In addition, I express my gratitude to Hertford College, especially the chapel community and choir, for providing me with a second home at Oxford as an associate chaplain. I warmly thank Mia Smith, the current chaplain, and Gareth Hughes, the former chaplain, for their support and friendship.

I thank Trinity College, University of Glasgow, as well as to the several Oxford foundations and the St Luke's College Foundation that provided research funding.

Lastly, I thank my mother, Alice M. Matarazzo, for her unfailing love, encouragement, and support for this project. This book is dedicated to the memory of my father, James M. Matarazzo, Sr. (1941–2018), one-time Dean and Professor of the School of Library and Information Science, Simmons College, Boston. From my parents, I learned what it means to be a scholar and a Christian. Indeed, their values and *praxis pietatis* inform this entire book.

Oxford, June 2018
James M. Matarazzo, Jr.

Abbreviations

AV	*Authorised (King James) Version of the Holy Bible.* London: 1611.
CCC	*Catechism of the Catholic Church.* London: Geoffrey Chapman, 1994.
CH	Marilyn McCord Adams, *Christ and Horrors: The Coherence of Christology.* Cambridge: Cambridge University Press, 2007.
DS	Heinrich Denzinger and Adolf Schönmetzer, eds., *Enchiridion symbolorum definitionum et declarationum de rebus fidei et morum.* Freiburg: Herder, 1965.
DWH	Hans Urs von Balthasar, *Dare We Hope 'That all Men be Saved'?* with *A Short Discourse on Hell.* Translated by David Kipp and Lothar Krauth. San Francisco: Ignatius Press, 1988.
HE	Marylin McCord Adams, *Horrendous Evils and the Goodness of God.* Oxford: Oxford University Press, 1990.
IEG	J. A. T. Robinson, *In the End God . . . The Christian Doctrine of the Last Things.* 1950. Special edition. Eugene, OR: Cascade, 2011.
NA	Sergei Bulgakov, *The Bride of the Lamb* [Neviesta Agntsa]. Translated by Boris Jakim. Grand Rapids: Eerdmans, 2002.
NIV	*The Holy Bible: New International Version.* Grand Rapids: Zondervan, 2011.

NRSV	*New Revised Standard Version of the Bible.* Washington, DC: National Council of Churches of Christ in the USA, 1989.
SV	Søren Kierkegaard, *Samlede Værker*. Edited by A. B. Drachmann, J. L. Heiberg, and H. O. Lange. Copenhagen: Gyldendal, 1901–6.

CHAPTER I

Introduction

The eschatological office is mostly closed these days.
  —Ernst Troeltsch[1]

If Christianity be not altogether thoroughgoing eschatology, there remains in it no relationship whatsoever to Christ.
  —Karl Barth[2]

IN THIS BOOK, I shall investigate the proposal that divine judgment is the judgment of love, that the judgment is salvific, and that the judgment is the event of absolute recognition of God, the self, and the other. Since this is an exploration of Christian eschatology (the study of the last things), it is first necessary briefly to discuss the theological tasks involved.

The quote above attributed to the German Protestant theologian Ernst Troeltsch (1865–1923) which was made before the onset of World War I shows how quickly the theological landscape can change, especially after two world wars destroyed the theological and social optimism of what was then deemed liberal Christian theology.[3] It is not surprising that

---

1. "... dass eschatologische Bureu sei heuzutage zumeist geschlossen." Cf. Troeltsch, Troeltsch, and von Le Fort, *Glaubenslehre*, 36.

2. Barth, *Epistle to the Romans*, 314.

3. However, while Troeltsch was not interested in biblical miracles, he did hold to a strong belief in life after death: "We must therefore decide in favor of life after death if we are fully to affirm the image of God. It alone can make great heroism possible. A good portion of the plaintiveness and resignation of the human race stems from its lack of courage to affirm this belief. Belief in immortality was indispensable for Goethe too, although he thought it applied only to the highest in humanity. But it holds true for this highest, too: The inner voice does not lie." Cf. Troeltsch, *The Christian Faith*,

Karl Barth (1886–1968), also quoted above, reacted to the horrors of the Great War with the second edition of his commentary on the *Epistle to the Romans* (*Die Römerbrief*) in 1922. He re-wrote *Die Römerbrief* while he was a professor at the University of Göttingen. Barth was also the lead author of the Barmen Declaration (1934), which opposed National Socialism's interference in the German Protestant churches through the Nazi-affiliated German Christian movement.[4] The carnage of the twentieth century not only reopened the "eschatological office," but it has stayed firmly open in the twenty-first century.

The word "eschatology," the study of the *eschata* (ἔσχατα, "last things"), was coined from the Greek by German Protestant theologians during the period of Lutheran Orthodoxy in the seventeenth century. Markus Mühling argues that Philipp Heinrich Friedlieb (1603–63) was one of the first Protestant theologians to use the term.[5] The earlier Latin term for the study of the last things is *De novissimis* ("concerning the last things"). These "last things" were enumerated as the *quattuor novissima* ("the four last things"): death, judgment, heaven, and hell.[6] By the nineteenth century, the word eschatology had generally supplanted the Latin term.[7]

Before continuing, *eschatology* needs to be defined. For this, I turn to Mühling in his fivefold definition:

1. A description of the doctrine of all possible conceptions of the future and the afterlife;

2. The doctrine of the last things, the final events. These can be understood in either a *temporal* or an *ontic* sense;

3. The doctrine of that which is ultimate, the ultimate things. This may be understood in a *temporal* sense but is generally expressed

---

240.

4. Cf. Barth, *Die Römerbrief*, 2nd ed. The standard English translation of the second edition is that by Hoskins cited above. The Barmen Declaration (Theologische Erklärung zur gegenwärtigen Lage der Deutschen Evangelischen Kirche) is readily available in English translation. Cf. "Barmen Declaration (1934)," in Leith, ed., *Creeds of the Churches*, 3rd ed., 518ff.

5. Cf. Mühling, *The T. & T. Clark Handbook of Christian Eschatology*, 3. Original German title: *Grundinformation Eschatologie: Systematische Theologie aus der Perspektive der Hoffnung* (Göttingen: Vandenhoeck & Ruprecht, 2007).

6. It should be noted that the Catholic doctrine of purgatory is not a "last thing" but a pre-eschatic intermediate state of purification.

7. Mühling, *T. & T. Clark Handbook of Christian Eschatology*, 4.

in other categories such as the ontically transcendent meaning of an event, as in Tillich;

4. A historical term for the future-oriented or apocalyptic character of the teachings and life of Christ, whether this is understood in a historicizing way (Albert Schweitzer) or in a systematic and positive way; and

5. A description of the doctrine of the ultimate person, Jesus Christ.[8]

Using this definition, Christian eschatology is a vast subject. Other religions have their own respective eschatological doctrines, further broadening this discipline. Nonetheless, in this book, I am attempting to make a proposal that adds to the existing Christian eschatological corpus. Mühling considers Friedrich Daniel Ernst Schleiermacher (1768–1834) to be one of the most important of the first "modern" systematic theologians to engage in a critical exploration of the *eschata* in his summary of dogmatics *Der christliche Glaube nach den Grundsätzen der evangelischen Kirche im Zusammenhange dargestellt* (1830/1831). This work is usually referred to as *Die Glaubenslehre* (*The Christian Faith*).[9] It is modern in the sense that it is post-Enlightenment. Schleiermacher did not feel bound to adhere to Reformation orthodoxy. Rather, he takes the creedal and confessional statements of the early church and the Reformation and reinterprets them, including the topic of eschatology.

Schleiermacher's theology could be termed a "theology of experience."[10] In a limited sense, Schleiermacher echoes the Methodist Quadrilateral based on the works of John Wesley (1703–91): that Christian doctrine is to be formulated on the basis of Scripture, tradition, reason, and experience.[11] However, while for Wesley Scripture is primary,

---

8. Mühling, *T. & T. Clark Handbook of Christian Eschatology*, 6–13. I have paraphrased and condensed Mühling's five definitions. Emphasis original.

9. Mühling, *T. & T. Clark Handbook of Christian Eschatology*, 7. Cf. Schleiermacher, *Der christliche Glaube*, 2nd ed. (Berlin, 1830–31); ET: *The Christian Faith* (1928/1989).

10. However, Schleiermacher actually does not speak of experience (*Erfahrung*). His terms are *Gefühl*, *Sinn*, and *Geschmack*. In German, the term *Bewußtseinstheologie* ("theology of consciousness") rather than *Erfahrungtheologie* is used when referring to Schleiermacher. I am grateful to Ulrich Schmiedel for this insight.

11. For example, the United Methodist Church (USA) defines the Quadrilateral in this manner: "[John] Wesley believed that the living core of the Christian faith was revealed in Scripture, illumined by tradition, vivified in personal experience, and confirmed by reason. Scripture is primary, revealing the Word of God 'so far as it is necessary for our salvation.'" Cf. *The Book of Discipline of the United Methodist Church*, 82.

for Schleiermacher the primary aspect for doctrinal definition is the experience of God-consciousness—all other sources (Scripture, tradition, reason) must be interpreted through the experience of the believer. This means that, since the future cannot be experienced now, Schleiermacher does not consider eschatology to be a study of the "last things." He does, however, critique the *novissima* in a way that was unthinkable for the magisterial reformers.[12] What should be noted is that Schleiermacher, as a post-Kantian theologian, does not really allow for eschatological speculation (as it is beyond human experience) as such, even though he does offer opinions about the possibility of *post mortem* redemption.

Mühling opines that Philip Melanchthon (1497–1560) essentially forbade speculation about the "last things" in the Augsburg Confession (*Confessio Augustana*, 1530) by its curt treatment of the topic and condemnation of radical reformers that proposed eschatological innovations:

> It is also taught among us that our Lord Jesus Christ will return on the last day for judgment and will raise up all the dead, to give eternal life and everlasting life to believers and the elect but to condemn ungodly [humans] and the devil to hell and eternal punishment. Rejected, therefore, are the Anabaptists who teach that the devil and condemned [humans] will not suffer eternal pain and torment.[13]

Interestingly, Melanchthon not only asserts salvific dualism, but also condemns universal salvation and an early (and violent) antecedent of the social gospel movement of the nineteenth century.[14] Thus, most treatments of the *novissima* in pre-Enlightenment Lutheran and Reformed orthodoxy were short, as if to prevent speculation. It is noteworthy that this article in the *Augustana* does not differ from the received teaching of Catholicism and Eastern Orthodoxy, although Eastern Christianity has a stronger tradition of theological dissent that favors universalism, i.e., that all persons will be reconciled to God and that no one will be damned eternally.[15]

---

12. Mühling, *T. & T. Clark Handbook of Christian Eschatology*, 6–7.

13. Article 17, "Augsburg Confession," in *The Book of Concord*, 38–39. Cf. Mühling, *T. & T. Clark Handbook of Christian Eschatology*, 8.

14. Article 17 is referring, respectively, to the universalist thought of German Anabaptist leader Hans Denk (1495–1527) and to the Münster Rebellion (1532–35) where millennialist Anabaptist leaders attempted to create a communal theocracy by force. The anti-Judaic aspect is noteworthy.

15. For a contemporary example, cf. Alfeyev, *Christ the Conqueror of Hell*.

Schleiermacher was aware of this dogmatic inheritance and he cites liberally throughout the *Glaubenslehre* various creedal and confessional statements prior to critiquing them. It is interesting that Schleiermacher's creative treatment of the *eschata* (even though restricted as noted above) leads to a universalist outcome that dispenses with hell in favor of an intermediate state, i.e., the *post mortem* state of a disembodied soul that inhabits a state that is neither corporeal life on earth nor resurrected life at the second coming of Christ. In this state, the human being is given a second chance to be reconciled with God—and such reconciliation will happen universally because God has eternally decreed it. In his reversal of Reformed supralapsarian double predestination to a singular divine decree to blessedness for humanity, Schleiermacher makes a theological turn that was roughly simultaneous with the late eighteenth- and early nineteenth-century American Universalist movement.[16] The salvific optimism of Schleiermacher has never been successfully quashed in mainline Protestant theology and his twentieth-century neo-orthodox critics seem to have their own universalist inclinations (e.g., Karl Barth).

In twentieth-century eschatology, Mühling notes that German-American Protestant theologian Paul Tillich (1886–1965) brought the word *eschaton* into popular usage. In his 1930 essay *Eschatologie und Geschichte* (*Eschatology and History*), Tillich writes that he favors the word "eschaton" (ἔσχατον; "the last thing") over *eschata* ("the last things") because he does not think of the "last things" as a series of events that happen in order, but the singular, transcendental, and atemporal goal of creation in God.[17] In so doing, Tillich, after a fashion, completes a task opened up by Schleiermacher positing that the eschaton can be understood not as a chronological event in earthly time-space, but rather as atemporal and transcendent.

Another option would be to conceive of the eschaton as neither a future event nor an atemporal event, but as a this-worldly, realized experience ("realized eschatology"). This approach, taken up by theologians such as British Congregationalist theologian C. H. Dodd (1884–1973) dispenses with the idea of an eschatic reality separate from

---

16. Supralapsarian double predestination is the concept that God eternally decided before the fall (*supra lapsum*), the salvation of every person, either to heaven or hell without regard to human faith or merit. For the history of American Universalism, cf. Howe, *The Larger Faith*.

17. Cf. Tillich, "Eschatologie und Geschichte," in *Religiöse Verwirklichung*, 291n4. Cited and translated in Mühling, *T. & T. Clark Handbook of Christian Eschatology*, 10.

earthly time-space—it can be experienced today.[18] However, Dodd did not deny the general resurrection or eternal life, but rather that God's realm can be a possession of the Christian *now* and not as something that must be awaited.[19] The German Lutheran theologian Rudolf Bultmann (1884–1976) began a project to demythologize the New Testament that effectively dispenses with miracles and eternal life (in the literal sense) and concentrates on an existentialist Christianity that can only be experienced within human finitude on earth.[20] He thus goes far beyond Dodd's project. The Swiss Reformed theologian Emil Brunner (1889–1966) criticizes Bultmann's eschatology as "a faith without hope."[21]

> What in Bultmann's view remains as eschatology is no longer a hope in an eternal future, but merely a new self-understanding for present-day man [sic], arrived at through ultimate decision, and which therefore can only be termed "eschatological" in a sense quite other than that of the New Testament "eschatological"—having reference to the last things. In this re-interpretation, the dimension of the future has quite simply fallen out of the New Testament kerygma.[22]

Brunner's critique is important because he raises the crucial issue of *hope*. If the eschatological hope for humanity is some sort of existentialist-naturalist response to the ethics of the kingdom of God, proclaimed by a demythologized gospel, then it is either secular humanism or a variant of ethical monotheism that does not postulate an "afterlife." Theism, a belief in God or a Supreme Being, is certainly possible without positing an "afterlife" for human beings, but in this case the apostle Paul's admonition is operative: "If for this life only we have hoped in Christ, we are of all people most to be pitied" (1 Cor 15:19 NRSV).[23]

I speculate that Bultmann's answer might be that one can only hope for the futurity of mortal humanity and its ethical development—which is more or less analogous to a Marxist *Reich der Freiheit* and thereby reduces eschatology to anthropology, which has echoes of the philosophy

---

18. Generally, I use the term "eschatic" when referencing an aspect of the world-to-come as an object of hope within the context of Christian faith. The term "eschatological" is used to refer to objects of academic discourse.

19. Cf. Dodd, *Interpretation of the Fourth Gospel*, 144ff.

20. Cf. Bultmann, "New Testament and Mythology" (1941).

21. Brunner, *Eternal Hope*, 214. Cited in Hoye, *The Emergence of Eternal Life*, 68.

22. Brunner, *Eternal Hope*, 214.

23. All scripture quotations are from the NRSV unless otherwise noted.

of Ludwig Feuerbach (1804–72). Feuerbach understood Christianity to be the dislocation of human relationality directed "upwards" to an imaginary God rather than an interpersonal relationality that overcomes the worldly problems between mortal human beings.[24]

The above introduction to eschatology is "Protestant" because the term "eschatology" came into being through German Lutheran theologians. However, the question of eschatology is hardly confined to one branch of Christianity. Therefore, my investigation will explore the wider Christian tradition. My book thereby contributes to *Christian* eschatology more generally, beyond denominational considerations.

1. Eschatology as an Exercise of Hope

Christian eschatological theology is above all an exercise of hope for the future of creation. It is also about asking questions: What will happen in the future? What will happen when we die? How do we relate to God? How can God exist if there is so much suffering? Is there an "afterlife"? These ultimate questions could be boiled down to Immanuel Kant's (1724–1804) *Critique of Pure Reason* (1781/1787) in his third question: What may I hope?[25] Hope, according to German Protestant theologian Jürgen Moltmann (b. 1926), is neither presumption nor despair. It finds its ground in trust:

> Presumption is a premature, self-willed anticipation of fulfilment of what we hope for from God. Despair is the premature, arbitrary anticipation of the non-fulfilment of what we hope for from God. Both forms of hopelessness . . . cancel the wayfaring character of hope. They rebel against the patience in which hope trusts in the God of promise.[26]

Moltmann's concept of hope as "wayfaring" is compelling. It is resonant with the concept of life as an earthly pilgrimage on the way to our true home. Just as the Israelites wandered in the desert for forty years (cf. Num 32:13) and just as Jesus wandered in the wilderness for forty days (cf. Luke 4:1), all humans wander this earth as *transitory* beings. No matter our wealth and perceived security or poverty and insecurity, all

---

24. Cf. Feuerbach, *Das Wesens des Christentums* (1841); ET: *The Essence of Christianity*.

25. Cf. Kant, *Critique of Pure Reason*, A804–805/B833. For a recent study on this question, cf. Chignell, *What May I Hope? (Kant's Questions)*.

26. Moltmann, *Theology of Hope*, 23.

human beings are finite with death as a universal endpoint. This deathward orientation of human life begs Kant's third question cited above.

An answer could be naturalistic, as American philosopher Holmes Rolston III (b. 1932) and Anglican theologian Arthur Peacocke (1924–2006) suggest in their idea of "cruciform naturalism": that biological life is a continuous series of birth and death and that this cycle is a necessity. To be alive on earth means to be born and to die.[27] Yet, this "cruciform" cycle is also the story of the incarnation of Christ. If the answer to the deathward orientation of human life is metaphysical, Luther's *Larger Catechism* (1529) gives part of a possible answer: "That to which your heart clings and entrusts itself is, I say, really your God."[28] To entrust oneself to God in love is also to entrust God with the finitude of human life: to die into God as an act of hope. The Barmen Declaration puts this idea in more forceful terms in its most famous sentence: "Jesus Christ, as he is testified to us in the Holy Scriptures, is the one Word of God, whom we are to hear, whom we are to *trust* and obey in life and in death."[29] Thus, to trust Jesus Christ is to entrust him with our death as well as our life. For a Catholic perspective, the 1992 document *De quibusdam quaestionibus actualibus circa eschatologiam* published by the International Theological Commission locates hope in the resurrection of Christ.[30] The English version was published as *Some Current Questions in Eschatology*.[31] While the document asserts the traditional aspects of Catholic eschatology, such as the separation of the soul at death, purgatory, and the affirmation of a bodily resurrection on the Last Day, the document begins with hope focused on the resurrection of Christ:

> Without the affirmation of Christ's resurrection Christian faith is in vain (cf. 1 Cor 15:14). Since there is indeed an intimate relationship between the fact of Christ's resurrection and our hope of our own future resurrection (cf. 1 Cor 15:12), the Risen Christ also constitutes the foundation of our hope, which opens itself up to horizons far beyond the limits of this earthly life. For "if our hopes in Christ are limited to this life only, we are

---

27. Cf. Holmes Rolston III, "Kenosis and Nature," in *The Work of Love: Creation as Kenosis*, ed. John Polkinghorne (London: SPCK, 2001), 57–8; cf. Arthur Peacocke, "The Cost of New Life," in ibid., 21–41. Cited in Thiselton, 10.

28. Cf. "Larger Catechism," in *The Book of Concord*, 365.

29. Cf. Leith, ed., *Creeds of the Churches*, 520. Emphasis mine.

30. Cf. *Gregorianum* 73 (1992), 395–435.

31. Cf. *The Irish Theological Quarterly* 58 (1992), 209–43.

the most pitiable of men" (1 Cor 15:19). Yet without this hope it would be impossible to lead a Christian life.[32]

This statement asserts that Christian faith *demands* both the resurrection of Christ and a hope that goes "far beyond" human mortality. This is a seemingly absurd twofold statement from the vantage point of twenty-first-century secularism: (1) that Jesus Christ rose from the dead (body, soul, and divinity) and (2) that human biological finitude is not the *ne plus ultra* of human being. Yet, this is the heart of the Christian faith. There is a reason for the aphorism *credo quia absurdum* misattributed to Tertullian (c. 155–240 CE).[33] Tertullian was not promoting fideism, but rather he was challenging the received Hellenistic philosophy of early Christianity's critics.[34] In other words, Tertullian was challenging the equivalent of today's scientific realism, i.e., that the world as described by the scientific method is the *real* world and there is nothing else. Thus, for the scientific realist, a metaphysical description of reality is false. However, human beings are limited by time, space, and language, and in their intellectual capacities and technologies. It is therefore debatable whether human beings have the ability to observe (never mind comprehend) "reality" if this is defined as the state of things as they actually exist. My investigation is unapologetically metaphysical, making the assumption that whatever "reality" is, it is not and cannot be restricted by scientism.

Although he is deeply critical of metaphysical approaches, the Italian philosopher Gianni Vattimo (b. 1936) challenges concepts of reality that claim to have abolished religiosity:

> The "end of modernity," or in any case its crisis, has also been accompanied by the dissolution of the main philosophical theories that claimed to have done away with religion: positivist scientism, Hegelian and then Marxist historicism. Today there are no longer strong, plausible reasons to be an atheist, or at any rate to dismiss religion.[35]

---

32. *The Irish Theological Quarterly* 58 (1992), 209.

33. The actual statement by Tertullian is "prorsus credibile est, quia ineptum est" ("it is by all means to be believed, because it is absurd"). Cf. *De Carne Christi*, V, 4 in *Ante Nicene Fathers*, ed. A. Cleveland Coxe and trans. Alexander Roberts and James Donaldson (Buffalo, NY: Christian Literature Company, 1885), 3:919.

34. Cf. Robert Sider, "Credo Quia Absurdum?"

35. Vattimo, *Belief*, 28.

Vattimo asserts that the twentieth-century project of anti-theistic rationalism, i.e., the demythologizing of human thinking so that truth and reason "triumph," has been "defeated."[36] In other words, Vattimo claims that scientism and a belief in utopian human progress must also be demythologized: "demythification has finally turned against itself, realising that even the ideal of elimination of myth is a myth."[37] For him, atheism itself is a myth and it has lost its currency. In place of the atheist myth, Vattimo claims that love is the manifestation of the "kenotic Being" (i.e., the self-emptying God) and it is in this love that we find the 'really real."[38] He is thus claiming that "God is love" (1 John 4:8).

Returning to the statement of the International Theology Commission, if it is combined with the sentence from the Barmen Declaration, it gives us a unique assertion: *Jesus Christ is the one Word of God incarnate, crucified, and risen, whom we are to hear, whom we are to trust and obey in life, in death, and in the hope of eternal life.* In other words, our hope that goes beyond our finitude is found in our relationship with the living God as manifested in the Risen Christ "in whom the whole fullness of deity dwells bodily" (Col 2:9).

The Human Need for an "Afterlife"

Yet, there is also an anthropological need concerning the "afterlife" that is often overlooked in statements of faiths. The Spanish author and philosopher Miguel de Unamuno (1864–1936) writes in a letter to a friend:

> I do not say that we merit an afterlife, or that logic demonstrates it; I say that we have need of it, whether or not we merit it, and that's all. I say that that which passes does not satisfy me, that I have thirst for eternity, and that without it everything is indifferent to me. I have need of it, I have need of it! Without it there is no more joy in living and the joy of living no longer has anything to give me. It is too easy to affirm: "It is necessary to live, one must be content with life." And those that are not content with it, what then?[39]

---

36. Vattimo, *Belief*, 28–29.
37. Vattimo, *Belief*, 29.
38. Vattimo, *Belief*, 93ff.
39. Unamuno, "Cartas inéditas de Miguel de Unamuno y Pedro Jiménez Ilundain," 135. Translation mine.

This honest statement could apply to human persons of any faith or none. While it is true that any concept of eternal life cannot be proven, certainly not by a scientific method, it can be described as a basic human need; a need to believe that finitude is not the final aspect of what it means to be human. There are already scientists such as British biomedical gerontologist Aubrey de Grey (b. 1963) who are seeking effectively to "cure" human mortality.[40]

Yet, biological life extension is not what Unamuno desires. He desires eternity, which is not the same thing as more or unending earthly time-space, but rather it is "life" that is supra-temporal and unlimited. It is the *need* to believe that eternity (meaning the possession of unlimited life) will be the next phase of human *being*. This is what Unamuno needs because it alone gives joy to earthly life. To put this another way, earthly joys are fleeting. Only eternal life can guarantee that joy is both meaningful and preserved. Yet, whether grounded in faith or not, the "afterlife" is always an object of hope and never one of facticity.

The existentialist philosopher Friedrich Nietzsche (1844–1900), perhaps surprisingly, alludes to this need in his novel *Also Sprach Zarathustra* ("*Thus Spoke Zarathustra*") in the poem "Zarathustras Rundgesang" ('Zarathustra's Roundelay'):

O Mensch! Gib acht!	Oh mankind, pray!
Was spricht die tiefe Mitternacht?	What does deep midnight have to say?
"Ich schlief, ich schlief—,	"From sleep, from sleep
Aus tiefem Traum bin ich erwacht: -	From deepest dream I made my way:
Die Welt ist tief,	The world is deep,
Und tiefer als der Tag gedacht.	And deeper than the grasp of day.
Tief ist ihr Weh—,	Deep is its pain—,
Lust—tiefer noch als Herzeleid:	Joy—deeper still than misery:
Weh spricht: Vergeh!	Pain says: Refrain!
Doch alle Lust will Ewigkeit—,	Yet all joy wants eternity—
will tiefe, tiefe Ewigkeit!"	Wants deep, deep eternity!"

This is then the mystery: earthly joy is fleeting, but human beings desire unending joy which can only be achieved if human finitude is overcome by "deep eternity."[41]

---

40. Cf. de Grey, *Ending Aging*.
41. Nietzsche, *Also Sprach Zarathustra* (1885), no.12; ET: Nietzsche, *Thus Spoke*

2 The Task

As can be understood by the title of this book, my task is an investigation of divine judgment within Christian eschatology. My task is further narrowed by limiting my project to three assumptions:

- That divine judgment is *issuant* from God's love;
- That divine judgment is *salvific*; and
- That Jesus Christ is the eschatic *Judge*.

Thus, I seek to develop a constructive contribution to the Christian eschatology based on these premises.

3. The Methodological Approach

For my constructive contribution to Christian eschatology, I shall dialogue with proponents as well as opponents of my theological claim that God's judgment and justice is issuant from God's love and is therefore salvific. My methodological approach is to engage in a historical and hermeneutical interpretation of theological and philosophical thinkers in relation to Christian eschatology. However, it is not possible for me to investigate all eschatologies. I have therefore heuristically chosen some who agree and some who disagree with my thesis. The rationale for this is entirely pragmatic. However, I also wish to achieve an ecumenical overview and thus I engage with thinkers from Protestantism, Catholicism, and Eastern Orthodoxy. While some of these thinkers are classical and well known, others have been largely forgotten in the theological academy.

For this dialogue, I enumerate my approach in a fourfold manner. My four points are a system of coordinates into which I shall chart the positions of the thinkers I cover. These coordinates allow me to investigate thinkers that agree with my thesis as well as those who do not. However, I shall advance my core argument through my historical-hermeneutical reading of all of these thinkers.

Zarathustra, 264.

God is Love Precisely in Judgment

Any statements about God's judgment must be interpreted through the revelation of God in the incarnation and earthly ministry of Jesus Christ and summarized in the words of 1 John 4:8b: God is love (ὁ Θεὸς ἀγάπη ἐστίν). Reflecting on the fact that my eschatological project is within the context of postmodernity, my understanding of God as love may be best captured by Anglican theologian Graham Ward:

> The postmodern God is emphatically the God of love, and the economy of love is kenotic. Desire, only possible through difference, alterity, and distance, is the substructure of creation. It makes transcendence both possible and necessary. In specific Christian communities—communities defined and created by narratives of Christ's life and work, the creedal teachings of the church and liturgical practices—the operation of this love provides a redescription of the trinitarian God and the economy of salvation.[42]

Thus, my methodological starting point is always that divine judgment is the judgment of love.

Iudicandus est salvandus

In my constructive exploration of divine judgment, I make the methodological assumption that judgment is salvific rather than destructive. I therefore created the aphorism *iudicandus est salvandus* ("to be judged is to be saved") as a second methodological approach. My provocation to Christian eschatology is that human beings are not "saved" *from* judgment, but are "saved" *within* it. This requires that I oppose an Augustinian single predestination (and its variants) which understands most of humanity as non-elect and thus a *massa damnata*. While this inheritance has been reformulated and challenged in Western Christianity (and largely rejected in the Christian East), its theological legacy remains palpable. My proposed reversal is to deem humanity a *massa amata*, the object of divine love, and to place divine judgment within this context.

---

42. Ward, "Postmodern Theology," 335.

Non-sectarian Approach to Theological Sources

My investigation has its locus in Christian eschatology, but I maintain a denominational neutrality and freely explore Roman Catholic, Eastern Orthodox, and Protestant sources. I also refer to Judaic and atheological sources. While my approach is Christian, the subjects of salvific judgment are not *ante mortem* Christians, but all human beings, both individuated and as a collectivity. While the eschatic event is inclusive of the entirety of the created order, my focus is on the divine judgment of human beings.

Heuristic Approach to Primary Sources

The Christian theological corpus is immense. In order to select primary source material, I have adopted a heurism that seeks sources that advance my concept of salvific judgment as issuant from divine love. Where possible, I recover works that are less well known in today's academy. I also discuss sources that oppose my thesis thereby to engage with them. This provides a necessary limit to the number of sources I employ.

The Limits of the Human Understanding of "Reality"

As alluded to above, I do not accept human restrictions on the concept of reality. In effect, I assert that only God comprehends things in the totality of their ontology. However, the earthly limits of the human understanding of reality (e.g., "for now we see in a mirror, dimly," cf. 1 Cor 13:12a) are changed by the eschatic event when such limitations will be removed (e.g., "but then we will see face to face. Now I know only in part; then I will know fully, even as I have been fully known.," cf. 1 Cor 13:12b).

4. Argument for Disposition and Exclusions

> *I have no wit, no words, no tears;*
> *My heart within me like a stone*
> *Is numb'd too much for hopes or fears;*
> *Look right, look left, I dwell alone;*
> *I lift mine eyes, but dimm'd with grief*
> *No everlasting hills I see;*
> *My life is in the falling leaf:*
> *O Jesus, quicken me.*

My life is like a faded leaf,
My harvest dwindled to a husk:
Truly my life is void and brief
And tedious in the barren dusk;
My life is like a frozen thing,
No bud nor greenness can I see:
Yet rise it shall—the sap of Spring;
O Jesus, rise in me.
—Christina Rossetti[43]

The main argument that this book seeks to make is that the gospel of Jesus Christ is inclusive of a divine judgment that is salvific, reconciling, and "quickening" (life-giving)—the quickening that the English poet Christina Rossetti (1830–94) longs for in her melancholic poem. Thus, the function of divine judgment is ultimately creative, hopeful, and non-dualistic. Dualistic soteriology that divides human beings into two camps, the saved and the damned, is the dominant inheritance of the Christian tradition. I argue that this dualism must be rejected both on the grounds that it destroys the coherence of the doctrine of God as omnipotent, omniscient, and omnibenevolent as well as the ontological ascription of God as that of love itself. It also presents a problem of theodicy because the eternal punishment or destruction of the damned is an eternalization of evil in the kingdom of God and a defeat of the victory of Christ over sin, death, and the devil. While this may lead to a charge that I am advocating universal salvation as the solution to the problems cited, this would be an oversimplification. The concept that divine judgment is salvific and creative does not yield *ex opere operato* what is commonly understood as universalism. Rather, it yields an argument that no human being is "lost" but the post-eschatic constitution of that person is by no means a glorified version of the same individual in her earthly instantiation. The creative judgment yields both continuity and discontinuity in terms of earthly human lives—and it *excludes* sameness. Thus, the eschatic person, depending on *ante mortem* factors, may or may not "resemble" that person as known on earth. In effect, universal salvation is both true and false for each human person and humanity as a collectivity. It is thus antinomic.

---

43. Rossetti, "A Better Resurrection," 164. The poem alludes to Hebrews 11:35.

I therefore argue against a dualistic soteriology that requires a binary eternal outcome of divine judgment. This means that the sources I employ that support my argument are thin on the theological ground. *Salvific judgment* is not explicitly promoted by any major theologian (past or present). Furthermore, my concept cannot be construed as a reinstatement of Origen's (c. 184–254 CE) concept of the *apokatastasis ton panton* (ἀποκατάστᾰσις των πάντων; "restoration of all things") or similar concepts as promoted by Clement of Alexandria (c. 150–215 CE) and Gregory of Nyssa (c. 335–95 CE). Origen understands universal salvation in terms of restoration to a *status quo ante* the Edenic fall.[44] However, my own eschatological thought has no retrograde trajectory, but rather is rooted in a creative understanding of divine judgment that yields not a return to purity, but a new creation that could be expressed as the *semper novum*.

---

44. Cf. Greggs, *Barth, Origen, and Universal Salvation*, 54–84.

CHAPTER 2

The Symbols and Problems of Judgment

1. Introduction

Where there's life, there's hope and only the dead have none.
—THEOCRITUS[1]

Now, this bell tolling softly for another, says to me: Thou must die.
—JOHN DONNE [2]

In the midst of life, we are in death.
—BOOK OF COMMON PRAYER[3]

ALL CHRISTIAN ESCHATOLOGIES BEGIN with a discussion of death and I shall follow suit. Death, which is understood as the "last enemy" that will be destroyed (cf. 1 Cor. 15:26), is understood by those who hold to the concept of an "afterlife" as, in effect, the gateway to judgment. For those that do not believe that life continues beyond biological death, it is the cessation of a human life in the sense of annihilation. So, death

---

1. τάχ' αὔριον ἔσσετ' ἄμεινον ἐλπίδες ἐν ζωοῖσιν, ἀνέλπιστοι δὲ θανόντε; cf. Theocritus (fl. c. 270 BCE) in Gow, ed. and trans., *Theocritus*, Idyll 4, line 42, 1:37.

2. John Donne (1572–1631), Devotions XVII "Nunc lento sonitu dicunt, morieris."

3. "Order for the Burial of the Dead," Book of Common Prayer (London: 1549/1662). From Thomas Cranmer's translation of *Media vita in morte sumus*, the medieval antiphon to *Nunc dimittis* at Compline for the third Sunday in Lent. Author unknown. Cf. *Codex Sangallensis* 546, f.319 (Abbey Library of St. Gallen, 1510); cf. *Processionale Monasticum* (Solesmes: Abbaye Saint-Pierre, 1893), 45.

is a universal problem for human beings regardless of one's respective metaphysics. The intermediate state is the proposed "place" where the dead "go" between death and resurrection. It is almost always understood as discarnation. In the discarnate state, some traditions hold to the doctrine of the *particular* judgment which determines the destiny of each disembodied soul. It may offer the possibility of purification (i.e., purgatory). The concept of a pre-eschatic intermediate state poses a number of problems which shall be explored.

Lastly, I explore the most problematic of all symbols of judgment: hell. Hell, no matter how it is defined, presents the dilemma that certain persons are beyond God's reconciliation and thus must enter an eternal state of sub-optimality. This condition varies in description from simply undesirable to one of horrendous misery. Hell is certainly problematic, especially when one posits that it is a loving God that destines persons for this eternal fate. The limit of this study is that it can only propose possibilities, but not assert actual solutions. It will be noted that I do not treat on the subject of "heaven" in this chapter as it is not a *problem* per se.

2. The Symbol and Problem of Death

In this section, I shall explore human death from secular, philosophical, and theological vantages. First, it should be noted that death is also one of the chief symbols of judgment ("the wages of sin is death" Rom 6:23). As a symbol and problem of divine judgment, death represents the first judgment against the first sin recorded in Abrahamic sacred text. In the Garden of Eden, Adam was warned not to eat from a certain tree: "but of the tree of the knowledge of good and evil you shall not eat, for in the day that you eat of it you shall die" (Gen 2:17). Having disobeyed God's command, Adam and Eve are expelled from the garden and death enters the world: "you are dust, and to dust you shall return" (Gen 3:19). This is referred to in Christian theology as "the fall of humanity." It is noteworthy that Judaism has no concept of "the fall" or original sin. The expulsion from Eden is seen as exile rather than fall.[4] Fall or exile, what the Garden of Eden represents is immortality and humanity's forced exit from it represents mortality. This is a mythical explanation of why human beings experience death, but it says nothing about what happens after death.

This is the dilemma: no one can *know* what happens after death. Paul's mirror analogy is apt: "For now we see as in a mirror dimly..."

---

4. Cf. Morris, "Exiled from Eden: Jewish Interpretations of Genesis."

(1 Cor 13:12a). Therefore, all statements about what happens after death are propositions. Appeals to positivism that death is the absolute end of life are no more factual than appeals to metaphysics. The attributed last words of the American Congregationalist theologian, Henry Ward Beecher (1813–87), are perhaps the more modest: "Now comes the mystery . . . ."[5] We may know what death is biologically, but not what happens in the moment of death (*hora mortis*) or after death (*post mortem*). In the context of Christian theology, death belongs to the rubric of hope. In effect, to die as a Christian is to die *into hope*. And yet, it cannot be denied that death is a radical challenge to human life and to the Christian gospel. There is no denial of this fact in the biblical record: "You do not know what will happen tomorrow. For what is your life? It is even a vapour that appears for a little time and then vanishes away" (Jas 4:14).

Ludwig Wittgenstein (1889–1951) makes a salient comment on this "not knowing" about death: "Suppose someone said: 'What do you believe, Wittgenstein? Are you a sceptic? Do you know whether you will survive death?' I would really, this is a fact, say 'I can't say. I don't know,' because I haven't any clear idea what I am saying when I am saying, 'I don't cease to exist.'"[6] Indeed, what does it mean that a person "survives" death? Wittgenstein's thanatological agnosticism points to another aspect of death: it is a *mystery*. Science can tell us that biological functions cease at death, but it cannot go beyond this. Thus, death as complete annihilation is a belief, not a fact. The opposite is also true. Plato's *Apology of Socrates* critiques the belief of an annihilationist view of death in this well-known quotation: "To fear death . . . is none other than to think oneself wise when one is not, to think one knows what one does not know. No one knows whether death may not be the greatest of all blessings for a [human being], yet [humans] fear it as if they knew that it is the greatest of evils."[7]

Yet the concept that death is the total destruction of a human person must be explored because it is increasingly held, at least in some intellectual circles, as the normative understanding of mortality in the post-Christian world.[8]

---

5. It is unknown whether Beecher actually said these words just before his death.

6. Wittgenstein, *Lectures and Conversations on Aesthetics, Psychology and Religious Belief*, 70.

7. Plato, "Apology of Socrates" 29b, in West and West, eds., *Four Texts on Socrates*, 80.

8. For example, cf. Martin and Augustine, eds., *The Myth of the Afterlife*.

Death as Annihilation

> *Laßt euch nicht verführen*
> *Zu Fron und Ausgezehr!*
> *Was kann euch Angst noch rühren?*
> *Ihr sterbt mit allen Tieren*
> *und es kommt nichts nachher.*
> —Bertolt Brecht[9]

"You only live once." This is a common English maxim. Death is both a theological and a secular problem, socially and existentially. For many, the problem of death can be neatly summarized by Bertolt Brecht's (1898–1956) poem (imitating a Lutheran chorale): "we die with all the animals and nothing comes after." Death until the early twentieth century in Western industrialized countries was deemed a normal aspect of life. The dying died at home, ideally surrounded by family and loved ones. Today, death is sanitized and hidden; the dying die in hospitals, nursing homes, and eldercare facilities far more often than they do in their own bed. Dietrich Bonhoeffer's (1906–45) aphorism (itself condensed from a maxim of Hugo Grotius) that in a "world come of age" we must live *etsi Deus non daretur* ("as if God did not exist") has come about, but not in the way Bonhoeffer imagined. We now also live *etsi mors non daretur* ("as if death did not exist").[10]

The practice of *memento mori* as being a part of one's interior reflection is now a relic of a previous age. Denial of death is the cognitive norm. The genre of *ars moriendi* is hardly a popular one today, with some notable exceptions such as the work of the Swiss-American psychiatrist Elizabeth Kübler-Ross (1926–2004) in her 1969 watershed book *On Death and Dying*.[11] Nonetheless, death is inevitable for human beings and indeed all lifeforms. We are mortal, finite beings. As to the denial of

---

9. Bertolt Brecht, "Gegen Verführung," in *Bertolt Brechts Hauspostille*. ET: "Don't allow yourselves to be seduced | To drudgery and emaciation! | Can fear tremble you anymore? | You die with all the animals | And nothing comes after." Translation mine.

10. Cf. Hugo Grotius (1583–1645), *De jure belli ac pacis* (Amsterdam: 1629); cf. Lenehan "*Etsi deus non daretur*." The maxim by Grotius in full is: Et haec quidem quae iam diximus, locum aliquem haberent etiamsi daremus, quod sine summo scelere dari nequit, non esse Deum, aut non curari ab eo negotia humana. ("What we have been saying would have a degree of validity even if we should concede that which cannot be conceded without the utmost wickedness: that there is no God, or that the affairs of men are of no concern to him.")

11. Cf. Kübler-Ross, *On Death and Dying*.

death, Jürgen Moltmann (b. 1926) comments that "[t]o push away every thought of death, and to live as if we have an infinite amount of time ahead of us, makes us superficial and indifferent. . . . To live as if there were no death is an illusion."[12] Moltmann also takes note that graveyards used to be in the center of the village, but today are more likely to be at the edge of town, out of sight.[13] Reminders of human mortality are kept at a distance. With the exception of the death of famous persons, public reaction to the death of ordinary people is usually one of avoidance, if at all possible. Death has become taboo. This taboo may be the result of the post-war decline in religiosity in the developed countries of the West where belief in "life after death" is in seeming parallel decline.

The presumption of an "afterlife," often conceived as the immortality of the soul, might seem to be in decline in industrialized countries based on the decline in attendance at religious services. However, a lack of interest in attending the formal worship services of organized religion does not always translate into a denial of the possibility of the "afterlife." For example, the Pew Research Center's "Religious Landscape Study" (2014) conducted a survey that showed that American Millennials (those born from 1981 onward) are less religious, but just as spiritual as older generations. What was more striking is that the study showed that while 52% of Millennials believe in God with absolute certainty, 67% believe in "heaven." Non-theism does not in itself necessarily deny the "afterlife" as a possibility, at least in the United States.[14]

Yet, a scientific materialism (or neo-positivism) is increasingly promoted in certain intellectual circles, as in the New Atheist movement.[15] It was also the default position of Marxism-Leninism. Vladimir Lenin (1870–1924) wrote that:

> Those who toil and live in want all their lives are taught by religion to be submissive and patient while here on earth, and to take comfort in the hope of a heavenly reward. But those who live by the labour of others are taught by religion to practise charity while on earth, thus offering them a very cheap way of

12. Moltmann, *The Coming of God*, 50.
13. Moltmann, *The Coming of God*, 56.
14. Cf. Alper, "Millennials are less religious than older Americans, but just as spiritual." For an example of non-theistic ideas about the afterlife, cf. Staume, *The Atheist Afterlife*.
15. The most well-known publication in his genre is by Richard Dawkins in his book *The God Delusion* (2006).

justifying their entire existence as exploiters and selling them at a moderate price tickets to well-being in heaven. . . . Our Programme is based entirely on the scientific, and moreover the materialist, world-outlook.[16]

For the materialist (regardless of political orientation), death is indeed the annihilation of the person once known. Bertrand Russell (1872–1970) captures this materialist approach to human death in a well-known quotation:

> I believe that when I die I shall rot, and nothing of my ego will survive. I am not young and I love life. But I should scorn to shiver with terror at the thought of annihilation. Happiness is nonetheless true happiness because it must come to an end, nor do thought and love lose their value because they are not everlasting. Many a man has borne himself proudly on the scaffold; surely the same pride should teach us to think truly about man's place in the world. Even if the open windows of science at first make us shiver after the cosy indoor warmth of traditional humanizing myths, in the end the fresh air brings vigour, and the great spaces have a splendour of their own.[17]

From a materialist point of view, then, it can be argued that to avoid the thought of death, to fear it, is illogical, agreeing with Russell who did not "shiver" at the thought of his own mortality. Death should not be feared because it is simply oblivion—which is painless.[18]

Wittgenstein, whose theism or lack thereof is an open question, offers a philosophical counterpoint to Russell and Epicurus: "Death is not an event in life: we do not live to experience death. If we take eternity to mean not infinite temporal duration but timelessness, then eternal life belongs to those who live in the present. Our life has no end in the way in which our visual field has no limits."[19] For Wittgenstein, to be in the

16. Lenin, "Socialism and Religion" (1905).

17. Russell, "What I Believe" (1925), 348.

18. The quotation ascribed to Epicurus (341–270 BCE) is well known: "So death, the most frightening of bad things, is nothing to us; since when we exist death is not yet present, and when death is present, we do not exist" (Epicurus, "Letter to Menoeceus").

19. "Der Tod ist kein Ereignis des Lebens. Den Tod erlebt man nicht. Wenn man unter Ewigkeit nicht unendliche Zeitdauer, sondern Unzeitlichkeit versteht, dann lebt der ewig, der in der Gegenwart lebt. Unser Leben ist ebenso endlos, wie unser Gesichtsfeld grenzenlos ist." Cf. Wittgenstein, "Logisch-philosophische Abhandlung," 6.4311; ET: *Tractatus Logico-Philosophicus*, 6.4311, p. 185.

present moment is to experience eternal life. Timelessness or rather being in the perpetual present is a symbol of divine eternity: "Jesus said to them, 'Very truly, I tell you, before Abraham was, *I am*'" (cf. John 8:58). The Johannine tradition thus associates Jesus with God as revealed to Moses ("I am who I am"; cf. Exod 3:14). The phrase "I am" as identifying the God of Israel is associated with the divine name YHWH (יהוה—the Tetragrammaton) in the Hebrew Bible. YHWH, the self-existent One, is not subject to measurable time, but is rather eternal.[20] However, I would dare add a prefix to Wittgenstein on this point. Death may not be an event in life—we do not live to experience death, but dying *is* an experience *in* life, even from a materialist point of view.[21] If we bifurcate the time before death from the moment of death, then we can say that the death itself is not an event *in* life.

In his book, *Death and Immortality* (1970), the Welsh philosopher of religion D. Z. Phillips (1934–2006) argues that Christianity has misunderstood the true meaning of "eternal life." In an expression, reminiscent of Wittgenstein's at the beginning of this chapter, Phillips remarks that: "If one understands what is meant by 'survival' and what is meant by 'death,' then one is at a loss to know what it means to talk of surviving death."[22] Rather than "more life" after death, Phillips comments that "Eternity is not *more* life, but *this life* seen under certain moral and religious modes of thought. . . . [E]ternal life for the believer is participation in the life of God."[23] However, believers who participate in the life of God and thereby experience "eternity" can only do so finitely. Their participation ends with death and thus "eternal life" also "ends" with them. For Phillips, death for a theist who denies an "afterlife" would be the same as death for the atheist-materialist. The end of human life is nothingness. Arguably, the theist of this typology can believe in a Supreme Being who created the universe with a purpose and that the gift of one life is of sufficient worth that we as creatures should be thankful that we exist at all. The materialist cannot share this view. Their universe is accidental and without inherent meaning. The American poet and novelist Sylvia Plath (1932–63) captures this sentiment in a negative context:

20. Cf. Wilkinson, *Tetragrammaton*, 129ff.

21. For an interesting discussion of the "afterlife" from a materialist perspective, see Johnston, *Surviving Death*.

22. Cf. Phillips, *Death and Immortality*, 15. It should be noted that Phillips was a Wittgenstein scholar.

23. Phillips, *Death and Immortality*, 49; 54–55. Emphasis mine.

> The human mind is so limited it can only build an arbitrary heaven—and usually the physical comforts they endow it with are naively the kind that can be perceived as we humans perceive—nothing more. No: perhaps I will awake to find myself burning in hell. I think not. I think I will be snuffed out. Black is sleep; black is a fainting spell; and black is death, with no light, no waking.[24]

It may seem that Plath's view is indeed dark (or "black"), but there are materialists who counsel bravery and even peacefulness in the face of what for them is annihilation and oblivion. This is not a new understanding, as the Epicureans counselled the same attitude along with the Stoics. The argument is simply that if at death the brain ceases to function, then there can be no fear, suffering, or pain because these are functions of the brain. Death is therefore the ultimate event of a painless, dreamless "sleep." While a materialist may regret the collapse of all relationality and sensation, she will not be aware of such regret at death. The only suffering could be in the dying process, but death itself would be the release from all suffering—forever.

Death as the Result of Sin

As noted at the beginning of this chapter, for the Abrahamic faiths, death enters the world in the allegory of the fall/exile of humanity; the expulsion from the Garden of Eden. The judgment against disobedient humanity is mortality: humans will "return to the ground" (Gen 3:19). This doctrine of original sin can be captured in the simple couplet from *The New England Primer*—"In Adam's Fall / We sinned All."[25] However, there is a difference between "fallen humanity" and "fallen nature." In Eastern Orthodox theology, original sin is referred to as ancestral sin (προγονικὴ ἁμαρτία) which results in humanity's disordered passions. However, there is no Eastern Orthodox concept that humanity bears the inherited *guilt* of Adam and Eve. Infants are born sinless, but are still subject to moral disorder. In other words, human persons are born into a sinful or disordered world and one of the consequences of this is human finitude.[26]

---

24. Plath, *The Unabridged Journals of Sylvia Plath*, 45.

25. *The New England Primer* was first published in Boston in 1690 by Benjamin Harris (1673–1717) with several editions made after this imprint. Cf. *New England Primer: Improved for the More Easy Attaining the True Reading of English*.

26. Cf. Ware, *The Orthodox Way*, 43–67.

In the Pauline understanding, the Edenic judgment that results in death is reversed through the obedience of Christ (the "New Adam"). This is summarized in universalistic terms: "For since death came through a human being, the resurrection of the dead has also come through a human being; for as all die in Adam, so all will be made alive in Christ" (1 Cor 15:21–22). However, this reversal is incomplete. Human beings *shall* all be made alive at the eschaton—and not before. The "curse" of death remains until the Last Day: "The last enemy to be destroyed is death" (1 Cor 15:26). Thus, as corporeal, material beings, humanity is finite and remains subject to sickness and death until the final consummation. Death is the "enemy" not simply because it ends a human life, but also because it is the end of a human being's relationships to others, the world, and the earthly self. Even if we presume that there is an "afterlife" that precedes the general resurrection, it will not be the corporeal existence that the deceased person knew. Hence, death is the end of earthly self-relation. The incarnation, ministry, death, and resurrection of Jesus constitute the beginning of the eschatic process, but the problem of death, even in the light of the Easter event, is that it will be the *last* problem of human life to be solved.

Even if death is a punishment for collective human sin, there is a wealth of literature, especially in the contemplative and mystical traditions, that welcome death as a liberator—which seems to contradict the concept of death as the last enemy. St Francis of Assisi's (1181–1226) well known hymn "Canticle of the Sun" (1224) thanks God "for our sister Bodily Death / from whose embrace no living person can escape" (Umbrian: *per sora nostra morte corporale / da la quale nullu homo uiuente pò skappare*).[27] However, for Francis it liberates only those who die in a state of grace or in need of purification; but for those who die without having repented any "mortal" sin, death is the gateway to hell: "Woe to those who die in mortal sin!" (Umbrian: *Guai a quelli ke morrano ne le peccata mortali!*).[28]

The scriptural antidote to the fear of death, within the context of Christian faith, is Jesus Christ, by whose death on the cross he frees "those who all their lives were held in slavery by the fear of death" (Heb 2:15). Christian or not, few human beings are truly fearless before death. For those that hold to the concept of an "afterlife," many believe that some

---

27. Cf. Armstrong and Brady, eds., *Francis and Clare*, 37ff.
28. Armstrong and Brady, eds., *Francis and Clare*, 37ff.

26 THE JUDGMENT OF LOVE

sort of judgment or reckoning awaits them *post mortem*. Thus, in the Western medieval responsory *Libera me* of the Office of the Dead, we find these fearful words: *Tremens factus sum ego, et timeo, dum discussio venerit, atque ventura ira*.[29] In the tradition of *ars moriendi*, Caroline divine and Anglican bishop Jeremy Taylor (1613–67) advises in his devotional book *The Rules and Exercises for Holy Dying* (1651) that renouncing the world is the path to fearlessness in the face of dying and death:

> He that would willingly be fearless of death must learn to despise the world; he must neither love anything passionately nor be proud of any circumstance of his life. "O death how bitter is the remembrance of thee to a man that liveth at rest in his possessions to a man that hath nothing to vex him and that hath prosperity in all things yea unto him that is yet able to receive meat" said the son of Sirach. But the parts of this exercise help each other. If a man be not incorporated in all his passions to the things of this world, he will less fear to be divorced from them by a supervening death; and yet because he must part with them all in death, it is but reasonable he should not be passionate for so fugitive and transient interest.[30]

Taylor advises that it is attachment to the world that causes us to fear death, thus renunciation is the path to be released from this fear. This allows us to transition forward two centuries to post-Enlightenment existentialist philosophy and one of its principle exponents, Søren Kierkegaard, who would agree with Taylor that self-denial and worldly renunciation are preparatory for death and eternal life.

Søren Kierkegaard's Philosophy of Death: Fearsome Transcendence

Immortality is Judgment.[31]

Søren Kierkegaard (1813–1855), the Danish philosopher, "father of existentialism," and critic of Hegelianism, died at the age forty-two, yet his

---

29. "I am made to tremble, and I fear, as I await the judgment and the coming wrath." Cf. "Absolutione pro Defunctis," Abbaye Saint-Pierre de Solesmes, *Graduale Romanum* (Paris: Desclée and Co., 1922), 103*. Note that the asterisk is part of the pagination.

30. Taylor, *The Rules and Exercises for Holy Dying*, 382. The biblical passage is from Ecclesiasticus 41:1 in the Apocrypha of the Authorised Version (1611).

31. *"Thi Udødeligheden er Dommen.* Udødelighed er ikke et fortsat Liv, saadan et i

oeuvre is notable for its vast output for a relatively short lifespan. As befits an existentialist philosopher, Kierkegaard's thanatology deals directly with the dread that death causes in human beings.[32] Kierkegaard's influence on twentieth-century Western theology and philosophy is widely acknowledged to be vast.[33] Thus, Kierkegaard provides an essential reflection on death that does not deny its terrors, but also sees in death an eschatic event: death yields to "immortality" and "immortality" yields to judgment.

In her 1990 essay "Kierkegaard's View of Death," Julia Watkin describes his approach to death as transcendentalist (transcending this world) and thus opposed to an immanentalist approach (rooted in this world). This is the case even though some of his writings describe an immanentalist understanding of death.[34] Such views are not however his personal view, but rather they are the understandings of his various characterizations, such as the "young aesthete" in *Either/Or* (Danish: *Enten-Eller*, 1843). The young aesthete despairs of humanity's finitude: "No one returns from the dead, no one has come into the world without weeping; no one asks one if one wants to come in, none when one wants to go out."[35] This is, however, not Kierkegaard's understanding of human mortality. In fact, for Kierkegaard "immortality" is real. Yet, he tends to take a contrarian attitude towards his audience regarding the issue of human death. Those who feel secure about their own "immortality" will be challenged and those who demand "proof" of an "afterlife" will not be

---

det Evindelige fortsat Liv, men Udødelighed er den evige Adskillelse mellem de Retfærdige og de Uretfærdige; Udødelighed er ingen Fortsættelse, som uden videre følger, men en Adskillelse, som følger af det Forbigangne"; cf. Søren Kierkegaard, "De Dødes Opstandelse forerstaare, de Retfædiges—og de Uretfædiges," in *Samlede Værker*, vol. 10, 206; ET: "For immortality is judgment. Immorality is not a continued life, a continued life as such in perpetuity, but immortality is the eternal separation of the righteous and the unrighteous; immortality is no continuation that results as a matter of course, but a separation that results from the past," in Søren Kierkegaard, "There will be a Resurrection of the Dead, of the Righteous—and of the Unrighteous," 207.

32. Cf. Kierkegaard, "At the Graveside" (1845), 69ff.

33. For an overview of Kierkegaard's major works, see Hampson, *Kierkegaard*. For Kierkegaard's twentieth-century reception, see Hannay and Marino, eds., *The Cambridge Companion to Kierkegaard*, 48ff.

34. Watkin, "Kierkegaard's View of Death," 65–66.

35. Quotation in Watkin, "Kierkegaard's View of Death," 66. Translated by the author from the original Danish of "Diapsalmata," *Either/Or* in Søren Kierkegaard, *Samlede Værker*, vol. 1, 4. Hereafter cited as "SV" with volume and page number with Watkin as translator.

given the comfort they desire. Rather, Kierkegaard insists that there is no such proof and no reason to take "immortality" for granted. Human life is transitory—it, like everything else in the created order, will pass away. Since there is no proof that there is such a thing as an "afterlife," human beings must *choose* what they believe regarding mortality.[36] To choose to believe in eternal life is an act of faith. In this, Kierkegaard is showing his Lutheran inheritance in spite of his open disdain for the Danish State Church. We can only believe in eternal life, as it were, *sola fide*. This "leap of faith" is often criticized as fideism, but one could argue that it is rather orthodox Lutheranism of which Kierkegaard was an adherent.

Kierkegaard uses Socrates as a starting point for dialogue about the "afterlife" in *Concluding Unscientific Postscript to the Philosophical Fragments* (Danish: *Afsluttende uvidenskabelig Efterskrift til de philosophiske Smuler*, 1846) where Kierkegaard writes under the pseudonym of Johannes Climacus (although as in other pseudonymous works, the words of Climacus do not always equate to the views of Kierkegaard). The *Postscript* is best known as an attack on Hegelianism and Hegel's deterministic philosophy.[37] In this work, Kierkegaard explores the Greek, Jewish, and Christian concepts of the human response to death—which, according to Watkin, can be seen, through Kierkegaard, as immanentalist, semi-immanentalist, and transcendentalist respectively.[38] He understands the early Greek view of life to be one where earthly happiness is prized and death is deemed an affliction and a consignment to the shadow-life of Hades. The later Platonist concept of immorality is for Kierkegaard still immanentalist and non-transcendent. Elysium is still part of the natural world: it is an insubstantial "immortality" that is "totally predicateless and indeterminate" which transcends nothing. It is thus nihilistic.[39]

For Kierkegaard, Judaism has elements of transcendence and thus can be described as semi-immanentalist. However, its focus is resolutely this-worldly and the blessings from God are blessings on earthly life. Beyond the grave awaits little more than what awaits the early Greeks, a shadow state called Sheol. Where resurrection of the community is asserted, Kierkegaard sees it as immanentalist because it implies

---

36. Watkin, "Kierkegaard's View of Death," 65–66.

37. Cf. Kierkegaard, *Concluding Unscientific Postscript*, SV vol. 7; for a discussion of the *Postscript*, see Hampson, *Kierkegaard*, 140ff.

38. Watkin, "Kierkegaard's View of Death," 68.

39. Cited in Watkin, "Kierkegaard's View of Death," 69. Cf. Kierkegaard, *The Concept of Irony*, SV vol. 13, 157; 166–70.

a restoration to *status quo ante mortem*. There is no transformation or transcendence.[40] It should be noted that Kierkegaard does not make reference to Rabbinical Jewish concepts of the "world to come" (עולם הבא; *olam ha-bah*). While it is true that the focus of life in Rabbinical Judaism is "this world" (עולם הזה; *olam ha-zeh*), Jewish eschatology does admit a more robust transcendentalist concept of "afterlife" than Kierkegaard is willing to admit.[41] He thus labels Judaism as the religion that is "closest to ordinary human life" which is apparently, for him, a negative concept.[42] Kierkegaard considers Christianity as the truly transcendentalist religion because, according to Watkin, it points to "an absolutely transcendent realm above all time, past, present and future. Both for the individual and in itself as a whole, immanence culminates in eternity so that unlike Judaism, Christian eternity is not in 'simple continuity' with the present but in transcendent continuity."[43]

The main thrust for Kierkegaard is that Christianity demands that we die to sin. It is through this dying (self-denial) that eternal life is opened to us.[44] Thus, what Kierkegaard requires of the Christian is "an absolute relationship to the absolute" and this means that the person must totally renounce (die to) immanence: "Those who try to make their life secure will lose it, but those who lose their life will keep it" (Luke 17:33 NIV).[45] In this context, Kierkegaard issues his famous warning in "The Resurrection of the Dead" in *Christian Discourses* (Danish: *Christelige Taler*, 1848) to believers and doubters: "Nothing is more certain than immortality; you are not to worry about, not to waste your time on, not to seek escape by—wanting to demonstrate or seeking to have it demonstrated. Fear it, it is only all too certain; do not doubt whether you are immortal—tremble, because you are immortal."[46]

For Kierkegaard, the grave is certainly real, but "immortality" and judgment are "more real" because at death immanence gives way to transcendence. He is unconcerned with the method of this continuance, be it

---

40. "Kierkegaard's View of Death," 70.

41. Cf. Raphael, *Jewish Views of the Afterlife*, 117ff.

42. Watkin, "Kierkegaard's View of Death," 70; cf. Kierkegaard, *Papirer*, eds. P.A. Heiberg et al. (Copenhagen: Gyldendal, 1968–70), vol. 10, 3A 139.

43. Watkin, "Kierkegaard's View of Death," 71.

44. Watkin, "Kierkegaard's View of Death," 73.

45. Watkin, "Kierkegaard's View of Death," 73.

46. Cf. Kierkegaard, "There will be a Resurrection of the Dead, of the Righteous—and of the Unrighteous," 205; cf. SV vol. 10, 203–7.

as a disembodied immortal soul or a resurrection of the body. He is also not concerned with body-soul dualism. His focus could be described as a type of transcendental immediate resurrection that is divorced from questions about corporeality. The way he describes the moment of death is dramatic:

> There is something very specific I have to say, and I have it so much in my conscience that I feel as if I dare not die without having said it. For in the instant I die and leave the world, I will—so I understand it—I will in the same second—so fearfully fast it goes!—still in the same second I will be infinitely far from here, at another place, where still in the same second—fearful speed!—the question will be put me: Have you carried out the errand, have you said what you had to, *very decidedly*? And if I have not done so, what then![47]

I would suggest that, for Kierkegaard, because death is the moment of judgment, it is also the moment of a *fearsome transcendence*. It is at this moment that we must answer whether we have "carried out the errand" or not. The errand is the command of Christ—to love the neighbor; to deny the self for the sake of the other; to be selfless. In other words, the judgment is based on whether we have loved the other rather than loved only ourselves (Luther's *cor curvum in se*). In this sense, "immortality" *is* judgment and that judgment is immediate: "it is appointed for mortals to die once, and after that the judgment" (cf. Heb 9:27).

Kierkegaard seems to allow for the possibility of damnation in hell for the one who does not deny the self and love the other: "everything is lost for you, eternity does not acknowledge you, it never knew you—or, even more terrible, it knows you as you are known, it binds you fast to yourself in despair."[48] However, Watkin notes that for Kierkegaard the use of "hell" is more a device to "awaken [people] from their complacency" rather than an inevitable fate for those that did not carry out the "errand" in their earthly instantiation.[49] In spite of the fear that "immortality" should cause, because it is absolute judgment by God of each and every person, Kierkegaard admits that he is in fact a universalist: "If others go to hell, then I will go too. But I do not believe that; on the contrary I believe

---

47. Cited in Watkin, 74. Cf. *Papirer*, vol. 10, 6 B 232. Emphasis original.
48. Cited in Watkin, 74. Cf. *Sickness unto Death*, SV vol. 11, 122.
49. Watkin, 74–5. Watkins notes that Kierkegaard views on the possibility of damnation are conflicted as at times he seems to advocate an unlimited grace that yields to universalism.

that all will be saved, myself with them—something which arouses my deepest amazement."[50]

The way that Kierkegaard phrases this universalist statement is important: "But I don't believe that . . . ." How each human being existentially views life and death determines his or her immortal destiny. If we choose to despair of life as meaningless, we will be judged for this category mistake (although saved in the end). If we choose to believe that God calls us to deny self and carry the cross in love for the other, then salvation already belongs to us in this life. Yet, no one escapes the judgment. So, one could say that for Kierkegaard the judgment itself is the event of salvation. This is crucial because in this Kierkegaard hints at something like salvific judgment. The moment of death is also the moment of a fearful transcendence (judgment) that will result in salvation—in fact, universal salvation.

Martin Heidegger's Philosophy of Death: Sein zum Tode

I now turn to the German existentialist philosopher Martin Heidegger (1889–1976), certainly influenced by Kierkegaard, but with a largely areligious orientation. Heidegger continues to impact both theology and philosophy in spite of his membership in the Nazi Party (1933–45) and the 2014 publication of the "Black Notebooks" (*Schwarze Hefte*) which contain some damaging anti-Semitic content.[51] It is alleged that he said privately that his Nazi affiliation was the "the biggest stupidity of his life," but he never expressed in public any regret.[52] However, for the purposes of this study, it is Heidegger's earlier work, specifically his book *Being and Time* (1927), that is of interest—and indeed it is this work that arguably asserts the strongest influence in the academy, including theology, to this day.[53] Heidegger began his career as a Roman Catholic academic and studied theology at the University of Freiburg. It was at Freiburg that he switched to the study of philosophy. Heidegger's philosophy is effectively non-theistic, but it is not at all clear that Heidegger would accept the label that he is an atheist. He seems to refute this in his *Letter on Humanism*

---

50. Kierkegaard, *Søren Kierkegaard's Journals and Papers*, 6:557.

51. Cf. Trawny, ed., *Martin Heidegger: Überlegungen II-VI (Schwarze Hefte 1931–1938)*.

52. "die größte Dummheit seines Lebens" cited in Petzet, *Auf einen Stern zugehen*, 43.

53. Cf. Heidegger, *Sein und Zeit*; ET: *Being and Time*.

(1947).⁵⁴ He also met with a priest before his death and was buried in the Catholic parish cemetery in his native town of Meßkirch.

The validity of Heidegger's philosophy has been debated for several decades, but what is of interest here is his approach to human death and his influence on theology. Two prominent theologians that are indebted to Heidegger are Rudolf Bultmann (1884–1976) and Karl Rahner SJ (1904–84).⁵⁵ Rahner will be the focus of the next section of this chapter. Heidegger's principal concept regarding human death as articulated in *Being and Time* is *Sein zum Tode* ("Being towards Death"). The sentence most often quoted to describe *Sein zum Tode* is this: "As soon as man comes to life, he is at once old enough to die."⁵⁶ The word that Heidegger uses to refer to human existence is *Dasein* ("Being There") which in colloquial German is used to refer to presence. Heidegger uses *Dasein* ontologically: *Dasein* is "the entity which each of us himself is" and "the being of man." Heidegger prefers using the word *Dasein* because it does not commit him to any one typology of human existence (e.g., biological, psychological, rational, etc.). It is simply existential.⁵⁷ Returning to humans as "beings towards death," *Dasein* is a state of being that has the inherent quality of 'thrown-ness' toward death. George Pattison translates *Sein zum Tode* as "running towards death" in his theological essay on Heidegger's thanatology.⁵⁸ Thus, mortality is an essential and inescapable part of what it is to be human. *Sein zum Tode* as a concept is non-theistic and, at least functionally, denies an "afterlife" for human beings. For Heidegger, authentic human existence is achieved only when we confront and accept our *Dasein* as "being towards death." However, though this may be true, death itself often ends in non-fulfilment:

> With its death, Dasein has indeed "fulfilled" its course. But in doing so, has it necessarily exhausted its specific possibilities? Rather, are not these precisely what gets taken away from Dasein? Even "unfulfilled" Dasein ends. On the other hand, so little is it the case that Dasein comes to ripeness with its end, that Dasein may well have passed its ripeness before the end. For

---

54. Cf. Heidegger, "Letter on Humanism," 253–54.
55. Cf. Inwood, "Martin Heidegger," 385.
56. Heidegger, *Being and Time*, 289.
57. Cf. Inwood, "Dasein," 189.
58. Pattison, *Heidegger on Death*, 13ff.

the most part, Dasein ends in unfulfilment, or else by having disintegrated and been used up.[59]

Pattison notes that for Heidegger, death is that which is always impending. This may seem as if Heidegger's view of human existence (*Dasein*) is totally negative. But this is not the case. Heidegger rejects every attempt to describe his *Being and Time* as a philosophy of death.[60] For Heidegger, it is just the opposite: "With death, Dasein stands before itself in its ownmost potentiality-for-Being. This is a possibility in which the issue is nothing less than Dasein's Being-in-the-world."[61] In Pattison's analysis of Heidegger, Pattison quotes the Russian Orthodox theologian and monk Sophrony Sacharov (1896–1993):

> My inevitable death was not just mine, someone of no account, "one of the little ones." No. In me, with me, all that had formed part of my consciousness would die: people close to me, their sufferings and love, the whole historical process, the universe in general, the sun, the stars, endless space; even the Creator of the world Himself—He, too, would die in me.... The fact that with his death the world, even God, dies is possible only if he himself, of himself, is in a certain sense the centre of all creation.[62]

As Pattison notes, Heidegger would not have used the same language as Sakharov. However, it is true that human death is the "end of the universe" for that person. Death then, for Heidegger, is "the possibility of the absolute impossibility of Dasein. Thus, death reveals itself as that possibility which is one's ownmost, which is non-relational, and unsurpassable."[63] This utter non-relationality in death will make an appearance again in the discussion of *Ganztodtheorie* ("total death theory") that will be discussed in later sections of this chapter.

Since death is the inevitable and inescapable annihilation of *Dasein*, it is understandable that this realization will cause a human being fear and dread. Heidegger comments on this by saying:

> Anxiety in the face of death must not be confused with fear in the face of one's demise. This anxiety is not an accidental or random mood of "weakness" in some individual; but as a basic

---

59. Heidegger, *Being and Time*, 288.
60. Cf. Pattison, *Heidegger on Death*, 4.
61. Heidegger, *Being and Time*, 294. See also Pattison, *Heidegger on Death*, 24ff.
62. Pattison, *Heidegger on Death*, 23. Cf. Sakharov, *We Shall See Him as He Is*, 12.
63. Cited in Pattison, *Heidegger on Death*, 25; cf. Heidegger, *Being and Time*, 294.

state-of-mind of Dasein, it amounts to the disclosedness of the fact that Dasein exists as thrown Being towards its end.[64]

Anxiety about death is *required* for authentic *Dasein*. In fact, a consciousness of our *thrown-ness* towards death is essential to realizing all the possibilities one's *Dasein* is capable of while alive.[65] Thus, this anxiety should not impede a full, rich life. However, most of us do not embrace this anxiety in our "everydayness" (*Alltäglichkeit*). Rather, we seek "tranquillization" of this anxiety, often by transferring our own anxiety onto a person who is dying:

> The evasive concealment in the face of death dominates everydayness so stubbornly that, in being with one another, the "neighbours" often still keep talking to the "dying person" into the belief that he will escape death and soon return to the tranquillized everydayness of the world of his concern.[66]

Heidegger's insistence that an active, conscious, even anxious, awareness of our thrown-ness towards death is the only way we can have authentic *Dasein* runs counter to the well-known statement of Wittgenstein mentioned previously: human beings *do not* live to experience death.[67] Dying may be part of life as a momentary and finite occurrence, but a *living-towards-death* is another matter. It could be argued forcefully that this is no way to live at all. Yet, for Heidegger, death-awareness is the path to true human freedom and self-understanding, or to put it in his own words, it is the only path to "impassioned freedom towards death."[68] This concept brings us to a student of Heidegger, the Jesuit Catholic theologian Karl Rahner (1904–84).

Karl Rahner's Theology of Death: The End of Being-in-Time

Karl Rahner is one of the most important Roman Catholic theologians of the twentieth century. Like the Protestant New Testament scholar Rudolf Bultmann, Rahner was influenced by Heidegger's existentialism. In fact, Rahner attended Heidegger's lectures in Freiburg, 1934–39, while he was working on his doctorate. His dissertation on Thomistic epistemology,

---

64. Pattison, *Heidegger on Death*, 26; cf. Heidegger, *Being and Time*, 295.
65. Pattison, *Heidegger on Death*, 26.
66. Pattison, *Heidegger on Death*, 27; cf. Heidegger, *Being and Time*, 297.
67. Cf. Wittgenstein, *Tractatus Logico-Philosophicus*, 6.431
68. Cf. Pattison, *Heidegger on Death*, 35; Heidegger, *Being and Time*, 311.

Geist in Welt ("Spirit in the World"), shows the influence of Heidegger's thought (which caused it to be rejected by his supervisor).[69] It is perhaps not surprising that among the vast corpus of his writings is an earlier work from 1958 entitled *On the Theology of Death*.[70] However, it would be incorrect to think of Rahner as in any way a "Heideggerian" theologian. He certainly found Heidegger's notion of *Sein zum Tode* compelling, but he interpreted this along Christian theological lines. Also, it is arguable that the philosophy of Heidegger's *Being and Time* concerning human mortality is self-evident: human beings are indeed always moving towards biological death from the moment of birth, but Heidegger finds an active confrontation with this fact as a path to human freedom. Rahner uses this concept, but in a very different way from Heidegger, above all, because death is not the absolute end of human existence (*Dasein*). For Rahner, *Dasein* is eschatological—which could not be less Heideggerian. In addition, death has a cause for the early Rahner and the cause is original sin: "Death is guilt made visible."[71] It is collective human guilt that "causes" death for beings-in-time. This post-Edenic death is a universal phenomenon that affects the *whole person*: "We do not mean that 'things go on' after death, as though we only changed horses, as Feuerbach puts it, and rode on. It is not a continuation of the peculiar distraction and vagueness of temporal existence.... No, in this regard death puts an end to the *whole* man [sic]."[72]

However, death, while it does end human life in the temporo-spatial reality of this world, is *not* the "end of everything"—which for Rahner "is really impossible and would be worse than hell . . . ."[73] It is here we can see the difference between Rahner and Heidegger because for Heidegger death is indeed the "end of everything." For Rahner, death is the end of the whole human being in the sense that it causes a definitive and final end to a human being as a being in time and freedom. Thus, death is a *personal* act. Human beings have freedom in time (in this universe of time and space) to choose to do good or evil, to as it were give into sin (including original sin) or to respond to God's grace in loving action to neighbor. This results in an historical process whereby human beings ex-

69. Cf. Rahner, *Geist in Welt*; ET: *Spirit in the World*.

70. Cf. Rahner, *Zur Theologie des Todes*; ET: *On the Theology of Death*.

71. Rahner, *On the Theology of Death*, 49.

72. Rahner, *Theological Investigations*, vol. 4, 347. Cf. Rahner, "Das Leben der Toten." Emphasis original.

73. Rahner, *Theological Investigations*, vol. 4, 347.

ercise their freedom in time. It is this historical "accumulation" of actions (for or against God) that ends at death and is judged.[74]

For Rahner, human freedom is not simply the ability to choose whatever one wishes (e.g., *liberum abitrium*), but rather it is the freedom to respond *for* grace (the good) or *for* sin (evil). This does not mean that human beings are deemed good or bad based on a laundry list of good works vs. sins that are enumerated at death. Rather, it is about how human beings have actualized love, especially for neighbor, throughout their earthly lives. It is this *being* now outside freedom-in-time (i.e., dead) that will "stand" before God:

> . . . the achieved final validity of human existence which has grown to maturity in freedom comes to be *through*, and not *after* death. What has come to be is the liberated, final validity of something which was once temporal, and which came to be in spirit and in freedom, and which therefore formed time in order to be, and not really in order to continue on in time.[75]

Rahner would agree with Heidegger that "tranquilizing" the awareness that to be a human being is to be *Sein zum Tode* leads to inauthentic existence. Therefore, seeking after worldly pleasures and self-indulgences which anaesthetize our death anxiety leads not only to an unfulfilled life, but has eschatic import. Since it is God that has made human beings mortal as free beings in time, we should rather embrace this fate and truly live. We must say "yes" to death to be truly free: "Wherever there is real liberty, there is love for death and courage for death."[76] But the prescription for such love and courage in the face of death is not an existential stoicism as would be recommended by Heidegger. Rather, it is the life of selfless, unconditional love for the other which results in an authenticity of life. For Rahner, human beings are *more than time*. Our terror before death, especially for those who live in loveless inauthenticity, is based on our innate self-understanding:

> It is only because we have become immortal in our life that death with its menacing and impenetrable mask of destructivity

---

74. Cf. Phan, "Eschatology," 179–81.

75. Phan, "Eschatology," 181. Cf. Rahner, *Foundations of the Christian Faith*, 437. Phan notes that the *Foundations* are not a true summary of Rahner's theology or eschatology (Cf. Phan, "Eschatology," 190n2). For a fuller treatment cf. Rahner, *Theological Investigations*, vol. 4, 347–54.

76. Phan, "Eschatology," 181. Cf. Rahner, *On the Theology of Death*, 87.

is for us so deadly. A beast dies a less deadly death than we. These and similar experiences would be impossible if the reality which we experience were, of its nature and essence, something that perished, something that wished to be no more.[77]

For Rahner, *pace* Brecht, we *do not* die like all the animals and something *does* come after (admittedly, the word "after" implies we remain beings-in-time rather when in fact, for Rahner, we become timeless). Yet, death, as a natural aspect of being-in-time, is still something we must *suffer*. In commenting on Rahner's christological approach to dying, Peter Phan writes that "in dying with Christ, the Christian undergoes the same dialectical experience of remoteness from and nearness to God, of doubt and faith, despair and hope, rebellion and love. Furthermore, she and he can do this not only at the moment of death but throughout their lives, especially in the sacraments . . . ."[78]

While Rahner does understand human ontology as possessing a material body and personal spirit (he prefers to avoid the word "soul"), he does not accept the simplistic definitions of body-soul dualism as taught in some catechisms.[79] However, the un-resurrected dead do have "life." He writes: "it cannot be denied that there is an 'intermediate state' in the destiny of man between death and bodily fulfilment . . . ."[80] The intermediate state will be discussed in the next chapter, but this is an important point. For Rahner, unlike for some of his Protestant contemporaries, the dead are not *ganz tot* ("entirely dead"). However, without discussing now about what sort of "life" the dead possess, Rahner comments this way:

> There is no place in Catholic Christianity for intercourse with the dead as individuals, as spiritualism aims at. There is not because the dead do not exist, not because they are really separate from us, not because their fidelity and love, made perfect before God, does not watch over us, not as if their existence were not

77. Rahner, "The Life of the Dead," *Theological Investigations*, vol. 4, 349.

78. Phan, "Eschatology," 182.

79. Cf. "Q. How does 'the resurrection of the body' comfort you? A. Not only will my soul be taken immediately after this life to Christ its head, but also my very flesh will be raised by the power of Christ, reunited with my soul and made like Christ's glorious body," *Heidelberg Catechism* (1563) Q. 57, see Schaff, ed., *Creeds of Christendom*, vol. 3, 326; cf. "What is 'rising'? In death, the separation of the soul from the body, the human body decays and the soul goes to meet God, while awaiting its reunion with its glorified body," *Catechism of the Catholic Church*, 997. Hereafter cited as CCC. See also Klein, "Karl Rahner on the Soul," 2ff.

80. Rahner, "The Life of the Dead," in *Theological Investigations*, vol. 4, 352–53.

truly embedded by death above all in the silent, secret ground of our own existence. But [because] *we* are still creatures *in time*.[81]

Rahner presents a theology of death that seeks to both affirm the radicality of human death as the death of the whole person (body and soul) as far as its existence as a being-in-time. Thus, the dead are *ganz tot* in their active relationship to beings-in-time (human *Dasein*). They are not however *ganz tot* outside of this-worldly time. In the timelessness of God, they live and await bodily fulfilment in the resurrection. However, while Rahner might advise a stoicism before the inevitability of death, death also entails suffering (*passio*). I therefore turn to Joseph Ratzinger (b. 1927) for a reflection on this aspect of death who appeals that we not seek analgesic solutions to death, but accept it as an essential aspect of human life.

Joseph Ratzinger's Theology of Death: Loving Assent to Life as a Whole

Pope Emeritus Benedict XVI (Joseph Ratzinger), agrees that "Bourgeois society hides death away."[82] He laments that death is now

> ... deprived of its character as the place where the metaphysical breaks through. Death is rendered banal, so as to quell the unsettling which arises from it. Schleiermacher once spoke of birth and death as "hewed out perspectives" through which man peers into the infinite. But the infinite calls his ordinary life-style into question. And therefore, understandably, humankind puts it to the ban. The repression of death is so much easier when death has been naturalized.[83]

He notes the words of the Litany of Saints in the petition *a subitanea morte, libera nos, Domine* ("from sudden death, deliver us, O Lord") and comments that in contemporary society this petition would actually be reversed. The request would be that God grants us a *sudden* death, above all to avoid suffering.[84] This is the key for Ratzinger: contemporary society desires the avoidance of suffering at all costs, not only physical pain but also *meta*physical fear. It is far better to die suddenly without

---

81. Rahner, "The Life of the Dead," 353–54.
82. Ratzinger, *Eschatology*, 69.
83. Ratzinger, *Eschatology*, 70–71.
84. Ratzinger, *Eschatology*, 71.

the experience of pain or the contemplation of impending annihilation and oblivion. For Ratzinger, however, this attitude about death is not humane, but dehumanizing. Indeed, such a sanitization of death results in a technological approach to human life which risks utilitarian solutions, such as the euthanizing of the incurably ill or the disabled. He thus comments: "The mounting callousness towards human life which we are experiencing today is intimately bound up with the refusal to confront the question of death."[85] Ratzinger is thus proposing that both theology and society engage in new forms of non-reductive (or non-positivist) thanatological enquiry: "Since positivist and materialist answers leave us finally perplexed as this crucial juncture, it should be clear that the issues of life and death are not among those which progress in a way the exact sciences can clarify."[86]

Ratzinger believes that human suffering is a requisite part of earthly life; even though we should do all we can to lessen it. The technocratic goal of contemporary humanity is the elimination of all suffering and this is, for Ratzinger, a human attempt to achieve its own "definitive redemption."[87] One can also argue that this is an implied critique of Marxism and its concept of the "realm of freedom." The reason we cannot and should not attempt to achieve a totally analgesic humanity is that it would result in "a ban on love and therewith the abolition of man. Such attempts constitute a pseudo-theology. They can only lead to an empty death and a vacuous life."[88] In other words, one should reduce suffering by all means, but the goal of the utter elimination of earthly suffering of any kind is anti-life: "Flight from suffering is flight from life."[89] The question that could be asked is whether suffering equates to pain. If so, is pain something that is good for human beings? Ratzinger never claims that pain or suffering are good things. Rather, he claims that one cannot escape either in this life. An attempt to live a totally painless life would mean not to be alive and not to love.

For Ratzinger, the fullness of life involves passion. The opposite of the passionate life is *apatheia*: "While faith does not deliberately seek out suffering, it knows that without the Passion [of Christ] life does not

85. Ratzinger, *Eschatology*, 72.
86. Ratzinger, *Eschatology*, 72.
87. Ratzinger, *Eschatology*, 103.
88. Ratzinger, *Eschatology*, 103.
89. Ratzinger, *Eschatology*, 103.

discover its own wholeness, but closes the door on its own plenitude. If life at its highest demands the Passion, then faith must reject *apatheia*, the attempt to avoid suffering, as contrary to human nature."[90] Thus, part of human nature in its earthly instantiation is at least some degree of suffering. Hence, an analgesic humanity would not be capable of passion, compassion, or love. In order to love truly, one must truly feel. A loveless humanity would no longer be truly human. Ratzinger also seems to imply that anxiety (metaphysical or otherwise) is a necessary aspect of a fully human life and in this he is echoing Kierkegaard, Heidegger, and Rahner. The agony in the garden of Jesus before his crucifixion, when he pleaded that the cup be passed from him (cf. Luke 22:42), is exemplary of the "plenitude" of the human experience of life: "Christ does not die the death of the philosopher. He dies in tears. On his lips was the bitter taste of abandonment and isolation in all its horror. Here the hubris that would be the equal of God is contrasted with an acceptance of the cup of being human, down it its last dregs."[91]

Ratzinger proffers that human beings must "assent to life as a whole."[92] The entirety of human life includes joy and suffering—and it is within this bittersweet context that human beings are able to engage in "loving service" to one another and thereby "acquire true riches and liberty."[93] Ratzinger concludes: "The only sufficient answer to the question of man is a response which discharges the infinite claims of love. Only eternal life corresponds to the question raised by human living and dying on this earth."[94]

In terms of the body-soul relationship in the human person, it is assumed that Ratzinger follows the "catechetical" teaching that restates a Thomistic concept of the soul as *forma corporalis* and that it separates from the body at death in the "Orphic-dualistic sense."[95] However, this is not necessarily what Ratzinger means. In fact, one could argue that Ratzinger's conception is monistic in at least some aspects.

> [God] *is* immortality, being the actuality of the relationship which is Trinitarian love. God is not "atomic": he is relationship,

---

90. Ratzinger, *Eschatology*, 101.
91. Ratzinger, *Eschatology*, 102.
92. Ratzinger, *Eschatology*, 101.
93. Ratzinger, *Eschatology*, 101.
94. Ratzinger, *Eschatology*, 103.
95. Cf. Mühling, *The T&T Clark Handbook of Christian Eschatology*, 195.

since he is love. It is for this reason that he is life. . . . The signal we derive from this view of being tells us: relation makes immortal. . . . Matter as such cannot provide the underpinning for man's continuing identity. . . . Hence the indispensability of the body-soul distinction. Nevertheless, the Christian tradition, with an ever increasing consistency of purpose . . . has conceived this duality in such a way that it is *not dualistic* but rather brings to light the worth and unity of the human person as a whole.[96]

Ratzinger's anthropology as a duality that is not dualistic is a compelling restatement of a traditional, Thomistic concept of death: there is indeed an immaterial soul that "separates" from the body at death, not as a separate entity but as the part of a human being that continues *postmortem* as the relational aspect of the whole person. It is this aspect of the human being that is before God at death. For Ratzinger, this is what Aquinas actually taught. The soul is however tethered; it remains connected to the body in anticipation of resurrection, but it is also 'active' apart from it. For Ratzinger, this intermediate state is only understandable from an earthward and temporal perspective.

The "between" only exists in our perspective. In reality the "end of time" is timeless. The person who dies steps into the presence of the Last Day and of the judgment; the Lord's resurrection and the parousia. As one author put it, "The resurrection can be situated in death and not just on the 'Last Day.'"[97]

This statement raises several questions about the intermediate state (the state between death and resurrection). But what Ratzinger is above all insisting is that human death in its relation to Christian theology cannot be anaesthetized. Human beings must in some manner *suffer* death as part of the path to eternal life which is an analogy to the crucifixion and resurrection of Christ. This is what Ratzinger means to wholly assenting to life. While it can be argued that suffering of any kind is a bad thing, Ratzinger is only stating what remains factual about human dying. Yet, the tethered soul is also capable of joy and suffering in the intermediate state. Thus, for Ratzinger, death does not equate to the end of joy and suffering and this issue will be discussed in the next sections.

---

96. Cf. Ratzinger, *Eschatology*, 157–59. Emphasis original.

97. Ratzinger, *Eschatology*, 108. Ratzinger is quoting Gisbert Greshake (b. 1933) and his idea of an immediate resurrection in death. Cf. Greshake, *Auferstehung der Toten*, 387. It should be noted that Ratzinger does not agree with Greshake's notion.

Eberhard Jüngel's Theology of Death: Total Death and Resurrection

Eberhard Jüngel (b. 1934) is perhaps the best known of the Protestant theologians of the twentieth century associated with *Ganztodtheorie* ("total death theory"). The *Ganztod* concept argues against the concept of the soul separating from the body at death (*anima separata*). This could never be accepted by Ratzinger and would go too far even for Rahner. For Jüngel, however, the human person is entirely dead and must await the resurrection at the end of time: "The person who is dying does not return home to God: he returns to the dust from which he was created. In this sense, death marks the end of a man's relationship to God."[98]

Ganztodtheorie began to develop with theologians such as Paul Althaus (1888–1966), Oscar Cullmann (1902–99), and Carl Stange (1870–1959). Cullmann famously stated his case against the immortality of the soul in his 1955 Ingersoll Lecture on the Immortality of Man given at Harvard Divinity School. For Cullmann, an immortal soul is unbiblical and was not part of primitive church teaching. It is rather the result of Platonizing dualism that should be expunged from Christian eschatology. Since the human soul is mortal, both body and soul as a unity of the human person will be resurrected. Cullman's assertion merits being stated in full:

> For Socrates and Plato no new act of creation is necessary. For the body is indeed bad and should not live on. And that part which is to live on, the soul, does not die at all.
>
> If we want to understand the Christian faith in the Resurrection, we must completely disregard the Greek thought that the material, the bodily, the corporeal is bad and must be destroyed, so that the death of the body would not be in any sense a destruction of the true life. For Christian (and Jewish) thinking the death of the body is also destruction of God-created life. No distinction is made: even the life of our body is true life; death is the destruction of all life created by God. Therefore it is death and not the body which must be conquered by the Resurrection. Only he who apprehends with the first Christians the horror of death, who takes death seriously as death, can comprehend the Easter exultation of the primitive Christian community and understand that the whole thinking of the New Testament is governed by belief in the Resurrection. Belief in

---

98. Jüngel, *Death: the Riddle and the Mystery*, 77.

the immortality of the soul is not belief in a revolutionary event. Immortality, in fact, is only a negative assertion: the soul does not die, but simply lives on. Resurrection is a positive assertion: the whole man, *who has really died*, is recalled to life by a new act of creation by God.[99]

Cullmann wrote in the preface to the English publication of the lecture that "[n]o other publication of mine has provoked such enthusiasm or such violent hostility."[100] His lecture was published in several books and journals beginning with a Festschrift for Karl Barth's seventieth birthday in 1956.[101]

This theory of "total death" was restated by Eberhard Jüngel in his concise book *Tod* ("Death") first published in German in 1971. Sixteen years after Cullmann's lecture, Jüngel was as equally emphatic: "There is no immortality of the soul" (*Eine Unsterblichkeit der Seele gibt es nicht*).[102] Like his predecessors, Jüngel wants to find a non-Platonizing concept of death and create what he believes to be a thoroughly biblical understanding of human mortality. The various passages in the Hebrew Bible that allude to the utter finality of death are mentioned frequently throughout the book, e.g., "The dead do not praise the LORD" (Ps 115:17).[103] All human relationality whatsoever ends with death—it is a tripartite death to self, to neighbor, and to God:

> To have died means not only that a man no longer has any relationship to everything apart from himself. First and foremost, he no longer has any relationship to himself: "For the living know (at least) that they will die, but the dead know nothing" (Eccl. 9:5). . . . Sin exerts a pressure in the absence of relationships. It renders man relationless. Death thus becomes one facet of this pressure which drives him towards relationlessness. . . . When death has actually occurred, then man's life has become completely relationless. The dead person is then forever alienated from God. Apart from God, everything becomes relationless.[104]

---

99. Cullmann, *Immortality of the Soul or Resurrection of the Dead?* 12. Emphasis mine.
100. Cullmann, *Immortality of the Soul or Resurrection of the Dead?* 1.
101. Cf. Cullmann, "Unsterblichkeit der Seele und Auferstehung der Toten."
102. Jüngel, *Death*, 120; Cf. *Tod*, 152.
103. Jüngel, *Death*, 77.
104. Jüngel, *Death*, 78.

If death as a curse is the consequence of man's drive toward relationlessness, then any deliverance from this death must consist in the creation of a new foundation for those relationships in which alone human life can find its fulfilment.[105]

Christian mortalism is not new to theology. However, the concept that soul-sleep or anything approaching *Ganztodtheorie* was held by Martin Luther (1483–1546) is questionable. Although many "total death" theologians were and are German Lutherans, it cannot be argued that this concept was taught by Luther himself in any consistent way:

> For how is Abraham a servant of God after his death? Will God not be able eventually to forget Abraham? Today he certainly still serves God, just as Adam, Abel, and Noah serve God. And this must be carefully noted; for it is divine truth that Abraham is living, serving God, and ruling with Him. But what the nature of that life is, whether he is asleep or awake, is another question. We do not have to know how the soul rests. *It is certain that it is alive*.[106]

Luther here, as elsewhere, is writing about a state of dormition (sleep) and not "total death": the soul *lives to* God. For Jüngel, the soul *dies* with the body. He understands body and soul monistically and not in a dualism of mortal flesh and immortal soul. Death enters the world for human beings because they desire to be in non-relation to God; to be free from God.[107] Like Rahner, Jüngel understands death as the result of sin (for Jüngel, sin is relationlessness). The curse of death is the curse of human non-relationality. Yet, through the resurrection of Jesus Christ, death no longer retains its absolute power: "Through Christ, life and death are placed in a new relationship to one another.... Life and death are therefore no longer the criteria which define man's relationship to God. Jesus Christ and faith in him is the one criterion for defining that relationship."[108] This explains the apostle Paul's reversal of the paradigm of the Hebrew Bible which sees death as an absolute end with no remedy. Paul writes that "to live is Christ and to die is gain" (Phil 1:20). This is a reversal of Hebrew Bible texts which understand death as total, inevitable loss.

---

105. Jüngel, *Death*, 89.

106. Martin Luther, "Lectures on Genesis: Chapters 26–30," in *Luther's Works*, vol. 5, 74. Emphasis mine.

107. Cf. Mühling, "Eschatology," 190ff.

108. Mühling, "Eschatology," 83.

The restoration of any relationship that leads to life is God's act, not humanity's. It is here that Jüngel disagrees with a key point made by Rahner (and he mentions Rahner by name)—that in death "a human being makes a final decision, the act which consummates human life."[109] For Jüngel, this concept is not biblical because man is passive before death and death ends not only the being-in-time of the human person, it ends the human being *in toto* in spite of the new relationship between God and humanity in Christ. Markus Mühling summarizes the "total death" concept of Jüngel and its problems in this way:

> Understanding human death in terms of "total death," i.e. as total relationlessness, appears to approximate to biblical understandings of death[;] . . . it is compatible with sociological, historical, and also biological understandings of human being and it takes [biological death] very seriously. . . . [However,] the understanding of death as total relationlessness can be questioned from the standpoint of the faithfulness of God, the identity of the human person, as well as for empirical reasons and can be modified in such a way that death is understood as the end of capacity for active relationality, whereas passive relationality, according to Härle, is preserved primarily in the relationship to God.[110]

Mühling is referring to the German Protestant theologian Wilfried Härle (b. 1941) who sought to modify Jüngel's stance in an effort to defend the coherence of the doctrine of God. For Härle, God cannot be said to be in relation with us if God allows the annihilation of the human person at death. In addition, total annihilation at death would mean that individual identity is lost. The person resurrected at the eschaton would be discontinuous with the annihilated dead person. Such a resurrection amounts to a re-creation or a duplication. Thus, the dead person X is not the resurrected person Y, but rather person Y is a replicant. Härle disagrees with the premise that the will of God could guarantee or retain a person's identity within the divine mind. While an omnipotent Being could do so, it would mean that the divine will and not God's love is operative. If God loves dead person X, then God cannot allow her total death. Härle also argues against the concept of divine preservation of the identity of the dead because it would mean that God could create two or more of the same persons of the same identity *by sheer will*. However, this also violates God's love because God is *in relation* to each and every

109. Mühling, "Eschatology," 91.
110. Mühling, "Eschatology," 191; 194.

created person. In addition, the judgment that accompanies resurrection would not be possible or valid because the judged person would be discontinuous with the resurrected person. Such a judgment could be the equivalent of creating a resurrected scapegoat—the person judged and any consequence of that judgment would be actioned upon an entirely different person. It would seem that Härle is proposing not "total death," but dying *into* God. The continuity required is maintained because in death we enter into a new relationship with God that is essentially *intra Deum* ("within God"). Interestingly, Mühling notes that Jüngel did not feel that Härle's modification of his concept of "total death" contradicted his own theory. This is because Härle's alteration did not require a dualistic human ontology.[111]

Jüngel and others in the tradition of *Ganztodtheorie* want to present a non-Platonizing, biblical eschatology that they insist demands "total death" with no continuity *post mortem* of the human person unless one allows for Härle's modification. In doing so, it, at least partially, can claim a concordance with modern biological science. The human dead are indeed totally dead from the vantage of biology and *Ganztodtheorie*. However, this de-mythologizing exercise creates insuperable problems for the doctrine of God and God's relationality to the dead, our own relationship with the dead, and the problem of continuity of resurrected persons at the eschaton—at least without Härle's modification.

Antje Jackelén's Theology of Death: Ganztod Revisited

Antje Jackelén (b. 1955), currently Archbishop of Uppsala and Primate of the Church of Sweden, is critical of the concept of death as transition and denies the immortality of the soul in her book *Time and Eternity* and can be said to accept the "total death theory" as described in the previous section.[112] The concept that death is merely a change from one form of existence to another trivializes the radicality of death: "The notion of the immortality of the soul is incompatible with Pauline theology because, in the final analysis, it does not take death seriously."[113] This is perhaps the most important aspect of her understanding of the seriousness of death.

---

111. Cf. Mühling, "Eschatology," 192ff; cf. Härle, *Dogmatik*, 629–33.

112. Cf. Jackelén, *Time and Eternity*, 217ff. First published in German as *Zeit und Ewigkeit* (2002).

113. Jackelén, *Time and Eternity*, 111.

For Jackelén, death must be "neither less nor more than death."[114] Death as simply a transition where the soul departs the body to experience a particular judgment with its rewards, purifications, or punishments or to enter the spirit world of a dualist Gnosticism is not true death and is to be rejected: "The New Testament is not about conjuring away death, but rather about suffering and overcoming death."[115] In addition, death-as-transition compromises the understanding of eternity: "To the extent that the conception of death as transition relativizes death per se, the character of eternity, as something radically different from time, is eroded. Eternity becomes a kind of prolonged time, an eternalized time. This outlook lacks the possibility of making eternity conceivable as the Other of time."[116] In this, Jackelén refers to the overall theme of her work in question: time and eternity. One of the reasons for rejecting body-soul dualism with death as a "transition" is because it denigrates the concept of eternity into some sort of inconceivable infinity of time. This results in the deconstruction of the concept of eternal life within the context of modernity.[117] Thus, deconstructed and discarded, "modern" human beings have no relationship with God thereby rendering the very concept of eternity as meaningless.[118] Quite literally, the only thing that remains is death itself, unless it can be overcome through technology. In this system, "the *now* is the only place for happiness."[119] Jackelén seeks to avoid both trivializing death and the loss of eternity and eternal life which leaves only death as the ultimate outcome of human existence through a theology of time, which she describes as "conceiving eternity as the Other of time."[120]

However, my interest in Jackelén's oeuvre concerns her theology of death rather than time. She defines death as "absolute non-relationality":

> Death is the collapse of all relations; it is the beginning and the event of absolute non-relationality, and, as such, it must be taken seriously and suffered as the "anthropological passive." That death is not more than death, however, means it has to be reduced to that limit which humans cannot set, for humans

114. Jackelén, *Time and Eternity*, 115; 217.
115. Jackelén, *Time and Eternity*, 112.
116. Jackelén, *Time and Eternity*, 112.
117. Jackelén, *Time and Eternity*, 113.
118. Jackelén, *Time and Eternity*, 113.
119. Jackelén, *Time and Eternity*, 114. Emphasis original.
120. Jackelén, *Time and Eternity*, 108.

cannot abolish it. Thus, death must be and become what Jesus Christ made of it: the limit to human beings that is set by God alone, who, in our total powerlessness, never abuses divine power.[121]

Within her overall project, Jackelén seems to propose that eternal life requires an antecedent total death followed by resurrection. The intermediate period between death and resurrection for the human person is non-relational: the dead human has ceased to exist in totality. The question then arises: how can there be preserved identity (and/or selfhood) if a person is annihilated by death and then resurrected (recreated) by God in the life of the world-to-come? Jackelén posits, using an analogy of a computer with a vast memory capacity, that human identities (and/or selves) are retained in the memory of God. This yields to an obvious discontinuity between the earthly life and eternal life of a human being. Jackelén acknowledges this. Her solution to the maintenance of continuity of the "self" of the dead is by means of its relationship to the God: "From the human perspective of our dependence on time, death must be described as non-relationality, as well as deprivation of the self. The person who had died is deprived of herself. What she will be, she cannot make; she can only receive it."[122] The selfhood of the dead is preserved in the memory of God. Jackelén is aware that this means that the dead person has no independent continuity of self—it is only held in the divine mind of God and it must be received by the dead at the resurrection. She argues that any continuity of self that is maintained *within* the dead person means that such identity is

> ... continuously bound by the timeline. ... [T]his eschatological model remains anthropocentrically restricted from the outset and thus leaves little room for cosmic dimensions. ... In contrast I would propose to understand eschatology as a hope that is precisely not hope in oneself. The preserved identity does not lie in a static conservation of one's own sameness along an infinite timeline, but is rather found in relation to the Other. ... I do not see selfhood as being constituted primarily through self-conservation, but rather through self-reception, that is,

---

121. Jackelén, *Time and Eternity*, 115. Here Antje Jackelén is referring to Werner G. Jeanrond (b. 1955) in *Call and Response*, 60; and more generally to Jüngel's *Tod*. The reference to the "anthropological passive" ["Der Tod ist ein anthropologishes Passiv"] is found in Jüngel, "Der Tod als Geheimnis des Lebens," in his *Entsprechungen*, 345.

122. Jackelén, *Time and Eternity*, 218.

through receiving oneself. Only in this way is it possible to come to oneself and find oneself; and, indeed, eternal life then presumably has to do with more than finding oneself. Identity becomes a question of relation.[123]

Jackelén then understands any personal continuity as relational, the passive relationship of the created person to the active relationship that God as the Other has with that person.[124] What is unclear is whether Jackelén's approach to eschatology allows for human beings to experience resurrection subjectively. Yet, it could be argued that the preservation of human individuality should not be the desire of the Christian.

Jackelén asserts that her theology of death and resurrection "is not ... an assertion of the dissolution of identity."[125] Identity is a difficult concept in eschatology because of its association with fixity: a static earth-bound self-understanding that cannot be maintained in the resurrected state. Resurrection is radical transformation: "flesh and blood cannot inherit the kingdom of God; nor does the perishable inherit the imperishable ... we shall all be changed." (1 Cor 15:52b). I would speculate that what Jackelén actually means is that human *subjectivity* is not dissolved. So, in spite of what I think are severe challenges to continuity between death and resurrection, Jackelén can affirm the words of Jesus to the good thief on the cross: "Truly I tell you, today you will be with me in Paradise" (Luke 23:43). Yet, it cannot be denied that her approach to eternal life for the individual is attenuated and deemphasized. In this regard, Jackelén keeps company with Jüngel and the twentieth-century existentialist theologians.

Jackelén's theology of death takes death as a biological fact—it is indeed the end of life of the human person and nothing "happens" after death until the resurrection. It also allows for a rational approach to death and eternal life that is perhaps more intellectually compatible with modern science, echoing the concept of resurrection posited by physicist Frank Tipler (b. 1946) and his proposal of a cosmological singularity he termed the Omega Point (*pace* Teilhard de Chardin).[126] The de-emphasis on personal survival accords with Eastern religions, in particular Buddhism. However, collectivizing eschatologies that radically attenuate

---

123. Jackelén, *Time and Eternity*, 218.
124. Jackelén, *Time and Eternity*, 219.
125. Jackelén, *Time and Eternity*, 219.
126. Cf. Tipler, *The Physics of Immortality*.

human subjectivity have significant problems. While there was a strong trend in twentieth-century liberal theology to depersonalize the "afterlife" and to dismiss individual salvation as trivial, this approach does not square with the gospel narratives that God in Christ comes to *persons* as well as communities. If not, the dialogue between Jesus and the thief on the cross is rendered meaningless. The danger of this type of eschatology is that the "good thief" will only be with Jesus in paradise in an amalgamated, discontinuous way that is unilateral and not relational; the thief will be with Jesus only as part of the human singularity, but it seems impossible that the thief would be aware of this paradisiacal reunion.

I would suggest that Jackelén's theology of death, while possessing certain advantages, is strongly reductive on the question of human subjectivity in the world-to-come. She insists on relationality as the remedy to the problems of eschatic discontinuity and resurrection as replication, but fails to explain how human subjectivity is maintained, unless the eschatic receiving of the self from God is analogous to a maintenance of subjectivity. If pre-eschatic relationality is unilateral, the question that remains is how depersonalization and dissolution of the human subject in the eschaton is avoided. However, her concept of eschatic self-reception is an intriguing possible remedy and I shall return to this later in this book.

Conclusion: Death as an Eschatic Event

> *As swimmers dare*
> *To lie face to the sky*
> *And water bears them,*
> *As hawks rest upon air*
> *And air sustains them,*
> *So would I learn to attain*
> *Freefall, and float*
> *Into Creator Spirit's deep embrace,*
> *Knowing no effort earns*
> *That all-surrounding grace.*
> —Denise Levertov[127]

---

127. Levertov, "The Avowal," 184.

The various approaches to the issue of human death could be broken down into two categories: a metaphysical nothingness and a metaphysical somethingness after death. Either "we die with all the animals and nothing comes after" or death is "Shakespearean" in that "all that live must die, passing through nature to eternity."[128]

I have engaged with those that hold to a materialist understanding of death and thus hold to the concept that death is the event of the annihilation of the human organism, such as Bertolt Brecht and Bertrand Russell. Others have advocated a metaphysical approach, such as the Christian existentialist approach to "immortality" of Kierkegaard, the non-theistic (or atheological) existentialist position of Heidegger in his *Sein zum Tode* concept, and the Christian reinterpretation of humanity's "thrownness-towards-death" by Rahner. Rahner, using Heidegger and Aquinas, seems to imply that death is itself a duality—that one is entirely dead and yet also eternalized or made timeless. In the approach by Ratzinger, there is an attempt to dialogue with the existentialist theology of the twentieth century through a reinterpretation of Thomas Aquinas that attempts to tighten the body-soul duality of scholastic theology.

A decidedly different approach to the interpretation of human death is given by Eberhard Jüngel in his concept of "total death" that eliminates dualism altogether and focuses on the promise of future resurrection. Antje Jackelén partly reaffirms the concept of "total death" and denies any separate existence of an immortal soul after biological death. For Jackelén, the death and resurrection of Jesus provide the blueprint that human beings must follow: death can only be "suffered and overcome." In addition, Jackelén remains agnostic about the possibility that individual human subjectivity is maintained in the eschaton, although she does not argue for the dissolution of the individual.

Returning to the opening sentence of this chapter, I wrote that no one knows what happens after death. Thus, one could argue that all of the concepts—from Bertrand Russell's proposal that we simply rot in the grave to Kierkegaard's transcendentalist leap of faith—are simply human viewpoints concerning mortality. The question "what happens when we die?" cannot be approached by claims of fact.

Embracing the argument that "something" happens at death is an act of faith which is not based on proof because "faith is the substance of things hoped for, the evidence of things not seen" (Heb 11:1 AV). To

---

128. William Shakespeare, "Hamlet," Act 1, Scene 2, lines 72–73.

believe in the "afterlife" or rather that a human being is not annihilated at death, but rather "overcomes" death is a radical act of hope. So, I do not approach this investigation by way of facts, but through faith, hope, and love within the context of Christian theology. Martin Luther wrote "That to which your heart clings and entrusts itself is . . . really your God."[129] So, this belief is, above all, grounded in the faithfulness and love of God. In this understanding, human death is an eschatic event because it is the moment when our relationality with this-worldly time-space is severed and we fall into divine love as intimated by Denise Levertov's (1923–97) poem quoted above. Thus, to die is to be in a state of absolute dependence on God. What happens in this moment is not known, but it is within the realm of speculative theology to explore, which is what this investigation seeks to do. Thus, it is the proposal of this dissertation that death is the *moment* of the eschatic event of salvific judgment. Yet, before this can be investigated, I must move through other problems associated with death.

3. Discarnation: The Problem of Intermediate Eschatology

> *A soul in this state makes its way to the invisible, which is like itself, the divine and immortal and wise, and arriving there it can be happy, having rid itself of confusion, ignorance, fear, violent desires and the other human ills and, as is said of the initiates, truly spend the rest of time with the gods.*
> —Socrates[130]

> *Flesh and blood cannot inherit the kingdom of God, nor does the perishable inherit the imperishable.*
> —1 Corinthians 15:50

> *Souls are immaterial subjects of mental properties. They have sensations and thoughts, desires and beliefs, and perform intentional actions. Souls are essential parts of human beings, and humans have sensations etc. and perform intentional actions in virtue of their souls doing so.*
> —Richard Swinburne[131]

---

129. Martin Luther, "Large Catechism," in *The Book of Concord*, 365.
130. Socrates in Plato's *Phaedo*, sec. 81a, in Cooper, ed., *Plato: Complete Works*, 71.
131. Swinburne, *The Evolution of the Soul*, 145.

In this section, I shall explore the concept discarnation (*discarnatio*) and its problems. By discarnation, I mean the concept in substance dualism that at death a human being is divided: the soul separates from the inanimate corpse and is capable of independent existence. If death is the irreversible failure of the human bio-organism as a whole with the *terminus ad quem* being the cessation of brain activity ("brain death"), I propose an alternative to discarnation. Rather than the separation of the soul from the fleshly body (*sarx*), I suggest that the moment of death is an eschatic event. My proposal is that the psychosomatic unity of the human being (body and soul; *soma* and *psyche*) is separated from earthly time-space. I therefore will argue against the traditional understandings of the separated soul (*anima separata* to use the Thomistic phraseology). Instead, one could see death as the moment that human beings enter the state of *vita separata* ('separated life') as far as their relationship with earthly time-space.

However, the concept of soul separation at death has a long history and it can be explained in several ways: the Platonist concept of a soul as the "true self" and the body as alien; Origen's understanding that the soul is imprisoned in the body as punishment for sin; the Thomistic modification of Aristotle's definition of the soul, that the soul is a substance and the form of the body (*forma corporis*) that together with the body constitute the human unity, yet the soul may still be severed from the body by death as *anima separata*; and the later simplified anthropological dualism by Renée Descartes (1596–1650) that the human being is comprised of two separable substances: *res cogitans* (soul) and *res extensa* (body).[132] For a modern definition of body-soul dualism, Charles Taliaferro (b. 1953) gives this definition:

> ... the thesis that persons are souls or minds in causal interaction with and yet remaining distinct from their material bodies, as well as the more modest thesis that a person has consciousness, experiences, or subjective states ... that are not identical with bodily, physical states, things, or events. Both forms of dualism hold that there is more to you than your neuroanatomy.[133]

---

132. Cf. Cross and Livingstone, eds., *The Oxford Dictionary of the Christian Church*, 1520-21; cf. Aquinas, *Summa Theologiae* Ia, 77, 8: *utres omnes potentiae animae remaneant in anima a corpore separata* ('whether all the powers of the soul remain in the soul when it is separated from the body') in *Summa Theologiae*, vol. 11, "Man" (Ia. 75–83), 114–15.

133. Charles Taliaferro, "Human Nature, Personal Identity, and Eschatology," in Walls, ed., *The Oxford Handbook of Eschatology*, 536.

I agree with Taliaferro that we are more than our neuroanatomy. Yet, in advocating my position I am not denying or mitigating the radicality of human death. I agree with Karl Rahner that human death is the death of the "whole man" (sic) as far as a human being's instantiation on earth.[134] I also agree with Antje Jackelén that this event is "neither less nor more than death."[135] Even so, I am likewise *not* resorting to the "total death theory" of Oscar Cullmann and Eberhard Jüngel as described previously in the chapter and partially affirmed by Jackelén.[136] By not affirming "total death" I assert that there is a continuity of human subjectivity after death. However, I do not resort to a separated soul, sustained by God after biological death that can then be reassembled and reunited with a "resurrection body in the resurrection world."[137] Rather, I suggest that the human being is and *remains* a psychosomatic unity, i.e., a unity of *psyche* (soul, mind) and *soma* (body) *post mortem* but not of the flesh (*sarx*) which remains in the grave in earthly time-space. Thus, I differentiate the earthly incarnate body from the transphysical eschatic body, although I do not discount the possibility of a reunification of a transubstantiated flesh with the eschatic body at the final consummation.

I can agree with those that assert variants of the "total death" concept in that human death is a radical event, an event that radically *dislocates* the psychosomatic unity of the human being. However, death does not dissolve or split this unity. Rather than a division resulting in a separated soul and an inanimate corpse, I propose that death results in a life *separated* from its this-worldly instantiation. In a tentative sense, this is a completion of the Heideggerian "thrown-ness towards death" discussed in the previous chapter: that in death the person is "thrown out" of earthly life. Thus, death is the eschatic event of separation from earthly time-space because separated life is ejected from it, body and soul, but it is also immediately "raised up" into an eschatic, transphysical instantiation.[138] However, before my proposal can be discussed, the intermediate state must be explored in its traditional forms.

---

134. Rahner, *Theological Investigations*, vol. 4, 347.

135. Jackelén, *Time and Eternity*, 115; 217.

136. Jackelén, *Time and Eternity*, 217.

137. Cf. Hebblethwaite, *Philosophical Theology and Christian Doctrine*, 117.

138. Cf. Prusak, "Bodily Resurrection in Catholic Perspective." I have borrowed the word "transphysical" from Prusak's article.

The Hellenistic Inheritance of the Immortal Soul

The concept that death results in a bifurcation of the human person into two components, body and soul, and that the latter half continues to exist has its origins in prehistory. Animism posits that not only humans, but non-human animals, plants, and inanimate objects have souls. Edward Burnett Tylor (1832–1917), the British founder of cultural anthropology, described animism as "one of anthropology's earliest concepts, if not the first."[139] It is beyond the scope of this investigation to explore the concept of the human soul among the world religions and its prehistoric antecedents. However, what can be said is that it is a concept that cannot be easily dismissed. Since Judaism and Christianity were both deeply influenced by Hellenism, my investigation will begin with a brief overview of what could be called the "Orphic-Hellenistic" concept of the soul, to borrow the term used by Markus Mühling.[140] Plato, speaking through Socrates in the *Apology*, provides a summary of ancient Greek thought about death and the afterlife:

> Let us reflect in this way, too, that there is good hope in that death is a blessing, for it is one of two things: either the dead are nothing and have no perception of anything, or it is, as we are told, a change and a relocating of the soul from here to another place. If it is a complete lack of perception, like a dreamless sleep, then death would be a great advantage. . . . If on the other hand death is a change from here to another place, and what we are told is true and all who have died are there, what greater blessing could there be?[141]

The first witnesses to the influence of Greek religious thought on Judaism can be seen in the Apocrypha or deuterocanonical books of the Bible such as the Book of Wisdom and extra-biblical writings such as 4 Maccabees.[142] It is this "Hellenism" that was rejected by certain Protestant theologians of the twentieth century. However, one can question whether the origins of a concept invalidate it. Is the "Orphic" concept of the soul invalid because it is of "pagan" origin and not of "biblical" origin? It is interesting to note that Rabbinical Judaism, already in its infancy at the

---

139. Cf. Bird-David, "Animism Revisited," 67.
140. Cf. Mühling, *The T. & T. Clark Handbook of Christian Eschatology*, 181–82.
141. Plato, "Apology" (40c-e) in Cooper, ed., *Plato: Complete Works*, 181.
142. Cf. Wis 1:15; 3:4; 4:1; 8:13, 17; 25:3; and 4 Macc 10:8, 22; 10:15; 14:5; 15:2, 16:13; 17:5, 18.

time of Jesus, had no such qualms in its own development concerning the concept of an immortal (and thus separable) soul as pagan and thus antithetical to Judaism. Modern Orthodox Judaism deems the immortality of the soul (*hasharat ha-nefesh*) to be an article of faith and is seemingly unconcerned that it may be the result of contact with Hellenism. The reason for this may be the concept that the Torah is two-fold: Written Torah (*torah shebichtav*) and Oral Torah (*torah sheba'al peh*). The written law (the Pentateuch) was given as a whole at Sinai, but the oral law, also given in full to Moses at Sinai, was passed down verbally through the generations until it was codified as Talmud. In other words, the concept of the immortal soul evolved in Judaism through the process of *tradition*.[143]

This tradition of soul separation at death was also passed down to Christianity. It remains the "orthodox" Christian doctrine to this day in most churches. Yet, it was harshly criticized by certain neo-orthodox Protestant theologians in the twentieth century and this resulted in the concept of the "total death theory" discussed in the previous chapter. While "total death" theologians usually did not speculate on what sort of body the resurrected human would possess, their concept begs the question whether their position equates to literal, fleshly reassembly of the body at the general resurrection. In other words, whether it agrees with the Fourth Lateran Council (1215) which decreed that resurrected human beings will retain their very same fleshly bodies.[144]

Thomas Aquinas and the Separated Soul

Thomas Aquinas (1225–74) is often credited and criticized as the medieval scholastic theologian *par excellence* in the assertion that an immortal soul separates from the body at death and thus exists in an intermediate state. However, Aquinas, who did not invent this concept, looks to Aristotle (385–23 BCE) and not Plato for his basic understandings and reinterpretations in the *Summa Theologiae*. Aristotle in his *De Anima* certainly believed that human beings had souls, but he did not believe that human souls could survive death.[145] Aristotle could be said to be one

---

143. Cf. Nickelsburg, *Resurrection, Immortality, and Eternal Life in Intertestamental Judaism*.

144. Qui omnes cum suis propriis corporibus resurgent, quae nunc gestant. Cf. Lateran IV: Constitution 1, "On the Catholic Faith," in Tanner, ed., *Decrees of the Ecumenical Councils* 1, 230.

145 Cf. Frede, "On Aristotle's Conception of the Soul."

of the first "total death" philosophers because for him death was indeed the cessation of life with no Platonist option of a spiritual continuation *post mortem* and no Judaic concept of bodily resurrection at the Last Day. It is thus not surprising that for Aquinas the discarnate soul is not "true life." It is at best an attenuated form of life. In other words, when a human person dies, it ceases to exist because a human being is by definition a unity of body and soul. A soul without a body is not actually a full person for Aquinas, but rather a *part* of a person. The soul is the form of the body (*forma corporis*) and this "form" is incorruptible and thus immortal. However, the *forma corporis* separated from its physical body is incomplete. It is thus nothing like the Orphic ideal of a spirit freed from its (undesirable) fleshly body so it may enjoy spiritual beatitude in Elysium.[146]

In fact, there is perhaps nothing desirable about being in the Thomistic state of *anima separata* with one exception: the enjoyment of the beatific vision of God (at least for the saints). One could argue that to "see God" is to experience the fullest blessing possible. Yet, even those souls that do experience this divine vision still desire to be reunited with their bodies at the resurrection.[147] It is far better, from a Thomistic sense, to be an enfleshed human being transformed into a glorious substance at the resurrection of the dead than to be a discarnate soul. Aquinas could therefore be said to be a reluctant dualist. He insists that the soul cannot exist without the body—which means it maintains its relationship to its corpse after death, either literally or figuratively in its connection to the material world. Some critics have argued that Aquinas is ultimately incoherent on this issue and that he, by default, actually holds that human beings cease to exist at death *in toto* and must await resurrection. Others (the majority) maintain that Aquinas' concept of the separated soul existing in an intermediate state is both coherent and valid.[148]

---

146. For a more detailed discussion on whether Aquinas can equate the separated soul to a human being, see Eleonore Stump's discussion of the separated soul in "Resurrection, Reassembly, and Reconstitution: Aquinas on the Soul."

147. Cf. Butera, "Incomplete Persons," 72.

148. For the argument that Aquinas actually teaches that humans cease to exist at death, see Toner, "St Thomas Aquinas on Death and the Separated Soul." For the opposing argument, see Stump, "Resurrection and the Separated Soul."

The Post-Thomistic Inheritance

One of the outcomes of the Thomistic tradition in the medieval period can be found in Pope Benedict XII's dogmatic constitution *Benedictus Deus* (1336) on the beatific vision:

> ... all these souls, immediately (*mox*) after death and, in the case of those in need of purification, after the purification mentioned above, since the ascension of our Lord and Saviour Jesus Christ into heaven, already before they take up their bodies again and before the general judgment, have been, are and will be with Christ in heaven, in the heavenly kingdom and paradise, joined to the company of the holy angels. Since the passion and death of the Lord Jesus Christ, these souls have seen and see the divine essence with an intuitive vision and even face to face, without the mediation of any creature by way of object of vision; rather the divine essence immediately manifests itself to them, plainly, clearly and openly (*nude, clare et aperte*), and in this vision they enjoy the divine essence. Moreover, by this vision and enjoyment the souls of those who have already died are truly blessed and have eternal life and rest. Also the souls of those who will die in the future will see the same divine essence and will enjoy it before the general judgment.[149]

This concept of the *visio beata* of the separated soul, at least for those "in heaven" and not in purgatory or hell, is described as enjoyment. It would seem that *Benedictus Deus* is unconcerned with the downside of the Thomistic separated soul. It simply continues the Hellenistic concept of the soul inherited from the early church. To this inheritance, it adds the beatific vision as one of the "benefits" of discarnate existence. This is a belief that has continuous currency and is not confined to Roman Catholicism. The tradition that death is a blessed release from the body with far better things to enjoy as a separated soul is summarized by Marilyn McCord Adams (1943–2017):

> Many metaphysical dualists have advertised death as a good thing, because it sheds the body which drags us down. Remember how Socrates welcomes it in the *Apology*. Remember

---

149. Cf. original in Denzinger and Schönmetzer, eds., *Enchiridion symbolorum definitionum et declarationum de rebus fidei et morum*, DS 1000. Hereafter cited as DS. ET: Benedict XII, *Benedictus Deus* in Neuner and Dupuis, eds., *The Christian Faith in the Doctrinal Documents of the Catholic Church*, 685. Latin original words in ET supplied.

Origen's characterization of the body as a prison, or Ambrose's denunciation of the body as "a bag of shit," which it would be idiotic to want back! Post mortem, we will be able to concentrate on higher things—on Platonic forms, on God and Divine ideas—unencumbered by sensory distractions.[150]

As discussed in the previous chapter, Martin Luther appeared to advocate (at times) a form of psychopannychism ("soul sleep") with no intermediate state. However, his later followers did not adopt his stance and it is not part of the Lutheran confessional tradition. In Reformed circles, John Calvin (1509-64) was a resolute defender of the separation of the soul from the body at death. He also insisted that these discarnate souls (of the elect) 'lived in the presence of Christ' in a state of enjoyment in the intermediate state.[151]

Purgatory: Chief Symbol of the Intermediate State

Purgatory is hope.
—Jacques Le Goff[152]

The very mention of an intermediate state demands discussion of purgatory. However, a discussion of the history and development of a doctrine held in the Western church up until it was declared *de fide* at the Second Council of Lyons (1274) is beyond the scope of this section.[153] It is held as dogma by no other Christian church and it has historically been excoriated as heretical by both Eastern Orthodoxy and Protestantism. That said, purgatory as some form of *post mortem* purification or redemption has retained its currency in spite of "non-Roman" rejections. The concept of an intermediate state that seems resonant with purgatory has made regular appearances outside of Roman Catholicism.[154]

---

150. Adams, *Christ and Horrors*, 212. The reference to Ambrose cited by Adams is taken from his *De excessu fratris sui Satyri*, II. 20.

151. Cf. John Calvin, "Psychopannychia" which was published in 1542 in Strasbourg as *Vivere Apud Christum non dormire animis sanctos, qui in fide Christi decedunt, Assertio Ioannis Calvini*; cf. Calvin, *Ioannis Calvini Opera Supersunt Omnia*, 165–232.

152. Le Goff, *The Birth of Purgatory*, 305. Le Goff's book remains the classic reference work on the origins of the doctrine.

153. For a concise history of purgatory, cf. Walls, *Purgatory*, 9–33.

154. Cf. Walls, *Purgatory*, in the chapters "Protestant Objections and Alternatives to Purgatory," 35ff and "Models of Purgatory," 59ff.

As the quotation by Jacques Le Goff (1924–2014) at the start of this section suggests, purgatory evolved, at least in part, under the rubric of hope in the medieval Western Church. Since the concept of the particular judgment, the judgment of the discarnate soul immediately at its death, became accepted doctrine, purgatory in effect offered hope to those who died without mortal sin (sin that demands damnation), but still died with venial sins ("forgivable sins"). In the *Catechism of the Catholic Church*, this definition a venial sin is offered:

> Venial sin weakens charity; it manifests a disordered affection for created goods; it impedes the soul's progress in the exercise of the virtues and the practice of the moral good; it merits temporal punishment. Deliberate and unrepented venial sin disposes us little by little to commit mortal sin. However venial sin does not break the covenant with God. With God's grace it is humanly reparable. "Venial sin does not deprive the sinner of sanctifying grace, friendship with God, charity, and consequently eternal happiness."[155]

Thus, one did not need to die a "saint" (in a state of unsullied grace) to achieve "eternal happiness." In other words, purgatory at least for the medieval Western Christian, offered a means for ordinary women and men to be admitted to heaven after the "temporal punishments" demanded by venial sin were transferred to the intermediate state to be purged. Venial sins demand *temporal* punishments. This led to the understanding that one spent *measurable time* in this state. Thus, purgatory was thought of as a time-space that was similar if not identical to the nature of earthly time. To put it another way, one could think of purgatory as a place where a soul might spend ten years or a thousand years in order for her sins to be fully expurgated. Yet, the rationale for "spending time" in purgatory, according to Jerry Walls (b. 1955), is "that the souls in purgatory are changing and being transformed, as opposed to the damned in hell who are unalterably fixed in their wickedness."[156] In other words, transformation requires the passage of "time" of some sort. The wicked in hell are changeless in their state and thus time would have no utility for them. Walls is here not citing his own opinion, but reviewing the introduction to Dorothy Sayers (1893–1957) translation of

---

155. Cf. CCC1863; the quotation within is from the Apostolic Exhortation *Reconciliatio et paenitentia* (December 1984) of John Paul II.

156. Walls, *Purgatory*, 74.

Dante's *Purgatorio*.[157] However, this is not part of Catholic doctrine and never was. The doctrine is simply that one must be purged of venial sin—which could be instantaneous or could be in a state that is not bound by time-space.[158] Ordinarily, purgation was understood to be a suffering that would involve hell-like flames, but the nature of the sufferings imposed in purgatory were likewise never magisterially defined. However, the idea of purifying fire does have a scriptural basis:

> ... the work of each builder will become visible, for the Day will disclose it, because it will be revealed with fire, and the fire will test what sort of work each has done. If what has been built on the foundation survives, the builder will receive a reward. If the work is burned up, the builder will suffer loss; the builder will be saved, but only as through fire. (1 Cor 3:13–15)

Even so, the saving fire that Paul refers to in 1 Corinthians implies the burning up of the *works* of the builder. Whether the builder must also pass through fire to be saved is open to interpretation. Since no concrete definition as to the nature of purgatorial sufferings was given by the Western church, there was ample room for speculation on the nature of these *post mortem* punishments and the speculator-in-chief (already mentioned above) concerning purgatory was Dante Alighieri (1265–1321).

Dante's influence as to the nature of purgatory is so dominant that hardly any academic study fails to cite *Purgatorio* within his famous work *The Divine Comedy* (c. 1301–20). In fact, it could be argued that Dante has become an unofficial authority concerning the doctrine to the present day. For Sayers, the genius of Dante's interpretation of purgatory was that "Dante has grasped the great essential which is so often overlooked on arguments about penal reform, namely, the prime necessity of persuading the culprit to accept judgment."[159] Thus, purgatory is the divine analogue to the original concept of a modern penitentiary; a *temporary* prison that seeks to reform the criminal until that person accepts judgment. Walls uses Sayers' translation to illustrate one of the reformatory

---

157. Cf. Sayers, ed. and trans., *The "Comedy" of Dante Alighieri the Florentine. Cantica II: Purgatory*.

158 Cf. CCC 1030: "All who die in God's grace and friendship, but still imperfectly purified, are indeed assured of their eternal salvation; but after death they undergo purification, so as to achieve the holiness necessary to enter the joy of heaven."

159. Sayers, *The "Comedy" of Dante Alighieri the Florentine*, 15; cited in Walls, *Purgatory*, 74.

punishments inflicted on a soul who in his earthly life was guilty of the sin of pride:

> I am Humbert; and my arrogance beguiled
> To loss not only me, but all my kin
> It dragged down with it, ruined and reviled.
> Therefore, till God be satisfied for sin,
> It here behooves me bear among the dead
> The load I bore not among living men.[160]

In Dante's interpretation, the soul who on earth was called Humbert must pay his debts and remain in purgatory until God is satisfied. It also shows how Dante crafted punishments in purgatory to fit the sin of each soul in need of purgation. Humbert must carry a heavy stone (i.e., the load he must bear) as *post mortem* penance until such a time as God relents and permits him to enter heaven.[161] However, there is hope in these lines from Dante. Humbert knows that God will eventually receive him into paradise. No matter how long he must carry his heavy stone, Humbert always has the assurance that heaven will be opened to him. Thus, as Le Goff asserts, "purgatory is hope."

The Problem with Purgatory

However, purgatory as an intermediate state has real difficulties. The first problem concerning purgatory as an intermediate state is that it demands a particular judgment of *individual* discarnate souls. Thus, if purgatory is accepted, this implies that there are two judgments, particular and general. This has no firm basis in the New Testament, but rather evolved as post-biblical tradition and the particular judgment remains part of the dogmatic inheritance of both Western and Eastern churches. It is also accepted by many branches of Protestantism, with the noted exception of those minority traditions that teach Christian mortalism ("soul sleep" or psychopannychism). Yet, the scriptural record would seem to consider divine judgment to be a singular eschatic event. Not only this, but it is mentioned as a *public* event that happens collectively. In other words, *individual souls are not judged, but a resurrected humanity is judged together*:

160. Sayers, *The "Comedy" of Dante Alighieri the Florentine*, 11, 67–72. Cited in Walls, *Purgatory*, 75.

161. Walls, *Purgatory*, 75.

> When the Son of Man comes in his glory, and all the angels with him, then he will sit on the throne of his glory. All the nations will be gathered before him, and he will separate people one from another as a shepherd separates the sheep from the goats, and he will put the sheep at his right hand and the goats at the left. (Matt 25:31-33)

In citing the Parable of the Sheep and the Goats, I am not implying a literal interpretation, but rather I wish to illustrate that the Gospels strongly favor a single, collective judgment.

The second problem with purgatory is not that it is an event of purgation (which could also happen in a singular judgment), but that it demands a sharp metaphysical dualism that splits the human being at death into mortal flesh (*sarx*) and immortal soul (*psyche*) with the result that the discarnate soul is depersonalized into a sort of phantasm that retains traces of its former humanity, but cannot be said to be a "true" human being. Thus, it can be argued that the intermediate state (regardless of its "location") is of souls in a dehumanized state.

A third problem is the issue of pseudo-corporeality. While a discarnate soul does not have a body in the fleshly sense, Le Goff insists that for the medievals the soul in purgatory did have a sort of materiality: "Once separated from the body, the soul was endowed with a materiality sui generis and punishment could then be inflicted upon it in Purgatory as though it was corporeal."[162] Thus, there is a sense in which discarnate souls become quasi-incarnate in the intermediate state to enable them to experience sensuality, for better or worse. However, this seems to defeat the very definition of discarnation: that the soul is fleshless. In Mark Corner's book *Death be not Proud: The Problem with the Afterlife* (2011), he notes that the Bishop of Paris, William of Auvergne (1180/90–1249), "states that purgatorial fire 'corporeally and really' (*coporaliter et vere*) torments what he calls 'the bodies of souls' (*corpora animarum*). Aquinas himself (at least according to the *Supplement* to the *Summa*) declares that 'separated souls can suffer from a corporeal cause.'"[163]

This typology of an intermediate state demands a corporeality that logically should not be possible. In other words, the problem of purgatory is a problem of the flesh where there is no flesh. Corner refers to this conundrum as implying that these are "somatomorphic

---

162. Le Goff, *The Birth of Purgatory*, 6.

163. Corner, *Death Be Not Proud*, 170-71. Corner is citing Aquinas in the *Supplement*, 70.3.

souls"—disembodied souls that somehow still have a "body" that can be punished in a time-space.[164] Le Goff comments on Dante's *Purgatorio* in terms of its time-space as follows:

> ... a symphony: the time in Dante's journey is superimposed upon time as it is experienced by the souls in whose midst he is travelling. Time is a congeries of various tempi, a composite of the experience of each of the souls undergoing trial in the space between earth and Heaven and in the interval between earthly life and eternity.[165]

Thus, as traditionally construed, purgatory is not simply a state of measurable time, but of measurable *times* and distinct *trials*. This again raises the question of multiple judgments with souls in an assembly-line fashion passing before Christ as Judge and being assigned punishments (except, as always, the saints), be they finite or infinite in duration. While this may be "symphonic" and perhaps poetic, I would argue that such a scheme does not accord with God's love.

A fourth objection that can be raised is that discarnation divides the *imago Dei* of the person *post mortem*. If human beings are created in the image of God (צֶלֶם אֱלֹהִים; *tzelem Elohim*; cf. Gen 1:26–28), is this divine image preserved in a discarnate soul or is the image lost? According to Aquinas, the soul is the form of the body, so it might be argued that this form retains the *imago*. However, the language of Genesis is distinctly bodily and fleshly. Adam is, after all, made from the dust of the earth (cf. Gen 2:7). It would not seem possible for a discarnate soul to be considered as having this divine image maintained. Even for the saints who enjoy the vision of God in an intermediate state, they would still not possess the fullness of the divine image until reunited with their flesh at the general resurrection. This again implies that discarnation results in a dehumanized existence. This raises the serious question as to whether God could will the dehumanization of any person created in the divine image.

Mark Corner offers a compelling alternative to purgatory that resonates with my proposal at the start of this chapter, that death is the immediate separation of a life from earthly time-space. He argues "that at death a person neither waits nor wanders but is translated into the presence of

---

164. Corner, *Death Be Not Proud*, 186ff.

165. Le Goff, *The Birth of Purgatory*, 353. Cited in Corner, *Death be not Proud*, 175. It should be noted that Corner does not agree with this concept.

God in God's time which is eternity. Being thrust into God's presence, a person is tormented by the exposure to God's love, and suffers—this is the pain of Purgatory which is also the pain of Hell. But this is not an 'interim experience'."[166] I shall return to this theme later in this chapter.

Friedrich Schleiermacher's Zwischenzustand

Moving from medieval understandings, I now seek to explore an Enlightenment response to Reformed theology, inclusive of John Calvin's neo-Augustinian approach to salvation as supralapsarian double predestination, in the theology of Friedrich Schleiermacher. His eschatology merits exploration because he developed a concept of an intermediate state (*Zwischenzustand*). To begin this exploration, Calvin's *decretum horribile* ("horrible decree") merits citation in full:

> As Scripture then clearly shows, we say that God once established by his eternal and unchangeable plan those whom he long before determined once for all to receive into salvation, and those who, on the other hand, he would devote to destruction. We assert that, with respect to the elect, this plan was founded upon his freely given mercy, without regard to human worth; but by his just and irreprehensible but incomprehensible judgement he has barred the door of life to those he has given over to damnation.[167]

Calvin's famous formulation asserts that God eternally decreed, and therefore always knew, the salvific fate of every human being.[168] It should be noted that Calvin does not refer to humanity in the collective, but only as individuals. He admits that this decree is "horrible," but that it must nonetheless be just as it was authored by God.[169] Calvin's predestinarian soteriology resulted in a number of reactions. It was condemned by the Council of Trent, it has no traction whatsoever in Eastern Christianity where Augustinianism is already held in suspicion, and it was not accepted by many Reformation movements, notably the Lutherans and Anabaptists.[170] Nonetheless, its influence on Christianity persists to

---

166. Corner, *Death Be Not Proud*, 175.
167. Calvin, *Institutes*, 3.21.7.
168. Calvin, *Institutes*, 3.21.5.
169. "Decretum quidem horribile, fateor." Cf. *Institutes*, 3.23.7.
170. "If anyone shall say that men are justified either by the sole imputation of the justice of Christ or by the sole remission of sins, to the exclusion of the grace and the

the present day. The Dutch theologian Jacobus Arminius (1560–1609) sought to soften the harshness of this variant of predestination by basing it on God's foreknowledge (similar to the confessional Lutheran position) and insisting that all human beings may benefit from God's prevenient grace and accept the gospel of Christ. However, the Remonstrant movement in the Netherlands was unsuccessful in altering the stance of the Dutch Reformed Church. Its English counterpart, the Arminian faction in the Church of England, remained in the minority until the nineteenth century, with the notable exception of the Wesleyan-Methodist movement of the late eighteenth century.[171]

Schleiermacher reinterpreted the Reformed tradition at a time when orthodox Calvinism was being attenuated by the Enlightenment and German idealism. Although technically from a German Reformed background, Schleiermacher was educated in a Moravian community and dates his experience of conversion to 1783 at age fourteen.[172] He was a staunch advocate for the unification of Reformed and Lutheran churches in Germany.

Schleiermacher comments on the first question of the *Heidelberg Catechism* (1563):

> Q. What is your only comfort in life and in death?
>
> A. That I belong, body and soul, in life and in death, not to myself but to my faithful Saviour Jesus Christ, who at the cost of his own blood has fully paid for my sins.[173]

In his *Sendschreiben,* Schleiermacher wrote that the answer to this question "proceeds immediately from the basic Christian feeling."[174] However, not all have this feeling which is produced by one's God-consciousness. Jesus, for Schleiermacher, had absolute God-consciousness while human beings possess this in varying degrees. This is made explicit in the *Glaubenslehre*: "In accordance with the laws of the divine government of

---

charity that is poured forth in their hearts by the Holy Spirit and remains in them, or also that the grace by which we are justified is only the good will of God-anathema sit." Council of Trent, Canon VI of the Decrees on Justification. DS 1561.

171. For an overview of the theology of Jacobus Arminius, see McCulloh, ed., *Man's Faith and Freedom.* For a summary of its influence in England, see Tyacke, "The Rise of Arminianism Reconsidered."

172. Gerrish, *Tradition in the Modern World,* 16.

173. Schaff, ed., *Creeds of Christendom,* vol. 3, 307.

174. *Schleiermachers Sendschreiben über seine Glaubenslehre an Lücke* as cited in Gerrish, *Tradition in the Modern World,* 33.

the world, so long as the human race continues on earth, all those living at any one time can never be uniformly taken up into the kingdom of God founded by Christ."[175]

There will be some who die outside the Christian church at any one given time. Yet, Schleiermacher also insists that "all other fellowships of faith are destined to pass into Christian fellowship."[176] However, there is a problem with this assumption: some persons have no faith and members of other faiths will undoubtedly die before they are absorbed into Christian fellowship. This problem is acknowledged by Schleiermacher:

> While the Christian sympathy is not disquieted by the earlier and later adoption of one and another individual into the fellowship of redemption, yet on the other hand there does remain an insoluble discord if, on the assumption of survival after death, we are to think of part of the human race as entirely excluded from this fellowship.[177]

Yet, he maintains that "the incarnation of Christ is analogous to the regeneration of the whole [human] race considered as a unity."[178] It is here that Schleiermacher develops his concept of a positive, single predestination for humanity for "each man, when his time is fully come, will be regenerated...."[179] This single predestination must include those who have died: "We infer from [the death of an unregenerate person] that for such a one this foreordination has not been fulfilled during his lifetime, but not by any means that a different foreordination is being fulfilled by his death; rather, the state in which he dies is only an intermediate state [*Zwischenzustand*]."[180]

And here it appears—the intermediate state, which any contemporary reader could have understood as a type of purgatory, although Schleiermacher makes no mention as to the nature of such a state. He also acknowledges that the Reformed confessions do not allow for an intermediate state. These confessional statements cited by Schleiermacher, as with the majority of witnesses to the Christian tradition, assert

---

175. Schleiermacher, *Der christliche Glaube* (1830-31). ET: *The Christian Faith* (1928), para. 117, 536.

176. Schleiermacher, *The Christian Faith*, para. 117, 536.

177. Schleiermacher, *The Christian Faith*, para. 118, 539.

178. Schleiermacher, *The Christian Faith*, sec. 1, 540.

179. Schleiermacher, *The Christian Faith*, sec. 1, 540.

180. Schleiermacher, *The Christian Faith*, para. 119, sec. 3. 549.

that if a person does not enter Christian communion before death and repent of her sins, such a person will be damned for all eternity. Schleiermacher rejects this outright. There is for him only one divine decree to blessedness for the whole human race, thus it must be possible to attain Christian consciousness *post mortem*.[181] This "afterlife" attainment of Christian consciousness (i.e., conversion and repentance) is not explored by Schleiermacher, but one can theorize that it would be the same process as the one which happens in earthly life, since this fits with the logic of Schleiermacher's understanding of the one positive decree for humankind. Note that unlike Calvin who postulates his double predestinarian decree for individuals, Schleiermacher insists on a collective approach. God does not predestine *individuals* to blessedness, but rather the whole human race. He explains this in terms analogous to universalism:

> From whatever side we view it, then, there are great difficulties in thinking that the finite issue of redemption is such that some thereby obtain the highest bliss, while others (on the ordinary view, the majority of the human race) are lost in irrevocable misery.... [W]e ought to at least admit the equal rights of the milder view, of which likewise there are traces in the Scripture; the view, namely, that through the power of redemption there will one day be a universal restoration of all souls.[182]

It can be speculated that for those who die before their "regeneration," the process will be the same for those living: they will be drawn within into the circle of preparatory grace, they will respond to that grace or resist that grace. To resist might be a sort of temporary self-imposed hell (although Schleiermacher does not suggest this). After their response to God's irresistible grace (either immediately or after a futile attempt to resist it), they will be sanctified and enter the "highest bliss." Schleiermacher's Platonist leanings make him unconcerned with bodily resurrection, that of Christ's or of humanity as a whole. The resurrection of Christ (the historicity of which he *does* affirm in the *Glaubenslehre*) may be a prototype of glorification in heaven, meaning a type of theosis, but the death and resurrection of Jesus is not itself salvific for human beings because the universal decree to blessedness has already been decreed eternally.[183] Yet, it remains noteworthy that for Schleiermacher the

---

181. Schleiermacher, *The Christian Faith*, 550.
182. Schleiermacher, *The Christian Faith*, para. 163, 722.
183. For a discussion of Schleiermacher on the resurrection, see Dieb, "The

incarnation of Christ is the analogue of humanity's redemption, rather than the cross or the Easter event.

Schleiermacher posits a very different sort of intermediate state than is common to received tradition. This state for the "unregenerate" would seem to be one of *growth* for presumably discarnate souls that is analogous to the redemption experienced by human beings on earth. What is striking is that this sort of intermediate state does sound like a form of Elysium (or a "middle heaven") where such souls are allowed to develop their Christian consciousness in order to enter the "bliss" which is presumably within the communion of saints.

Brunner's critique that Schleiermacher veers towards "heathenish mysticism" may be accurate if one is prepared to equate Christian Platonism with paganism.[184] Yet, this mildest of purgatories (if the word can even be used for his *Zwischenzustand*) provides a sharp contrast to the more harrowing account of the purgatorial intermediate state in traditional interpretations. One thing that is striking is Schleiermacher's lack of any mention of the degrees of human sin as far as it may impact an intermediate state. This may be explained by the fact that for Schleiermacher "sin" is simply the lack of God-consciousness. Unregenerate souls may be those of persons who have engaged in heinous crimes in their earthly lives, but the degree of their evil equates to their lack of God-consciousness. If the growth that would happen in this "middle heaven" would be such that those who acted wickedly on earth would have a "long climb" to attain regeneration, then it would be the sort of intermediate state that somewhat accords with the opinions held by Origen and Clement of Alexandria. That said, what Schleiermacher provides is a permanently discarnate state for those in "middle heaven" and those in "highest bliss"—one without a body (*soma*) and one without a general resurrection. Thus, while Schleiermacher's "purgatory" does no damage to the doctrine of God as the One who is ontologically love itself, it also drifts so far from the idea that human beings are only human as psychosomatic unities that it echoes the words of Marilyn McCord Adams quoted previously: that we will be blissful souls "unencumbered by sensory distractions." Yet, if the prototype of human glorification is the incarnation and resurrection of Christ and that this glorified humanity is both bodily and

---

Precarious Status of Resurrection in Friedrich Schleiermacher's *Glaubenslehre*."

184. Cf. Brunner, *Die Mystik und das Wort*, 388.

sensuous, participants in a heavenly banquet, then Schleiermacher does not seem to allow for this divine sensuality in the eschaton.

Sergei Bulgakov's Theology of an Intermediate State as Bodily Dormition

The focus so far has been on Western, scholastic, and Enlightenment approaches to an intermediate state. However, Eastern Christianity has its own teachings about this possibility. Platonism has never been deemed problematic in the Eastern theological tradition and thus there has been nothing like a "total death" theology in Eastern and Oriental Orthodoxy. The Russian Orthodox theologian Fr. Sergei Nikolayevich Bulgakov (1871–1944), who will be discussed more fully in chapter 3, defines death in the context of mystery:

> The existence of death, just like birth, shrouds in *mystery* the being of man and of all living things. Man can hide from this mystery only by ceasing to feel or by fleeing from all thought of it, but this is possible only for a time. This mystery is inaccessible to knowledge. It is therefore an object of belief, whatever the content of the latter. Not to believe in immortality is also a kind of belief, impossible to verify within the limits of this life and, in the formal sense, it does not differ from belief in immortality.[185]

For Bulgakov, the meaning of death is not open to knowledge-based enquiry (i.e., science). However, Bulgakov writes that a belief in immortality "can become self-evident" to those who encounter God's love spiritually. Such a spiritual encounter with divine love ends all doubt on the matter.[186]

Bulgakov lived in a time when positivism was in its first ascendency and he comments on this phenomenon in terms of its denial of an "afterlife":

> What is most incomprehensible in what can be called the ontology of death is disbelief's assertion that death is the total annihilation of life. It is an axiom for positivism that *ex nihilo nihil fit*, together with the law of the conservation of energy. Positivism therefore rejects the idea of the creation of the world

---

185. Bulgakov, *The Bride of the Lamb*, 349. Emphasis original.
186. Bulgakov, *The Bride of the Lamb*, 349.

out of nothing and proclaims the eternity of the world, while admitting the spontaneous generation of life.[187]

The eternity of the universe is no longer held to be a given in science as it was in Bulgakov's time. However, Bulgakov's critique still retains its overall logic: "positivism proclaims the ultimate ontological absurdity of a double annihilation: an appearance out of nothing and a return to nothing, a soap bubble that has burst, whose real content is emptiness."[188] The denial of immortality is therefore the ontology of nihilism, which for Bulgakov is the biblical "outer darkness"—"a double nonbeing: *before* death and *after* death."[189]

It is impossible for Bulgakov to conceive of what he called "autonomous nonbeing," "absolute death," and "outer darkness." The reason for this is that God did not create death. He quotes from the Jewish Hellenistic scriptures: "God did not make death, and he does not delight in the death of the living. For he created all things so that they might exist" (Wisdom of Solomon 1:13–14).[190] It is also not possible for Bulgakov to envision that death entails anything approaching the concept of *Ganztodtheorie* ("total death theory"), a concept already discussed in the previous chapter. The dead are, in fact, still *in* life:

> In the tripartite structure of man, death's dividing sickle passes between the spirit and the soul (which are therefore usually combined under the general notion of soul) on the one hand and between the spirit and the body on the other. It is very important to take into account this indivisibility of the spirit and the soul in death, for it confirms the principle of creaturely immortality in the continuing connection to the world. The soul is an intermediate principle connecting the spirit with the creaturely world. The soul is creaturely, like the "blood" that animates the body. The physical blood dies and decomposes together with the body. But the suprahysical energy of life . . . abides. . . . [Resurrection] is not only a restoration but also a continuation of life, which supposes a continuous identity and

---

187. Bulgakov, *The Bride of the Lamb*, 349.
188. Bulgakov, *The Bride of the Lamb*, 350.
189. Bulgakov, *The Bride of the Lamb*, 350.
190. Cited by Bulgakov in part. Version of the Wisdom of Solomon here is from the NRSV.

unity of life before death and after resurrection. Once again this compels us to understand *death as a state of life*.[191]

What is interesting in Bulgakov's take on what would seem to be a traditional understanding of *anima separata* is that there is a permanent connection between earthly life and the life in the intermediate state. The "state of life" between physical death and resurrection is psycho-spiritual—and the soul maintains its connection to the body even though it is in essence cut in half when the spirit departs the body at death. It is not *anima separata* in the Thomistic sense. The human spirit does indeed depart the body at death, but the soul maintains a connection to the body and the earth even as it maintains a connection to the spirit. Thus, this intermediate "state of life" is bipartite—the fullness of humanity being tripartite. In effect, the intermediate state of human life is not the fullness of life, which is always tripartite (body, soul, and spirit), but it is still a form of life. In addition, Bulgakov rejects the idea that the human spirit has its own power of being apart from the body. On the one hand, "the human spirit has a divine origin and can participate in divine life"[192] and on the other, "[the] human hypostasis does not have a spiritual, supermundane being, nor, in this being, an immortality independent of incarnation. The human spirit is not created as a fleshless spirit . . . like the angels. *No human spirit can exist independently of the world.*"[193]

The pre-eschatic afterlife, for Bulgakov, is one of reduction to a "state of potentiality, a shadow state. It loses the fullness of life."[194] This is analogous to the understanding of Aquinas. While by no means the same thing, this "shadow state" does allude to the early Israelite concept of Sheol where human life after death was reduced to a sort of shade. Nonetheless, the dead are still *in* life, however attenuated they may be in their discarnate form. This is why Bulgakov uses the term "dormition" for the state of "life" of the dead. In this dormition, "[t]he soul does not die, but is only relatively potentialized. In this sense (but only in this sense), one can refer to the dead as those who are 'asleep,' and there are different modes and degrees of this dormition."[195] The question is whether the "different modes and degree of this dormition" imply some sort of punishment for

---

191. Bulgakov, *The Bride of the Lamb*, 354. Emphasis mine.
192. Bulgakov, *The Bride of the Lamb*, 355.
193. Bulgakov, *The Bride of the Lamb*, 355. Emphasis mine.
194. Bulgakov, *The Bride of the Lamb*, 356
195. Bulgakov, *The Bride of the Lamb*, 356.

the impure or wicked. Eastern Orthodoxy does not accept the doctrine of purgatory, but Bulgakov does comment on the role of divine judgment in the pre-eschatic intermediate state. This topic will be explored in chapter 4, section 3. However, Bulgakov would not suggest that the intermediate state is a place of punishments, but rather a place where spiritual growth is still possible.

Paul Griffiths' Theology of the Discarnate Intermediate State

> Présence de Dieu. . . . La première présence est la présence de création. La seconde est la présence de dé-création. (Celui qui nous a créés sans nous ne nous sauvera pas sans nous. Saint Augustin.)
> —Simone Weil[196]

In Paul Griffiths' book *Decreation: The Last Things of All Creatures*,[197] the Warren Professor of Catholic Theology at Duke Divinity School presents a novel approach to eschatology that seeks to stay within the confines of Catholic magisterial teaching. He takes his title "Decreation" from a poem by the French philosopher and mystic Simone Weil (1909–43) cited above. For Griffiths, the *novissima* (last things) are exactly that: there is no novelty possible upon a creature's (animate or inanimate) reaching its *novissimum*. The "Father's house" may have many mansions (John 14:2), but for Griffiths there is no further growth, opportunity, or change possible there.[198] He allows for only three possibilities: annihilation, simple stasis, and repetitive stasis.[199] He summarizes this as follows:

> Every creaturely last thing falls under one of these three heads: annihilation, simple stasis, or repetitive stasis. There is no fourth possibility. To deny all three of these to a creature is exactly to deny it its last thing. The same is true of the last thing, if there is one, of the ensemble of creatures that is the world: that will be

---

196. Weil, *La pesanteur et la grâce*, 48–49; ET: "The presence of God. . . . The first presence is the presence of creation. The second is the presence of de-creation. (He who created us without us will not save us without us. —Saint Augustine)," in Weil, *Gravity and Grace*, 38. English translation altered.

197. For a review of this book, cf. Tanner, "God's Umpire." Tanner takes issue with Griffiths' concept of heaven as a form of stasis.

198. Griffiths, *Decreation*, 5, 7–13.

199. Griffiths, *Decreation*, 15–23.

either annihilation or its entry into one of two kinds of stasis. A creature with an endlessly novel future lacks a *novissimum*.[200]

It is important in this context to note that for Griffiths, the discarnate state is a form of "temporary annihilation" because "[e]very human creature ceases at death: that is Christian doctrine."[201] In other words, echoing both Aquinas and Bulgakov, a human being that is discarnate ceases to be a human being. It is an *anima*, but it is not a human person. In this context, the function of the discarnate intermediate state is in effect the place where discarnate souls are assigned their eternal destiny:

> Death in the devastation is the separation of the soul from the flesh; each of our souls will undergo judgment immediately upon death that will destine us either for a *novissimum* of eternal and ecstatic intimacy with the LORD, or for one of eternal separation from him. Our discarnate souls begin, at death, to move toward our allotted *novissimum* . . . .[202]

What is striking about Griffiths' understanding of the intermediate state is that it is one of movement: moving towards God (Griffiths' preferred term for the triune God is "LORD") or away from God.[203] For those who die in a state of grace without the need of further purification, this forward movement is instantaneous in that the separated soul enjoys the beatific vision immediately. For presumably most forward-moving souls *ad Deum*, purification is necessary and thus this "slower" movement is purgatorial. For those humans that die in a state of mortal or damnable sin, the regressive movement of their souls is away from God along with the agony that this separation implies. Thus, the intermediate state for Griffiths is tripartite. He constructs this in part by referring to the 1336 Constitution *Benedictus Deus* of Benedict XII which for Griffiths is to be deemed binding (*de fide*) on Catholic Christians.[204]

As mentioned before, the first possible state for the discarnate soul is immediate entry into a heavenly state where they experience the

---

200. Griffiths, *Decreation*, 25.

201. Griffiths, *Decreation*, 175.

202. Griffiths, *Decreation*, 173. Note that the term "devastation" is Griffiths' preferred term for the post-Edenic fallen world. Cf. Griffiths, Griffiths, *Decreation*, 4.

203. The capital letters are important. "LORD" is commonly used in English translations of the Hebrew Bible for the tetragrammaton YHWH.

204. Griffiths, *Decreation*, 174.

THE SYMBOLS AND PROBLEMS OF JUDGMENT 75

beatific vision "face to face."[205] The second possible state is purgatory. While the nature of purgation is not a matter that has been magisterially defined, it presumably involves some sort of cleansing of what *Benedictus Deus* refers to as *aliquid purgabile* ("something to be purged")[206]. For a self-proclaimed orthodox Catholic work on the last things, it is striking how Griffiths is sparing in his use of the words "purgatory" and "purgatorial." In fact, the words are not listed at all in the voluminous index. Griffiths rather prefers "intermediate state" throughout his treatment of the subject. The nature of purgation is painful in that the soul, although moving toward God and its consummation, is still separated from God. Griffiths refers to this separation as "pain" (in as much as a discarnate soul can experience pain).[207] In his continuing exploration of *Benedictus Deus*, Griffiths asserts that the soul in this second intermediate state can be cleansed before the general resurrection and thus enter the first state of discarnation and enjoy beatitude with the saints. The third possible state is for the damned. They enter into hellish punishments (*ubi poenis infernalibus cruciantur*) which may or may not be continuous until the general resurrection.[208] This tripartite scheme of the intermediate state that Griffiths posits is entirely traditional and seems to be without novelty. However, what was noted at first was the concept of *movement* within this discarnate realm. These souls are on the move, toward or away from God.

Another interesting aspect of Griffiths' intermediate eschatology is that discarnate souls, although not enfleshed, do have "bodies." For Griffiths, a "body" is "the capacity for location in time-space, and thus for availability and responsiveness to other creatures with such location; any creature with such capacity has, or is, a body."[209] Thus, the souls in the intermediate state are *bodily* creatures. Also, the intermediate state, like heaven and hell, are time-spaces. While the nature of time-space in heaven or hell may not be the same as the time-space of the world (the "devastation"), the time-space of the intermediate state is according to

---

205. "visione intuitiva et etiam faciali" from *Benedictus Deus*, cited in Griffiths, *Decreation*, 178.
206. Griffiths, *Decreation*, 178. Cf. index, 394.
207. Griffiths, *Decreation*, 179.
208. Griffiths, *Decreation*, 179.
209. Griffiths, *Decreation*, 5.

Griffiths "metronomic."[210] There are two types of time for Griffiths: systolic and metronomic. Metronomic time, which can be measured, is

> ... devastated time, and, according to the axioms of Christian theology, to be devastated is to be damaged, to be lacking in good or goods that would, absent devastation, be present. The damage in question is exactly loss of intimacy with the LORD. Time intimate with the LORD is folded upon his passion and inspired by the LORD's creative breath.[211]

In other words, God's time is not metronomic, but systolic (or systolic-diastolic). Metronomic time, time that can be measured, is "fallen" time. Systolic time is divine time—it is in effect the "breathing" of God and this already is the case in the time-space of heaven:

> In heaven . . . [t]he annihilation there of metronomic time is coincident with the full expansion of the systole into the diastole. The indrawn breath is exhaled; the resurrected and ascended flesh of Christ sits now, fully present, at the center of the faithful; the time of heaven is a constant, endless, back-and-forth of praise and love between the saints and the LORD, an inbreath and outbreath of gift-given and gift-received-by-being-returned. This endlessly repeated but temporally structured cycle is the temporal form of the beatific vision: it is how temporal creatures see the LORD, the maximal extent of creaturely participation in the LORD's eternity.[212]

In this above passage, Griffiths' highly speculative project can be fully glimpsed. Yet, it shows how he conceives of the two types of time—damaged time (metronomic) and healed time (systolic). In the context of his proposal of the time-space that is the intermediate state, the type of time experienced by the discarnate souls is metronomic—until and if they enter a participation in the beatific vision ("heaven") and are freed from damaged time.

In the intermediate state, all "suffer" from a separation from the flesh that they left behind on earth. In the case of the saints in heaven, Griffiths prefers to term this as "longing." This is fully in accord with Aquinas who also said that even those souls who experience the beatific

---

210. Griffiths, *Decreation*, 180.
211. Griffiths, *Decreation*, 106–7. See also 89–93.
212. Griffiths, *Decreation*, 108.

vision long to be reunited with their fleshly bodies at the general resurrection.[213] It is questionable whether this can be said of the damned since even if reunited with the body at the general resurrection their fate it still annihilation in hell. It is noteworthy to mention here that Griffiths, in spite of his attempts at maintaining Catholic magisterial orthodoxy, is in the end an annihilationist. The damned *do not* suffer eternally. While hell will be discussed in the next chapter, it is important to mention Griffiths' unique definition of hell:

> . . . the time-space during which creatures, according to their kinds, are maximally and irreversibly separated from the LORD and from one another. The speculative position taken in this book is that such a time-space is utopia, timeless and placeless, and that creatures who enter it therefore *come to nothing as creatures* who are necessarily spatio-temporal must when they become timeless and placeless.[214]

Now that we have a full picture of the three destinations in the intermediate state, it is possible to analyze Griffiths' contribution to intermediate eschatology. First off, it must be said that Griffiths gives what might be called a slightly "softened" orthodox approach to the problem of discarnation. He retains *anima separata* fully, but he gives it a bodily dimension that goes beyond the *forma corporis* of Aquinas, not unlike the somatomorphic souls mentioned by Corner. Thus, separated souls are bodily creatures. Griffiths does not go so far as to imply that such souls are somehow pseudo-incarnate and he certainly does not imply anything like immediate resurrection in his eschatology.[215] Rather, Griffiths implies a harrowing account of the intermediate state that is within metronomic (damaged) time-space. Only those persons who die in a state of grace without the need of purgation are spared this time-space where the "clock" ticks as the soul moves painfully closer to God (although as-

---

213. Cf. Eberl, "Do Human Persons Persist between Death and Resurrection?" 189.

214. Eberl, "Do Human Persons Persist between Death and Resurrection?" 5. Emphasis mine.

215. Griffiths is aware of this concept: "Christian thought need not have gone in this direction. Had the flesh's resurrection been understood to occur immediately upon death in the devastation, which is the position that some Christians, ancient and modern, have held, so that there was no interval between the one event and the other, there would be no time, metronomically speaking, when the world was absent of human creatures so resurrected, and thus no doctrine of temporary annihilation. But that is not the way things went..." Cf. Griffiths, *Decreation*, 174–75.

sumedly the pain lessens with each advance) or painfully away from God with annihilation in hell as its endpoint. The only softening aspect of this is the fact that hell for Griffiths is, he opines, not eternal.

In a book that is written with exquisite prose that almost succeeds in masking some of its disturbing content, I find it impossible to square Griffiths' account of the intermediate state with the doctrine of God. I accept that the concept of the separated soul is part of Catholic teaching and I did not expect any modification of this pattern. I also accept that the concept of the particular judgment would be maintained by Griffiths, but the end result in this mobile intermediate state is, to use a word Griffiths favors, devastating. He suggests a purgatorial or infernal intermediate discarnate state that is a rollercoaster ride *bound by measurable time* towards eventual bliss or destruction. For the souls in purgatory, Griffiths' account could seem like a modern version of Dante's *Purgatorio* with the upward movement of the souls through the seven terraces of Mount Purgatory. However, Griffiths' account maximizes the concept of the passage of time, resulting in an excruciating and seemingly unlimited passage of time for the soul's progress towards God. The reason it has an almost unlimited quantity of metronomic time is that according to *Benedictus Deus* while *some* souls may progress and enter heaven before the general resurrection, others will not and will be in a purgatorial state until the Last Day (as in the Last Day of earth's time-space).

In my judgment, Griffiths' purgatory does not square with the doctrine that God is love and the argument that God is love precisely in judgment. Even in the particular judgment, if accepted, the Judge of discarnate souls is Christ. As such, God in Christ who is perfect love is the one who casts out all fear (1 John 4:18). This is the paradox—that the divine judgment can be one without fear. Griffiths does not deny that God (the LORD) is love, far from it. However, it is strangely non-operative in the damaged metronomic time-space of his intermediate state. For the damned, the "rollercoaster" is one of agony in metronomic time until annihilation, presumably at the general resurrection. Griffiths elaborates that

> ... souls in the third, hellish, state lack utterly the most profound good in the order of being, which is the love of the LORD—they are, as Augustine likes to say, *animae deo desertae*, (discarnate) souls deserted by the LORD.... [T]he lacks of the souls suffering hellishly will not be made good, for even when the resurrection of the flesh occurs and they become thereby

human creatures once again, they remain enduringly separate from the LORD.[216]

Despite the softening of the orthodox doctrine of eternal hell into a finite annihilation, the damned are destined for a journey of agony in measurable time towards their destruction. While Griffiths acknowledges that it is not certain that anyone will be damned or consigned to hell/annihilation and thus no soul may endure this hellish movement away from God and God's love, he nonetheless provides a third path in the intermediate state assuming that some might be damned.[217]

By no means do I think that Griffiths is intentionally implying that God is sadistic towards impure or damned souls. He is adhering to the magisterial tradition that he believes is binding. However, in his schema of intermediate eschatology, unless one is among the saints who dies *sine macula*, the intermediate state that Griffiths proposes is one of unimaginable suffering, even for those who will eventually be admitted into heaven. If we accept as axiomatic for Christians that we know the character of God only in the witness of Jesus Christ, I suggest it would be contrary to the divine purpose for God to devise an intermediate state such that Griffiths defends.

Considering that this type of intermediate state is (for most discarnate souls) partially or fully nightmarish, the question must be raised: is the problem itself the issue of eschatological intermediacy? In other words, is it the requirement that at death souls discarnate and enter a required intermediate state which in turn creates the problem of how such a state operates? It would seem that the nightmare that Griffiths proposes, which in some aspects makes Dante's speculations about purgatory seem preferable, is based on the temporo-spatial demands to make the intermediate state viable—it is a place where stained souls and damned souls in a state of pseudo-corporeality "spend time" in an agonizing progression or regression towards heaven or hell.

The Problem of Discarnation as a bonum

> *For to me, living is Christ and dying is gain. If I am to live in the flesh, that means fruitful labor for me; and I do not know which I*

---

216. Griffiths, *Decreation*, 184.

217. For a full treatment on Griffiths' concept of hell, its inhabitants or lack therefore, and his idea of annihilationism, cf. Griffiths, *Decreation*, 241–50.

> *prefer. I am hard pressed between the two: my desire is to depart and be with Christ, for that is far better.*
> —Philippians 1:21–23

Moving away from the doctrine of purgatory, there is still a concept of an intermediate state that is perhaps favored in some variants of Christianity in terms of death being a blessed release from earthly sufferings and constraints. The famous prayer, often attributed to John Henry Newman (1801–90), but actually dating from the sixteenth century, is suggestive: "May [God] support us all the day long till the shades lengthen and the evening comes and the busy world is hushed and the fever of life is over and our work is done. Then in his mercy may he give us a safe lodging and a holy rest and peace at the last."[218]

Yet, the idea that death is a blessing because it is better to be with the Lord in "holy rest and peace," in a limited and contextual sense, is Pauline. Yet, note that Paul says that "living is Christ." It is deeply problematic to disparage earthly incarnate life, in spite of the suffering that such life clearly entails. It is even more problematic to think of death in the form of discarnation as "far better." Referring back to Aquinas, Griffiths, and Bulgakov, I doubt any of them would imply that discarnate "life" is a true good (*bonum*), with the possible exception of those discarnate saints who enjoy the beatific vision (yet even they are said to long to be reincarnated at the general resurrection). While certain neo-orthodox Protestant theologians of the twentieth century attacked the belief in the discarnate soul as unbiblical, they also attacked it for its low view of material existence. Karl Barth (1886–1968) advocates an anthropological monism against the inherited dualism: "Through the Spirit of God, man is the subject, form and life of a substantial organism, the soul of his body—wholly and simultaneously both, in ineffaceable difference, inseparable unity, and indestructible order."[219] For Barth, a separated soul existing in an intermediate state is impossible. The only solution to death is resurrection. Barth's reaction can be interpreted as an antidote to the form of denial of death that was common in the late nineteenth and early twentieth centuries.

However, as was discussed in the previous chapter, death is *not* a blessing. Death is a radical event and one that dissolves our earthly relationships. Whatever reunification is possible in the world-to-come

---

218. Cunningham, ed., *John Henry Newman*, 59.
219. Barth, *Church Dogmatics III.2*, 119.

between loved ones, it is most emphatically not a repetition of earthly life in perfected form. The life of the world-to-come (*vita venturi saeculi*; Hebrew, *olam ha-ba*) by definition will not be life as we know it now. Werner G. Jeanrond (b. 1955) provides a helpful critique: "as long as we, so to speak, prepare our stamp collection for eternal inspection, as long as we expect to be carried to eternity on the wings of a well-groomed soul, we have missed the point of Jesus' death and resurrection. And most disturbingly, we have missed the point of our own life and death. It is dangerous to speak carelessly about our death."[220] As Antje Jackelén notes, "The New Testament is not about conjuring away death, but rather about suffering and overcoming death."[221] The death event terminates earthly relationality, at least in a way that we know it now—as enfleshed psychosomatic human beings. It is a universal human phenomenon to experience the death of those we love. So, human experience is certainly aware of death's radicality in terms of its impact, emotional and otherwise. The problem of death denial is theological, or perhaps more accurately, ecclesiastical. The comforting words to the bereaved are indeed that their departed loved ones are, as Jeanrond wrote, "carried to eternity on the wings of a well-groomed soul." The belief that humans are transformed into angels at death is a common Christian funerary motif. No one wants to be reminded that death must be "suffered and overcome" nor do we want to be told that the departed are radically separated from our earthly time-space. Yet, the truth of the matter is that we *do* know it. Human beings are deeply aware of the void left by the death of those we love.

While death is a radical event, I would argue that death does not terminate the separated life's relationship with God. Brian Hebblethwaite (b. 1939) notes that "the soul's immortality as a disembodied state beyond death is not popular amongst Christian theologians or among Christian philosophers today."[222] Indeed, and I would argue it is also undesirable. Thus, there is a conundrum: how is the concept of a soul-only *post mortem* existence (i.e., discarnation) avoided? In other words, how is the concept that the dead are not "totally dead" (awaiting reassembly in resurrection at the Last Day), but rather radically transformed at the moment of death asserted? For a possible solution, I turn to the German Catholic theologian Gisbert Greshake (b. 1933).

---

220. Jeanrond, *Call and Response*, 60.
221. Jackelén, *Time and Eternity*, 112.
222. Hebblethwaite, *Christian Hope*, 113.

Recovering Gisbert Greshake's "Resurrection in Death"

Gisbert Greshake sought to overcome the problem of the intermediate state by introducing the argument that at death the human being is immediately resurrected. This is often termed as "resurrection in death."[223] As a Catholic theologian, he went against the received (and indeed magisterial) tradition of both soul separation and an intermediate eschatology. He also went against the concept of a particular judgment at death for each human person. Thus, his position runs contrary to the dogmatic constitution of *Benedictus Deus* and the belief that the beatific vision is enjoyed by the separated soul (if the person died in a state of grace). Greshake is in effect engaging in a Catholic response to the "total death" theology of his Protestant contemporaries, but also arguing against anthropological dualism. He uses Philippians 1 as cited above as biblical support that the dead enter into immediate fellowship with Christ. However, immediate fellowship could still mean non-somatic fellowship, but Greshake wants to preserve the whole person without bifurcation. He also wants to demand continuity between *ante mortem* and *post mortem* life. The continuity problem is one that haunts the theology of "total death"—if a person dies totally at death, what is resurrected at the eschaton? Is it a copy? Can there be true continuity with total death? Greshake's solution to both the total death problem and the continuity problem is that death is the event of resurrection for the whole person, body and soul. Therefore, there is no moment when the person ceases in being.

However, Greshake does not mean that in an immediate resurrection at death human flesh (*sarx*) is resuscitated for he states that "matter in itself" cannot inherit God's kingdom.[224] It is obvious that corpses remain in their graves. The process by which resurrection of the body (*soma*) happens is *relational*. Our bodies are the means of our "being in the world" and it is through the body that we have relationality and history. Bernard Prusak gives this summary of Greshake's proposal:

> For Greshake, "resurrection in death and resurrection on the last day are nothing but two successive event points, united together through a dynamic progressive process." Every individual "body" thus becomes a member moving toward the completion

---

223. Greshake, *Auferstehung der Toten*, 360–414; ET: cf. Prusak, "Bodily Resurrection in Catholic Perspective," 82.

224. Cf. Greshake, "Die Leib-Seele-Problematik und die Vollendung der Welt," 175. Cited in Schärtl, "Bodily Resurrection," 104.

and fullness foreshadowed by the Resurrection of Christ. We ultimately bring before God what we have each done in love, which is inscribed on the person or self we have become, and also on the process of the world inasmuch as it is affected by our actions.[225]

Thus, for Greshake, there is no interval between death and eternal life, and yet there is no separation of body and soul. He calls this the human "continuum" that is raised by God in faithfulness and love.[226] The body is defined not by its material flesh, but by its relationships in the world. It is the "being in the world" that is resurrected and this is somatic, but not according to the flesh (*kata sarka*), but rather according to the spirit (*soma pneumatikon*). The dead are thus transphysically somatic (i.e., glorified and incorruptible) rather than bodies of corruptible flesh. This of course asks the question of whether Greshake has "over-spiritualized" an immediate resurrection.[227] In other words, it appears that he dispensed with any sense that matter can be redeemed at the eschaton, at least as far as human flesh and blood. However, I interpret Greshake as not so much saying that the flesh will not be redeemed and perhaps reunited with resurrected human beings, but rather any such flesh will be radically transformed in the same way as the flesh of Christ was transformed at his resurrection.

For Thomas Schärtl (b. 1969), Greshake's concept has significant advantages. It avoids substance dualism, avoids the problem of reassembly at the resurrection, and also avoids more unusual proposals, such as Peter van Inwagen's (b. 1942) "body snatcher" concept (the concept that at death God provides a simulacrum for the corpse and translates the corpse to the eschaton).[228] Even so, Greshake's proposal did not gain traction in mainstream Catholic theology. Joseph Ratzinger gives this disapproving summary of the argument for immediate resurrection in death:

> This starting point is then utilized to explain resurrection: when a person, by his dying, enters into non-time, into the end of the

---

225. Prusak, "Bodily Resurrection in Catholic Perspective," 83.

226. Cf. Greshake and Kremer, *Resurrectio mortuorum*, 251–53; and Greshake, "'Seele' in der Geschichte der christlichen Eschatologie," 146–47; cf. Prusak, "Bodily Resurrection in Catholic Perspective," 82.

227. Cf. Schärtl, "Bodily Resurrection," 104.

228. Cf. Schärtl, "Bodily Resurrection," 105 and for the full discussion, 103–26. For Peter van Inwagen's idea, see his "The Possibility of Resurrection," in Inwagen, ed., *The Possibility of Resurrection*, 45–51.

world, he also enters, by the same token, into Christ's return and the resurrection of the dead. There is, therefore, no "intermediate state." We have no need of the soul in order to preserve the identity of the human being. "Being with the Lord" and the resurrection from the dead are the same thing. A solution of striking simplicity has been found: resurrection happens in death.[229]

I disagree with Ratzinger's argument against resurrection-in-death as obviating the need for a soul. Even if the idea of immediate resurrection is affirmed, human beings remain psychosomatic: body and soul in an "inseparable unity, and indestructible order" according to Barth. Of course, resurrection-in-death does obviate the intermediate state and a "metronomic" purgatory. It is therefore no surprise that Ratzinger disagrees with Greshake, although one could argue that there is nothing that prevents "purgatory" from being an eschatic event that takes place *within* the judgment. In other words, purgatory as part of divine judgment can be preserved if it is seen as happening *at the eschaton itself*. The objection that the dead are immediately translated to the eschaton—such that all who have died are always already before Christ in his second coming at the consummation of the cosmos—as "striking simplicity" is overstated. Such a concept is complex because it forces an entirely different understanding of time-space as it pertains to God. If God is Lord of time and if eternity is understood as properly belonging only to God, then just as the incarnation, life, death, and resurrection of Christ is a breaking in of eternity into earthly time-space, so one could argue that death is the event when human beings break into God's 'time-space." Such a breaking in would be radical—as radical as the doctrine of the incarnation of Christ. What Greshake is advocating is not discarnation, but rather the *translation* of human beings at death (body and soul) to the eschaton, transformed into the spiritual beings that bear the image of the "man of heaven" (cf. 1 Cor 15:49).

The question that could be asked is whether there is a reunification with earthly flesh in the eschaton such that we are truly in the image of the resurrected Christ as glorified *sarx-soma-psyche* human beings. If not, is this not Platonism carefully disguised, as in Brunner's concerns about Christianity adopting "heathenish mysticism"? As mentioned above, the proposal is that human beings "arrive" at the eschaton in a transphysical state. The eschaton itself is the consummation of the cosmos which

---

229. Ratzinger, *Eschatology*, 252.

implies that everything will be made new and the old order will pass away (Rev 21:4–5). Therefore, part of this consummation is the transformation of materiality itself. It could then be argued that eschatic humanity would incorporate an imperishable materiality (i.e., flesh) as the final aspect of its transformation (1 Cor 15:53). Then, human beings would fully reflect the *imago Christi* in the world-to-come.

Karl Rahner's Consideration of "Resurrection in Death"

Karl Rahner appears to have adopted the position of Greshake concerning an immediate resurrection in death in his later years. This is recorded in his foreword to Silvano Zucal's book *La teologia della morte* which was published two years before Rahner's death.[230] Earlier, in his *Investigations*, he also modified his positions on the whether a human being could be "perfected" after death or whether it could occur in the moment of death. This change meant that Rahner was no longer as committed to death as the moment when a person's final validity as history in freedom is determined:

In other words, it may remain an open question whether the perfecting of an individual takes place "later," as his personal perfecting, or whether it takes place when he dies; i.e. whether we have to expect the resurrection of the individual "in the body" as part of a general resurrection of all men at the end of history, or whether it is "co-existent" with historical time, which meanwhile continues to run its course.[231]

Thus, Rahner allows for at least the possibility that immediate resurrection can be "co-existent" with historical time—that for the dead the resurrection has always already happened while for those in earthly time-space "historical time ... continues to run its course." This led Rahner to revisit the idea of the intermediate state and the problems posited by *anima separata*. His original solution to this problem was to propose that the soul at death is pancosmic. Prusak summarizes the pancosmic solution: "In [Rahner's] pancosmic perspective, the soul's relation to matter would still remain and be preserved even when the precise way the body is formed during its earthly life, through this relation of matter and spirit,

---

230. Zucal, *La teologia della morte in Karl Rahner*, 6. Cf. Prusak, "Bodily Resurrection in Catholic Perspective," 84.

231. Cf. Rahner, *Theological Investigations* 17, 17. Cited in Prusak, "Bodily Resurrection in Catholic Perspective," 85.

ceased to exist."[232] However, Rahner began to think of the intermediate state (together with purgatory) as a stage in theological development during the medieval period when the Western church developed this state as "an attempt to reconcile the collective and the individual view of eschatological perfection."[233] Instead, Rahner wants to focus on the collective, cosmic transformation at the eschaton, inclusive of the whole of humanity yet also allowing for the preservation and the reconciliation of the individual within the collective, but *without* an intermediate state: "For we ought at least to read what we have said about the individual into the concept of the final consummation, as one element of a progressive transformation of world history and the cosmos in general."[234]

Rahner then goes on to consider Greshake's concept of immediate resurrection since both the intermediate state and the separated soul no longer seem viable:

> [P]robably no metaphysically thinking theologian would continue to maintain today (for either philosophical or theological grounds) that the identity of the glorified body and the earthly body is only ensured if some material fragment of the earthly body is found again in the glorified body. For this kind of identity cannot even be found in the earthly body, because of its radical metabolic processes. And this kind of thinking is completely inconceivable with a modern conception of matter. . . . How would it in any way serve the identity between the earthly and the glorified body if we were to think into the resurrection body a material particle of this kind, which had earlier been the "property" of the earthly body? . . . For us, identity consists, now and in the future, of the identity of the free, spiritual subject, which we call "the soul." That is why even empirical evidence of the corpse in the grave can no longer provide an argument for there having been no "resurrection." . . . So why should we not put the resurrection at that particular moment when the person's history of freedom is finally consummated, which is to say at his death?[235]

Thus, Rahner argues that there is no need for the earthly body to be equated with the glorified body in the material sense, i.e., that the same

---

232. Prusak, "Bodily Resurrection in Catholic Perspective," 86.

233. Rahner, *Theological Investigations 17*, 118. Cf. Prusak, "Bodily Resurrection in Catholic Perspective," 86.

234. Rahner, *Theological Investigations 17*, 118.

235. Rahner, *Theological Investigations 17*, 120. Cf. Prusak, 86–7.

material flesh we possess now will be somehow recombined and resurrected on the Last Day. Rather, Rahner wants to locate human subjectivity in the "soul" but by using this word, he does not mean the metaphysical dualism of a discarnate soul. He acknowledges that the corpse remains in the grave, but that this does not mean the resurrection has not occurred. I interpret Rahner when he refers to the "free, spiritual subject" as meaning that that which is resurrected is the *soma pneumatikon*.

Rahner thus gives a radically different interpretation to humanity's *post mortem* state than is provided by the Thomistic tradition. It is an approach that is holistic rather than individualistic. It also defends a doctrine of God in which God's love remains universally operative. While Rahner never asserted universal salvation as something that can be held *de fide*, the overall thrust of his theological discourse is towards the glorious transformation of the entire cosmos which includes earthly history and humanity.[236]

Conclusion

In this section, I have discussed the concept of the discarnate soul starting with the Hellenistic background and then explored various aspects that succeeded it. The scholastic understanding of Thomas Aquinas of the "separated soul" has dominated Western Christian theology to the present day, whether or not the doctrine of purgatory is accepted. Looking at purgatory itself, I have shown that the substance dualism requires a pseudo-incarnate soul that can experience sensuality and the passage of time and that these aspects are deeply problematic as far as what it does to the doctrine of God's love. This is evident in the magisterial Catholic definitions, in Dante's poetic treatment, and in Griffiths' speculative descriptions. It is also posited (without a purgatory) in the theology of the magisterial Reformation. Schleiermacher offers an Elysian intermediate state that does ample justice to God's love, but seemingly denies any possibility of embodied sensuality in the life to come due to its strongly Platonist inclinations. Bulgakov offers an intermediate state that is an attenuated form of the tripartite human being where the soul acts as an intermediary between the earthly realm and the spiritual realm. In this attenuated state, the human spirit may experience growth that is pre-eschatic so that the person that died is not the same as the eschatic person

---

236. For an exploration of universal salvation in Rahner's works, see Ludlow, *Universal Salvation*.

that experiences resurrection. Greshake and Rahner offer entirely different interpretations that seek to solve the substance dualism and the issue of reassembly at resurrection demanded by "total death" eschatology. The weakness with both is that they can be accused of an over-spiritualized understanding of the resurrection body that makes no room for a reunification with transubstantiated and glorified human flesh.

My proposal to the symbol and problem of discarnation is to recover Greshake's concept of immediate resurrection in death, amplified by Rahner, and echoing Corner, which I have interpreted to mean "separated life." By proposing that at death, the psychosomatic unity of a life lived on earth is separated from earthly time-space and translated to the God's time-space at the eschaton, I suggest that all "separated lives" stand collectively and immediately before God in Christ. It is in God's time-space that the judgment takes place. In doing so, I am also suggesting that the entire history of every "separated life" is transformed, embodied and presented to the Lord. Thus, human history in freedom always matters, individually and collectively. It is this personal and collective history which must endure divine judgment. My argument also seeks to avoid the inherited dualism of *anima separata* that can seem to denigrate earthly life and celebrate disembodied existence as that of a blissful separated soul (at least for the saints). I thus suggest that one can say that the dead are "separated lives" in that they are separated from us in this earthly temporo-spatial existence. However, they are not separated from God and indeed, assuming that they endure the judgment, they are not separated from the communion of the saints.

Returning to the concept of Corner that at death the human person is "thrust" before the divine presence and "suffers" on account of the radical exposure to divine love, I would argue that this constitutes the purgation of the human being. To stand before God's love is thus the actual "state" of purgatory. Thus, my proposal can allow for something called purgatory in this eschatic context. Speculation on how God's judgment is operative is reserved for chapter 4 of this book. However, the argument that motivates this dissertation is that divine judgment is always the judgment of love and that we are not "saved" from judgment, but reconciled to self, the other, and God *within* it. The question of whether a person will not endure the judgment or can refuse the offer of divine love at the judgment is a question about hell—since such an outcome would be hell. That will be discussed in the next section.

4. Pessimistic Eschatology and the Problem of Hell

To despair is to descend into hell.
—Isidore of Seville[237]

In this section, I shall argue that the doctrine of eternal, retributive hell which subjects its denizens to endless torment is not consistent with the goodness and love of God. Hell, if such a "place" has denizens, must have a function that accords with God's ontic love. It is noteworthy that there is no such thing as "anti-canonization" in Roman Catholicism (or for the Eastern churches, "anti-glorification") that would declare someone damned *de fide* (the opposite of being declared a saint). Excommunication cuts a person off from the reception of the sacraments of a church (and in some cases its fellowship), but it is in no way a sentence of damnation. An attributed saying of Mahatma Gandhi (1869–1948) is that "only God decides who goes to hell."[238] In fact, no person or ecclesial community may declare that someone is damned, whether that person be Cain or Judas Iscariot.[239] Such a decision, if it is ever made, belongs to the sovereignty of God.

The fact that such a decision belongs to God alone creates a particular problem in orthodox Reformed soteriology where it is asserted that God did decree that a certain portion of humanity will be damned. In other words, the Reformed magisterial reformers *de facto* asserted that such a decision was made by God from eternity. Karl Barth, in his twentieth-century restatement of Reformed theology, gives this answer to this issue of divine election in his *Church Dogmatics*: "If we are to respect the freedom of divine grace, we cannot venture the statement that it must and will finally be coincident with the world of man as such (as in the doctrine of apokatastasis). No such right or necessity can be deduced.

---

237. Isidore of Seville, *Sententiae [De Summo Bono]*, Liber II 14.2: "desperare vero in infernum descendere." Cf. Lindsay, ed. *Isidori Hispalensis Episcopi Etymologiarum sive Originum libri XX.*

238. Cf. Browning, ed., *Universalism vs. Relativism*, 141. It is not known if Gandhi ever said these words, although the words appear in a dialogue in the 1982 film *Gandhi*.

239. Cf. Cf. Council of Orange II (529): DS 397; Council of Trent (1547): DS 1567; CCC 1037: "God predestines no one to go to hell; for this, a wilful turning away from God (a mortal sin) is necessary, and persistence in it until the end. In the Eucharistic liturgy and in the daily prayers of her faithful, the Church implores the mercy of God, who does not want "any to perish, but all to come to repentance."

Just as the gracious God does not need to elect or call any single man, so he does not need to elect or call all mankind."[240]

Barth while overturning supralapsarian double predestination does not do so by substituting it with universal salvation, although it *could* be true that God has indeed elected every human being from eternity for salvation. However, assuming that God opts not to elect a human being, what is the result of this "non-election"? If it is not hell, then what is it? Barth offers a possible answer in his commentary on John Calvin's Catechism (1537):

> The Creed discusses the things to be believed. To believe. It is important to finish with faith. We believe in the Word of God and it is the word of our salvation. The kingdom, the glory, the resurrection, the life everlasting, each one is a work of rescue. Light pierces through the darkness, eternal life overcomes eternal death. We cannot "believe" in sin, in the devil, in our death sentence. We can only believe in the Christ who has overcome the devil, borne sin and removed eternal death. Devil, sin, and eternal death appear to us only when they are overcome.[241]

Hence the church does not confess is its creeds a statement such as *credo in infernum et mortem aeternam*. Indeed, Christians do not *believe in* such things, and from a Barthian perspective we are not required to have faith in the existence of hell because hell is not an object of faith. The answer to the question, for Barth, is that such speculation should not be part of Christian theology.

Peter Phan (b. 1946) notes that Karl Rahner, for example, considered that hell

> ... could not be spoken of as a factual reality, but as a serious possibility. With regard to the eternity of hell and the connected theme of the *apokatastasis*, Rahner rather says that the two biblical statements about God's universal will of salvation (e.g., 1 Tim 2:1–6) and the *possibility* of eternal self-loss must be affirmed together. How these two dialectical statements can be reconciled with each other remains unclear to us. The nature of human freedom forbids one to state with apodictic certainty that all will be saved. On the other hand, Rahner points out, to deny a priori the possibility of universal salvation would be

---

240. Barth, *Church Dogmatics* II.2, 417.
241. Barth, *The Faith of the Church*, 171–74.

tantamount to imposing arbitrary limits upon the supreme sovereignty of God's will.[242]

While hell may be a possible state, this does not mean it is an *actual* state. Thus, I argue that as a possibility, hell must have a function that accords with an omnibenevolent God that desires the good of every creature. If hell is possible, then I agree with Paul Griffiths in a very limited sense that it is *utopia*: a state where human beings are happiest in being indefinitely separated from God and the company of the blessed. In other words, they are happiest in the pleasure of their own radical inwardness (Luther's *cor corvum in se*) that desires no reconciliation with self, the other, and God.[243] I am dubious as to whether such a state exists, but I agree with Rahner that I cannot claim with "apodictic certainty" that universal salvation is true and that no human being would choose separation from God. If hell is to be maintained as a possibility, then I shall argue that its existence must accord with the supreme goodness of God. To do otherwise is to posit that there is a limit to God's benevolence which is not congruent with God's ontic love.

A Hell of a Problem

The problem of hell is that it assumes that an omnipotent, omnibenevolent Creator eternally turns against a creature's good in eternal retribution. Not only does the traditional concept of hell do this, but it does so in a specifically horrendous way. The traditional concept of hell can be reduced to the belief that a finite sin deserves an infinite punishment. The *Westminster Confession of Faith* (1647) summarizes this: "As there is no sin so small but it deserves damnation; so there is no sin so great, that it can bring damnation upon those who truly repent."[244] In the case of the orthodox Reformed tradition as summarized in the Westminster Confession, there is no distinguishing between types of sin, such as venial and mortal. However, it does imply that the smallest offence is damnable, while the most heinous crimes are forgivable to the one who

---

242. Peter C. Phan, "Roman Catholic Theology," in Walls, ed., *The Oxford Handbook of Eschatology*, 224. Emphasis original.

243. Cf. Griffiths, *Decreation*, 5. I have borrowed the idea of hell as "utopia" from Griffiths. However, I otherwise disagree with his definition of hell. This will be discussed later in this chapter.

244. Westminster Confession of Faith 15:4. Cf. Schaff, ed., *Creeds of Christendom*, 3:632.

sincerely repents *ante mortem*. Yet, the issue here is finitude. Human sin, no matter how heinous, is finite. It must end. Eternal punishment in hell as traditionally understood is infinite. It will never end. There is an irony here as far as the Westminster divines and their formulations. In the *Westminster Shorter Catechism* (1647), the first question and answer are well known:

> Q. What is the chief end of man?
> A. The chief end of man is to worship God and enjoy him forever.[245]

Yet, the existence of hell and the damned (or reprobate) that are its denizens, which the *Confession* and *Catechism* affirm, flatly deny this answer. The chief end of humanity cannot be eternal enjoyment, since some or most of humanity will be consigned to damnation. If Augustine of Hippo's (354–430) teaching that most of humanity is a *massa damnata* is held to be true, then it is only the predestined elect that have this "chief end." The answer to the first question in the *Catechism* accords with God's omnibenevolence, but this is not maintained, just as it is not maintained in any Christian tradition apart from a minority that overtly assert universal salvation.

The problem of hell as eternal retribution was addressed by the Scottish philosopher David Hume (1711–66) in his essay *On the Immortality of the Soul* (1755). Hume was well acquainted with the Calvinism of the Church of Scotland and takes issue with the concept of eternal retribution:

> Punishment, without any proper end or purpose, is inconsistent with our ideas of goodness and justice, and no end can be served by it after the whole scene is closed. Punishment, according to our conception, should bear some proportion to the offence. Why then eternal punishment for the temporary offences of so frail a creature as man?
>
> [He then concludes that] The damnation of one man is an infinitely greater evil in the universe than the subversion of a thousand million kingdoms.[246]

---

245. Schaff, ed., *Creeds of Christendom*, 3:676. The official Latin translation reads: "Quaestio: Quis hominis finis est praecipuus? Responsio. Praecipuus hominis finis est, Deum glorificare, eodemque frui in aeternum."

246. Cf. Wollheim, ed., *Hume on Religion*, 266–67; for a discussion on Hume's case against hell, cf. Corner, *Death Be Not Proud*, 68ff.

As Hume would have it, hell is radically disproportionate to the temporal offences of human beings. Thus, even in the case of the villains of history, a God who imposes an infinite punishment imposes an infinite evil. The villains of history have committed heinous, yet finite crimes. If they are punished, it must logically be of finite duration. Capital punishment, although it means the execution of the criminal, is still a finite act in earthly time-space. However, the proponents of the traditional doctrine of hell insist that any offence against an infinitely just God, no matter how small, deserves an infinite punishment. As Anselm of Canterbury (1033–1109) wrote in his *Monologion*: "the guiltiest soul would be in the same state as the most guiltless."[247] For Anselm, as for Augustine and Aquinas, divine honor must be avenged and the only vengeance appropriate to offending the honor of an Infinite Deity by means of sin is an infinite penalty.[248] However, this creates a problem of God's justice overriding God's love and mercy. If "mercy triumphs over judgment" (cf. Jas 2:13b), it would seem eternally inoperative when it comes to maintaining divine honor.

Thus far, hell seems to be the destination of the wicked (those who commit wicked acts without repentance before death). But there is an added problem. Within the framework of Christian exclusivism, hell is a divine sentence, but it is not directed solely at those who are inherently wicked, but also against human creatures (of whatever virtue) who are unbelievers (wicked or not). There is no consequence of sin to the one who truly repents before death (not matter the magnitude of the sin), but for the righteous unbeliever, her *post mortem* fate is one of unending agony—because that person has not accepted the Christian revelation. She is damned because *extra ecclesiam nulla salus*, to cite the famous dictum attributed to Cyprian of Carthage (c. 200–258). However, it must be cautioned that the church belongs to Jesus Christ, its sole head, and it can be argued that he alone decides who is a member of his assembly: "I have other sheep that do not belong to this fold" (cf. John 10:16a). The Belgian Catholic theologian Edward Schillebeeckx (1914–2009) restates Cyprian's formula as *extra mundum nulla salus* to emphasize God's love in Christ for the world (*cosmos*) and all humanity (*humanum*).[249] In a Gospel dialogue with Thomas the Apostle, Jesus says "I am the way, and

---

247. Cf. Anselm, *Monologion*, chapter 72, "Eternal unhappiness for the soul that rejects the supreme essence," in Davies and Evans, eds., *Anselm of Canterbury*, 76.

248. For a discussion on Anselm's position, cf. Seymour, *A Theodicy of Hell*, 183ff.

249. Cf. Schillebeeckx, *Church*, 5–13.

the truth, and the life. No one comes to the Father except through me" (cf. John 14:6). However, what does it mean to come to God through Christ? Scripture and tradition seem to give emphasis to a confessional approach. However, it is perilous to insist on whom Christ will admit to God's presence and thereby into eternal life.[250]

Fundamentally, these *quaestiones disputatae* are reducible to a single question: can an omnibenevolent God damn some and not others for eternity, regardless of the reason? If the answer is affirmative, is God wholly good? The theodicy of hell in this question is, of course, not new. However, the doctrine that God saves some and damns others could be construed as pseudo-Manichaean—for such a God is dualistic, a God who loves and hates rational creatures simultaneously (e.g., *simul amor et odio*). In spite of all of these objections, Jerry Walls notes that there is an epistemological problem in the dismissal of an eternal hell. He quotes Peter Geach (1916–2013) who argues that:

> We cannot be Christians, followers of Christ, we cannot even know what it is to be a Christian unless the Gospels give at least an approximately correct account of Christ's teaching. And if the Gospel account is even approximately correct, then *it is perfectly clear* that according to that teaching many men are irretrievably lost. . . . It is less clear, I admit, that the fate of the lost according to that teaching is to be endless misery rather than ultimate destruction. But universalism is not a live option for the Christian.[251]

However, it is certainly not "perfectly clear" that many are lost. As a counterpoint to this position, the German Lutheran theologian Christoph Blumhardt (1842–1919) wrote in his "confession of hope":

> [t]hat God might give up on anything or anyone in the whole world—about that there can be no question, neither today nor in all eternity. . . . The end has to be: Behold, everything is God's! Jesus comes as the one who has borne the sins of the world. Jesus can judge but not condemn. My desire is to have preached

---

250. It is beyond the scope of this chapter to explore what amounts to universal salvation (be it for the wicked, those of other faiths, or those of no faith). For resources on this issue (and there are many), cf. Parry and Partridge, eds., *Universal Salvation? The Current Debate*. For a more focused study, cf. Ludlow, *Universal Salvation*.

251. Geach, *Providence and Evil*, 123–24; cited in Walls, *Hell*, 6.

this to the lowest circles of hell, and I will never let myself be confounded.²⁵²

This statement of hope stands in opposition to the belief that many are lost—and the very term "lost" is simply a code word for "damned." However, even Blumhardt's universalism does not deny the existence of hell. Hell is a problem only if it has permanent "residents" within it who are eternally tormented. An empty hell, which also means that it is emptied of the devil and his angels and not simply human beings, presents no stumbling block to belief in an omnibenevolent God. But an empty hell, while possible, is not the obvious inheritance of scripture and tradition. The question remains whether there is an alternative to hell, one that seems to accord with divine benevolence.

Hell as Traditionally Construed

> *Abandon every hope, you who enter here.*
> —Dante Alighieri²⁵³

In order to investigate the idea of hell as a possible state, the traditional definitions of what this state is like must be explored. There are numerous accounts within the Christian tradition, some less hellish than others. However, the concept of hell that has been inherited often lacks the subtle degrees of Dante's *Inferno* and is at odds with the various counterproposals such as those given by C. S. Lewis (1898–1963) in his book *The Great Divorce* that consider hell as eternal separation rather than eternal torment.²⁵⁴ Rather, the received tradition that is still held in the popular imagination is the hell of "fire and brimstone." The seventeenth-century scholastic Lutheran theologian Johannes Quenstedt (1617–88) gives a description of hell that could pass the test of orthodoxy in some Christian churches, even to this day:

> Death Eternal, or damnation, is that most unhappy state in which, from the just judgment of God, men who remain unbelieving to the end, being excluded from the beatific sight of

---

252. Cf. Harder, ed., *Blumhardt*, Vol. 2, 131.

253. "Lasciate ogni speranza, voi ch'entrate," Dante Alighieri, *The Inferno*, Canto III, Line 9. For the Italian text with English translation, cf. *The Divine Comedy of Dante Alighieri: Inferno*, trans. Mandelbaum, 21–22.

254. "All that are in Hell, choose it. Without that self-choice there could be no Hell." Cf. Lewis, *The Great Divorce*, 75ff.

God, and associated in the infernal prison with the devils, will be tortured eternally ... with the most severe and ineffable torments, *to the praise of divine truth, and the glory and exultation of the godly.*[255]

Yet, this concise, if horrific, account by Quenstedt pales in comparison to the description given by the nineteenth-century German Catholic theologian Matthias Joseph Scheeben (1835–88) in his *Die Mysterien des Christentums*.[256] Scheeben is interested in whether the fires of hell can be deemed to be material fire in his chapter "Die negative Verklärung oder das Mysterium des höllischen Feuers."[257] Scheeben uses violent language to portray the state of the damned: God will "degrade them below their nature, to devastate and consume them [*zu vernichten, zu verzehren*]."[258] Paul Griffiths' summary of Scheeben's concept of hell merits citation:

> The LORD's punitive power reduces the damned *bis an den Rand des Nichts* (almost to the edge of nothing), and later, *den Leib an den Rand der Vernichtung bringt* (brings the body to the edge of annihilation). And this intense punishment, carried out by the LORD with a material fire (Scheeben makes a good deal of this; unconvincingly), is a necessary concomitant of the LORD's saving grace: *Die unendliche mächtige Kraft der Gottheit muß* ... and *muß* is repeated again and again. The LORD must punish the wicked with torments that bring them almost to nothing. Justice demands it.
>
> For Scheeben, privation is not enough. The final and irreversible separation of the damned from the LORD, which is what would happen if they were to go out of existence (as his language says they almost do) in the intermediate state before the general resurrection, would not satisfy the LORD's honor, which has been damaged by the supernatural offence of sin. Such satisfaction requires fleshly punishment, thinks Scheeben—there is *poena sensus* as well as *poena damni*—which is the *umgekehrte Bild der göttlichen Verklärung*, the reverse picture, or mirror-image, of divine transformation.... Scheeben goes so far as to say that for the damned the LORD's love is transformed without remainder into wrath (*in diesen Zorn sich verwandelt*

---

255. Quenstedt, *Theologia Didacto-Polemica* I,565 (1685); in Schmid, *The Doctrinal Theology of the Evangelical Lutheran Church* (1843), 657. Emphasis mine.

256. Cf. Scheeben, *Die Mysterien des Christentums* (1865).

257. For a more detailed description of Scheeben's concept of hellfire, see Griffiths, *Decreation*, 244ff.

258. Cited in Griffiths, *Decreation*, 244.

hat . . .); this is a transformation that he seems to take to mark a real change in the LORD rather than a self-wrought change in the human creature.[259]

Thus, in Scheeben's view, which goes well beyond Quenstedt, God's ontology as love is transformed into ontological hate when it comes to the damned—for "justice demands it." The damned must be punished to the point of almost being destroyed in an intermediate hell only to be resurrected and subjected to hellfire in the flesh, eternally and corporeally. To Scheeben, this is *"ein Wunder der Strafgerechtigkeit Gottes*—a miracle of God's punitive justice; it is he writes, a *Mysterium der Qual, der Pein und des Schreckens*—a mystery of agony, of pain, and of fear."[260] Griffiths, in his comparison between Augustine's and Scheeben's concepts of hell summarizes this as follows: "It is only the LORD's deliberate and supernatural intervention that prevents sinners from ceasing to be; and it does this exactly by establishing and maintaining a domain of endless pain. This is not a pleasing picture."[261]

Indeed, it is not pleasing at all, whether that of Quenstedt or Scheeben. In fact, it is impossible not to consider that God is a sadist of the worst possible kind in the eternal treatment of the damned. The question that must be asked is this: if faith, hope, and love abide forever (cf. 1 Cor 13:13), how can this be reconciled with a state of eternal despair and hate? I would suggest that it is not possible to hold to God's omnibenevolence and admit what is tantamount to dystheism (i.e., the belief that God is malevolent). Such a theistic dualism cannot stand for it implies that God's love fails, even though the Pauline tradition claims that this is not possible because "Love never fails" (cf. 1 Cor 13:8). The barbarity of the traditional hell is discordant with the God who is proclaimed to love the cosmos (cf. John 3:17).

Sergei Bulgakov and Hell as Universal Purgatory

Bulgakov has already been cited in this chapter on the intermediate state and he will be explored in more depth in chapter 3 of this book. However, it is useful to explore what the nature of hell is for Bulgakov whose

---

259. Griffiths, *Decreation*, 245. It should be noted that Griffiths does not agree with Scheeben's speculations.

260. Griffiths, *Decreation*, 246.

261. Griffiths, *Decreation*, 247.

eschatology ultimately results in universal salvation. Bulgakov offers a unique alternative to hell that in some ways bridges the hell of tradition with more recent modifications of the doctrine.

It may seem unusual that a universalist writes so freely about hell, but Bulgakov does just that. The Eastern Orthodox theologian Paul Gavrilyuk in his study on Bulgakov's universalism notes that Bulgakov uses the term "universal purgatory" (Russian: *vseobshchee chistilishche*) as a way to describe hell and Gavrilyuk considers this the best definition of a Bulgakovian hell.[262] Bulgakov never uses this term again in his last theological work *The Bride of the Lamb*. In fact, he rejects the idea of purgatory as a third state since it is incompatible with Eastern Orthodox doctrine. What is interesting is that for Bulgakov hell is purgatorial, remedial, and finite. In other words, hell and purgatory are the same thing.[263] He makes reference to the works of Isaac the Syrian (c. 613–700; also known as St Isaac of Nineveh) which he quotes from the Russian translation:

> I say that those tormented in gehenna are struck by the scourge of love. And how bitter and cruel is this agony of love, for, feeling that they have sinned against love, they experience a torment that is greater than any other. The affliction that strikes the heart because of the sin against love is more terrible than any possible punishment. It is wrong to think that gehenna are deprived of God's love. Love is produced by knowledge of the truth, which (everyone is in agreement about this) is given to all in general. But by its power love affects human beings in a twofold manner: It torments sinners, as even here a friend sometimes causes one to suffer, and it gladdens those who have carried out their duty. And so, in my opinion, the torment of gehenna consists in repentance. Love fills with its joys the souls of the children on high.[264]

Isaac the Syrian uses the Hebrew term "gehenna" (Hebrew: *Ge Hinnom*, "Valley of Hinnom") reflecting his own Semitic background and the fact that the word Gehenna is the word that Jesus uses (translated as "hell" in almost all versions of the New Testament). However, Isaac the Syrian is using Gehenna to mean hell in the conventional sense and not as a geographical location outside Jerusalem.[265] In effect, hell is God's love

262. Gavrilyuk, "Universal Salvation in the Eschatology of Sergius Bulgakov," 125.
263. Gavrilyuk, "Universal Salvation in the Eschatology of Sergius Bulgakov," 125.
264. Cf. Bulgakov, *The Bride of the Lamb*, 466.
265. For a discussion of the Jewish origins of the use of Gehenna as a *post mortem*

as experienced by those who must be purified of sin. It is the same divine love enjoyed by the "children on high" (the saints). Thus, to be in the presence of Christ, who is both Judge and Lover, is to be assailed by the torments that offenses against love demand. What is interesting in this hellish love or loving hell is that for the person standing before Christ, the attitude of that person is not fear, but—in spite of torments—love: "A human being cannot fail to love the Christ that is revealed to him, and he cannot fail to love himself as revealed in Christ."[266] This is extremely important. For Bulgakov, libertarian free will is not thwarted by this irresistible love because it is an ontological experience. God in Christ is, literally, love itself. Human beings are made in the image of God and thus a direct encounter with Christ is an encounter with God's perfect image. But, the sin that is revealed to the human being in this encounter (and sin always offends love) results in the "scourge" of hell. The "fires" of hell are not inflicted by God nor are the sufferings desired by God. Rather, to be in the presence of divine love simply causes this purgatorial effect. God cannot be less loving in order to lessen the anguish of this encounter just as God cannot be less divine. Thus, Bulgakov makes this strange statement: "Hell is love for God, though it is a love that cannot be satisfied. Hell is a suffering due to emptiness, due to an inability to contain this love for God."[267]

The reason for this is that a human being for the first time sees herself in the mirror of Christ (the mirror of the perfect image of God) and sees absolutely for the first time how the *imago Dei* in her has been deformed by sin. This is the purgatorial judgment—the seeing of the deformity is the experience of the judgment of love which is a form of hell:

> Judgment as separation expresses the relation between image and likeness, which can be in mutual harmony or in antinomic conjugacy. Image corresponds to the heavenly mansions in the Father's house, to the edenic bliss of "eternal life." Likeness, by contrast, corresponds to that excruciating division within the resurrected human being where he does not yet actually possess what is his potentially; whereas his divine proto-image is in full possession of it. He contemplates this image before himself and in himself as the inner norm of his being, whereas, by reason of his proper self-determination and God's judgment, he cannot

---

state, cf. Raphael, *Jewish Views of the Afterlife*, 140ff.
266. Bulgakov, *The Bride of the Lamb*, 459.
267. Bulgakov, *The Bride of the Lamb*, 492.

encompass this being in himself. He cannot possess part (and this part can be large or small) of that which is given to him and loved by him in God (cf. St Isaac the Syrian); and this failure to possess, this active emptiness at the place of fullness, is experienced as perdition and death, or rather as a perishing and a dying, as "eternal torment," as the fire of hell. This ontological suffering is described only in symbolic images borrowed from the habitual lexicon of apocalyptics. It is clear that these images should not be interpreted literally. Their fundamental significance lies in their description of the torments of unrealized and unrealizable love, the deprivation of the bliss of love, the consciousness of the sin against love.[268]

In other words, the agony of hellish love, is also the only way that the image of God can be restored in a human being. For Bulgakov, everything that is non-love must be purged away in this eschatic encounter. There is no escape from this purification, although the degree of the purifying "fires of love' corresponds to the offenses committed against it. The purgatory of love experienced by a saint might be minimal. However, for the truly wicked, the torments caused by the encounter with divine love would be horrendous.

Bulgakov believes in the paradox that all human beings will experience both hell and heaven in the eschatic encounter with Christ:

> We must therefore conclude that the very separation into heaven and hell, into eternal bliss and eternal torments, is internal and relative. Every human being bears within himself the principle of the one and the other, depending upon the measure of his personal righteousness. Since no human being is without sin, there is no one who does not have the burning of hell within himself, even if only to a minimal degree. Conversely, there is no human being whose soul is not illuminated by the light of paradise, even if only at a single point or by a distant reflection.[269]

Thus, no matter the degree of goodness or evil within any human being, salvation will be the end result because divine love will burn away all that is non-love and "save" that which is love, even if it is only a "single point" of love in a wicked person. As horrendous as the torments of God's love may be, this same love will enable human beings to participate in eternal life.

268. Bulgakov, *The Bride of the Lamb*, 474–75.
269. Bulgakov, *The Bride of the Lamb*, 465. Cf. Gavrilyuk, *Decreation*, 124.

Bulgakov presents an eschatic purgatorial hell that retains the retributive element, but the retribution is caused by an encounter with the love of God. The "flames" are not material fire, but the embrace of God that restores the *imago Dei* that has been marred by sin in a human being back to its "prototype" which is represented by Christ, the perfect image of God. The experience of hell is the means to that restoration. It would seem that no one, not even the saints, will escape universal purgatory: "For all of us must appear before the judgment seat of Christ, so that each may receive recompense for what has been done in the body, whether good or evil" (cf. 2 Cor 5:10). While Bulgakov's high Mariology states that she is exempt from judgment, it would seem that she too must pass before the judgment seat even though she would not suffer any purgation, but only the happy embrace of God's love. Thus, even the saints who die "in a state of grace" will still have some purgation to endure since they do not possess the perfect image of God that belongs to Christ alone. The simplest way to conceive of a Bulgakovian hell is to think of Christ as the Judge who holds a mirror before each human being reflecting back to them the deformities to their God-given divine image. It is the terribleness of this experience that is both judgment and hell and it is this encounter that purges and restores that image which results in theosis, union with God.

Bulgakov presents a unique unification of judgment, purgatory, and hell that results in universal reconciliation. None of the terribleness of hell is attenuated, but its source is always God's love. The same love that "burns" also is the joy of the saints in eternal life. Thus, for Bulgakov, hell is not a place, but an event. It is infinite only in the same way that God's love is infinite. It is finite because for Bulgakov it is implausible that any human being will reject the passionate embrace of God's love forever. While not official dogma in Eastern Orthodoxy, Bulgakov's approach has a long history in Eastern Christianity and, unlike in the West, the doctrine of universal salvation has remained a tolerated (if "heterodox") belief.

Hell: Recent Modifications

Some recent works of eschatology often seek to soften the traditional, retributive concept of hell, while not abandoning the doctrine. The Catholic theologian William Hoye (b. 1940) gives a classic example of what might be called hell without hellfire: "Hell is neither hatred nor disappointed love. It can be nothing other than deficient love. In hell, there can be no conscious suffering for that would be itself a kind of desire.... Hell is lack."[270]

Granted, not all theologians are willing to remove suffering from hell, regardless of denominational affiliation. However, the speculations on the nature of hell offered by Quenstedt and Scheeben would probably be deemed repellent by many contemporary Christian theologians, even those who do hold to the traditional understanding that hell involves some sort of endless suffering. Yet, Hoye is trying to remedy the punitive typology of hell. It would seem heretical to assert something about the revealed divine character that is hateful. God may hate sin, but God undeniably loves the sinner within the context of Christian tradition. Bulgakov's alternative to hell as universal purgatory may be harrowing, but the end result is beatitude. However, Bulgakov's alternative stands largely alone within the theological corpus: he renders hellfire into love-fire and unites retributive suffering with universal salvation.

Joseph Ratzinger notes that eternal damnation cannot be avoided in Christian theology: "*No quibbling helps us here*: the idea of eternal damnation ... has a firm place in the teaching of Jesus, as well as in the apostolic writings."[271] Indeed, hell cannot be dismissed, no matter how offensive the concept may be to some Christians. However, the contradiction that God hates those in hell when the fundamental attribute of the God of Christian monotheism is love seems to demand a remedy. In fact, there has always been a minority tradition even in the Christian West that hell can only be purgative and finite. Yet, this tradition was never dominant and was at least partly condemned by the Fifth Council of Constantinople in 553 CE. Even so, a desire to attenuate hell fills the modern theological corpus. The *Catechism of the Catholic Church* states that the "definitive self-exclusion from communion with God and the blessed is called 'hell.'"[272] The Russian Orthodox archbishop Hilarion Alfeyev (b. 1966) goes further in saying that Christ descended into hell as a conqueror and thus renders Hades as a place where God is emphatically present and its occupants have the opportunity to convert *post mortem*

---

270. Hoye, *The Emergence of Eternal Life*, 109.
271. Ratzinger, *Eschatology: Death and Eternal Life*, 215. Emphasis mine.
272. CCC 1033.

so that universal salvation is possible. Alfeyev, similar to Bulgakov, thus changes hell into a form of purgatory with an open door.[273]

In the post-conciliar Catholic definition, hell is modified as "self-exclusion"—the damned person excludes him- or herself from the beatific vision and any suffering would be resultant from this lack. In the second more radical example of Alfeyev, the focus is on *Christus Victor* and the *descensus*—where Christ conquers hell and thus transforms even Hades into a place where the divine presence is manifested. The Protestant theologian Jerry Walls gives perhaps the best contemporary example of a mollified version of hell that sits between the more epistemically modest definitions of the *Catechism of the Catholic Church* and the optimism of Alfeyev. Walls dispenses with eternal torments, although he admits that hell is a miserable, endless state:

> Generally speaking, the reason hell can be freely chosen is that it is a distorted mirror image of heaven. There is no righteousness or holiness in hell, but it does offer the alternative of self-righteousness. It offers no real joy or happiness, but it does offer the deformed sense of satisfaction from holding on to bitterness, resentment, and hurt. There is no real fulfillment, but it does offer the illusory triumph of getting one's way, self-destructive though it is. Hell is an empty shell of which heaven is the pulsating, vibrant reality. But the shell is not without its pleasures, miserable though they are.[274]

In this concept of hell, God's love could be said to remain intact because hell is a choice and God respects the libertarian free will of human beings. While this eternal state of separation from God is not one of happiness, it can be said to contain pleasures: the perverse pleasures that some human beings derive from holding onto arrogance, hatreds, rebellion, and a refusal to conform to God's divine policies. Thus, hell is an eternal state of willful separation from God. To the saints, hell would be a place of agony since their desire is eschatic union with God and one another, and indeed all creation. However, to the damned, hell may be utopian as it offers them a place where they can continue in their sinful pleasures.

It could be argued that hell is a place that God creates out of love for obstinate sinners who would find heaven to be hellish and prefer the

273. Cf. Alfeyev, *Christ the Conqueror of Hell*.

274. Walls, *Heaven, Hell, and Purgatory*, 90. For Walls' original academic study of hell, cf. Walls, *Hell*.

perverse freedom of perpetual rebellion against God, the other, and the cosmos in the "infernal world." Thus, hell is their heaven, as John Milton (1608–74) alludes to in *Paradise Lost*: "The mind is its own place, and in itself can make a heaven of hell, a hell of heaven."[275] Hell may be a place of eternal misery, but it is the place that certain human beings prefer. However, if this view is taken, God's salvific project is defeated if we assume that the salvation and reconciliation of all things is within this project. God will not be "all in all" at the eschaton if some created beings remain eternally separated from the divine presence. (cf. 1 Cor 15:28)

Further Modifications: Paul Griffiths and Annihilationism

Paul Griffiths provides this speculative definition of hell that he believes stays within the restraints of Roman Catholic magisterial teaching:

> *Hell*: the time-space during which creatures, according to their kinds, are maximally and irreversibly separated from the LORD and from one another. The speculative position taken in this book is that such a time-space is utopia, timeless and placeless, and that the creatures who enter it therefore come to nothing as creatures who are necessarily spatio-temporal must when they become timeless and placeless.[276]

Griffiths does not assert his definition of hell is true, only that it is possible and coherent. The first aspect of traditional hell that he deems problematic is that of endless torment: "pain is a feature, an artifact, of the fall, and as such belongs properly to the devastation; its occurrence for human creatures is inseparable from metronomic time that belongs to the devastation, and to say that it can continue after the general resurrection is just to say that the devastation is not fully and finally healed."[277]

The reader is reminded from the previous section that, for Griffiths, the "devastation" is the fallen world that we now inhabit which is bound by measurable time. So, while finite torment is possible for the hell-bound in the discarnate intermediate state, it is not possible after the general resurrection. It is noteworthy that for Griffiths the concept of "enfleshed inhabitants of hell" who suffer would mean that God did not achieve the

---

275. Cf. "Paradise Lost," Book I, in Milton, *The Poetical Works of John Milton*, vol. 1, 12.

276. Griffiths, *Decreation*, 5. Emphasis original.

277. Griffiths, *Decreation*, 242.

THE SYMBOLS AND PROBLEMS OF JUDGMENT 105

eschatic healing of the cosmos: "This is reason enough by itself to pause before the doctrine of an inhabited hell."[278] A restored cosmos should be one that is totally free of suffering and "fallen time"—for Griffiths, metronomic time is devastated time. The ticking of the clock is an aspect of the devastated world we inhabit. It has no place in the eschaton. Suffering in the flesh would logically require metronomic time to occur, but this should not be an eschatic possibility. However, Griffiths is well aware that Scripture and tradition seem to state the opposite: that endless torment in hell is a post-eschatic possibility. Griffiths turns to Augustine of Hippo to explore an account of how this possibility is justified. He uses the twenty-first book of Augustine's *City of God* (*De civitate Dei*) as the basis of his exploration.[279]

Augustine attempts to provide an explanation on how human flesh can suffer endlessly in hell by referring to examples of how the dead peacock's flesh does not rot (*Quis enim nisi Deus creator omnium dedit carni pavonis mortui ne putesceret?*) and the belief that the Sicilian mountain salamander lives in fire (*Quapropter si, ut scripserunt qui naturas animalium curiosius indagarunt, salamandra in ignibus vivit et quidam notissimi Siciliae montes, qui tanta temporis diuturnitate ac vetustate usque nunc ac deinceps flammis aestuant atque integri perseverant*).[280] Such ancient beliefs were false, but Griffiths responds that even if they were true they do not justify Augustine's claim.[281] Human flesh does not endlessly suffer on earth—its sufferings are either finite or the human being dies. Likewise, a salamander that was thought to live in fire was not thought to be tormented by it. Augustine then moves from animal examples to the simple proposition that God is able to do anything God wants (*aliquid vult potest*). If God wants human beings to suffer endless bodily torment in hell (*igne aeterno crucientur corpora damnatorum*), God will simply make

---

278. Griffiths, *Decreation*, 242.

279. Griffiths, *Decreation*, 243ff. Griffiths does not use footnotes or endnotes in his book. He does however provide sources after each chapter. For all the work of Augustine, Griffiths consulted the Latin texts available at *S. Aurelii Augustini Opera Omnia: Patrologiae Latinae Elenchus*, www.augustinus.it/latino/. His citations from *De civitate Dei* come from this source.

280. Griffiths, *Decreation*, 243ff. Cf. *De civitate Dei*, 21.1. Latin citations are mine not Griffiths' but from the same web source supra.

281. Griffiths, *Decreation*, 243ff.

this happen by virtue of divine omnipotence.²⁸² Griffiths disagrees with Augustine because he does not think that Christian orthodoxy demands

> ... that there are, or may be, human creatures suffering eternal fleshly torments forever.... The most we can say is that Christian doctrine requires that the eternal, irrevocable, and maximal separation from the LORD's prevenient love be a possibility for human beings, and that condition is met as well by postulating annihilation as a possibility for human creatures as by postulating a fleshly and torturous hell as a possible last thing for them.²⁸³

While hell as annihilation rather than eternal torment is not new to theology, it is interesting to see it proposed by a Catholic theologian. Another term for annihilationism is conditional immortalism. The conditionalist argument is that while the torments of hell may be of "long duration," they are finite and that at their conclusion the conscious torment ceases and the human being is destroyed.²⁸⁴ Thus, human beings are conditionally immortal: for the righteous or those who are made righteous by justification, they meet the "conditions" for immortality and are admitted to eternal life. For the wicked, be it for their crimes, non-acceptance of Christ, or both, they do not meet these conditions and their immorality is denied. Thus, humanity is divided between those who possess the preconditions of eternal life and those who do not.

Griffiths' account of the trajectory of the damned, if there are any, is that they suffer hellish torments in the intermediate state as discarnate souls. However, he does not think it is possible for the damned to be re-enfleshed at the general resurrection when metronomic time is healed and the clocks stop ticking. Likewise, suffering and pain, which are artefacts of the devastation (the fallen world) are also healed and thus cease. Unlike the saved, the damned are not resurrected in the flesh, but consigned to a state that is timeless and placeless. Such a state results in their dissolution because human beings can only exist in a time-space, whether it is the devastated time-space of the world or the healed

---

282. Griffiths, *Decreation*, 244. Latin citations provided by Griffiths from *De civitate Dei*, 21.7.

283. Griffiths, *Decreation*, 244.

284. There are numerous proponents for the species of hell that results in annihilation. Among the most prominent holder of this view is Clark Pinnock in his "The Destruction of the Finally Impenitent." For the discussion, cf. Spiegel, "Annihilation, Everlasting Torment and Divine Justice"; and cf. Brown and Walls, "Annihilationism: A Philosophical Dead End?"

time-space of eternal life with God. The devastation that is the unhealed cosmos is transformed at the eschaton and thus there is only one divine time-space, *ergo* the damned cannot exist. While Griffiths does not assert that his species of conditional immortalism is true and the doctrine of endless torment, as held by the received tradition, is false, he states that his proposal is "more beautiful and more fully articulated with tradition's deep grammar" and that the alternative "suffers from a profound ugliness in the order of knowing."[285] He clearly finds the barbaric aspects of traditional visions of hell both theologically dubious and morally repellent.

Griffiths seems to want to modify the post-Vatican II emphasis on hell as eternal separation from God to be inclusive of annihilation of the damned. This proposal is not asserted as *de fide* and his proposal should be understood as a hope, rather than any defiance to scripture, tradition, or the magisterium. However, Griffiths notes that whatever version of hell may be true for its possible denizens, an inhabited hell represents "the success of the project of sin, which exactly is a project of self-extrication from the LORD, who is the condition of the possibility of being for all human creatures."[286] If God, to use the well-known phrase of Paul Tillich (1886–1965), is the "Ground of Being," then hell is the "place" where this divine ground is absent. The damned "fall" into nothingness at the eschaton.[287]

Griffiths affirms that all suffering has its roots in sin and that sin has its roots in the fall. The "devastation" is a world deformed by sin. Death and pain are earthly reminders that our world is fallen. Thus, evil in the world is analogous to hell on earth. Bad things, whatever they may be, are in effect manifestations of hell. Only union with God in the life of the world-to-come heals the devastation and all its ill effects. To follow the sin project to the end means that a human being willingly brings herself to nothing.[288]

Griffiths believes that the Christian tradition generally assumes that hell is inhabited, although it never asserts it. He notes that the Roman Catholic Church is characteristically "chaste" in its silence on whether human beings are in hell, and this dogmatic chastity is even more

---

285. Griffiths, *Decreation*, 247.

286. Griffiths, *Decreation*, 247.

287. I am merely borrowing Tillich's phrase and not asserting anything about Tillich's soteriology. For a concise, if dated, discussion on the topic of God as the Ground of Being, cf. Hammond, "Tillich on the Personal God."

288. Griffiths, *Decreation*, 248.

pronounced for specific individuals. However, he notes Christians do not seem to possess this virtue. He writes that "[i]t appears to be a deep-seated desire among Christians, even if an unedifying and unnecessary one, to name the damned."[289] Griffiths concludes his speculations on hell in a paragraph that unifies his understanding of both hell and the intermediate state:

> Annihilation, which is hell under its proper name, is, then, a possible *novissimum* for human creatures (and for angels), though not one who actuality is known for any individual. Any humans who arrive at it do so by failing to be resurrected for eternal life; what is, for the saved, a temporary loss of self during the intermediate state, a loss produced by the absence of the flesh, becomes for the damned permanent and beyond the possibility of reversal. The postmortem sufferings of the damned, those approaching nothing, undergo as discarnate souls progressively reduce those souls beyond the point at which reunion with the flesh is possible, and at that point it will have become the case that those sufferings were hellish, hell-bound. They are then truly dead souls, *animae deo desertae*. By contrast, there are discarnate souls whose postmortem sufferings purify them and ready them exactly for reunion with resurrected flesh. When this happens, it will be apparent, to them and to others, that their postmortem sufferings were purgatorial rather than hellish.[290]

In this passage, Griffiths makes it clear that the damned are not resurrected and sent as fleshly human beings into hell. In the intermediate state, their sufferings reduce their souls to the point that they cannot be reunited to their bodies at the eschaton. They thus cannot be true human beings again. Since re-incarnation does not happen and hell is timeless and placeless, they cannot have existence. They are dissolved or, perhaps more accurately, erased. In God's time-space, it would be as if they never existed. For the souls in purgatory, their agony seems to be extreme

---

289. Griffiths, *Decreation*, 248.

290. Griffiths, *Decreation*, 250. The phrase *animae deo desertae* is from Augustine's City of God. Cf. *De civitate Dei*, 13.2: "Impiorum namque in corporibus vita non animarum, sed corporum vita est; quam possunt eis *animae* etiam mortuae, hoc est *Deo desertae*, quantulacumque propria vita, ex qua et immortales sunt, non desistente, conferre. Verum in damnatione novissima quamvis homo sentire non desinat, tamen, quia sensus ipse nec voluptate suavis nec quiete salubris, sed dolore poenalis est..." Cf. *S. Aurelii Augustini Opera Omnia: Patrologiae Latinae Elenchus*, www.augustinus.it/latino/, accessed 11 June 2016. Emphasis in Latin quotation mine.

because they do not know their sufferings are purifying until they are resurrected—or if released prior, until they behold the beatific vision. In effect, Griffiths constructs an intermediate state that equates to a traditional concept of hell with only the souls of the saints being exempt. It is only at the end that the damned realize that they will cease to exist and the souls being purified will rejoice that they will attain eternal life.

Thus, the only mollification that Griffiths offers is that hell is finite and the damned will be spared eternal torment by being annihilated. Griffiths states that it is possible, if dubious, that endless torment for the damned is true. Thus, in the end analysis, Griffiths offers only the hope that hell is finite for the damned. He is pessimistic, based on the weight of Scripture and tradition, that hell might be uninhabited. However, the logic of Griffiths' eschatological speculations is grounded in his concepts of fallen time-space and healed time-space. Since the parousia of Christ reverses the fall and heals time-space universally, it would seem that Griffiths cannot allow for a hell that "continues." There is no metronomic time in the world-to-come, only a systolic "breathing" of an eternal liturgy of praise and love that is never changing, but assumedly never boring. There is no liturgy in hell because there is no systolic time-space there. Hell is a non-time-space and as such it is nothingness. Human beings, be they enfleshed or discarnate, cannot exist outside of a time-space. Thus, the damned *must* come to nothing. Due to the doctrinal constraints that Griffiths self-imposes, he cannot *assert* that hell will be destroyed at the eschaton, along with any inhabitants. However, the logic of his theological thought seems to demand this. Thus, Griffiths leaves the reader only with the speculative hope that hell is finite.

However, I would argue that a hope that hell is finite is not enough to overcome the problem of what an eternal hell or the annihilation of the damned does to the doctrine of God. It would seem that if either option is true, the "sin project" succeeds and succeeds eternally. If God is ontic love, as my thesis asserts, I suggest that neither possibility is viable.

Hell on Earth: The Problem of Despair

> For the world is hell, and human beings are on the one hand the tormented souls and on the other the devils in it.
> —Arthur Schopenhauer[291]

291. Arthur Schopenhauer (1788–1860): *Die Welt ist eben die Hölle, und die*

As illustrated by the quotations from Isidore of Seville and Dante previously, and now Schopenhauer, hell is, in addition to its other problems, a problem of despair; it is a place without hope. Hope is fundamental to the Christian gospel—and is central to the Pauline message that faith, hope, and love abide forever (cf. 1 Cor 13:13). The belief that God in Christ would consign even the worst of sinners to perpetual despair seems at odds with the character of God as revealed in Jesus Christ. The earthly despair that humans can and do experience is also a type of hell. It seems incoherent to propose that God would *eternalize* despair in the eschatic reality. Moltmann describes the problem of hell in secular, this-worldly terms:

> The logic of hell seems to me ... extremely atheistic: here the human being in his freedom of choice is his own lord and god. His own will is his heaven—or his hell. God is merely the accessory who puts that will into effect.... Is that "the love of God"? Free human beings forge their own happiness and are their own executioners. They do not just dispose over their lives here; they decide on their eternal destinies as well. So they have no need of God at all.... Carried to this ultimate conclusion, the logic of hell is secular humanism.[292]

The proposal that the concept of hell is atheistic is striking. One of the appeals of contemporary nihilism is that it implies total freedom. If the universe has no meaning and humanity's existence is accidental, then our actions for good or ill are also meaningless. This in turn frees human individuals to act in whatever way they please for quite literally nothing matters. I am by no means saying that theism is necessary for morality—clearly it is not. However, Moltmann's claim that the logic of hell is actually a form of secular humanism is an interesting one. Human beings are their own "lords and gods" and God simply actualizes their decisions. Yet, secular humanism and its cousin nihilism both allude to a serious problem in contemporary society—despair. Despair is an earthly, real problem and Isidore is absolutely right—to experience despair *is* to descend into hell, and that hell can be here on earth. Karl Barth makes this comment about hell being a reality of earthly life:

Menschen sind einerseits die gequälten Seelen und andererseits die Teufel darin. Cf. Schopenhauer, *Essays and Aphorisms*, 48.

292. Moltmann, "Logic of Hell," 43–47.

And let us not add: "Yes, but sin is a grievous thing"—as though hell and so many horrors were not on earth already! If one does really believe, one cannot say: "But!" this terrible and pitiful "but." I fear that much of the weakness of our Christian witness comes from this fact that we dare not frankly confess the grandeur of God, the victory of Christ, the superiority of the Spirit. Wretched as we are, we always relapse into contemplation of ourselves and of mankind, and, naturally, eternal death comes up no sooner than we have looked on it. The world without redemption becomes again a power and a threatening force, and our message of victory ceases to be believable. But as it is written: "The victory that triumphs over the world, this is our faith" (1 Jn 5:4).[293]

Barth was certainly aware that hell can happen on earth. He witnessed the atrocities of World War II, even if from the relative safety of his native Switzerland. The litany of earthly evils should be readily apparent to anyone. The world's newspapers and television reports are filled with news of terrible things, be they of natural causes or human design. Marilyn McCord Adams in her book *Horrendous Evils and the Goodness of God*, provides a concise example of earthly horrors:

> I define "horrendous evils" as "Evils the participation in (the doing or suffering of) which gives one reason *prima facie* to doubt whether one's life could (given their inclusion in it) be a great good to one on the whole." Such reasonable doubt arises because it is so difficult humanly to conceive how such evils could be overcome. . . . I offer the following list of paradigmatic horrors: the rape of a woman and axing off of her arms, psychophysical torture whose ultimate goal is the disintegration of personality, betrayal of one's deepest loyalties, cannibalizing one's own offspring, child abuse of the sort described by Ivan Karamazov, child pornography, parental incest, slow death by starvation, participation in the Nazi death camps, the explosion of nuclear bombs over populated areas, having to choose which of one's children shall live and which will be executed by terrorists, being the accidental and/or unwitting agent of the disfigurement or death of those one loves best. I regard these as paradigmatic, because I believe most people would find in the doing or suffering of them *prima facie* reason to doubt the positive meaning of their lives. . . . For better and worse, the by now standard

---

293. Barth, *The Faith of the Church*, 174.

strategies for "solving" the problem of evil are powerless in the face of horrendous evils.[294]

All of the horrors listed by Adams could be deemed a form of hell on earth. According to the World Bank, 2.1 billion people on earth (35 percent of the population) live on less than US $3.10 per day.[295] It is self-evident that poverty leaves its victims open to many hellish possibilities, for example: famine and starvation, lack of medical care, human trafficking, or powerlessness before the apparatus of the state. Adams' concern is partly the physical toll of evils on a human person, but more so the psychological cost: hellish happenings make its victim doubt the goodness of the person's life. Such a circumstance results in despair and the maxim of Isidore of Seville becomes operative. Wealth may safeguard its beneficiaries from certain evils, but not all. All human beings are subject to horrors and no one escapes death.

The reason that it is necessary to explore the theme of "hell on earth" is because in the Christian exclusivist-retributivist version of the doctrine of hell, the vast majority of the human race has been or will be consigned to hell. This means that for many they will leave an earthly hell only to enter an eternal hell, and both places are attributed to God's creation. The "from hell to hell" view of the human race as a *massa damnata* is massively problematic. I would suggest that it leaves the doctrine of God in a shamble. Thus, what is called the soteriological problem of evil (i.e., the problem of hell) is all the more important for theological engagement. Yet, I would also remind the reader that most theology, ancient and modern, is elitist. It is elitist because most theologians are part of the wealthy or northern world, whether it is Augustine, Luther, Calvin, Tillich, or Barth. I do not deny that there have been theologians in developing countries whose works have been recorded, but they are as yet not normative. Thus, the state of the world as containing elements of the traditional doctrine of hell must (I suggest) cause us to reflect on what sort of eschatic hell we are willing to attribute to God's design. It is with this caveat that I engage in an exploration of eschatic or *post mortem* hell as a problem of evil.

---

294. Adams, *Horrendous Evils and the Goodness of God*, 211–12.

295. The World Bank, Poverty data, http://www.worldbank.org/en/topic/poverty/overview, accessed 11 June 2016.

Hell and the Soteriological Problem of Evil

Hell, as a problem of evil, has elicited a wide-ranging response starting since the nineteenth century. Some have sought to reconcile a retributive, eternal hell with a loving God, thus exonerating God from being the author of evil. Others have attempted various modifications, from attenuation to what amounts to universal salvation. Marilyn McCord Adams, whose eschatology will be discussed in depth in chapter 3 of this book, has labelled hell as a fundamental problem of evil for the Christian. In fact, she asserts that hell is the *chief* problem of evil for Christians according to the following schema:

I. God exists, and is essentially omnipotent, omniscient, and perfectly good; and

II. Evil exists; and

III. Some created persons will be consigned to hell forever

Concerning the above illustration, Adams states: "My own view is that hell poses the principal problem of evil for Christians. Its challenge is so deep and divisive, that to spill bottles of ink defending the logical compossibility of (I) with this-worldly evils [II] while holding a closeted belief in (III) is at best incongruous and at worst disingenuous."[296] I agree with Adams that there is no way to avoid thinking that the traditional retributive hell is an evil—and one of eternal duration, even if we accept as valid the claim that "there exists no dogmatic definition on the nature of the punishments of hell."[297] There may be no definition, but the punishments, whatever they are, will never end. However, the claims of Quenstedt and Scheeben have a longer pedigree, inclusive of the concept that the redeemed will look upon the torments of the damned and rejoice in God's justice.

Thinkers such as Augustine, Quenstedt, and Scheeben have attempted various defensive solutions to retain the traditional doctrine of hell. As Adams notes, they have spilled "bottles of ink in their efforts to do so." Adams is quite clear that for her hell, as traditionally conceived, is not a viable Christian doctrine. Indeed, she discards hell in favor of universal salvation. However, in this chapter, I shall not discard the possibility of hell. I shall rather investigate selected approaches to the soteriological

---

296. Adams, "The Problem of Hell," 401.

297. Ratzinger, *Hölle*, 446–47, cited in Hoye, *The Emergence of Eternal Life*, 105.

problem of evil as represented by hell in search of a possible solution that still allows hell as a possibility.

John Hick and the Pluralist Solution

John Hick (1922–2012) moved from evangelical Christianity to a theistic pluralism during his long career as a theologian. Since the 1960s when Hick still deemed himself within the Christian tradition, he has commented on hell as a problem of evil. However, his major contribution on eschatology is in his work *Death and Eternal Life*, first published in 1976 and revised in 1994. There are certain caveats when using Hick as a source for Christian eschatology. The Bible is not authoritative for Hick in the traditional sense, and he does not give credence to the understanding that the New Testament is in any way an eyewitness account of the ministry of Jesus of Nazareth. Thus, he moves beyond an allegorical interpretation of Scripture to one that is more in line with mythos. For the later Hick, Jesus was a prophetic, existential preacher who called individuals away from destructive, self-centered behaviors. "Damnation" results from behavior which is "heedless of neighbour or human need," which bears a similarity to Rahner's concept that love of God is love of neighbor.[298] The threats of damnation made by Jesus in the Gospels were existential, not eternal and Hick rejects the concept of hell on moral grounds: "I . . . believe that the needs of Christian theodicy compel us to repudiate the idea of eternal punishment . . . [because] the suffering of the damned in hell, since they are interminable, never lead to any constructive end beyond themselves and are thus the very type of ultimately pointless and endless anguish."[299]

Hick believes that Jesus is only salvific in the Christian community and thus for Hick human "salvation" is not a soteriology, but a "phenomenon."[300] Salvation for Hick has nothing to do with the work of Christ and everything to do with the transformation of the individual and society. Thus, it is not at all surprising that the problem of hell is no problem at all—it can be jettisoned in the same way that Paul Tillich rejected the God of traditional monotheism in favor of the "God above the God of theism."[301]

298. Ratzinger, *Hölle*, 248.
299. Hick, *Evil and the Love of God*, 377–78.
300. Hick, "A Pluralist View," 43.
301. Cf. Tillich, *The Courage to Be*; my page citation is taken from the second edition by Yale University Press (2000) in the section entitled "The God above God and the Courage to Be," 186ff.

Since Hick has moved to a post-Christian perspective, his reinterpretation of the concept of hell with the God as revealed in Jesus Christ can be readily challenged by the "orthodox," but he provides a plausible corrective that hell is an existential threat and not a threat of eternal punishment. Thus, as my focus lies within Christianity my exploration of Hick has been brief. For a sharp contrast to Hick's pluralism, I turn to the evangelical Protestant theologian and analytic philosopher William Lane Craig (b. 1949).

William Lane Craig: Hell and Transworld Damnation

> *There is salvation in no one else, for there is no other name under heaven given among mortals by which we must be saved.*
> —Acts 4:12

William Lane Craig may be the most notorious defender of the traditional concept of hell in the theological academy. His paper entitled "No Other Name" (1989) seeks to use the concept of "middle knowledge" as developed by the Jesuit theologian Luis de Molina (1535–1600) as a defense for limited salvation and an eternal, punitive hell. It remains a target of theological criticism to this day.[302] The basis of his title is taken from the citation from the Books of Acts above. For Craig, because sin is universal (i.e., the doctrine of total depravity), "all persons stand morally guilty and condemned before God, utterly incapable of redeeming themselves through righteous acts."[303] Thus, Craig, countering liberal attenuations or denials of the doctrine of hell, states emphatically a *sola fide* soteriology:

> To reject Jesus Christ is therefore to reject God's grace and forgiveness, to refuse the one means of salvation which God has provided. It is to remain under condemnation and wrath, to forfeit eternally salvation. For someday God will judge all men, "inflicting vengeance upon those who do not know God and upon those who do not obey the gospel of our Lord Jesus. They shall suffer the punishment of eternal destruction and exclusion from the presence of the Lord and from the glory of his might" (II Thessalonians 1.8–9).[304]

---

302. Cf. Craig, "No Other Name."
303. Craig, "No Other Name," 172.
304. Craig, "No Other Name," 173.

Thus, human behavior has no real bearing on one's eternal destination. *Faith alone* is what is required and no one can self-redeem by good works. Craig criticizes John Hick's pluralistic universalism as an overturning of Christian orthodoxy. He cites Hick who writes that

> [i]f Jesus was literally God incarnate, and if it is by his death alone that men can be saved, and by their response to him alone that they can appropriate that salvation, then the only doorway to eternal life is Christian faith. It would follow then that the large majority of the human race so far have not been saved. But is it credible that the loving God and Father of all men has decreed that only those born within one particular thread of human history shall be saved?[305]

While this proposal is not credible for Hick, it is for Craig: "I do not see that the very notion of hell is incompatible with a just and loving God."[306] Not only does Craig not see this as a problem, but he argues that human beings alone bear the responsibility for the loss of heaven "[by] spurning God's prevenient grace and the solicitation of the Holy Spirit...."[307] However, the question that must be asked is in what way do persons of lapsed faith, other faith or no faith "spurn" God's prevenient grace? In a critique of Craig's exclusivism, David B. Myers writes that "Craig seems to assume that anyone who is fully informed of the Gospel could not, on cognitive grounds, reject its truth."[308] While Craig uses the Arminian-sounding phrase "prevenient grace," this seems to be a veiled form of irresistible grace pertaining to the elect. Craig writes in his book *Reasonable Faith: Christian Truth and Apologetics* that not accepting the gospel is tantamount to ignoring the Holy Spirit:

> When a person refuses to come to Christ it is never because of a lack of evidence or because of intellectual difficulties: at root, he refuses to come because he willingly ignores and rejects the drawing of God's spirit on his heart. No one in the final analysis fails to become a Christian because of lack of arguments; he fails to become a Christian because he loves darkness rather than light and wants nothing to do with God.[309]

305. Cf. Hick, "Jesus and the World Religions," 180. Cited in Craig, "No Other Name," 175–76.
306. Craig, "No Other Name," 176.
307. Craig, "No Other Name," 176.
308. Myers, "Exclusivism, Eternal Damnation, and the Problem of Evil," 415.
309. Craig, *Reasonable Faith*, 35–36. Cited in Myers, "Exclusivism, Eternal

THE SYMBOLS AND PROBLEMS OF JUDGMENT   117

This is a very strong claim for it implies that anyone who is not a Christian is *ipso facto* a willful child of darkness. Craig, in a reply to Myers, states that his views are not based on theodicy, but on plausibility. However, Myers rejects this and replies that in his use of Molina's account of God's middle knowledge as a means to explain why some are damned and others saved, Craig is very clear that "no person who is informed about Christ and freely rejects him does so only for evidential reasons."[310] This demands an exploration of Craig's Molinist account of God's middle knowledge in solving the soteriological problem of evil that claims a just and loving God saves some human beings and damns others. Molina proposes that God possesses three types of knowledge: natural knowledge, middle knowledge, and free knowledge. Middle knowledge is that knowledge that lies between God's natural knowledge and free knowledge: the former being God's knowledge of necessary truth and the latter being knowledge of a creature's free choice. In essence, Molina absolves God of predestining any human being to damnation. Thus, as Craig would have it, God is blameless for the damnation of any human being. Molina proposes that God creates human beings without predestining what choices they will make in their lives. However, God knows all things fully and thus knows what human beings will freely choose under every possible circumstance (i.e., counterfactual knowledge). This is how God's middle knowledge operates.[311] Craig then develops a Molinist account of predestination:

> Prior to the divine decree, God knows via His middle knowledge how any possible free creature would respond in any possible circumstances, which include the offer of certain gifts of prevenient grace which God might provide. In choosing a certain possible world, God commits Himself, out of His goodness, to offering various gifts of grace to every person which are sufficient for his salvation. Such grace is not intrinsically efficacious in that it of itself produces its effect; rather it is extrinsically efficacious in accomplishing its end in those who freely cooperate with it. God knows many will freely reject His sufficient grace and be lost; but He knows that many others will assent to it, thereby rendering it efficacious in effecting their salvation. . . . There is no risk of [those who assent to God's grace] of being

---

Damnation, and the Problem of Evil," 417.
   310. Myers, "Rejoinder to William Lane Craig," 428.
   311. For a discussion of Molinism, cf. MacGregor, *Luis de Molina*.

lost; indeed *in sensu composito* it is impossible for them to fall away. But *in sensu diviso* they are entirely free to reject God's grace; but were they to do so, God would have had different middle knowledge and they would not have been predestined. Similarly, those who are not predestined have no one to blame but themselves. It is up to God whether we find ourselves in a world in which we are predestined, but it is up to us whether we are predestined in the world in which we find ourselves.[312]

Thus, Craig's Molinist argument lets God off the hook for what would appear to be supralapsarian double predestination. Middle knowledge saves God from being the author of damnation. Within this approach, Craig develops a theory known as "transworld damnation." Any person who does not accept Christ is damned in every feasible world that God could create. He states this proposition in these two formulae:

- There is no world feasible for God in which all persons would freely receive Christ [ergo][313]
- God has actualized a world containing an optimal balance between saved and unsaved, and those who are unsaved suffer from transworld damnation.[314]

This world is the best God could create, given God's middle knowledge, even though this best of all possible worlds will still result in the damnation of many—and those many are trans-worldly damned: there is no possible world (assuming an infinite number of worlds) where they freely accept God's grace. Thus, Craig believes he has plausibly solved the soteriological problem of evil.

The difficulty in reconciling the God who is ontic love with the God postulated by Craig seems insurmountable. As Myers notes,

> If Craig is simply trying to make the case that it is *logically possible* that an omniperfect God justly condemns to hell every person who rejects Christ, then I do not see how this claim can be refuted. Moreover, I have not tried to refute this logical claim. A successful case for the logical consistency of the exclusivist view of salvation is not, however, a substantive achievement, and of

---

312. Craig. "No Other Name," 179.
313. Craig. "No Other Name," 182. This is proposition 7 in the article.
314. Craig. "No Other Name," 184. This is proposition 9 in the article.

course Craig claims to have achieved much more—namely to have established that the exclusivist view is plausible.³¹⁵

Indeed, and I agree with Myers and Craig: an omnipotent Being *could* actualize a world that Craig proposes in which transworld damnation occurs for some. Craig finds his conclusion regrettable: "No orthodox Christian likes the doctrine of hell or delights in anyone's condemnation. I truly wish universalism was true, but it is not."³¹⁶

Myers rejects that Craig has solved the soteriological problem of evil via a Molinist transworld damnation proposition because he believes disbelievers are inculpable. He thus rejects Craig's thesis that anyone who does not accept the gospel of Christ, either due to a different religiosity or a rational decision rooted in atheism or agnosticism, is indicative of transworld damnation. The simple fact for Myers is that transworld damnation, no matter how elegant the model for its plausibility, is in itself a problem of evil. The middle knowledge defense does not exonerate God for creating a world where some are unavoidably damned. For Myers, the worldly problem of evil (which is finite), pales in comparison to the eternal problem of evil because Craig's thesis results in the eternal suffering of human beings, no matter how virtuous they are in their earthly lives.³¹⁷

Thomas Talbott, professor emeritus of philosophy at Wilmette University, Oregon, is perhaps one of the best-known defenders of Christian universalism. Like Craig, his background is evangelical, but his eschatology is the polar opposite to Craig's.³¹⁸ It is thus not surprising that Talbott and Craig have a long history of scholarly disagreement. Talbott published an article in 1990 that sought to discredit the traditional doctrine of hell which elicited a response from Craig.³¹⁹ Talbott rejects Craig's notion of transworld damnation as "deeply incoherent" because Talbott's understanding of human libertarian free will differs from Craig's. Talbott rejects transworld damnation with his own counter-formula: "for any person S there are feasible worlds 'in which God undermines (over

---

315. Myers, "Exclusivism, Eternal Damnation, and the Problem of Evil," 418. Emphasis original.

316. Craig, "No Other Name," 186.

317. Myers, "Rejoinder to William Lane Craig," 430.

318. Cf. Talbott, *The Inescapable Love of God* (2nd ed., 2014; first published in 1999).

319. Cf. Talbott, "The Doctrine of Everlasting Punishment"; Craig, "Talbott's Universalism."

time) every possible motive that S might have for rejecting him.'"³²⁰ In other words, for Talbott, God's love will ceaselessly seek out the human being who rejects the offer of grace until the person finally relents and accepts it. Craig replies that this in effect corresponds to irresistible grace and overrides libertarian free will. His retort utilizes lines from the poem *Invictus* of William Ernest Henley (1849–1903):

> *It matters not how strait the gate,*
> *How charged with punishments the scroll,*
> *I am the master of my fate:*
> *I am the captain of my soul.*³²¹

Craig believes that perpetual "human rebellion against God" is logically possible and that God, no matter how ceaseless the effort, may not be able to win over a human being in any possible circumstance (or rather in any possible world).³²² Craig can thus not accept Talbott's counter-proposal that God would prevent a human being from making a choice that results in damnation.

Talbott, echoing Schleiermacher as discussed in the previous chapter, notes that those who have accepted Christ and possess eternal life would suffer knowing that other human beings are separated from them and subjected to eternal torment.³²³ If to be in heaven is to be in union with God, such persons would participate in God's omniscience. They would no longer see dimly and they would know fully (cf. 1 Cor 13:13). The reader will recall that for Quenstedt, the agonies of the damned were a source of "exaltation for the godly." However, this delight in suffering can be said to be an evil in itself and such an affect seems implausible for beings that are in union with God. Talbot summarizes this line of thought:

> In a nutshell, the argument is this. God necessarily wills that each created person should eventually receive a special kind of blessedness: a kind that (a) exists only when one is filled with love for others and (b) would survive even a full disclosure of the facts of the about the world. But such blessedness is simply

---

320. Talbott, "Providence, Freedom, and Human Destiny," 237. Cited in Craig, "Talbot's Universalism," 301. The first part of the formula is supplied by Craig.

321. William Ernest Henley, "Invictus," in Williams, ed., *Modern Verse*, 111. Cited in Craig, "Talbot's Universalism," 301–2.

322. Craig, "Talbot's Universalism," 302.

323. Cf. Talbott, "Human Destiny," 239.

not possible in a world in which some persons are eternally damned and therefore eternally miserable.[324]

Craig argues that it is possible that the "redeemed in heaven have no such knowledge. Perhaps God obliterates from their minds any knowledge of lost persons so that they experience no pangs of remorse for them."[325] For Talbott, however, this is a deception and thus an impossibility. God does not deceive the blessed.[326] Craig however sees this not as deception, but simply sparing the blessed from this unfortunate knowledge. Craig rather posits that those "in heaven" are not the ones who suffer the pains of knowing the state of the lost, but rather God alone bears this pain: "In fact, I see God's taking on Himself alone the suffering of knowing the state of the lost as a beautiful extension of Christ's suffering on the cross."[327] Craig goes even further than this. Not only does God suffer knowing the state of the lost, God *feels* the sufferings of those in hell:

> In shielding His redeemed people from the painful knowledge of the estate of the damned and bearing it in Himself alone, God extends the suffering of the cross into eternity. The terrible secret of the condition of the lost is buried for eternity deep within the breast of God, a burden whose gravity only He can fully feel and yet which He willingly takes upon Himself in order that He might bring free creatures into the supreme and unalloyed joy of fellowship with Himself.[328]

Craig's "solution" to the soteriological problem of evil involves an incredibly high cost. In creating the best of all possible worlds, God must damn some to save others. Thus, creation itself bears an infinite cost in that some, perhaps most, human beings must suffer for eternity due to their trans-worldly damned status. In addition, in order that those who are saved may supremely enjoy union with God with nothing impeding this bliss, God perpetuates the sufferings of the cross of Christ eternally by knowing and feeling the pains and despair of the damned in hell. It would seem that for Craig, God must enter hell in quasi-fellowship with the damned forever as the cost of creation. In doing so, certain human beings, who benefited from "transworld salvation," share the beatitude of

---

324. Talbott, "Human Destiny," 240. Cited in Craig, "Talbott's Universalism," 306.
325. Craig, "Talbott's Universalism," 306.
326. Cf. Talbott, "Human Destiny," 237–38.
327. Craig, "Talbott's Universalism," 306.
328. Craig, "Talbott's Universalism," 307.

heaven with God, blissfully ignorant that the price of their eternal happiness comes at the cost of an inhabited hell and a God that suffers its pains forever.

Without entering into any arguments about divine impassibility (or the "heresies" of theopaschitism and patripassionism), Craig's proposal to solve the soteriological problem of evil would seem utterly to defeat God's love, will, and plan. Not only is the "sin project" successful, but suffering itself, which as Griffiths reminds us is an artefact of an unhealed world in metronomic time, is perpetuated. Furthermore, Christ's crucifixion within the triune life of God, is likewise eternalized. For the redeemed, eternal life is the eternal Easter event. For God and the damned, their collective fate is a perpetual Calvary. Thus, Craig's Molinist methodology to justify supralapsarian double predestination based on God's middle knowledge is not only infinitely costly, but his proposals require the infinite self-damnation of God along with those human beings in hell who bear the *imago Dei*. While Craig may see this as part of the mystery of the Divine Majesty, not unlike Scheeben's "mystery of God's punitive justice," it perpetuates the evil of suffering and suggests that God must also bear this evil within God's self. There is no real *Christus Victor* in this proposal. Christ does not overcome death, sin, and the devil.[329] Rather, God in Christ must in effect incorporate and suffer all three aspects in the eschaton because death becomes eternal death, sin remains active, and the devil still "reigns" in hell. I suggest that Craig's proposal not only does not solve the soteriological problem of evil, but his solution perpetuates it to the point that this evil must be eternally suffered by God. This would mean that God in Christ fails to overcome evil at the eschatic judgment. Thus, God's love fails and does so eternally. I now turn to Jonathan Kvanvig (b. 1954) in search for another solution.

Jonathan Kvanvig and the Concept of an Issuant Hell

Jonathan Kvanvig in his book *The Problem of Hell* notes that the Christian tradition holds that God created human beings to be in loving fellowship with them, and yet God's attribute of love is quickly changed to the attribute of justice when it comes to human beings that in some way do not cooperate with divine policies. Defenders of the traditional, retributive doctrine of hell claim that God is both perfectly loving and perfectly just.

---

329. Cf. Aulén, *Christus Victor*, 20ff.

But as Kvanvig notes, this does not solve the problem of hell.[330] He observes that "[w]hereas God's love and grace predominate in a discussion of heaven, the focus shifts completely when turning to the topic of hell."[331] Kvanvig finds this shift problematic: "No longer does love seem to be part of the picture at all; instead, God's dominant motive is portrayed in terms of justice (at best) or vindictiveness (at worst)."[332] He cites a passage from Augustine's *Enchiridion* as illustrative:

> Now, who but a fool would think God unfair either when he imposes penal judgment on the deserving or when he shows mercy on the undeserving? ... The whole human race is condemned in its apostate head by divine judgment so just [*universum genus humanum tam iusto iudicio divino in apostatica radice damnatum*] that even if not a single of the race were ever saved from it, no one could rail against God's justice.[333]

Kvanvig also notes that a character shift toward creatures may be a trait of imperfect beings, but not of the God of traditional theism. Thus, Kvanvig proposes that "any adequate account of hell must begin with an understanding of the nature of God and present the possibilities of heaven and hell as flowing from this *one nature*; that is, a solution to the problem of hell can be obtained only by an *integrated* account of heaven and hell."[334] Kvanvig proposes that the nature of God, which is one of "love and beneficence" as manifested in the creation of the universe and the incarnation of Christ, must be manifested in both heaven and hell. However, Kvanvig is aware that some theological traditions do not view love as the chief characteristic of God. The above example of Augustine, partly based on the scriptural verse "I have loved Jacob, but I have hated Esau" (cf. Mal 1:2–3; Rom 9:13), suggests a division of the human race, one that is loved and one that is hated. However, this dis-integrates God's nature and creates an unacceptable dualism in the divine character.

---

330. Kvanvig, *The Problem of Hell*, 107–8.

331. Kvanvig, *The Problem of Hell*, 109.

332. Kvanvig, *The Problem of Hell*, 110.

333. Kvanvig, *The Problem of Hell*, 108. Kvanvig is citing from the *Enchiridion* 25.98–9 from *The Enchiridion of Faith, Hope and Love*, ed. and trans. Outler. I have supplied the Latin in brackets from *Enchiridion de fide, spe et caritate liber unus*, cf. *S. Aurelii Augustini Opera Omnia: Patrologiae Latinae Elenchus*, www.augustinus.it/latino; accessed 8 June 2016.

334. Kvanvig, *The Problem of Hell*, 112. Emphasis mine.

For another view that sees creation as God's self-glorification, he cites the Genevan Reformed theologian Theodore Beza (1519–1605) as an example: "God has created the world for his glory; his glory is not known, unless his mercy and his justice are declared: to this end, he has, as an act of sheer grace, destined some men to eternal life, and some, by just judgment, to eternal damnation. Mercy presupposes misery, justice presupposes guilt."[335] For Beza, creation's purpose is for God's glorification. But as the sole Being, the means of glory required created beings to actualize this glorification. Beza posits that God's glory demands a declaration or display of divine justice and mercy. The only way that God could be fully glorified is by the creation of rational human beings and predestining some to damnation (to declare divine justice) and some to eternal life (to declare divine mercy). Thus, God's love is not the source of creation. The chief attribute of God is glory, made manifest in salvation and damnation of created persons. It is obvious that this view of the divine nature is problematic. Kvanvig notes that "God could have made his justice known in a multitude of ways without damning anyone to hell."[336] In fact, the question must be asked: why does God need to be glorified at all? The Ultimate Being would seem to have no need of praise from creatures nor would such a Being need to "declare" divine justice and mercy, let alone randomly damn and save rational beings as part of this declaration. However, if Beza seems to take the Calvinist tradition to extremes, he is not alone.

Kvanvig notes that other Reformed theologians seemed intent on following this line of reasoning further to emphasize God's absolute sovereignty. The French Reformed theologian Pierre Jurieu (1637–1713) implies that God's sovereignty is best displayed by degrading human beings because such abasement "raises the Divine to the highest degree of greatness and superiority that can be conceived."[337] Jurieu seems perversely to argue that God's supremacy requires that God be above morality. Kvanvig argues that the price for this sort of theology is "inordinately high" because it means that, *pace* Friedrich Nietzsche, God is 'beyond

---

335. Cf. Theodore Beza, from the Colloquy of Montbelliard (1586), in Pierre Bayle, *Oeuvres Diverses*, T. III (La Haye, 1727). Cited in and translated by Kvanvig, *The Problem of Hell*, 112.

336. Kvanvig, *The Problem of Hell*, 113.

337. Cf. Pierre Jurieu, *Apologie pour les Réformateurs* (Rotterdam, 1683) as cited in Walker, *The Decline of Hell*, 199–200. Cited in Kvanvig, *The Problem of Hell*, 113.

THE SYMBOLS AND PROBLEMS OF JUDGMENT 125

good and evil."[338] However, this renders traditional theism meaningless because it claims that God is *essentially* good and thus perfectly moral. The "extreme sovereigntist" posits that God is good not in essence, but only in action. To Kvanvig, this radical emphasis on divine sovereignty is "truly malignant."[339] In effect, the divine self-glorification concept is descriptive of a God who is not ontic love, but inordinate self-love; a deity that is "unduly egocentric."[340]

Kvanvig argues that creation is not resultant from God's justice, but from God's love: "it arises out of the desire *to give of oneself to the other*."[341] Kvanvig further argues that justice cannot be the chief attribute of God because it is contrary to Scripture and tradition which understands God as the One "who continually postpones the visitation of justice in favor of demonstrations of love."[342] The incarnation of Christ was a mission of salvation, not condemnation (cf. John 3:17). Thus, the *missio Dei* is one of love for creation. Based on this argument, Kvanvig argues if hell exists, it must be an *issuant* concept; hell must issue from God's divine nature of love, the same divine nature from which heaven is derived.[343]

Kvanvig explores possible concepts of an issuant hell by focusing on the works of C. S. Lewis and Eleonore Stump (b. 1947). I shall briefly overview Kvanvig's assessments of these concepts. The conception of hell posited by C. S. Lewis is well known: the doors of hell are locked from the inside. In essence, the denizens of hell choose to remain there. Conversion in hell is possible, but it never happens, thus hell for the damned is eternal by their own volition.[344] Kvanvig summarizes Lewis' ideas as ". . . God's love extends as far as it possibly can, until any further extension would violate his justice. Hell, then [for Lewis], is what results when love can extend no further without being accompanied by injustice."[345] However, Kvanvig notes that Lewis's concept of hell is problematic, even if the gates are locked from the inside, because according to Lewis the results

---

338. Kvanvig, *The Problem of Hell*, 114. The reference to Nietzsche is my own.
339. Kvanvig, *The Problem of Hell*, 115.
340. Kvanvig, *The Problem of Hell*, 116.
341. Kvanvig, *The Problem of Hell*, 118. Emphasis mine.
342. Kvanvig, *The Problem of Hell*, 118.
343. Kvanvig, *The Problem of Hell*, 119.
344. Cf. Lewis, *The Problem of Pain*. Kvanvig refers to following edition: Lewis, *The Problem of Pain* (New York: Macmillan, 1973), 111. It is this edition that will be cited henceforth.
345. Kvanvig, *The Problem of Hell*, 120.

of a human being resident in hell is that he becomes "an ex-man [consisting] of a will utterly centred in its self and passions utterly uncontrolled by the will."[346] In other words, while to be in heaven is to be fully human, to be in hell is to be inhuman to the point that such a human being is almost annihilated. The denizens of hell are "remnants" of humans. Yet, Lewis denies annihilation is possible:

> Destruction, we should naturally assume, means unmaking, or cessation, of the destroyed. And people often talk as if the "annihilation" of the soul were intrinsically possible. . . . If a soul can be destroyed, must there not be a state of *having been* a human soul? And is not that, perhaps, the state which is equally described as torment, destruction, and privation [in hell]?[347]

Kvanvig comments that Lewis is confusing physics with metaphysics. If divine creation is *creatio ex nihilo*, then God who creates from nothing has the omnipotence to "decreate" something into nothing.[348] And yet, although Lewis insists that annihilation is impossible, he seems to contradict himself: ". . . but hell was not made for men. It is in no sense *parallel* to heaven: it is 'the darkness outside,' the outer rim where being fades away into nonentity."[349] Kvanvig notes that while Lewis provides an issuant view of hell that flows from God's love to those who reject divine fellowship, the end result of this willful non-communion is dehumanization to the point of non-entity. Kvanvig thus rejects Lewis's version of an issuant hell as flawed.

Kvanvig then explores Eleonore Stump's version of an issuant hell as quarantine. As a scholar of the theology of Thomas Aquinas, Stump attempts to use Aquinas's account of God's love to explain hell.[350] Kvanvig interprets Stump as asserting that, for Aquinas, God loves human beings by maximizing "the goodness of their acquired nature."[351] For Stump, annihilation in hell is impossible:

---

346. Lewis, *The Problem of Pain*, 113–4. Cited in Kvanvig, *The Problem of Hell*, 121.

347. Lewis, *The Problem of Pain*, 113. Cited in Kvanvig, *The Problem of Hell*, 121.

348. Kvanvig, *The Problem of Hell*, 112.

349. Lewis, *The Problem of Pain*, 114–15. Cited in Kvanvig, *The Problem of Hell*, 122.

350. Cf. Stump, "Dante's Hell, Aquinas's Moral Theory, and the Love of God." Cited in Kvanvig, *The Problem of Hell*, 123ff.

351. Kvanvig, *The Problem of Hell*, 125.

> Should [God] then annihilate [those in hell]? To annihilate them is to eradicate their being; but to eradicate being on Aquinas's theory is a prima facie evil, which as essentially good God cold not do unless there were an overriding good which justified it. Given Aquinas's identification of being and goodness, such an overriding good would have to produce or promote being in some way, but it is hard to see how the wholesale annihilation of persons could produce or promote being. . . . [Thus,] the annihilation of the damned is not morally justified and thus not an option for a good God. On Aquinas's account, then, it is not open to God to either fulfil the natures of such persons or eradicate them.[352]

Thus, God cannot annihilate a damned human being, for being itself is an essentially good thing. God's love for the damned is manifested in assigning them to a place, albeit in hell, where the greatest good for them can happen. This may seem contradictory as hell is not deemed a place where there is any goodness. However, Stump is using Dante's *Inferno* as a model. Since Dante provides many levels of hell, some approaching a level of quasi-benignity, it could be said that there is some semblance of goodness in hell. However, hell is also a quarantine: it separates the damned from the blessed to prevent the damned from harming those in heaven. Even so, hell is not a place of retribution or even a place of no escape, although she posits that no one ever leaves hell. It is the place that whatever goodness a damned human being has is amplified.[353] Thus, hell is issuant from God's love. God is maximally good even to those beings that by their acquired nature must be eternally separated from heaven. Kvanvig is not convinced. The problem with hell as quarantine is that while it keeps the blessed from harm by the damned, it does not prevent the damned from harming themselves or one another. Hell becomes a prison with no guards. Thus, while God may will that all possible goodness is preserved (albeit minimal) in the damned, there is nothing to prevent perpetual abasement of the damned as inflicted on themselves and one another. The damned thus become both the devils and the victims of hell. While Stump may argue that simply existing is a good in itself, it is difficult to see how this issuant version of hell truly flows from divine love. Yet, neither imposed residence in heaven nor annihilation are

---

352. Stump, "Dante's Hell, Aquinas's Moral Theory, and the Love of God," 196. Cited in Kvanvig, *The Problem of Hell*, 125.

353. Stump, "Dante's Hell, Aquinas's Moral Theory, and the Love of God," 198.

permitted for Aquinas or Stump because the former overrides libertarian free will and the latter is intrinsically evil. The God of Aquinas (and Stump) can do neither.[354] Since the end result of the quarantine version of hell is the continual abasement of human beings, it cannot be issuant from divine love. Therefore, for Kvanvig, another model must be sought.[355]

Kvanvig opts to find a solution that avoids the problems he finds in the Lewis and Stump proposals for an issuant concept of hell that claims to flow from the loving character of God. As was noted, Kvanvig believes that what C. S. Lewis actually proposes, in spite of his denials, is that hell results in human non-entity (i.e., annihilation). Kvanvig engages in an exhaustive philosophical investigation of earthly human analogues to hell as annihilation or quarantine. For annihilation, Kvanvig investigates capital punishment and rational suicide. By rational suicide, Kvanvig means that a human being could have adequate reasons to choose to end her life: "If the most significant goods for that person (i.e., those goods judged to be essential for a continued life to be worthwhile) *are rationally thought to be unachievable*, that person should be free to choose nonexistence."[356] This does not mean that Kvanvig is in favor of suicide, but rather that it could be deemed a rational human choice. For quarantine, he explores incarceration as life imprisonment.[357] What Kvanvig wants to do is find a unified theory of hell that can be said to accord both with God's love and the weight of Scripture and tradition. As he admits, "the problem of hell is not easily solved."[358] He labels the incarceration model as the "exile doctrine of hell" and the alternative "the annihilation doctrine of hell."[359] Kvanvig rejects the Thomistic stance that existence itself is an ultimate good in that eternal exile in hell must be preferred to nonbeing. Thus, for Kvanvig, "the teleological character of hell is properly described in terms of annihilation."[360] Since God is omnipresent, there is no place where God's presence is absent. The *telos* of hell, for Kvanvig, is the choice to exist independently of God. Since existence without God is

---

354. Cf. Kvanvig, *The Problem of Hell*, 127–29.
355. Kvanvig, *The Problem of Hell*, 130.
356. Kvanvig, *The Problem of Hell*, 142. Emphasis original.
357. Kvanvig, *The Problem of Hell*, 135–51.
358. Kvanvig, *The Problem of Hell*, 135.
359. Kvanvig, *The Problem of Hell*, 137.
360. Kvanvig, *The Problem of Hell*, 147.

impossible, the result would be non-entity.[361] This choice of non-entity would not be capital punishment as it is effected by the person and not by God. However, Kvanvig argues that while the end result of hell is annihilation, the "mechanistic" aspect of hell is a state of being *on the way to* nonbeing. Kvanvig proposes to unify incarceration and annihilation as a possible solution for an issuant hell:

> [H]ell is a composite system with a teleological component, which is annihilation, and a mechanical component, which involves continued existence. Hell is an afterlife journey toward annihilation. It may even be true that some never get to the end of the road toward annihilation; it may be, that is, that some eternally exist in hell, never coming to see the alternatives clearly or never changing their opposition to the heavenly community, and yet never achieving rationality for those beliefs and desires.[362]

This definition attempts not only to unify quarantine/incarceration and annihilation, but also avoids the traditional concept of hell as divine retribution that has no escape. As with Lewis, the option to leave hell remains open, but it would seem the option is never exercised. In fact, Kvanvig, seemingly agreeing with Lewis, does not believe that his concept implies a *post mortem* "second chance" at obtaining beatitude: "[the concept of a second chance at reconciliation after death] is to have certain consequences of one's choices deferred while one tries again to avoid those consequences. The account of hell presented here does not imply the existence of this kind of second chance."[363]

While the *telos* of hell is annihilation, it requires a rational decision by the inhabitant to choose non-entity as the only means to reject God eternally. The omnipresent God is present in hell, so the only escape from God and divine love is nonbeing which is self-imposed. Thus, for Kvanvig, God's perfect love and goodness are preserved and the soteriological problem of evil is resolved.[364] In fact, if rational suicide in hell is voluntary self-annihilation, Kvanvig proposes that this self-termination manifests the fullness of God's love: "The most radical expression of this love occurs in annihilation. In loving a person, one must be willing to suffer even total loss in allowing another to pursue what they most deeply

---

361. Kvanvig, *The Problem of Hell*, 148.
362. Kvanvig, *The Problem of Hell*, 152.
363. Kvanvig, *The Problem of Hell*, 156
364. Kvanvig, *The Problem of Hell*, 156.

want."[365] Thus, God permits this radical act of libertarian free will of the creature even though it will cause God horrendous pain, a pain that God will bear for eternity. Note that in this very narrow sense, Kvanvig can be said to agree with Craig.

However, Kvanvig is aware of the constraints of theology on his philosophical proposals and the demands of epistemic modesty that are required in speculations about eschatic states of being. Thus, he concludes his investigation with an agnostic caveat:

> If it is possible to be characterized by a determination to avoid heaven, then it is equally possible that no one is to be so characterized. So the doctrine of hell itself holds no promise that some persons will exist there. In addition, although it is possible for persons to have hell as a place of residence or state of existence, it is also possible that those consigned to hell undergo a complete and total eradication of being.[366]

Kvanvig offers in his issuant concept of hell a means to maintain that God is ontic love even if hell is populated. The punishment of hell lies in a creature's rejection of God's offer of grace, not in God's absence. The teleology of hell is voluntary self-extinction because to demand total separation from God is to not exist. God, in love, will permit this. However, Kvanvig is unwilling to assert that his argument is to be held as anything more than a possibility. He is far more modest than Craig or Griffiths, who seem to claim that their speculations are at least fully plausible or even, for Craig, "probably true." Kvanvig shares with Griffiths a certain concept of hell's trajectory—that to be in hell is to be on the road to annihilation, but he stops short of asserting that all the denizens are destroyed. Like Griffiths, Kvanvig admits that perhaps no one is consigned to hell. However, unlike Griffiths and certainly unlike Craig, hell is not separation from God, not retribution, and not eternal torment. It is in essence eschatic self-exile and/or self-extinction. God's love allows this because God will not force any creature into heaven, for to be in heaven would mean to be "governed by a love of God and a delight in his beauty."[367] Thus, Kvanvig agrees with C. S. Lewis in another well-known quotation from *The Great Divorce*: "There are only two kinds of people

---

365. Kvanvig, *The Problem of Hell*, 153.
366. Kvanvig, *The Problem of Hell*, 159.
367. Kvanvig, *The Problem of Hell*, 158–59.

in the end: those who say to God, 'Thy will be done,' and those to whom God says, in the end, '*Thy* will be done.' All that are in Hell choose it."[368] I find Kvanvig's interpretation compelling, but one aspect stands out that I find deeply problematic. If God allows eschatic suicide for the denizens of hell, God is also allowing the self-destruction of creatures whom God loves. In a sense, one could argue that eschatic suicide is a form of deicide because human beings possess the divine image. The divinity of humanity is not only in the human possession of an enfleshed spirit (the incarnation of the *ruach* or breath of God), but also in the divine image that each person possesses. The possibility of theosis or union with God, and in effect becoming part of God through the eschatic transformation into glorious form, is because human beings share God's image. Thus, eschatic suicide is not an option and defeats salvific judgment. I am thus compelled to look further for a yet another solution.

Possible Solution: An Open Hell or Eschatic Reconciliation

In their article "Escaping Hell: Divine Motivation and the Problem of Hell," philosophers Andrei Buckareff (b. 1971) and Allen Plug (b. 1976) propose a model that states that God "will provide opportunities for people in hell to receive the gift of salvation and such persons can decide to receive the gift."[369] In other words, the gates of hell are not locked from the inside (Lewis) or the outside (Griffiths and Craig) and there *is* an opportunity that amounts to a "second chance" *post mortem* for the damned (which Kvanvig does not support): "those who will be separated from God in the eschaton can, and perhaps some will, exercise their free will and respond affirmatively to God's gift of grace and be reconciled to Him."[370] The denizens of hell then always have an open door to beatitude. It is part of God's policies always to offer reconciliation to those who freely desire it, whether in this life or in the life to come. Buckareff and Plug also go beyond Christian exclusivism, thus in some ways agreeing with Hick, although they argue from a Christian vantage point. They are well aware that hell is the traditional destination not simply for the wicked, but for anyone who does not possess the "true faith" at the moment of death. This is a problem not just for the Christian exclusivist, but also for the Islamic and Jewish exclusivist, albeit with various interpretations. They

368. Lewis, *The Great Divorce*, 72.
369. Buckareff and Plug, "Escaping Hell," 45.
370. Buckareff and Plug, "Escaping Hell," 45.

note that Theodore Sider has argued that the traditional doctrine of hell is based on "arbitrary cut-offs" that seems to deny that God is perfectly just.[371] For example, a person who does not possess the Christian faith may be entirely virtuous and exemplify love of neighbor while another person who confesses Christ at the moment of death has until then lived a life of despicable cruelty, in effect hating his neighbor. The Christian exclusivist would have God assign the righteous person to hell and the wicked person to heaven.

The authors, however, do not make an argument against salvation *per Christum solum*. The question at hand is about a person's response to God's prevenient grace (towards or away from goodness). One can still hold that no one is reconciled to God except through Christ while denying that they must possess certain *ante mortem* beliefs. In effect, *post mortem* conversion at the eschaton—which would be to stand before *and* accept Christ in an instantaneous moment of recognition (i.e., faith) is possible for Buckareff and Plug. However, it is not guaranteed or forced. This too is an issuant concept of hell because it flows from God's ontic love. Admittedly, what the authors coin as "escapism" "is compatible with the hope that the vast majority of, and perhaps all, created persons will finally be saved."[372] Thus, it is not an assertion of universal salvation, but rather a hope that it may be true. This hope remains within Christian orthodoxy, even if it is held to be unlikely. Thus, the authors take a speculative step further than Kvanvig would not. As philosophical theologians, the authors make numeric assertions. The straightforward way to illustrate their propositions is to list them:

1. All of God's actions are just and loving.

2. If all of God's actions are just and loving, then no action of God's is motivated by an unjust or unloving pro-attitude.

3. If no action of God's is motivated by an unjust or unloving pro-attitude, then God's soteriological activity is motivated by His just and loving pro-attitudes.

4. If God's soteriological activity is motivated by His just and loving pro-attitudes, then God's provision for separation from Him is

---

371. Buckareff and Plug, "Escaping Hell," 40ff. Cf. Sider, "Hell and Vagueness."
372. Buckareff and Plug, "Escaping Hell," 41.

motivated by God's desire for the most just and loving state of affairs to be realized in the eschaton.[373]

Thus far, the authors agree with Lewis, Stump, and Kvanvig. Hell may be a miserable place, but its purpose is not retribution. It is not a place of torment for the sake of torment. But they differ with them in their assertion that "it would be out of God's character to create a place for Him to punish persons forever."[374] The authors take note of Karl Barth's position that "in [God's] freedom he actually does not desire to be without humanity, but with us, and in the same freedom to be not against us, but regardless and contrary to our dessert, to be for us—he desires in fact to be humanity's partner and our omnipotent pitying Saviour."[375]

Thus, Buckareff and Plug assert that there is a requirement for eschatic reconciliation based on God's "parental love." If God is the perfect Parent, then the door to heaven is always open to any of God's estranged children. The worst prodigal child is always received with open arms.[376] The authors' propositions therefore continue:

5. If God's provision for separation from Him is motivated by God's desire for the most just and loving state of affairs to be realized in the eschaton, then God will provide opportunities for people in hell to receive the gift of salvation and such persons can decide to receive the gift.

6. Therefore, God will provide opportunities for people in hell to receive the gift of salvation and such persons can decide to receive the gift.[377]

This then completes their argument. However, they are well aware that not only are they rejecting the traditional doctrine of hell, but that there will be serious objections to their issuant concept of hell that allows for eschatic reconciliation of the damned.

In their assessment of the objections to an escapist conception of an issuant hell, they reject the assumed reply of the sovereigntist that God

---

373. Buckareff and Plug, "Escaping Hell," 42–43.

374. Buckareff and Plug, "Escaping Hell," 43. The authors cite Micah 7:18–19 as biblical support on page 53n17.

375. Cf. Barth, "The Humanity of God," reprinted in Green, ed., *Karl Barth: Theologian of Freedom*, 56. Cited in Buckareff and Plug, "Escaping Hell," 44.

376. Buckareff and Plug, "Escaping Hell," 44.

377. Buckareff and Plug, "Escaping Hell," 45.

is not to be held to human standards of morality. They refer to this as the "Job objection." If God was not required to justify the arbitrary actions taken against Job in the biblical narrative, then God is most certainly not required to do so with us. They find this reasoning defective and make a bold retort: "God's moral obligations that provide Him with moral reasons for acting do not differ from ours."[378] They also reject that they have substituted an intermediate state or purgatory for hell.[379] It is important to note that purgatory in its traditional Western form is pre-eschatic, preparatory, and retributive. Its discarnate denizens are destined for heaven at the eschaton. While an escapist hell may have a purgatorial quality in that it is a miserable place to be, it is not a substitute for purgatory.

Buckareff and Plug freely admit that they hope universal salvation is true and they assert that "[s]uch a state of affairs is one that all Christians should desire."[380] However, their escapist hell is not one that guarantees universalism because some denizens may choose to remain there forever. The open-door policy that they propose does not imply that hell's denizens will opt to pass through it into the divine embrace. Milton's verse that it is "better to reign in hell than serve in heaven" could be the view of some of hell's occupants. Some may never be converted to God's policies and plans. To enter heaven entails not only a willing submission to God, but an alignment with God's love and purpose. So, an escapist concept of hell is only hopeful that all will enter into communion with God at the eschaton.

The authors conclude that their escapist-issuant hell is "immune" from the further objections that it is coercive and overrides libertarian free will or that it "cheapens grace."[381] In other words, God's grace is not degraded if it is accepted in hell rather than in earthly life. One interesting objection that followed the publication of Buckareff and Plug's article was a reply from Benjamin Matheson, at that time a postdoctoral researcher at the University of Gothenburg, entitled "Escaping Heaven."[382] Matheson responds that if one can escape hell, should not one also be able to escape heaven? In a response, Buckareff and Plug have summarized Matheson's objection as follows:

378. Buckareff and Plug, "Escaping Hell," 48.
379. Buckareff and Plug, "Escaping Hell," 49.
380. Buckareff and Plug, "Escaping Hell," 49.
381. Buckareff and Plug, "Escaping Hell," 51–52.
382. Matheson, "Escaping Heaven." Matheson is now a postdoctoral researcher in practical philosophy at Stockholm University.

1. If, according to escapism, there is no symmetry with respect to God's policies toward those in both heaven and hell, then escapism is not an adequate response to the problem of hell.

2. On escapism, there is no such symmetry.

3. Therefore, escapism is not an adequate response to the problem of hell.[383]

Buckareff and Plug reject Matheson's critique as "chimerical."[384] All three authors agree that the concept of a human being resident in the eschatic world-to-come ("heaven") escaping communion with God is "wildly implausible."[385] However, Buckareff and Plug reject the argument that symmetry is required and that heaven should be escapable in the same manner as hell. Part of the reason why heaven would not be escapable is that those who enter it are not only sanctified but also divinized (i.e., theosis). Their communion with God is of such intensity that their glorification results in a radical alignment with God's ontic love, policies, and plans. Matheson however counters that such a process would mean an end to libertarian free will in heaven.[386] Buckareff and Plug dissent because to be in union with God involves transformation and that this transformation also involves the will. In other words, human free will is aligned to the will of God and thus human beings will reflect this reality by becoming "orthonomous agents"—beings that, like God, always do what is right yet without sacrificing their autonomy.[387] Matheson also comments that if a person's character is settled *contra Deum* in her *post mortem* state, she will never exit hell because her psychology is fixed: "[i]t only takes one person to never have the option to leave Hell to cast doubt on the claim that God is all-loving and just." Buckareff and Plug agree that this is "troubling" but they are unwilling to agree that a person's psychological development ceases at death.[388] However, while even one person in hell is troubling, the authors affirm the hope that all will be saved, although they are agnostic as to whether this ideal state of affairs

383. Buckareff and Plug, "Escaping Hell But Not Heaven," 248.

384. Buckareff and Plug, "Escaping Hell But Not Heaven," 247.

385. Matheson, "Escaping Heaven," 201. Cited in Buckareff and Plug, "Escaping Hell But Not Heaven," 249.

386. Cf. Matheson, "Escaping Heaven," 202–3.

387. Buckareff and Plug, "Escaping Hell But Not Heaven," 250.

388. Matheson, "Escaping Heaven," 205. Cited in Buckareff and Plug, "Escaping Hell But Not Heaven," 252,

will occur. They conclude their reply to Matheson by reaffirming their issuant-escapist concept:

> [E]scapism's issuant commitments render hell a place provided by God out of love; it is not a place to exact retribution. Those in hell would be choosing separation from God. While the relevant state of affairs they would find themselves in is qualitatively inferior to communion with God, it does not follow that they experience negative well-being. Still, it is an inferior state of being. But it is one that an agent prefers, even if the preference is not objectively rational.[389]

Buckareff and Plug offer an interesting solution to the soteriological problem of evil. They do not, as Adams does, resort to overt universalism. They avoid a retributivist, annihilationist, or imprisonment concept of hell. For them, hell is a place that is created by a loving God for those who do not wish to reciprocate it. Some may remain there eternally, in spite of an open door and endless invitation. Others will experience eschatic conversion which presumably must involve repentance. Human beings are so transformed by their willing entry into eternal life that the stance that human beings can experience a satanic exile from heaven is rendered impossible. The denizens of heaven become incorporated into divine life in such a way that they become part of God's Being while still retaining autonomy.

The one thing that I think plagues the escapist-issuant version of hell as proposed by Buckareff and Plug is that it presupposes metronomic time at least as far as the time-space that is hell. Thus, the residents of hell, if there are any, are experiencing measurable time in order to decide or reject to take the open door before them. The horror of hell, even if not a place of retribution, is that those who refuse eschatic reconciliation will remain in the damaged time-space of the ticking clock. However, as Griffiths notes, time is one of the things that God in Christ heals at the eschaton. Hell would remain a place where the unredeemed remain in unhealed time. Even if hell is issuant from God's love, the final consummation would be thwarted so long as one person refuses God's grace and remains separate from the communion of heaven.

---

389. Buckareff and Plug, "Escaping Hell But Not Heaven," 252.

Conclusion

> *When I tread the verge of Jordan,*
> *Bid my anxious fears subside;*
> *Death of death, and hell's destruction,*
> *Land me safe on Canaan's side:*
> *Songs of praises, songs of praises*
> *I will ever give to thee.*
> *I will ever give to thee.*
> —"Cwm Rhondda," William Williams Pantycelyn[390]

In this section, I have investigated the problem of hell from several angles. I have explored the traditional doctrine of hell and its problems. I have also discussed recent attempts to modify the traditional understanding. The fact that the pre-eschatic world itself can be hellish was acknowledged. Hell and the soteriological problem of evil were explored at length with concepts ranging from universalism to transworld damnation. In the previous section, the idea of hell with an open door, or an escapist-issuant concept of hell was discussed. At the outset of this chapter, I proposed that if God is love in judgment, then any possibility of hell must flow from God's love. The issuant concept of hell fits this proposal, but some of its proponents devise a hell that either is a perpetual, degrading incarceration or an eventual annihilation of beings which bear the divine image. The issuant-escapist proposal provides an attractive alternative, but it does not deal with how a place in metronomic time, as hell would have to be, can exist in the eschaton when time and the cosmos are healed. While being in an inferior place called hell would be a *de facto*, if self-imposed, form of punishment, it would seem that earthly human sin does not have the consequences that it demands. But there is a danger in asserting that retribution as demanded by human beings accords with God's character. Human justice is not divine justice. One need only think of the saying of Jesus that one should forgive another person seventy times seven, meaning the one should *always* grant forgiveness (cf. Matt 18:12).

---

390. The Welsh hymn *Arglwydd, arwain trwy'r anialwch* often known by the name of its tune "Cwm Rhondda" was written by William Williams Pantycelyn (1717–91) was first published in 1762 and was translated into English by Peter Williams (1722–96) with the title "Guide me, O Thou Great Redeemer." The verse "death of death, and hell's destruction" come from the Welsh *Ti gest angau, ti gest uffern* ("you conquered death, you conquered hell"). Cf. Watson, *An Annotated Anthology of Hymns*.

I would argue that the issuant-escapist concept has merit, but it needs a dose of Bulgakovian purgation and a recognition of the problem of metronomic time-space in the eschaton that Griffiths elegantly illustrates. Thus, my speculative solution to the problem of hell is to suggest that hell is a state that is in essence an offshoot of heaven, created by God's love, for those human beings that persist in their refusal to be reconciled with God, the other, and the self. This means that at the eschatic judgment they refuse to be reconciled with the awful truth of the absolute recognition that occurs when they are confronted by Christ—the recognition of the history of their earthly existence as in a mirror, but perfectly, not dimly. This perfect knowledge is purgatory and the retribution is effected by repentance in its encounter with God's ontic love. It is not God that punishes, but rather the human being experiences the truth of her nature in the presence of God whose perfect love burns away the chaff of sin. Hell, then, would be a refusal to look into the "mirror" that is God in Christ. In love, God permits those who refuse this to depart to the misery that is non-communion with the Divine and the saints. However, the door to eternal life remains open. The denizens of hell know that if they enter God's presence ("heaven"), they must face Christ, which is to face the totality of their own being and suffer loving purgation. It may be that some will refuse this perpetually, thus thwarting universal salvation and the *apokatastasis ton panton*. However, this would mean that God in Christ would not achieve the final consummation—the perfection of all worlds, God that is "all in all" (cf. 1 Cor 15:28).

Bulgakov, as will be discussed in the next section, cannot accept that this is possible. Since for Bulgakov to see Christ is to love him, it would be impossible for a human being to resist eternally. For Adams, God as Parent would override libertarian free will just as a human parent would do so with her own child in order to achieve the greatest good for that child. For Griffiths, who maintains a more traditional concept of hell that results in annihilation, it is not possible for hell to survive the eschaton because it would require that measurable time (which is fallen time) be maintained in some sort of unredeemed antechamber of the world-to-come.

I would like to assert with Bulgakov that eternity in hell, even if it is a "loving hell" is impossible and universalism is true. I can assert the former (that hell is not eternal), but I cannot claim the latter in an absolute sense. I shall explore this concept later in the dissertation, but I should state that I cannot see how God's divine plan can be thwarted. As quoted above in the well-known Welsh hymn, *Cwm Rhondda*, the hope of the eschaton is that death and hell will be destroyed. However, this is only possible, following Griffiths and to an extent Kvanvig, if the denizens of hell are also destroyed. I agree with John Polkinghorne (b. 1930) that "God's offer of mercy and forgiveness is not withdrawn at death but, rather, divine love is everlasting. Nevertheless, no one will be carried into the kingdom of heaven against their will by an overpowering act of divine love."[391] Yet, how then is hell destroyed along with death?

I suggest that as heaven and hell are issuant from God's love, that they are actually *one in the same place*. Hell is not a state, but a *post mortem* experience. If hell is possible as an enduring state, then it means that eschatic refusal of human beings who turn away from the essential event that absolute recognition and reconciliation require to "enter" eternal life is eternalized. Eternal life ("heaven") is the state where after absolute recognition (judgment), purgation, and reconciliation occur, human beings "enter" the world-to-come and its wonders that "no eye has seen, nor ear heard, nor the human heart conceived" (cf. 1 Cor 2:9).

One possible solution, borrowing from Buckareff and Plug, is that that some human beings will remain in the "annex of heaven" forever, but the door to eternal life remains open and the divine invitation will never cease. For those that hate God, the open door and unyielding offer of grace would be the punishments of hell; for to such a denizen, they are despised, even "painful." The hope then is that in the "end of the end" no one will refuse this offer and God will truly be all in all. However, I do not think this "annex" solution is truly viable and rather it is more "spilled ink." Rather, if Christ has conquered and is Victor, there must be another solution. I shall attempt to explore such solutions in chapters 4 and 5.

5. Conclusion

In this chapter, I have explored three symbols and problems of judgment: death, the intermediate state, and hell. Death has been investigated from materialist and metaphysical perspectives. The materialist understanding as exemplified by Brecht and Russell is simple—death is annihilation of the person who once lived on earth. Any "afterlife" would have to be in biological progeny (if any), in memory (temporary), or in deeds that have a lasting impact on the world (ultimately temporary assuming information loss over time). Thus, death is oblivion in the truest sense of that

---

391. Polkinghorne, *The God of Hope and the End of the World*, 136.

word. This is possible even in a theistic context because one can believe in God while rejecting an 'afterlife." The alternative to atheistic or theistic materialism is not open to scientific verification. Heidegger provides a philosophical framework of thrownness-towards-death that was later picked up by Rahner, but theologized. Jüngel and Jackelén adhere to the 'total death' theory that presumes, as modified by Härle, that the self is preserved in passive relationality to God until the general resurrection. This involved the problem of continuity of individual personhood between death and resurrection.

The belief that biological death is not the permanent end of a human life is an act of faith, hope, and love. It is such an act whether one posits that the dead 'sleep' until the general resurrection or whether the dead experience some immediate life as a separated soul or in some other state. Thus, to die is always an act of trust; a falling into God's love in absolute dependence. In my understanding, death is an eschatic event because, for the dead, the eschatic event is immediate.

The intermediate state of discarnation, soul separation, was investigated in its various forms from Hellenism, Hellenistic Judaism, and medieval Christianity with Thomas Aquinas as the chief articulator of *anima separata*. Despite Luther's ambivalence, the Thomistic interpretation survived the Reformation. It was revised in the Enlightenment period in the Reformed tradition by Schleiermacher as a type of *post mortem* second chance. Bulgakov offers a tripartite intermediate state with the soul as the 'glue' between the corpse (or the earth) and the spirit (which inhabits a spiritual realm). For Bulgakov, spiritual growth is possible in this state, thus it is dynamic. Paul Griffiths gives a modern Catholic interpretation as a metronomic time-space of movement toward (which could be construed as growth) or away from God. Greshake offers a radical departure from Western Christian tradition by proposing resurrection-in-death with which the later Rahner seemed to resonate. Immediate resurrection dispenses with an intermediate state. My own understanding borrows from Greshake and Rahner and proposes that the life lived is transphysically resurrected and is immediately present with God at the eschaton, thus divine judgment is not something that the dead await, they are always already in the eschatic reality. I therefore do not hold to any intermediacy for the 'living dead."

The symbol and problem of hell is deeply challenging. It is a soteriological problem of evil and the belief that it has permanent denizens, in my opinion, is ruinous to the doctrine of God. When reading descriptions of the hell of tradition, the question that must be asked is: what sort of God has created such a place or state for creatures? The answer often yields a dystheism that cannot be sustained by Christianity. As Adams noted, spilling bottles of ink defending the omnibenevolence and love of God while maintaining the doctrine of eternal punishment is an exercise in futility. God is never victorious in such scenarios. Craig's concept of transworld damnation as an attempt to exonerate God for hell fails in its task. Attempts at modifying hell as annihilation (Griffiths); hell as self-imposed (Lewis); a hell issuant from God's love (Kvanvig); a hell as quarantine (Stump); and an escapist hell (a hell that one can leave freely) are all examples of spilled ink, although each tries to find a way to defend the doctrine of God without jettisoning the concept. In my own attempt to 'spill more ink,' I was left with an 'annex' in the eschaton that is ultimately unsatisfactory.

CHAPTER 3

The Larger Hope: Divine Judgment in Optimistic Soteriology

1. Introduction

IN THIS CHAPTER, I shall investigate the proposal that modern theologians of both the Western and Eastern church traditions who promote an optimistic soteriology—one that is either overtly universalist or is hopeful that God will save all rational creatures—are implicitly or covertly advocating the concept that divine judgment is, in itself, the act of salvation. Considering the vast twentieth-century theological corpus, I shall approach this topic in a selective manner. I have chosen four theologians, one Eastern and three Western, to engage in dialogue with and to critique: Sergei Bulgakov (1871–1944), one of the twentieth century's most important Eastern Orthodox systematic theologians; Hans Urs von Balthasar (1905–88), an equally important twentieth-century Catholic theologian; John A. T. Robinson (1919–83), a provocative theologian and Anglican bishop who is perhaps best remembered for his popular 1963-book *Honest to God*; and Marilyn McCord Adams (1943–2017), an American philosophical theologian and an Anglican priest. I shall first investigate each theologian's soteriology focusing on divine judgment and then engage in a comparison and critique.[1]

My rationale for choosing the above theologians is pragmatic. Each speaks to the issue of salvific judgment. Other philosophers and

---

1. Cf. *Honest to God* (London: SCM, 1963). Note that Robinson is usually cited by the initials of his three given names as J.A.T. Robinson and I follow suit.

theologians have written also about this concept, often indirectly—notably Nikolai Berdyaev (1874–1948), Karl Barth (1886–1968), Karl Rahner (1904–84), and Jürgen Moltmann (b. 1926). It is noteworthy at the outset that of the four theologians I am investigating, three are proponents of universal salvation and one, Balthasar, was accused of this stance by his theological opponents.

Prior to this comparison, it is necessary to propose a definition of salvific judgment in order to investigate it theologically. My proposal is that salvific judgment is the eschatological event of absolute recognition; the absolute recognition of human beings by God in Christ. In the moment of divine judgment, Christ recognizes each human being in his or her totality. Within this recognition, there is the judgment. In this judgment, each human being is radically confronted with his failure to actualize love in his mortal life. Salvation is therefore the purgative acceptance of this failure and subsequent reconciliation and union with God. This can be illustrated aphoristically as *iudicandus est salvandus* ("to be judged is to be saved"). While no theologian, including those mentioned above, has proposed this definition, I argue that their investigations in soteriology and eschatology lead to this ultimate conclusion. Before it is possible to make a case for salvific judgment as I have defined it, it is necessary to evaluate the soteriologies of judgment of the selected theologians. Salvific judgment will be further investigated in chapters 4 and 5.

2. Sergei Bulgakov: The Judgment of Love
Bulgakov's Cosmology, Use of Antinomy, and Sophiology

Before overviewing the eschatological teachings of Fr. Sergei Nikolaevich Bulgakov, it is necessary briefly to discuss his cosmology, his use of antinomy, and his controversial teaching on Divine Sophia, i.e., sophiology. The cosmology of Bulgakov is centered on the following themes:[2]

(1) The world (*cosmos*) is an organic unity animated by a "world soul" or entelechy. The term world soul (*anima mundi*) which originated with Plato refers to "an intrinsic connection between all living things in the world." The Aristotelian term "entelechy" refers to "that which realizes or makes actual what is otherwise merely potential." For Bulgakov, both terms refer to (and are the same things as) Sophia (divine wisdom).

---

2. The three themes are adapted from James P. Scanlon's entry on Sergei Bulgakov: "Bulgakov, Sergei Nikolaevich (1871–1944)" in *Encyclopedia of Philosophy*.

(2) God is the Absolute, who created the cosmos *ex nihilo*, not as something external or alien to him, but as an emanation of his own nature; the world is God as becoming (panentheism), the divine nature fused with nothingness.[3]

(3) Mediating between the Absolute and the cosmos, uniting them both within itself, is a "third being"—Sophia, the principle of divine wisdom. As the world of Platonic Ideas, Sophia is the ideal basis of the cosmos; as the object of divine love, purely receptive and conceiving everything within herself as the womb of being. She is a kind of "fourth hypostasis" in God. This suggestion of a fourth hypostasis (fourth person of the Trinity) was condemned as an error by both the Moscow Patriarchate and Russian Orthodox Church outside Russia (ROCOR) in the 1935 *ukaz* (decree). It should be noted that Bulgakov himself was not condemned as a heretic.

Sophiology has its origins in the Russian philosophical renaissance of the late nineteenth century—which has its origins in the Slavophile movement that began in the 1840s. It was a period when conservative forces that wanted to uphold the traditional Russian Orthodox faith confronted liberal and radical westernizers who wanted to abolish the old ways in favor of secular institutions. Vladimir Solovyov (1853–1900) attempted to bridge the gap between these two opposing factions through the concept of Sophia (Holy Wisdom). In this, he wished to merge Western European modernity with the traditional concept of Holy Russia. His means to do this were provided by incorporating Western philosophy, German idealism, and the rights of the individual into a political philosophy grounded in the spirituality of Russian Orthodoxy.[4] There are two components to this: divine-humanity and Sophia. Divine-humanity reflects the dyophysite Chalcedonian formula regarding the two natures of Christ, divine and human. Through theosis, humanity will be transformed and also possess a dyadic existence. Sophia for Solovyov is in effect the world soul that progressively and inexorably spiritualizes humanity and the cosmos. This concept of progressive, historical theosis through Sophia had a profound effect on Bulgakov. Whereas Solovyov's philosophy was overtly pantheistic, Bulgakov compensates for this and maintains a Christian particularity. Humanity is created in the divine image, and thus reflects the Divine Sophia. The creation is the manifesta-

---

3. Panentheism is the belief that God, though greater than the universe, also suffuses the universe. Thus, God is in everything and surpasses everything,

4. Cf. Kornblatt, *Divine Sophia*, 1–97.

tion of creaturely Sophia—thus the prototype of humanity is the Divine Sophia. Sophia, divine and creaturely, is the link between God and the cosmos. Humanity, as part of this creation, has both a divine origin and a divine finality. Bulgakov relates to this dyadic human nature as a parallel to the incarnation of Christ. For a concise definition, I turn to his principal eschatological work, *The Bride of the Lamb*, which was his last major theological study before his death in 1944. This therefore represents the most mature representation of his sophiology:

> The Incarnation, in which all human beings are co-resurrected in glory together with Christ, makes [the] sophianic proto-image of every human being transparent and clear. Resurrection in glory is therefore the definitive sophianization of man through the manifestation in him of his proto-image. In this sense, resurrection in glory is the manifestation of Divine Sophia in the creaturely Sophia, the completion of creation. . . . The image of the resurrected human being . . . is his proper eternal image in God hitherto hidden and obscure, but manifested in its power and glory in resurrection.[5]

One of the main aspects of Bulgakov's epistemology is his concept of a philosophy of antinomies.[6] For Bulgakov, all human rationality inherently involves antinomy. Bulgakov, in this engagement with Kantianism and German idealism, considered the problem of human knowledge as related to the antinomy of transcendence/immanence. Bulgakov argues that antinomy is especially characteristic of human religious consciousness attuned to the mystery of the transcendent world. He writes

> An antinomy simultaneously admits the truth of two contradictory, logically incompatible, but ontologically equally necessary assertions. An antinomy testifies to the existence of a mystery beyond which human reason cannot penetrate. This mystery, nevertheless, is actualized and lived in religious experience. All fundamental dogmatic definitions are of this nature. It is futile to attempt to dispel or remove an antinomy. In a logical contradiction, however, exactly the opposite is the case. Such a

---

5. *Neviesta Agntsa* [Невеста Агнца] (1945); ET: *The Bride of the Lamb*, 451. Hereafter cited as NA.

6. Cf. Gallaher, "Antinomism, Trinity and the Challenge of Solovĕvan Pantheism in the Theology of Sergij Bulgakov."

contradiction is always an indication of a mistake in reasoning which should be detected and removed.[7]

The concept that Bulgakov suggests is best suited to express this antinomy is Sophia, as understood in *her* two distinct aspects. As one can read in various biblical passages concerning divine wisdom, Sophia is laid as the foundation of creaturely existence. This foundation of the world is the *ousia* that underlies all of creation as its basis in divine reality. Although Sophia received divinity from God, Sophia is not God but the divine substance (*ousia*) resting at the first order of the created universe. She is antinomic because she is uncreated and created.

Bulgakov's Eschatology in Outline

While Bulgakov is a Russian Orthodox theologian and deeply bound to the dogmatic heritage of Eastern Orthodoxy, he felt at liberty to develop his own eschatological system because in his words "the church has not established a single universally obligatory dogmatic definition in the domain of eschatology."[8] Teleologically, Bulgakov understood the end of the world as the consummation of the created cosmos—its completion and its theosis. Thus, the *telos* of the world is not centered on judgment, although judgment is part of it. It is rather centered on ontological transformation and *not* on retribution.[9] In this way, Bulgakov is at odds with the juridical eschatology of the Western tradition—which he describes in characteristic style as a

> ... deformity of anthropomorphism. ... The mystery of the depth of the richness of Divine Wisdom is reduced to a manual of instructions for organizing an exemplary prison where the confinement is without end. These and similar pseudo-dogmas, which anthropomorphism unhesitatingly includes in dogmatics as the sole and final word, are the product of a meager theological reason and of a dry, egotistical heart.[10]

This critique applies to both Catholicism and Protestantism. Above all, for Bulgakov, divine judgment is centered in the love of God, not apart

---

7. Bulgakov, *Sophia*, 77n18. This book was translated from an unpublished Russian manuscript.
8. NA, 379ff.
9. NA, 368.
10. NA, 382.

from it. He warned that "the mysteries of God's love cannot be measured according to the penal code."[11] Thus, Bulgakov rejects the Latin models of atonement—both the Anselmian concept of Christ making satisfaction for the "dishonor" of human sin and Calvin's reformulation of Anselm's formula into penal substitution: "[Christ] made a substitute and a surety in the place of transgressors and even submitted as a criminal, to sustain and suffer all the punishment which would have been inflicted on them."[12] It would also be incorrect to assert that Bulgakov therefore favors the patristic models of atonement such as ransom or recapitulation. Rather, the atonement, the act at Calvary, is an ontological act of love.[13]

Another key aspect of Bulgakov's eschatology is human cooperation (synergism). Human beings are not passive participants in the economy of salvation. In this respect, Bulgakov dissents from Augustinianism and its Lutheran and Reformed manifestations. Rational creatures participate in the life of the world-to-come. Daringly, he argues that individual souls will cooperate with God in reconstituting their own bodies at the general resurrection, although he modifies this to say that these souls do this out of obedience to the will of God and by the power of God and not in the freedom of the human spirit (soul and spirit are distinct in Bulgakov's tripartite understanding of humanity).[14] It is here that the speculative nature of Bulgakov's theology is evident. He proposes that the general resurrection is applicable to all human beings; and all will uniformly "rise incorruptible and spirit-bearing."[15] The resurrected human beings participate together in the world soul and in a 'universal human corporeality.'[16] Bulgakov insists that

> ... the idea of two humankinds, divided and separated from each other at the Last Judgment, does not correspond to the

---

11. NA, 382.

12. Calvin, *Institutes*, 2.7.10.

13. "Here we have not a juridical but an ontological relation, which is based on the real unity of the human essence, given its real multiplicity in the multi-unity of the hypostatic centers. Christ assumed the entire human nature; He therefore can assume, in and through it, the entire sin of all human individuals, although personally He did not commit it. Thus, in His holy humanity, as well as in the universal human personality of the New Adam, every adamite can find and realize his justification and reconciliation with God." NA, 362.

14. NA, 440. Cf. 1 Cor 15:43–44.

15. NA, 457.

16. NA, 444–45.

fullness and connectedness of reality. Humankind is one. It is one in Adam and one in Christ, one in his Body, the Church: "so we, being many, are one body in Christ, and everyone members of one another" (Rom. 12:5). This unity is expressed in love.[17]

Divine Judgment

For Bulgakov, the second coming, general resurrection, and judgment are a *unitary act* and not separate events. He writes: "It is necessary to understand that the parousia, the coming of Christ in glory, that is, in the manifestation of the Holy Spirit, is, as such, *already* the judgment."[18] The Second Coming of Christ is humanity's collective "encounter with God, the entering into the realm of divine fire, [and it] is not something optional for human beings. It is inevitable."[19]

Bulgakov asserts that human beings, regardless of any previous acceptance or rejection of Christian faith, will immediately recognize Christ, the God-man (*theanthropos*), for whom he is—God the Word incarnate, crucified, resurrected, ascended, and now returned. It is this encounter with Christ "who will come again in glory" that *is* the judgment and this stance is also foundational to my own thesis. This stands in sharp contrast to the received (Western) tradition. Bulgakov asserts that at the parousia of Christ, which is synonymous with the resurrection and the judgment, human beings will be glorified without regard to their state of grace *in hora mortis*: "Incorruptibility and glorification are given to [each human] by God in resurrection *ex opere operato*, so to speak, and enter [sic] into life as an irresistible force, as a higher reality from which man cannot hide."[20] What human beings cannot hide from is Christ before whom they must stand. This confrontation results in each human being seeing her biography in its totality as it is reflected back to her by Christ. This results in self-judgment. However, this judgment does not happen alone. It is a relational judgment: "Both man's life and his responsibility are conditioned by and linked with the destinies of the whole human race."[21] Although human persons are in glorious form at the

---

17. NA, 515–16.
18. NA, 455. Emphasis added.
19. NA, 455.
20. NA, 457.
21. NA, 458.

judgment, they are simultaneously radically exposed before all creation: "In every human being, his own unreality or nakedness, his failure to wear the wedding garment at the wedding feast, is clearly distinguished from Christ's reality."[22]

Although in glorious form, human beings will experience judgment and intrapersonal separation through the eschatic confrontation with Christ:

> The judgement and separation consist in the fact that every human being will be placed before his own eternal image in Christ, that is, before Christ. And in the light of this image, he will see his own reality, and this comparison will be the judgment. It is this that is the Last Judgment of Christ upon every human being. In this judgment, the 'books' are opened, for the Holy Spirit gives the power to read them clearly. Human life in all its fullness and connectedness is manifested in the implacable, inwardly irrefutable light of justice. This is a global vista, referring to man not only as a personal being but also as a generic one. Both man's life and his responsibility are conditioned by and linked with the destinies of the whole human race. He is judged or rather he judges himself in Christ as belonging to all humankind, to the whole history of "all the nations," in the total connectedness of all-human, universal being. He now knows this being as the life of Christ's humanity, which [Christ] assumed in his double nature.[23]

Here it can be seen where Bulgakov departs from the traditional understanding of divine judgment as retribution. Rational creatures are not judged *by* Christ, rather each human being and humanity as a whole experience judgment *through the eschatic encounter* with Christ. In Christ, the person recognizes what he was in his or her mortal life and what he or she could have been—the reality of the person's existence on earth versus their proto-image in Christ. This, for Bulgakov, is the separation referred to in Matthew 25:31–33:

> When the Son of Man comes in his glory, and all the angels with him, then he will sit on the throne of his glory. All the nations will be gathered before him, and he will separate people one from another as a shepherd separates the sheep from the goats,

---

22. NA, 458.

23. NA, 457–58.

and he will put the sheep at his right hand and the goats at the left.[24]

Bulgakov writes: "The proto-image is Christ. Every human being sees himself in Christ and measures the extent of his difference from the proto-image."[25] Christ the Judge is the mirror in which all is revealed (cf. 2 Cor 3:18). In it, human beings recognize themselves fully without the possibility of denial, self-deception or retreat. Christ is the eternal proto-image of every person—and the contrast between the two, the actual and the ideal, results in unavoidable and irresistible self-judgment. This too is a form of synergy—human participation. Human beings will participate in their own final judgment. God is love *precisely* in this moment of judgment. He writes further:

> The judgment of love is the most terrible judgment, more terrible than that of justice and wrath, than that of the law, for it includes all this but also transcends it. The judgment of love consists of a *revolution in people's hearts*, in which, by the action of the Holy Spirit in the resurrection, the eternal source of love for Christ is revealed together with the torment caused by the failure to actualize this love in the life that has passed. *It is impossible to appear before Christ and to see Him without loving Him.* In the resurrection, there is no longer any place for anti-Christianity, for enmity towards Christ, for satanic hatred of Him, just as there is no place for fear of Him as the Judge terrible in His omnipotence and the fury of His wrath.[26]

For Bulgakov, the human being standing before the eschatic Christ engages in "ontological self-judgment" and the self-verdict is impossible to reject because it is "one's own truth."[27] Yet, since for Bulgakov any encounter with Christ is an encounter with divine love, the person who experiences judgment not only loves Christ the Judge but also herself as fully revealed: "A human being cannot fail to love the Christ revealed to him, *and he cannot fail to love himself* as revealed in Christ."[28] This applies universally to all who experience judgment, regardless of their sanctity

---

24. NRSV.
25. NA, 459.
26. NA, 459. Emphasis supplied.
27. NA, 459.
28. NA, 459. Emphasis supplied.

or villainy on earth. However, as this love is the Holy Spirit (divine fire), it is the judgment itself:

> Love is the Holy Spirit, who sets the heart afire with this love. But this love, this blazing up of the Spirit, is also the judgment of the individual upon himself, his vision of himself outside himself, in conflict with himself, that is outside of Christ and far from Christ. And the measure of the knowledge of this separation are determined by Love, that is, by the Holy Spirit. The same fire, the same love gladdens and burns, torments and gives joy.[29]

This is why Bulgakov claimed that love's judgment (which is really the Holy Spirit) is the most terrible of any judgment. The reason for its quality as *terribilis* is because it causes a separation within the human person. All that is outside of Christ (i.e., sin) is separated or rather excised by the fire of the Spirit.

This is the paradox of Bulgakov's soteriology—in the judgment there is wrath, but this wrath, though terrible, has no retributive function. There is no fear for perfect love casts out fear (1 John 4:18). This loving wrath is analogous to passion. Christ's passionate love results in torment in the person not due to any punishment inflicted, but due to the terrible understanding by the beloved that he did not actualize his love for Christ, the divine lover, in his past life. This encounter is "revolutionary" because the person is face to face with ontological Love, the uncreated source of love itself—love as being. For Bulgakov, justice is a form of love. He writes: "God-Love judges with love the sins against love."[30] The parable of the separation of the sheep from the goats does not, however, seem to square with Bulgakov's interpretation. It plainly states that there is an "eternal punishment" and this punishment is in the "eternal fire prepared for 'the devil and his angels.'" However, Bulgakov does not interpret this passage (or indeed any Scriptural text) in a literal manner. Rather, for him, the separation occurs *individually* in each rational creature—the creature is divided in the encounter with God-Love. The "goat" is sin against love and this must be burned away by the "eternal fire" of God's love. The "sheep" is the remainder—that which is purified by love. Hell, then, is the act of division (or separation) caused by the encounter with Christ. It is self-inflicted and terrible, but it is *not* eternal for rational creatures will "be saved, but only as through fire."(1 Cor 3:15)

29. NA, 459.
30. NA, 459.

Evaluation

> "God will punish all atheists. They will burn in everlasting fire."
> Obviously upset, the Staretz [St Silouan of Athos] said,
> "Tell me, supposing you went to paradise, and there looked down and saw somebody burning in hell-fire—would you feel happy?"
> "It can't be helped. It would be their own fault," said the hermit.
> The Staretz answered with a sorrowful countenance:
> "Love could not bear that," he said. "We must pray for all."[31]

Bulgakov's soteriology is highly original and he knowingly departs from the dogmatic definitions of his own church. Paul Gavrilyuk has critiqued his universalism, questioning whether his salvific optimism was a compensatory response to his experiences as an exile and the suffering of the Russian Orthodox Church under Communism, as well his last years being spent in German-occupied Paris.[32] However, I disagree with the argument that Bulgakov's soteriology is in some way an antidote to earthly sufferings. His overall philosophical and theological project insists that the world is in the process of both humanization and divinization (theosis) and that this process continues, despite the tragedies that accompany life on earth. The parousia is the crowning event of this evolution—and this evolution does not stop with the Second Coming. Glorified humanity continues to experience meta-history and further evolution in the world-to-come—going "from glory to glory." It may be argued that his is a Platonizing soteriology, but this can also be said of some of the Alexandrian and Cappadocian fathers (e.g., Clement of Alexandria, Gregory of Nyssa, Gregory of Nazianzus).

Gavrilyuk outlines Bulgakov's ontological universalism in this way:

(a) Rational creatures do not endure their resurrection and judgment passively, but cooperate with God synergistically.

(b) The last judgment consists in the confrontation between each resurrected individual and his or her eternal image in Christ.

(c) The goal of divine punishment is primarily medicinal and purgative, not retributive.

---

31. Sakharov, *Saint Silouan the Athonite*, 48.
32. Gavrilyuk, "Universal Salvation in the Eschatology of Sergius Bulgakov," 131.

(d) The ontological and moral unity of humankind makes the separation between the two parts of humanity impossible.

(e) Hence, the separation between good and evil occurs in each human being.

(f) All will undergo purgative suffering ("universal purgatory"), and;

(g) No one will endure such suffering eternally, for this would entail an ontological dualism between good and evil.

(h) After a suitable period of purgation all creation, including Satan and the fallen angels, will be restored to the union with God.[33]

While some of the above aspects are novel, some are views held by several church fathers of the Alexandrian school as well as the Egyptian desert fathers.

Bulgakov has been accused of failing to take full account of the role of human freedom in his concept of judgment.[34] For Bulgakov, it is true that it is ontologically "impossible" for a human being not to love Christ when confronted with him in the parousia. It is also impossible in Bulgakov's system for a human being to avoid recognizing his failings and to refuse to engage in self-judgment—which is itself the torment of hell. At one time Bulgakov claimed it was still possible for a human being to refuse divine grace perpetually. In his book *The Orthodox Church* (1935) Bulgakov writes: "God does not punish; he forgives. Sinful creatures may refuse his forgiveness. This refusal (which may be unending since human free choice can never be destroyed) makes hell to be hell. In a word, God has mercy on all—whether or not all wish it."[35]

Thus, in this example, universal salvation is not guaranteed, but it is desired by God. However, by the time Bulgakov wrote the *Bride of the Lamb* his eschatology left little room for human refusal. The charge that Bulgakov is less epistemically modest than the hopeful soteriological proposals of Hans Urs von Balthasar or Karl Barth is perhaps true.[36] It is true that Bulgakov asserts the salvific desire of God in ways Balthasar and Barth do not. Yet, Bulgakov does not insist that God's salvific grace is irresistible, but the thrust of his last work suggests that no creature can

---

33. Gavrilyuk, "Universal Salvation in the Eschatology of Sergius Bulgakov," 128.

34. Gavrilyuk, "Universal Salvation in the Eschatology of Sergius Bulgakov," 131.

35. Bulgakov, *Pravoslaviye* (1935); *The Orthodox Church*, xiii.

36. Cf. Balthasar, *Dare We Hope 'That All Men be Saved'?*; Bettis, "Is Karl Barth a Universalist?"

withstand God's love. Perpetually resisted grace by a rational creature in the eschaton would indeed make "hell to be hell" for that creature, but as God will never withdraw the free offer of grace nor the desire for universal reconciliation, Bulgakov is a universalist by default—human beings cannot resist God forever.

One could argue that Bulgakov's ontological universalism is a Christian eschatological redaction of the Marxist theory of progress, a theory he embraced in the 1890s.[37] While his eschatology is hardly consonant with the materialism of Marxist utopia, it is fair to note that his concept of God's desire for universal salvation is deterministic. As noted above, for Bulgakov, the rejection of God's saving grace by some members of resurrected humanity is possible in theory, but improbable. Thus, a level of salvific determinism is evident. In line with the above criticism of Bulgakov's eschatological determinism, the divine judgment at the eschaton is one where a human being is, it would seem, forced, by a "revolution" of the heart, to confront his own failing to become in earthly life what God had willed him to be (the proto-image in Christ vs. the reality of the life that has passed). But is this realization so compelling that all humanity will achieve *post mortem* repentance and conversion? It seems that Bulgakov allows that it could be resisted because he does not believe in divine coercion—human beings are truly free.[38]

Where there *is* a problem with Bulgakov's concept of divine judgment is his peculiar avoidance of the problem of evil. While he was acutely aware of the atrocities of the various wars and revolutions of his time, this reality does not intrude into his theology. Thus, for example, the question of what an eschatic encounter between Christ and a person who committed crimes against humanity (e.g., Hitler, Stalin, Mao) rather than just the "ordinary" sins of ordinary human beings is not considered or alluded to in his works. Paul Gavrilyuk notes the following:

> Paradoxically, Bulgakov's mature eschatological vision, unlike his earlier overtures on the chiliastic character of Marxism, was thoroughly disengaged from the apocalyptic events of his time. It is the inevitable conclusion of his system that no matter how much evil is actually committed in history, all will be saved in the end. A sympathetic critic could object that this very ahistoricity of Bulgakov's theology provided a consolation to those whose lives were split in half by the Bolshevik revolution and crushed

---

37. Gavrilyuk, "Universal Salvation in the Eschatology of Sergius Bulgakov," 129.
38. NA, 492.

by the Second World War. Still, Bulgakov's grasp of the problem of evil falls short of the profound insights of Dostoevsky....[39]

Bulgakov could counter the above objection by stating that human sin, individual and collective, does have eschatic consequence. For him, each human being is subject to the irresistible realization of their failings and each is subject to the "most terrible" judgment of love. The torment is in this revelation—the mandatory life review in which the sinner confronts his sin. This review is the fire and torment of hell. Since the act of divine judgment in the parousia is *outside* time, it is impossible to ascribe a temporal quality to this purgatorial process. However, one can postulate that this supra-temporal state is proportionate to the sins against love committed by each rational creature. Yet, even so, it is true that Bulgakov's eschatology provides a universally positive ending to human history. Unless one posits that some human beings will perpetually resist divine grace (which seems impossible based on his last work), there is no eternal hell to modify this "happy ending." But I must disagree with Gavrilyuk that Bulgakov's eschatology is unaware of the problem of evil. The purgation that Bulgakov envisions is harrowing and the transformation of evil into eschatic goodness that he proposes means that evil actions (sin) must be suffered through to the end before they are forgiven and purged. I therefore take no issue with the happy ending Bulgakov envisions, although the reinterpretation of hell as universal purgatory retains an eschatic violence veiled as God's love that I find troubling, but I think it would satisfy the imputed concerns of Dostoevsky.

3. Hans Urs von Balthasar: The Judgment of Hope

Theological Overview

In this section of the chapter, I shall argue that the Catholic theologian Hans Urs von Balthasar's (1905–88) claims on divine love as "absolute love" are soteriologically problematic in spite of a universalist salvific hope. He can only assert with 1 John 4:17 that *Christians* should have confidence concerning God's judgment (although he does not assert the opposite—that non-Christians should despair concerning the judgment). Before engaging in this critique, it is necessary briefly to explore both his theological and eschatological understandings.

---

39. Gavrilyuk, "Universal Salvation in the Eschatology of Sergius Bulgakov," 132.

It has been argued that Balthasar found the Catholic Thomism of the pre-Vatican II era of the interwar and post-World War II years to be lifeless and he sought to remedy this by delving into the writings of Augustine and the early church fathers. For Balthasar, theology was meant to be dynamic, dramatic and vital—and not the reiteration of old texts. The French philosopher Maurice Blondel (1861–1949) greatly influenced Balthasar's thought, especially through his 1893 work *L'Action* in which he warned against objectifying God as a static being, rather than the God of love who stirs the human heart and soul. To do otherwise, for Blondel, is to turn God into "nothing but a phantom and an idol."[40]

Balthasar's interpretation of God as a *living* God, active and present in the universe, caused him to develop his theological aesthetics which led further to his concept of theo-dramatics. God is the Beautiful, the Truth and the Good—as Balthasar explains in his multivolume work *The Glory of the Lord*:

> We no longer dare to believe in beauty and we make of it a mere appearance in order the more easily to dispose of it. Our situation today shows that beauty demands for itself at least as much courage and decision as do truth and goodness, and she will not allow herself to be separated and banned from her two sisters without taking them along with herself in an act of mysterious vengeance. We can be sure that whoever sneers at her name as if she were the ornament of a bourgeois past—whether he admits it or not—can no longer pray and soon will no longer be able to love.[41]

It is beyond the scope of this section to explore the entire corpus of Balthasar's oeuvre. However, especially in the context of his eschatology and concept of divine judgment, it is necessary to understand Balthasar's concept of God's love, which is a central theme in all his works. His short book *Love Alone Is Credible* sheds light on his overall approach.[42] At the centre of Balthasar's project is the theme that "God is love" (1 John 4:8). Within his theology of love there is also a feminine perspective which

---

40. The original quote in full: "Sitôt qu'on ne s'en étonne plus comme d'une inexprimable nouveauté et qu'on le regarde du dehors comme une matière de connaissance ou une simple occasion d'étude spéculative sans jeunesse de cœur ni inquiétude d'amour, c'en est fait, l'on n'a plus dans les mains que fantôme et idole." Blondel, *L'Action*, 352.

41. Balthasar, *The Glory of the Lord I*, 18.

42. Cf. Balthasar, *Glaubhaft ist nur Liebe* (1963); ET: *Love Alone Is Credible*.

perhaps owes something to his lifelong collaboration with Adrienne von Speyer. In *Love Alone Is Credible,* Balthasar writes:

> But whenever the relationship between nature and grace is severed (as happens where "faith" and "knowledge" are constructed as opposites), then the whole of worldly being falls under the dominion of "knowledge," and the springs and forces of love immanent in the world are overpowered and finally suffocated by science, technology and cybernetics. The result is a world without women, without children, without reverence for love in poverty and humiliation—a world in which power and the profit-margin are the sole criteria, where the disinterested, the useless, the purposeless is despised, persecuted and in the end exterminated—a world in which art itself is forced to wear the mask and features of technique.[43]

In his soteriology, Balthasar defines God's love in the context of the Trinity. In the example that follows, he uses the kenotic soteriology of Bulgakov, whom he knew from French translations of his works, to illustrate divine salvific love:

> In his doctrine of redemption, *Sergei Bulgakov* tries to grasp the kenosis of the Cross as the last of God's self-utterances. It begins within the Trinity, with God the Father's self-dispossession in favor of the Son, and proceeds via the kenosis involved in the creation. Christ will bear the world's sin: this is the rationale underlying all creation. It remains a mystery how Christ bears sin, but it takes place because, ontologically, the New Adam bears within him the totality of human nature—in this, Bulgakov is following the Greek Fathers—and because Christ's humanity, as a result of the Hypostatic Union with the whole of humanity (through kenosis), is empowered "in a supra-empirical manner" to appropriate all the sins of the world: . . . "naturellement *dans son essence, et* compassionnellement *dan son amour.*"[44]

Balthasar goes on to critique both Karl Rahner and Jürgen Moltmann as respectively too focused on the economic Trinity or too much of a process theological approach, favoring a soteriology centered on the "immanent Trinity." He refers again to Bulgakov:

---

43. Balthasar, *Love Alone is Credible,* 114–15.

44. Balthasar, *Theo-drama* IV, 313. Emphasis original. The French quotation is from Balthasar. He is quoting from Bulgakov's 1933 work *Agnets Bozhyi* ("Lamb of God") through the French translation, *Le Verbe incarné: Agnus Dei* (Paris: Aubier, 1943). Non-italicised words are Balthasar's. Cf. Bulgakov, *The Lamb of God.*

> The immanent Trinity must be understood to be that eternal, absolute self-surrender where by God is seen to be, in himself, absolute love; this in turn explains his free self-giving to the world as love, without suggesting that God "needed" the world process and the Cross in order to become himself (to "mediate himself"). It is possible to say with Bulgakov, that the Father's self-utterance in the generation of the Son is an initial "kenosis" within the Godhead that underpins all subsequent kenosis.... Inherent in the Father's love is an absolute renunciation: he will not be God for himself alone.... The Son's answer to the gift of Godhead (of equal substance with the Father) can only be eternal thanksgiving (*eucharistia*) to the Father, the Source.... Proceeding from both, as their subsistent "We," there breathes the "Spirit" who is common to both: as the essence of love, [the Spirit] maintains the infinite difference between them, seals it and, since he is the one Spirit of them both, bridges it.[45]

It is this speculative "dramatic Trinity" of absolute love that is salvific. Furthermore, for Balthasar, Christian revelation affirms that *Being is love*. Being is love because it is the love expressed within the triune God, the love of the Father and the Son in the Spirit. We experience Being-as-love therefore only in our relationship with God.[46] Relating this to Balthasar's eschatology, to be discussed below, Balthasar understands both the world's origins and its end (*telos*) to be in the context of the eternal community of love—creation united with the triune God. Thus, since the world is destined to unite with God, everything will be preserved. John O'Donnell, SJ writes that for Balthasar "[in] Christ, we see that our worldly loves are not to be left behind but are to be integrated into heavenly ones. Time will find its fulfilment in eternity."[47] This is by no means confined to Christians. Christ is unquestionably *salvator mundi* and therefore he is able to integrate humanity, with its several faiths and saviors, through his inescapable judgment *and* his divine power to bring all creatures and creation into the life of the world-to-come. The power of Christ to do so is love itself—which is invincible and cannot fail (cf. 1 John 4:16–18; 1 Cor 13:8).

---

45. Balthasar, *Theo-drama* IV, 323–24.
46. O'Donnell, *Hans Urs von Balthasar*, 7.
47. O'Donnell, *Hans Urs von Balthasar*, 7.

Balthasar's Eschatology

The purpose of this section is to understand Balthasar's concept of divine judgment, but this is not possible without understanding his overall eschatology. As Edward T. Oakes SJ and David Moss note, Balthasar was not invited to be an advisor (*peritus*) to the Second Vatican Council, so that the soteriological paradigm shift found in the conciliar documents cannot in any way be attributed to him.[48] Rather, Balthasar's contribution to Catholic theology is post-conciliar and it further amplifies *Gaudium et Spes* which stated that *every* human being has the possibility to be associated with the paschal mystery.[49] Balthasar's amplification of the conciliar text is that it is valid to hope that this association is universal.[50] Balthasar's eschatology is deemed to favor universal salvation (although Balthasar is not a universalist except in the sense of *hoping* that it *might* be true). It is thus at odds with a traditional understanding of salvation that presumes a more pessimistic soteriology: that some or even most of the human race is damned. As Oakes notes, well after Balthasar's death in 1988, that soteriological optimism within "liberal Christianity," including some Catholic theologians, had lost any semblance of the epistemic modesty that characterized Balthasar's approach. It also began to advocate a religiously pluralistic approach to human salvation. The response from the Vatican was the issuance of the highly controversial document produced by the Congregation for the Doctrine of the Faith in September 2000, under the title of *Dominus Iesus,* where pluralism was roundly rejected and Christian particularity reasserted.[51]

Balthasar's inclusive approach to humanity's participation in the paschal mystery is grounded in his unique Holy Saturday theology which focuses on the *descensus*, the descent of Christ into hell. Balthasar interprets Scripture and tradition, including Aquinas, as supporting the idea that Christ's descent was both atoning and redemptive for all humanity. Aquinas stated that the descent was *prima ut sustineret totam poenam peccati, ut sic totam culpam expiaret* ("First to take on the entire punishment

---

48. Oakes SJ and Moss, eds., *The Cambridge Companion to Hans Urs von Balthasar*, 5.

49. *Gaudium et spes*, "The Pastoral Constitution of the Church in the Modern World," paragraph 22, in Abbott, ed. *The Documents of Vatican II*, 221–22, cited in Oakes, "Christ's Descent into Hell," 386.

50. Oakes, "Christ's Descent into Hell," 386.

51. Oakes, "Christ's Descent into Hell," 387.

of sin and thereby to atone wholly for its guilt").[52] Taking this from scholastic theology, Balthasar fuses it with scriptures such as Galatians 3:13 ("Christ redeemed us from the curse of the law, by becoming a curse for us.") and 2 Corinthians 5:21 ("For our sake, he made him to be sin, who knew no sin, so that in him we might become the righteousness of God"). These statements in Scripture applied not simply to the cross, but also to the *descensus*. It is here we find the "innovation" of which Balthasar was accused.[53]

However, Balthasar's construct was hardly an innovation. In the medieval period, there were many cults devoted to the sufferings of Christ as salvific for humanity as a whole.[54] To this "fusion" one can also add a reappraisal of Origenism by Balthasar. Indeed, Balthasar was accused of promoting a sort of neo-Origenism in his later works on soteriology. However, there remains much uncertainty about the condemnation of Origen's eschatology in various councils in the sixth century CE. Even so, Balthasar never specifically promoted a so-called Origenist concept of the apokatastasis.[55] Returning to the *descensus*, what is compelling for Balthasar is best summarized by Oakes:

> But at least this can be said: *if* anyone remains in hell after Christ's descent, it is now only because Christ knows from inside what hell entails and *on that basis* has been given the powers of judgment: "For as the Father raises the dead and gives them life, so also the Son gives life to whom he will. The Father judges no one, but he has given all judgment to the Son. . . . For as the Father has life in himself, so he had granted the Son also to have life in himself, and has given him authority to execute judgment, because he is the Son of Man" (John 5:21–22; 26–27).[56]

In terms of teleology, Balthasar retains his focus on christology. Christ himself *is* the eschaton. Balthasar sees no conflict between human progress in history and the second advent of Christ. Christ, as the center of history, is in our midst *now* and when the Father wills it, Christ will

---

52. Aquinas, *Sermon-Conferences*, 78. Cited in Oakes, "Christ's Descent into Hell," 388.

53. Cf. Pitstick and Oakes, "Balthasar, Hell, and Heresy: An Exchange." This article is noteworthy as Pitstick critiques Balthasar as an innovator who has strayed from orthodox Catholicism.

54. Cf. Oakes, "Christ's Descent into Hell," 388n13.

55. Oakes, "Christ's Descent into Hell," 383ff.

56. Oakes, "Christ's Descent into Hell," 389. Emphasis original.

"come again" and fulfil human history rather than annul it. O'Donnell interprets Balthasar's concept of the future of humanity and the cosmos in this way:

> If it is the Spirit who opens up the future and if Jesus is permeated by the Spirit, then Jesus can be said to be the future of the world. In Christ, God has achieved his plan conceived before the foundation of the world. This is what we mean when we say that Jesus is the *eschaton*. In him eternity and time meet. The future of the world is already present. In a certain sense, a future beyond Jesus cannot be given. There is nothing more to await. As Balthasar puts it, "Now, when the absolute fullness has already been given, all that interpretation can do is to flow round it in never-ending circles, moving freely and without any compulsive line of development."[57]

With this view of the eschaton, the question that must be asked is: what then is human progress? Balthasar rejected any concept of a Marxist-human utopia as a possible future before the eschaton. Balthasar wrote that "In a hundred thousand years, humanity will be not one inch closer to the archetype [which is] Christ than it is today."[58] The reason for this is the mystery of human freedom.[59] Thus, there is a pre-eschatic pessimism in Balthasar's thought. The only hope for humanity is the resurrection and the journey with Christ to the Father—which culminates in what Balthasar describes as the *connubium*, the bridal union between creature and God. Thus, humanity's post-eschatological being will be a journey into the mystery of the triune God—and this will be a union of perfect love which for Balthasar makes any concept of growth or progress in the life to come irrelevant.[60]

Divine Judgment

There are many works that touch upon the subject of divine judgment in Balthasar's oeuvre, such as his seminal work *Mysterium Paschale* as well as his five-volume *Theo-Drama: Theological Dramatic Theory* where he uses

---

57. O'Donnell, *Hans Urs von Balthasar*, 146. The quotation from Balthasar is found in his *Theology of History*, 136.

58. Balthasar, *Du krönst das Jahr mit deinem Huld* (1982), 228. Translated in O'Donnell, *Hans Urs von Balthasar*, 151.

59. O'Donnell, *Hans Urs von Balthasar*, 151.

60. O'Donnell, *Hans Urs von Balthasar*, 152.

the metaphor of dramatic action to explore the interactions between God and humanity.[61] In assessing Balthasar's understanding of judgment, his key works are arguably his two short books which he wrote toward the end of his life: *Was dürfen wir hoffen?* and *Kleiner Diskurs über die Hölle*, published in German in 1986 and 1987 respectively.[62] In English, these were published in 1988 in a single volume as *Dare We Hope "That All Men be Saved" with a Short Discourse on Hell*.[63] Most of his key thoughts in his earlier works are reflected in this short combined book, although he quotes liberally from a large number of sources to strengthen his case. Balthasar was aware that *Dare We Hope* would cause controversy. Due to its implication that salvation *could* be universal (a universalism of hope), it was condemned by some as being at variance with Catholic dogma dating back to the condemnation of Origenism.[64] While the main issue in Balthasar's short book is the hope of universal salvation, the task here is to assess the role of judgment in his scheme rather than engage in full in this *quaestio disputata*. However, it is worth adding that Balthasar refused (as did Barth) to assert absolute universalism. He wrote in reply to his critics that

> ... he who voices such a hope [for the salvation of all] advocates the "universal redemption" (*apokatastasis*) condemned by the Church—something that I have expressly rejected: we stand completely and utterly *under* judgment, and have no right, nor is it possible for us, to peer in advance at the Judge's cards. How can anyone equate hoping with knowing?[65]

Oakes notes that for Balthasar "revelation forbids us to speak of either a populated or an empty hell. Revelation leaves the question open."[66]

Balthasar's view of judgment might be summarized in the following passage: "On his earthly pilgrimage on earth, man is, of course, placed between fear and hope, simply because he is *under* judgment and does

---

61. Balthasar, *Mysterium Paschale: Die Theologie der Drei Tage* (1970); ET: *Mysterium Paschale: The Mystery of Easter* (1990); and *Theodramatik* (1973–1983), ET: *Theo-drama: Theological Dramatic Theory* (1988–1998).
62. Balthasar, *Was dürfen wir hoffen?*; *Kleiner Diskurs über die Hölle*.
63. Hereafter cited as DWH.
64. DWH, 163ff.
65. DWH, 166.
66. Oakes, "Christ's Descent into Hell," 385.

not *know* . . . ."⁶⁷ Thus, Balthasar does not give human beings what might be called "blessed assurance"—rather human beings must live in tension between fear and hope. Balthasar notes that "[b]y no means are we above [judgment], so that we might know its outcome in advance and could proceed from that knowledge to further speculation."⁶⁸ There is thus no possibility that human beings can "know" that they are among the elect or that their election is secure. While we must all face judgment (cf. 2 Cor 5:10), we are able to have confidence (*parrhesia*) as well as hope because the One who is our Judge is the savior of the world.⁶⁹ Balthasar notes Philippians 2:12–13 to drive home this state of being in humanity under judgment: "Therefore, my beloved, just as you have always obeyed me, not only in my presence, but much more now in my absence, work out your own salvation with fear and trembling; for it is God who is at work in you, enabling you both to will and to work for his good pleasure." "Fear and trembling" co-exist with hope and confidence. This is at the heart of judgment for Balthasar. This approach to judgment finds several analogues in traditional Catholic prayers, notably in the prayers known as Acts of Contrition where the penitent confesses to be sorry for her sins because she fears the just punishment (judgment) of God, but above all because she has offended God, the *summum bonum* and the source of love.

Balthasar equates these two possibilities as being consistent with God's covenant with Israel: "See, I have set before you today life and prosperity, death and adversity" (Deut 30:15); "And to this people you shall say: Thus says the LORD: See, I am setting before you the way of life and the way of death" (cf. Jer 21:18).⁷⁰ For Balthasar, this begs the soteriological question of whether God depends on human choice even though God, in God's own freedom, wills only salvation (cf. 1 Tim 2:4). It is here that Balthasar first mentions that he understands that the divine quality of mercy is infinite and thus it is legitimate to hope that all human beings will be saved—a stance for which he was sharply criticized.⁷¹ Gerhard Hermes (1909–88) criticized Balthasar by writing that "[s]uch hope does not exist, because we cannot know hope in opposition to *certain knowl-*

---

67. DWH, 27. Emphasis original.
68. DWH, 13.
69. DWH, 13.
70. DWH, 14–15
71. DWH, 16–17

edge and the avowed will of God. . . . [It is impossible that] we can hope for something about which we *know* that it will *certainly* not come about. . . . [Thus,] there is no hope for the salvation of all."[72] Other critics used the example of Judas Iscariot as a person who is, they asserted, unquestionably damned for all eternity. However, Balthasar remained defiant in the face of his critics: "So be it; if I have been cast aside as a hopeless conservative by the tribe of the left, then I know what sort of dung-heap I have been dumped upon by the right. But back to matters of substance."[73]

Balthasar consistently rejects the idea that anyone can *know* the outcome of divine judgment. He takes issue with the concept that God judges humanity *ante* or *post praevisa merita* and criticizes the scholastic theology of the twelfth and thirteenth centuries for its strident pronouncements of how God will judge certain creatures. He cites the provincial councils of Orange 2, Quiercy 1, Lyon, Valence, Quiercy 2, Langres, et al., as promoting a twofold predestination that is "truly tragic, if not grotesque" but also veiled in the language of High Scholasticism which was in turn further amplified at the Reformation (most notably in its Swiss Reformed manifestation) and in its Catholic manifestation in Jansenism.[74]

Moving forward to the nineteenth century, Balthasar makes an interesting critique of John Henry Cardinal Newman's (1801–90) soteriology. He quotes from Newman's [Catholic] sermons the following: "I stood from all eternity before your eyes, O God. You see clearly, and have always seen, whether I will be saved or lost. At all times my fate hovered before you: in heaven or in hell. O terrible thought!"[75] Balthasar comments that Newman presumes to know too much about judgment. He asks what Newman could possibly *know* about how God will judge human beings. The answer from Newman's sermon follows:

> We are but few in number, and they are many; . . . O misery of miseries! Thousands are dying daily; they are waking up into God's everlasting wrath . . . and their companions and friends are going on as they did and are soon to join them. The father would not believe that God could punish, and now the son will not believe; the father was indignant when eternal pain was spoken of, and the son gnashes his teeth and smiles contemptuously

---

72. Cited in DWH, 18. Emphasis original.
73. DWH, 19–20.
74. DWH, 24.
75. Cited in DWH, 25.

...; myriads..., like the herd of swine, falling headlong down into the steep! O mighty God! O God of love! It is too much!⁷⁶

Balthasar notes that to believe, as apparently Newman did, that humanity is in essence (apart from a few) a *massa damnata*, is to reject the central theme of the gospel that Christ died for all humanity on the cross *with the full capacity* to redeem every human being.⁷⁷ For Balthasar, Newman seemed to hold the belief that hell is stronger than Christ.⁷⁸ He again asks: "How does Newman know this?" He ends his commentary on Newman's sermon by stating that "After this kind of theology of the Cross, where is there any room left for rejoicing?" ⁷⁹ Balthasar turns to the German Catholic philosopher Josef Pieper (1904–97) as offering a possible explanation of the problem of anticipating God's judgment:

> There are two kinds of hopelessness. One is despair; the other is *praesumptio*. *Praesumptio* is usually translated as presumption, although a translation as anticipation not only is more literal but also catches the sense quite precisely. *Praesumptio* is a perverse anticipation of the fulfilment of hope. Despair is also an anticipation of the nonfulfillment of hope "to despair is to descend into hell" (Isidore of Seville)....⁸⁰

Balthasar refers to this problem of anticipating damnation as something that "from a certain point in time onward, will cast itself as a great shadow over the history of the Church and of theology."⁸¹ This "great shadow" is perhaps best captured in the decrees of the Council of Florence (1439–45), which today strike one as utterly opposite to the spirit of the Sec-

---

76. DWH, 26.

77. Cf. Council of Trent, Session VI, Canon 17: Si quis iustificationis gratiam non nisi praedestinatis ad vitam contingere dixerit, reliquos vero omnes, qui vocantur, vocari quidem, sed gratiam non accipere, utpote divina potestate praedestinatos ad malum: an. s. ['If anyone shall say that the grace of justification is attained by those only who are predestined unto life, but that all others, who are called, are called indeed, but do not receive grace, as if they are by divine power predestined to evil: let him be anathema.']; DS 827.

78. Granted Newman would agree with Trent, but his thought seems to stray towards the idea that many are "predestined to evil."

79. DWH, 27.

80. Pieper, *Über die Hoffnung*, 49. ET: *On Hope*, 47. Cited in DWH, 28. Pieper is quoting from Isidore's *Sententiae [De Summo Bono]*, Liber II 14.2: "... desperare vero in infernum descendere." Cf. Lindsay, ed. *Isidori Hispalensis Episcopi Etymologiarum sive Originum libri XX*.

81. DWH, 28.

ond Vatican Council. Balthasar is certainly aware of this inheritance, an inheritance that undoubtedly informed Newman's own thought already mentioned. An example is illustrative in the "*firmiter*" decree of Florence:

> [This council] firmly [*firmiter*] believes, professes and preaches that all who are outside the Catholic Church, not only pagans but also Jews or heretics and schismatics, cannot share in eternal life and will go into the everlasting fire which is prepared for the devil and his angels (Mt 25:41), unless they are joined to the Catholic Church before the end of their lives.[82]

However, Balthasar notes that the New Testament offers several texts that are at variance with the severity and finality of this medieval conciliar decree. He notes the overtly universalist tone of 1 Timothy 2:3–6 as a counterpoint to the salvific pessimism of the Council of Florence, for in it Paul declares that "God our savior ... desires everyone to be saved and come to the knowledge of the truth. For there is one God and there is one mediator between God and humankind, Christ Jesus, himself human, who gave himself a ransom for all."[83] He also notes with approval the thought on this topic of the Protestant theologian Helmut Thielicke (1908–86) in his *Der evangelische Glaube*. Thielicke writes (seemingly referencing Balthasar's concept of the *descensus*):

> There are theological truths and circumstances—in this case, the situations of the "lost" [*apollumenoi*]—that cannot be subjects of dogmatic statement but only contents of prayer. Nothing prevents one from beseeching in prayer that those who have rejected Christ might themselves not be rejected, that their histories might continue together with God in eternity, and that the boundlessness of eternal love should not draw back even before *them*. Only in that case can the speculative question about the how—whether it is answered through the *Descensus ad inferos* or however—be left out of consideration, while any attempt to formulate a dogmatic proposition here would immediately lead to a profusion of supplementary hypothetical theses. At the next moment, we would already find ourselves in the midst of fantasy

---

82. "Firmiter credit, profitetur et praedicat, nullos extra catholicam Ecclesiam exsistentes, non solum paganos, sed nec Judaeos aut haereticos atque schismaticos, aeternae vitae fieri posse participes; sed in ignem aeternum ituros, qui paratus est diabolo et angelis eius (Mt 25, 41), nisi ante finem vitae eidem fuerint aggregate..." DS 1351, Council of Florence, Decree for the Copts and Ethiopians, "Cantate Domino," 4 February 1442. Cited in Oakes, "Christ's Descent into Hell," 385n8.

83. DWH, 35. Quotation is from NRSV rather than that in DWH.

and the manipulation of heavenly-hellish stage sets. But prayer for the *apollumenoi* can leave the legitimacy of the requested goal and the means of its attainment up to the hands that this request has been entrusted to. For this request, like all others, is included under the general proviso: "Thy will be done." This proviso is a declaration of trust.[84]

Thielecke brings into focus a central theme for Balthasar: it is God and God alone who decides who will be saved—we can only pray that the lost may through God's love partake in eternal life.

For Balthasar, part of the judgment of Christ is the division of the human race. Balthasar writes:

> In setting out to gather all men, Jesus relativizes all religion in the world, Jewish and Gentile. He thereby separates whatever is prepared to respond to his absolute summons from what resists it. So it comes about that the peace-bringing mission ("he is our peace," Eph. 2:14) introduces more division in the world than any other; not through fanaticism but because of an inherent logic: the very One who has come "not to judge but to save" utters that "word" that judges those who reject it (Jn 3:16-21; 12:47-48).[85]

There is a limit to Balthasar's salvific optimism. Hope for all in the face of judgment is not the same thing as *knowing* that—in the famous mystical mantra of Julian of Norwich (1342-1416)—"all will be well." However, he refers extensively to medievals such as Julian and later mystics to support his salvific optimism—and interestingly, they are almost entirely women.[86] It was only later that certain Protestants (e.g., Friedrich Schleiermacher) picked up on this theme by means of an Enlightenment reappraisal of Reformed soteriology. Human beings cannot know the outcome of judgment. Part of Christ's judgment is the division of humanity between those who accept the Gospel and those who reject it. However, Balthasar is not

---

84. Thielecke, *Der evangelische Glaube:Theologie des Geistes*, vol. 3, 610ff. Cited and translated in DWH, 36-37. Emphasis original.

85. Balthasar, *Theo-Drama* IV, 435. Cited in Oakes, "Christ's Descent into Hell," 391.

86. Oakes, "Christ's Descent into Hell," 384. In DWH, Balthasar quotes the medieval mystics Mechtilde of Hackeborn (1240-98), Angela of Foligno (1248-1309), Julian of Norwich (1342-1416); and later mystics such as Mary Magdalen of Pazzi (1556-1607); Marie de l'Incarnation (1599-1672); and, of course, Thérèse of Liseux (1873-1897). Cf. DWH, 97-113.

willing to consign those on the side of the "goats" to hell. It is here that Balthasar takes on Augustine with a sharp critique:

> [Augustine] signified a turning point in the Church history insofar as [he] interprets the relevant texts in such a way as to show that he plainly and simply *knows* about the outcome of divine judgment. And all those bowing to his authority, from Gregory the Great through the early and High Middle Ages—Anselm, Bonaventure, and Thomas [Aquinas] not excepted—to the Reformers and Jansenists, will become *knowers* in the same sense, taking this knowledge as a fully secure basis upon which to construct further speculations about God's twofold predetermination *post* or *ante previsa merita*.[87]

Nonetheless from the Renaissance onward, a shift towards a form of soteriological optimism away from the Augustinian heritage began to appear. Joseph Ratzinger notes this in his own book on eschatology, where he mentions the example of Thérèse of Lisieux (1873–97) who was willing to be plunged into hell so that others may escape it:

> Thus, in the history of holiness which hagiology offers us, and notably in the course of recent centuries, in John of the Cross, in Carmelite piety in general, and in that of Thérèse of Lisieux in particular, "Hell" has taken on a completely new meaning and form. For the saints, "Hell" is not so much a threat to be hurled at other people, but a challenge to oneself. It is a challenge to suffer, in the dark night of faith, to experience communion with Christ in solidarity with his descent into the Night. One draws near to the Lord's radiance by sharing in his darkness. One serves the salvation of the world by leaving one's own salvation behind for the sake of others.[88]

In this example, not only is there allusion to the descent of Christ into hell on Holy Saturday for the salvation of all, but also the imitation of Christ by the saints who are also willing to undertake such a *descensus* for the sake of other human beings. Thus, while human beings cannot *know* about the outcome of judgment, they *can* know that Christ has descended into hell and taken on the full judgment of God "for us humans and for our salvation" and that indeed this same Christ calls his disciples to follow him, without fear, in both his descent and his glorification.

---

87. DWH, 65. Emphasis original.
88. Ratzinger, *Eschatology*, 217–18.

For Balthasar, divine judgment is inescapable yet never hopeless—because the Judge is God in Christ, the source of hope. This is a Judge that humanity can wholly trust because it is a Judge who is Love itself:

> The seriousness that we are confronted with is the seriousness of a love that goes beyond all justice. God's love for every man is absolute; it is ineffable. Who can, "by rights," claim adequacy before it? No saint would presume to say, "I can." No one has loved God with his whole heart, with his whole soul, with all his strength. Everyone, without exception, has to say: "Lord, I am not worthy." All will someday have to stand before him, and then "every eye will see him, everyone who pierced him; and all the tribes of the earth will wail (for themselves). Even so. Amen" (Rv 1:7). Nothing is more serious than love, precisely because it is "abundance that goes beyond justice:" one must surrender oneself to it for better or for worse.[89]

Evaluation

> *I pray, Master, that the flames of hell may not touch me or any of those whom I love, and even that they may never touch anyone (and I know, my God, that you will forgive this bold prayer).*
> —Pierre Teilhard de Chardin[90]

The prayer of Teilhard de Chardin (1881–1955) is fully in accord with Balthasar's soteriology. To pray, to hope that no one will be lost or consigned to an eternal hell is not only acceptable, it is indeed obligatory. However, it is this boldness that caused concern among his contemporary critics and still does so today. Oakes summarizes the theological criticism associated with him in his reply to a critique by Alyssa Pitstick:

> Hans Urs von Balthasar is a disturbing theologian. Even among some of his most vocal enthusiasts, he seems "not quite right." Nor has this diffidence been much assuaged by John Paul II's evident admiration for the theologian, shown most incontrovertibly when the pontiff named him a cardinal in 1988. Nor are the anxiously orthodox much allayed by Pope Benedict XVI's praise of him in October 2005, on the occasion of the hundredth anniversary of his birth. And surely the central reason for that uneasiness is—despite his self-proclaimed orthodoxy—Balthasar's

---

89. DWH, 176.
90. de Chardin, *Le Milieu Divin*, 143.

claim that Christ descended into the depths of hell in order to rescue, at least potentially, all those "spirits in prison who disobeyed God long ago" (1 Pet 3:20).[91]

Much of the critique on Balthasar's concept of divine judgment and salvific optimism is that it does not square with the magisterial teaching of the Catholic Church, both in his innovation on the *descensus ad inferos* on Holy Saturday and in his insistence this descent of Christ into hell not only was salvific for "spirits in prison who disobeyed God long ago" but indeed that it is at least potentially salvific for the entirety of human race until the eschaton. For Balthasar, Christ has conquered and is now Lord of hell. The judgment of Christ is a judgment before the One who is the fullness of love and hope and who *knows* hell personally, including its agonies. Human beings in their earthly life are at all times under judgment. They cannot know what judgment awaits them. They therefore must radically trust Christ—whose judgment is perfect, all-loving and all-knowing. The ninth stanza of the sixth-century Latin hymn *Vexilla Regis Prodeunt* captures the nature of Balthasar's understanding of judgment and hope which prays that the "sins of the guilty" will be "removed" by the crucified Christ:

> *O Crux ave, spes unica,*
> *hoc Passionis tempore!*
> *piis adauge gratiam,*
> *reisque dele crimina.*[92]

My problem with Balthasar's hopeful soteriology is not his refusal to assert that all will be saved based on his reading of Scripture and tradition, or his obvious wrestling with the issue within the confines of Catholic dogma and its magisterium. It is rather his seeming failure to deal with divine judgment and the possibility of a "guilty verdict" as a problem of evil. As horrible as the idea of eternal torment is, Balthasar never follows through on this problem: that God in Christ as Judge will potentially condemn some creatures to hell—and that this is *in itself* an evil. This is in spite of the fact that he quotes sources that state that it is impossible that there is a God of love who permits the existence of an eternal hell.[93]

---

91. Pitstick and Oakes, "Balthasar, Hell, and Heresy: An Exchange," 25–29.

92. Anonymous, sixth century: "O hail the cross our only hope / in this Passiontide / grant increase of grace to believers / and remove the sins of the guilty."

93. E.g., "If God is love, as the New Testament teaches us, hell must be impossible.

Marilyn McCord Adams, with whom I shall engage in the fifth section of this chapter, states the issue in this way:

> Hell poses the principal problem of evil for Christians. Its challenge is so deep and decisive, that to spill bottles of ink defending the logical compossibility of [an all-powerful and all-loving God who permits] this-worldly evils while holding a closeted belief that ... some created persons will be consigned to hell forever, is at best incongruous and at worst disingenuous.[94]

It is here that Balthasar, who as a person who lived through the horrors of World War II, albeit within the security of neutral Switzerland, leaves what to me is a soteriological void. Balthasar never actually refers to hell as an evil in itself. Even in the attempts, after C. S. Lewis (1898–1963), to consider the proposal that hell is self-made by creatures who consign themselves to it by self-judgment, hell would still be an *eternal* evil permitted by God.[95] If hell is maintained as a "real possibility," how then can Balthasar's triune conception of God as "absolute love" be maintained? It would seem that Absolute Love is diametrically at odds with the existence, juridical sentence or even allowance of eternal torment. An example of what I see as Balthasar's conundrum of hell being a serious problem of evil can be seen in this passage where he notes that Scripture and tradition "force" him to retain hell as a possible outcome of divine judgment:

> If the threats of judgment and the cruel, horrifying images of the gravity of the punishment of sinners that we find in scripture and tradition gave any point, then it is surely, in the first instance, to make *me* see the seriousness of the responsibility that I bear along with my freedom. But do scripture and tradition also force me to assume from these threats of judgment, beyond what concerns me, that even only *one other* besides me has met ruin in hell or is destined to do so? Quite to the contrary, it seems to me that, initially, the following thesis can be advocated (only, however, from the perspective of practical-prescriptive and not theoretical-cognitive reason): "Whoever reckons with

---

At least, it represents a supreme anomaly. In no case can being a Christian imply believing more in hell than in Christ." Martelet SJ, *L'au-delà retrouvé*, 181ff. Cited in DWH, 55.

94. Adams, "The Problem of Hell," 302.
95. DWH, 91–94. Balthasar refers to C. S. Lewis, *The Great Divorce*, 69ff.

> the possibility of even only *one* person being lost besides himself is hardly able to love unreservedly . . . ."⁹⁶

Yet, the thesis quoted by Balthasar is surely applicable to God as absolute love—and could be restated this way: If God allows even one person to be lost, God is hardly able to be said to love unreservedly. If hell must be maintained as a possible outcome of divine judgment, then it is neither possible nor logical to assert that God is absolute love. Balthasar ends his short book with the following:

> Let us cast aside what leads to such dead-ends and limit ourselves to the truth that we all stand under God's absolute judgment. "I do not even pass judgment on myself," as Saint Paul says. "The Lord is the one to judge me. So stop passing judgment before the time of his return. He will bring to light what is hidden in darkness." (1Cor 4:3ff). Not forgetting Saint John: "We should have confidence on the day of judgment." (1 John 4:17).⁹⁷

As stated previously, Balthasar's claims on divine love fail at this point. He has hope, even a vague confidence, for the universal salvation of Christians, but he remains silent as to the fate of humanity as a whole. He refuses to give, in a manner similar to but more pessimistic than Barth, that word of certainty that indeed this God of absolute love will save all human beings at the judgment.⁹⁸ We can hope and pray that it is true, but we cannot and we will not *know* until that Day comes. This soteriology of God's love, in spite of all the arguments and the obvious tensions imposed by Catholic dogmatics, is not one of *absolute* love. It is conditional and uncertain.

4. John A. T. Robinson: Defending the Doctrine of God

Introduction

In this section, I shall explore an earlier work of J. A. T. Robinson, *In the End, God . . .* , which was published in 1950 and republished and revised

---

96. DWH, 211. The quote is unattributed, but appears to be taken from Verweyen, *Christologische Brennpunkte*, 119–22.

97. DWH, 254.

98. Karl Barth famously said toward the end of his life: "I cannot exclude the possibility that God would save all men at the judgment." Cited in "Witness to an Ancient Truth," *TIME* magazine, 20 April 1962, Cover story.

in 1968.⁹⁹ Robinson strongly asserts the idea that human beings will "in the end" *always* choose God. Thus, there is in the eschaton a choice that the resurrected person must make. For Robinson, hell is that which *must not* be chosen.¹⁰⁰ Robinson makes this assumption to defend the doctrine of God rather than simply to embrace a soteriological nicety. However, while he succeeds in making a case that it is God's will that all should be saved, I argue that he fails to explain how this divine fiat preserves human freedom (which he maintains) to make a decision for or against God.

Robinson's Eschatology

> Eschatology is the explication of what must be true of the end, both of history and of the individual, if God is to be the God of the biblical faith. All eschatological statements can finally be reduced to, and their validity tested by, sentences beginning: 'In the end, God . . .'¹⁰¹

According to Trevor Hart, Robinson's eschatological argument can be divided into four parts: the witness of Scripture; the nature of divine love; the relation between divine purpose and human freedom; and the abiding reality of hell.¹⁰² Hart's divisions will serve as a convenient means to explore Robinson's eschatological schema as mapped out in his *In the End, God. . .*

1. Witness of Scripture

Robinson is above all a biblical scholar and his later works focus entirely on the New Testament. However, as Hart notes, Robinson's approach to Scripture is Kierkegaardian: for the biblical text only "speaks" through the reader's encounter with the living God. Without this divine-human interaction, the texts are, says Hart, "inert and have nothing of significance to say to us."¹⁰³ Robinson's doctoral dissertation focused on Martin

---

99. The 1950 original edition was also published by James Clark. The second edition was published in 1968 (London: Fontana). The 2011 special edition is a reissue of the original 1950 edition with all the 1968 modifications noted in the footnotes, hereafter cited as IEG. The 1968 revised edition is referred to as *In the End God* (1968).

100. IEG, 111–16.

101. IEG, 23. This is Robinson's concise definition of eschatology.

102. IEG, xxi. Hart's introduction to the special edition originally appeared, in shorter form, in Gregory MacDonald, ed., *"All Shall be Well."*

103. IEG, xxiv.

Buber's "I and Thou" (*Ich und Du*, 1929) thus this approach to Scripture is consonant with his earliest scholarship. Even so, Robinson approaches the eschatological texts of the New Testament in exegetical fashion. Yet, by doing so, Robinson is not engaging in proof-texting. Rather, his premise is reminiscent of Schleiermacher's restatement of Reformed theology and its teleological focus on the "everlasting purpose of God."[104] For Robinson, this divine purpose is captured (without invoking Origen) in this way:

> The New Testament asserts the final *apokatastasis*—the restoration of all things—not as daring speculation, nor as a possibility, but as a reality—a reality that shall be and must be, because it already is. It already is because it is grounded in what has been, the decisive act, once and for all, embracing every creature. "In Christ *shall all* be made alive" (1 Cor 15:22), because "through one act of righteousness the free gift *came* unto *all men* to justification of life" (Rom 5:18).[105]

The universal restoration, which is also universal *reconciliation*, embraces every rational creature and the cosmos as a whole. It is through this lens that Robinson interprets biblical texts. Robinson has been accused by some of hubris in that he asserts as *fact* that universal restoration is indeed what the New Testament asserts, dispensing with the salvific dualism in many passages.[106] However, Robinson does acknowledge and engage with this dualism. He devotes an entire chapter to this issue.[107] Robinson explores the dualistic images in the New Testament, e.g., the parable of the separation of the sheep and goats in Matthew 25:31–46. For Robinson, borrowing the language of Bultmann, there are two salvific myths in the New Testament—one that promises universal salvation and one that promises an eternal separation of the righteous from the wicked. In exploring how these two myths are both possible, he reviews a series of soteriological models.[108]

---

104. Cf. Article 17 of the Articles of Religion of the Church of England (1563): "Predestination to Life is the everlasting purpose of God, whereby (before the foundations of the world were laid) he hath constantly decreed by his counsel secret to us, to deliver from curse and damnation those whom he hath chosen in Christ out of mankind, and to bring them by Christ to everlasting salvation, as vessels made to honour . . . ." in *The Book of Common Prayer* (1662).

105. IEG, 93. Emphasis original.

106. IEG, xli.

107. IEG,, 93–102.

108. IEG, 93–102.

Supralapsarian double predestination (the Calvinist inheritance) is, unsurprisingly, rejected outright and on exegetical grounds. Calvin (and Augustine) misunderstood the Pauline texts. Robinson notes that "[t]his solution need not detain us long."[109] The second solution is that there are two possibilities (salvation and damnation) that "eternally remain open" in order to preserve divine and human freedom. This is swiftly rejected as unscriptural. There cannot be two such possibilities because Scripture does not use the subjunctive in its eschatological statements: Christ *will* (*not* may) draw all humans to himself (John 12:32) and also some human beings *will* (*not* may) depart into eternal punishment (Matt 25:41). Thus, Robinson states that this is not a matter of two possibilities, but of two *realities*. His third solution explores the doctrine of God as either compatible or incompatible with this dualism. Here he dialogues with Emil Brunner and Aquinas. Brunner and Aquinas exemplify the traditional doctrine: God is love, loves all, but nonetheless does not save all and that some human beings will suffer eternal torment. Robinson rejects this as disingenuous: God is either love or God is not. If there is eternal torment for any created being, then God has failed, cannot be described as love itself (cf. 1 John 4:8), and is not the God revealed to us in Christ. The fourth solution is universalism, the reconciliation of all things. For his key text, Robinson, like his German-American contemporary Paul Tillich (whose theology Robinson tried to make accessible in his 1963 book *Honest to God*) focuses on 1 Cor 15:28: "When all things are subjected to him, then the Son himself will also be subjected to the one who put all things in subjection under him, so that God may be all in all."

11. Divine Love

For Robinson, to be saved is to love God or rather to respond to God's holy love. Yet for Robinson, divine love has a ferocity reminiscent of Bulgakov's understanding that the judgment of God's love is the "most terrible of judgments." Robinson defines divine love as "a love of cauterizing holiness and of righteousness whose only response to evil is the purity of a perfect hate. Wrath and justice are but ways in which such love must show itself to be love in the face of its denial. If it appeared in any other form, it would be less than perfect love."[110] In effect, while not denying human freedom, God's love is omnicompetent and omnipotent. Such a

---

109. IEG, 95.
110. IEG, 99.

love is then, by this definition, irresistible. If God is ontologically love, then God's love cannot fail (Cf. 1 Cor 13:8).

III. Human Freedom

Robinson was aware that his absolute universalism was a problem for human freedom. While he could make the case that God's will is universally salvific from at least part of the biblical tradition, he could not easily dismiss the possibility that a human being could refuse to reciprocate to God's love ante- or post-mortem. He defends human freedom within his universalist project:

> For without freedom love cannot be love. Love to be a force at all demands the exercise of freedom. One cannot move a chair by loving it, but only a person is perfectly free to not be moved if he does not wish to be. Love is peculiarly love and its power purely that of love only when this capacity to flout it is presupposed in all its integrity. Depreciate this in the least degree, and love is impotent.[111]

Robinson continues this theme insisting that the "rock of liberty then, must stand."[112] Yet, the "rock" has an Achilles' heel. While human beings are truly free, Robinson asserts in the form of a question that God's holy love is, in the end, irresistible: "May we not imagine a love so strong that ultimately no one will be able to restrain himself from free and grateful surrender?"[113] This is again strikingly similar to Bulgakov's approach. Human beings have free will, but God's love is relentless, overwhelming, and inexhaustible. Eventually, free human beings will "freely" yield and be conquered by this love. Robinson quotes a hymn by Charles Wesley as an illustration:

> *I yield, I yield,*
> *I can hold out no more;*
> *I sink by dying love compelled*
> *To own thee conqueror.*[114]

---

111. IEG, 104.

112. IEG, 105.

113. IEG, 106.

114. IEG, 106. The hymn is taken from Charles Wesley's poem "The Resignation," in *Hymns and Sacred Poems*, (London, 1740).

Robinson then engages in a reflection on the argument that an irresistible love nullifies true freedom.[115] His appeal is to anthropology—to human love: "We have all known what it is to be confronted by a love too strong to resist."[116] This sweeping statement is problematic for even Robinson in his 1950 privileged British context. He knew that the world has many people that know no love at all. He admits this, but recasts this irresistible love as a sort of *deus absconditus* that embraces all people. In a move redolent or imitative of Schleiermacher's use of confession statements in his *Glaubenslehre,* he cites Article 17 of the Thirty-nine Articles of the Church of England (1563) concerning predestination.[117] He recasts this as a singular, positive decree of election for all humanity, but roots this in divine love rather than simply divine goodness. This leads Robinson to entertain a paradox: "The strange compulsion of God's love and its necessary victory would not abrogate, but simply release, our freedom."[118] In other words, to surrender to the saving love of God is the consummation of freedom. He writes further that "to the Christian, in the personal relationship of faith to God, the knowledge that the divine victory of love is necessary brings, not conflict and debate, but joy and peace in believing. For he sees this necessity as in no way inimical to freedom, but rather its very substantiation and assurance."[119] It could be argued that for Robinson yielding to God's love is true freedom, while resisting this love, even as an act of free will is a form of bondage that will not be permitted by God to endure. However, Robinson does not intimate that human will is fallen and also in need of redemption.

iv. Reality of Hell

For Robinson, hell is an existential myth, but it is nonetheless real in terms of human decision. "To the man in decision—and that means to all men, always, right up to the last hour—hell is in every way as real a destination as heaven. Only the man who has genuinely been confronted by both alternatives can be saved."[120] This description that up to the moment

---

115. IEG, 106–10.

116. IEG, 107.

117. ". . . the godly consideration of predestination and our election in Christ is full of sweet, pleasant, and unspeakable comfort." Cited in IEG, 108. This quotation omitted in the 1968 revision.

118. IEG, 108.

119. IEG, 109. Cf. Rom 15:13.

120. IEG, 112.

of death—or indeed *in* that very moment—there comes a time for each human being to make an eternal decision for or against God bears a remarkable resemblance to the eschatology of Rahner and less well known Ladislaus Boros (1927–81), both contemporaries of Robinson. Robinson then goes on to state, unconvincingly, that "[t]here could be no greater calumny than to suggest that the universalist either does not preach hell or does so with his tongue in his cheek."[121] His explanation for this somewhat bizarre statement is that the two myths—universal salvation (hell is impossible) and dualism (hell is a real possibility)—are a paradox to be held in tension: "The two myths represent two different standpoints. The one says: 'Christ is all in all.' The other says: 'Christ has to be chosen.' One is the truth as it is for God and as it is for faith the further side of decision; the other is the truth as it must be to the subject facing decision."[122]

To make sense of this, Robinson proposes that any choice not for God is hell, whether in this life or the next. Thus, in the eschaton, hell is a reality for those who choose it. He also argues in a way reminiscent of Clement of Alexandria who recommended that the pains of hell be preached to the masses to put the fear of God in them, but to those more knowledgeable, it is safe to entrust them with the doctrine of the *apokatastasis*. In Robinson's own words: "they that choose [hell; eternal death] and as long as they choose it, it is something that must present itself to them ... as a choice which is final and irreversible."[123] Yet, the believer "knows" that God will not allow this situation to maintain. While hell is infinite to the one who has chosen it, it is not infinite to God. In effect, those in hell *do not know* it is temporary. Robinson's hell is an intermediate state, but not a purgatory. It is a seemingly eternal state of alienation to those in it, but God in Christ will continuously invite the denizens of hell to choose love. God as Omnipotent Love will not accept a populated hell. Divine love is "inexhaustible and ultimately unendurable: the sinner *must* yield."[124] It is the nature of God to save, to reconcile. And above all, for Robinson, God can never be untrue to God's nature.

---

121. IEG, 112. This sentence was omitted in the 1968 revision.
122. IEG, 113.
123. IEG, 113.
124. IEG, 113. Emphasis original.

A Response to Emil Brunner

Robinson began his exploration of eschatology in a response to the statement of Emil Brunner (1889–1966) in his *Dogmatics* (1946). Robinson, who spoke fluent German, cites Brunner in a 1949 article entitled "Universalism—Is It Heretical?"[125] In that article, Robinson quotes a sentence from Brunner about universal salvation as "a menacing heresy endangering the biblical faith."[126] Brunner also states that the *apokatastasis* is "the false alternative" (*die falsche Alternative*) to the problem of double predestination in Reformed soteriology.[127] Since Robinson is in dialogue with Brunner, it is worth exploring this section of Brunner's *Dogmatics*:

> The Church has good reason to reject the doctrine of universal salvation, not only on the formal "Biblical" ground, but also from the point of view of the actual teaching of the Bible. This does not mean that the final salvation of men must be denied as a possibility, but only that it cannot be established as a positive human doctrine. All that we would urge is that we should not allow ourselves to be lulled into a false security by taking the possibility of an incomprehensible, gracious decision of God for granted; we do not deny that this possibility may exist. The error of the doctrine of universal salvation is not that it leaves the door of divine possibility *open*, but that it leaves *this door only* open, and closes the door on the other possibility. That which is an incomprehensible divine *possibility* is here arrogantly taken for granted by man as a *certainty*. This is in absolute opposition both to the Biblical understanding of God and to the Biblical understanding of man and salvation.[128]

---

125. Robinson, "Universalism—Is It Heretical?" (Reproduced in Appendix 1, IEG).

126. Robinson, "Universalism—Is It Heretical?", 139. Robinson's translation of Brunner is not exact. Here is the original German passage in full: "Nun ist aber die Lehre von der doppelten Prädestination nicht das einzige Missverständnis, das der echten biblischen Erwählungslehre droht; auf der andern, entgegengesetzten Seite liegt die *nicht minder gefährliche, für den biblischen Glauben ebenso bedrohliche Irrlehre* von der ἀποκατάστασις τῶν πάντων, die Lehre von der Allbeseligung, der Satz: Alle sind von Ewigkeit erwählt, darum werden alle des ewigen Lebens teilhaftig." Brunner, *Dogmatik I*, 363. Emphasis in quotation mine. ET: Brunner, *The Christian Doctrine of God*, 334. Robinson re-uses some of his 1949 article in his book, *In the End God*, in chapters 8 and 9. Cf. IEG, 97ff.

127. Brunner, *Dogmatik I*, 363.

128. Brunner, *The Christian Doctrine of God*, 335. Emphasis original.

Brunner's statement on universal salvation is reminiscent of Balthasar's view, already discussed in section three of this chapter. It is also similar to the view of Karl Barth.[129] The restraint displayed by Balthasar and Brunner, albeit for different reasons, is not shared by Bulgakov, nor by Robinson. This eschatological restraint is also not shared by Marilyn McCord Adams who will be discussed in the next section. Brunner writes that to be faithful to the "biblical understanding" one cannot teach universal salvation as a given, but only as a hope. Robinson, who is above all a New Testament scholar, asserts that to be faithful to the biblical revelation one *must* conclude that universal salvation is true. The reason it must be true, as was alluded to above, is that the doctrine of God demands it. In other words, if some are lost, this perverts the doctrine of God: "In a universe of [God's] love there can be no heaven which tolerates a chamber of horrors, no hell for any which does not at the same time make it a hell for God. He cannot endure that, for that would be a mockery of his nature—and he will not."[130]

For Robinson, Brunner fails to hold together the holiness and love of God. He quotes Brunner in his 1949 article from the English translation of Brunner's *The Mediator*:[131] "[God] wishes to make himself known as love, as far as this is possible; but he must also make himself known as the holy righteous Judge when this is inevitable."[132] God is not simply Love. He *defines* himself as Love. Love is his will, not his nature, although it is his eternal will. As his nature, however, even in Christ we must worship his sovereign majesty and holiness.[133]

---

129. As previously cited in "Witness to an Ancient Truth," *TIME* magazine, 20 April 1962, Cover story. It is noteworthy that Brunner admits that he mainly agrees with Barth's doctrine of election, but he does criticize Barth for his well known, novel stance that Jesus is the only rejected human, the only human ever to suffer reprobation. Brunner acknowledges that Barth said that the church should not preach the *apokatastasis*, but he does claim that Barth's doctrine dares to "throw on the scrapheap the idea of a final divine Judgment, and the doctrine that a man may be "lost." Thus, Brunner accuses Barth not of absolute universalism, but of eliminating the Last Judgment for all humanity—which thus leads to a default doctrine of universal salvation, even if Barth refuses to admit it (or rather, refuses to *preach* it). Cf. Brunner, *The Christian Doctrine of God*, 348ff.

130. IEG, 116.

131. IEG, 130, n5.

132. Cf. Brunner, *Der Mittler*; ET: *The Mediator*, 551.

133. Brunner, *The Mediator*, 282.

Brunner is reflecting his Swiss Reformed theological inheritance which emphasizes the sovereignty of God. The rebuttal to Robinson's article by T. F. Torrance (1913–2007), who like Brunner is rooted in the Reformed tradition, was entitled "Universalism or Election?"[134] It appeared in the same journal as Robinson's article and it is in agreement with Brunner's soteriological dualism—that God is love *and* holiness; God still demands absolute justice. For Robinson, Brunner's approach (and Torrance's affirmation) result in "a dangerous distinction between the Being and Will of God."[135]

It however must be noted that both Brunner and Torrance are insisting on soteriological modesty. It is better to be hopeful, yet agnostic about universal salvation. But for Robinson this is an unacceptable form of dualism. As if taking a page from Luther, Robinson insists that God is solely the God as revealed in Christ. Thus, whether hubristic or not, Robinson asserts as "facts" that God's nature *and* will are love and that this love wills to save humanity—and will do so. His conclusion is christological. In his reply to T. F. Torrance, also in the same volume of the *Journal of Scottish Theology*, Robinson responds to Torrance that his assertion of universal salvation does not rest on human logic or analogy, but rather on "the *action* of God in Christ. For the Christian, the *eschaton has been revealed*, in the summing up of all things and all men in Jesus Christ."[136]

Hoc ita non evenit: The Nature of Divine Judgment in a Reply to Aquinas

However, it is not only Brunner and Torrance that Robinson takes to task on this issue. Thomas Aquinas (1225–74) is also a focus of his exploration. Just as there is a criticism of a key line in Brunner's oeuvre, so there is a particular sentence in the *Summa Theologiae* that Robinson engages. Robinson criticizes Aquinas' commentary on 1 Timothy 2:3–4: "This is right and is acceptable in the sight of God our Savior, who wills (θέλει) everyone to be saved and to come to the knowledge of the truth." Aquinas then comments on this text: *hoc ita non evenit*.[137] Aquinas states

---

134. Cf. Torrance, "Universalism or Election?" (reprinted in IEG, Appendix 2).

135. IEG, 131n5.

136. Cf. Robinson, "Universalism—A Reply" (reprinted in IEG, 153–56; quotation from 153). Emphasis original.

137. "It doesn't turn out this way." Aquinas, *Summa Theologiae*, I, 19.6.1. Cited in IEG, 128.

this simply as a fact—God may desire this, but it does not come to pass. Robinson criticizes the scholastic theology of Aquinas which seeks to differentiate the antecedent will of God from the conditioned will of God. The antecedent will of God, as declared in 1 Timothy 2:3-4 is that God wills to save everyone. However, as Aquinas notes "it does not turn out this way." This is due to God's conditioned or consequent will. Due to the demands of divine justice, the consequent will of God is that some will be damned eternally. Thus, God remains love, remains willing to save all, but God's nature—echoing Brunner—is not *only* one of love, but of holiness and justice. God must punish the wicked who do not repent as this is demanded by the divine nature. God does so in holy love—even if this holy love punishes some of God's creatures eternally. Unsurprisingly, Robinson rejects the distinction between an antecedent and conditioned divine will. For Robinson, God's justice is not separate from divine love, but is rather a component of it.[138] He writes:

> It is most important to hold to the fact that justice is in no sense a substitute for love, which comes into operation when the other has failed to be effective. . . . God has no power but the power of love, since he has no purpose but the purpose of love and no nature but the nature of love. If that fails, he fails. Justice is no second line defence: it has no power of its own. For it is nothing other than love being itself, love in the face of evil, continuing to exercise its peculiar power.[139]

This then, in his rebuttal of Aquinas's salvific dualism, leads to Robinson's understanding of the purpose of divine judgment. For Robinson, judgment is the confrontation of divine love with sin and evil: "Judgment is, indeed, absolutely necessary, as that through which alone sinful man can hear the word of mercy. But the sole possible function of judgment can be to enable men to receive mercy which renders it superfluous."[140] This statement is striking in that while Robinson tries to make use of the idea that God's love is one of "cauterizing holiness" yet in the end the judgment of God is the operation of mercy. There is no purgatorial fire or the ferocity of Bulgakov's terrible judgment, but rather a penetrative

---

138. "Rather is his justice a quality of his love, a characterization of its working." IEG, 99.

139. IEG, 99-100.

140. IEG, 100.

love that overwhelms and casts out sin from the sinner—in a seemingly gentle way.

Evaluation

I am sympathetic to Robinson's universalism and his insistence that God is merciful. It stems from his doctrine of God which is at its center christological. For Robinson, it is a fact that God is love and that all the attributes of the Divine Being are rooted in love. Robinson was a serious biblical scholar and most of his works focused on the New Testament. Yet, in this admittedly young work of theology, Robinson cites texts that serve his purposes and then casts those that do not as "existential myths" which results in a peculiar quasi-Bultmannian reinterpretation where it suits his aims, but where it does not, the texts are allowed to speak in a distinctly non-mythic way. I also appreciate his wrestling with dualism, both theistic and salvific. Yet, he insists his universalism rests on the proposal that God's love overwhelms eschatically intact human freedom. Teilhard de Chardin, as radical as he was, still could write: "You have told me, O God, to believe in hell. But you have forbidden me to think . . . of any man as damned."[141] Robinson could not write such a sentence, but at times it appears he could write the reverse: "I have told you, O God, that no one is damned." This then leads to the issue of Robinson's treatment of divine judgment. It has no hint of apocalyptic, but this is not surprising since Robinson's realized eschatology has no interest in the second parousia. Robinson was a student of C. H. Dodd (1884–1973) and he shared in Dodd's realized eschatology. For Robinson, everything is completed in Christ's incarnation and the second coming, resurrection, and last judgment are symbolic. Christ's advent is singular.[142] Yet, Robinson does allow for some measure of futurity and a concept of bodily resurrection on the last day. He refuses to speculate on what happens between death and resurrection, although he denies the concept that for the dead the resurrection has already occurred. The divine judgment for Robinson is notably tranquil, with the one exception of referring to God's love as "cauterizing." It is most certainly not the mystical ferocity of Bulgakov's second coming. However, if Robinson's eschatology locates the divine judgment exclusively to the cross, then what human persons experience

---

141. de Chardin, *Le Milieu Divin*, 143.

142. IEG, 51. Note also that for Robinson, the resurrection of the body is myth. Cf. IEG, 84.

is not actually judgment. It is rather a spiritual shepherding so that sinners "may hear the word of mercy." It bears a *slight* resemblance to the therapeutic eschatology of Marilyn McCord Adams whose schema will be discussed in the next section of this chapter.

Robinson's ideas about free will and judgment are problematic. Robinson seems to want to argue that human beings will in the end make the "right choice" and embrace God's salvific offer of reconciliation. Thus, human freedom is maintained. However, Robinson does not explain how free will is maintained when it is drowned in an overwhelming cascade of God's love. Robinson defends this conundrum by stating that we do not lose, but rather "find" our freedom in yielding to God's love.[143] Admittedly, there are biblical passages that allude to this concept (cf. John 8:36; Rom 6:8) as well as patristic sources, notably the maxim *cui servire regnare est* often attributed to St Augustine of Hippo. This maxim is usually translated "whose service is perfect freedom" rather than literally as "whom to serve is to reign." However, my concern is not that libertarian free will is preserved at the judgment, but rather that Robinson does not explain how human free will is transformed by it.

Considering the overall oeuvre of Robinson, it is not particularly helpful to call his works heterodox or controversial, especially in twenty-first century retrospective. Robinson knew that he was at variance with mainstream Christian doctrine when he wrote his 1950 essay and indeed this made him well known in his day, as a radical and a liberal. His later works, especially *Honest to God* confirmed this status. It is therefore not surprising that his eschatology, even as a young theologian, was forcefully optimistic, asserting universal salvation as fact and not merely as pious hope. The overall tone of Robinson's *In the End God . . .* is one of passionate assertion of God's nature as love and that this love is salvific for all. While he fails to address the function of judgment, the problem of eschatic human freedom, and the problem of evil, he does forcefully argue that God is revealed to us in Jesus Christ and what is revealed is holy love. After exploring Robinson, I realized that his theology is consonant with an earlier confession of faith from early nineteenth-century New England which perhaps will serve as the concluding word: "We believe there is one God, whose nature is Love; revealed in one Lord Jesus Christ,

---

143. Robinson, "Universalism—Is it Heretical?" 148.

by one Holy Spirit of grace, who will finally restore the whole family of mankind to holiness and happiness."¹⁴⁴

5 Marilyn McCord Adams: Horrors and Therapeutic Eschatology

Marylin McCord Adams, unlike the previous three theologians of this chapter, has the problem of evil at the heart of her theo-philosophical investigations. However, as will be seen below, I argue that she is reductionist when it comes to the role of divine judgment in her eschatology. While Adams does believe that there is a consequence for sin, the Judge that returns at the eschaton is more of a cosmic psychotherapist and hardly the God of Bulgakov's "terrible judgment" of love or the God of Balthasar, who places humanity "under judgment" the outcome of which cannot be known.

Adams' Christological Project

In order to understand Adams' conception of divine judgment, it is necessary to explore her overall christological project. In her book, *Christ and Horrors: The Coherence of Christology*, Adams continues her project on the problem of evil, a topic she has focused on since the beginning of her career.¹⁴⁵ Her previous book on this topic was published in 1999 as *Horrendous Evils and the Goodness of God*.¹⁴⁶ In all her works, Adams is consistent in her rejection of theodicy and "restricted-standard theism," the theism that upholds God as omnipotent, omniscient, and omnibenevolent. Rather, she turns to christology as a means to find solutions to the problems inherent in material reality. For Adams, Christ is the "explanatory posit" that solves the non-optimality problem of divine-human relations.¹⁴⁷ I shall use her book *Christ and Horrors* as my primary source for this investigation. In that book, she gives this summary of her project:

---

144. Winchester Profession of Faith (1803), Article II, 'General Convention of Universalists in the New England States at Winchester, NH' in Schaff, ed., *Creeds of Christendom*, vol. 1, 934.

145. Hereafter cited as CH. Adams first scholarly publication dates from 1967 when she was an Instructor in Philosophy at SUNY College of Cortland , cf. Adams, "Is the Existence of God a 'Hard' Fact?"

146. Here after cited as HE.

147. CH, 1.

> My topic is Christology; my thesis, the coherence of Christology; my theme, Christ as the One in Whom all things hold together. Existentially, Christ is the integrator of individual positive personal meaning; psychologically, our inner teacher; body-politically, the organizer of Godward-community. Christ saves us by virtue of being real and really present: Emmanuel, God with us, sharing our human condition; ascending to His most glorious throne in heaven and God's right hand; in the most blessed sacrament of the altar; and in the hearts of all His faithful people.[148]

Adams proposes a christological solution to the problem of horrendous evil through what she terms a three-stage "defeat" of horror by Christ (the "horror-defeater"). She seeks to do this by presenting a "high" or Chalcedonian understanding of the person of Christ. The dilemma that Adams tackles is the impossibility for human beings existentially to arrive at personal meaning in the face of horrors.[149] The goal is to "to re-present robust Christology as a viable competitor in the market place of religious and theological worldviews."[150] Her essay is thus a detailed christological synthesis that insists that through the incarnation God's horror-participation in Christ defeats horror (i.e., evil) and leads to the assimilation and union of humanity with God, i.e., an unapologetic affirmation of universal salvation.[151] Adams, a philosophical theologian, proffers as givens that the problem at hand is "the non-optimality of the human condition generally and divine–human relations in particular" and the "the solution" is Christ.[152] For Adams, human non-optimality is epitomized by the prevalence of horrors in human existence. Horrors or horrendous evils damage or destroy human meaning-making capacities: horrors, both committed and suffered, are evils that give "*prima facie* reason to doubt whether the participant's life could have positive meaning for him/her on the whole."[153] Adams asserts that vulnerability to horrors fundamentally characterizes human existence: "*God has created us radically vulnerable to horrors, by creating us as embodied persons, personal animals, enmattered spirits in a material world of real or apparent scarcity*

---

148. CH, 1.
149. CH, 32.
150. CH, 13.
151. CH, 49, 51.
152. CH, 18.
153. CH, 32.

such as this."[154] She breaks down these "systemic and metaphysical" issues into three aspects: (i) the developmental and biological aspects of human beings which yield to vulnerability to destruction and perversion; (ii) the inherent insatiability of human desire that outstrips the capacity of the material world to satisfy it; and (iii) "the metaphysical mismatch between Godhead and humanity, the enormous gap between Divine and human personal capacities" which makes "communication difficult and trust hard to win."[155] Thus, human sin is a symptom and a consequence of the fact that God has created human beings vulnerable to horrendous evils, but it is not the cause of human non-optimality.[156]

Adams remains consistent throughout *Christ and Horrors* and this leads to an inevitable conclusion: if human horror-participation is integral to this created universe, then God is *responsible* for such horror. While Adams agrees that God cannot sin, God nonetheless has been "setting us up for horror-participation."[157] This divine responsibility for our "non-optimality problems" carries several implications, each of which seems in some way problematic. First, the sacrifice of Christ on the cross is, in part, "something like an *expiation* by which God acknowledges and accepts responsibility for our plight."[158] The passion and death of Christ are thereby radically transformed into acts of divine self-redemption and a sacrificial offering *to* human beings rather than (or as well as) *for* human beings. Second, Adams posits that God desired our materiality. This is emphatic within Adams' writings—we are material beings in a material world, because God loves materiality. Thus, human bodily resurrection *kata sarka* is affirmed. Yet, the reason human beings are so vulnerable to horrors is because we are material, fleshly creatures. Third, if this foundational turn demands theodicy in response, Adams will not concede because "God has no obligation to creatures."[159] Adams tries to find a way out of this difficulty by insisting that she is simply giving *explanatory* (rather than *justifying*) reasons for God's actions. Her main explanatory reason is the hypothesis that God desired a material world and desired

---

154. CH, 37. Emphasis original.
155. CH, 38.
156. CH, 37.
157. CH, 275; 52, cf. CH, 270; 273.
158. CH, 309. Emphasis mine.
159. CH, 43.

to achieve assimilation and unity with it.[160] Even so, this explanatory approach does not eliminate the question of theodicy. In fact, the concept that God has no obligation to creatures seemingly demands rather than eliminates further elaboration. However, such elaboration is not given.

Soteriology of Horrors in Three Stages

Adams' soteriological argument is that in Christ, God has taken on human nature and by doing so has become vulnerable to the same horrors to which humanity is subject. To this end, she understands Christ in his earthly ministry to have shared all our weaknesses and temptations, but takes issue with the orthodox understanding of Christ's impeccability.[161] Here, Adams insists that Jesus must share our status as horror-participants, including sin. Indeed, for Adams, horror-participation is part of the sin problem. This causes her to make some unusual christological assertions: "if Jesus perpetrates horrors, it is not in the spirit of Hitler" and it is "extremely unlikely that He was a paranoid schizophrenic."[162] Nonetheless, the "Gospels give us a Jesus who was not only a victim, but also an *occasioner* and a *perpetrator* of horrors."[163] While Adams maintains a high christology in the metaphysical sense, she claims a "low" christology when it comes to the humanity of Jesus of Nazareth—for only someone who is truly like us in our horror-participation is able to defeat horror.[164] We are thus saved by the incarnation of a *humanly* fallible Savior.[165]

God overcomes horrors in Christ, offering the "only currency valuable enough to make good on horrors,"[166] namely Jesus Christ himself. This involves three stages. Stage I "turns merely human horror-participation into occasions of personal intimacy with God" and means that "materials for lending positive meaning to any and all horror-participation are already planted in the history of the world here below."[167] This connects individual horror-participation to the individual's relation to God.

---

160. CH, 44.
161. CH, 79.
162. CH, 72, 73.
163. CH, 71. Emphasis mine.
164. CH, 66.
165. For an interesting comparison, see Tanner, "Incarnation, Cross, and Sacrifice."
166. CH, 47.
167. CH, 47.

To accomplish this, "Christ must share *human vulnerability to horrors*."[168] For Adams, this means more than the traditional understanding of Christ carrying the sins of the world within him on the cross. Jesus not only suffers the horrors of the crucifixion (as the sin-bearer of the world), but he also occasions horrors. Adams understands the incarnation to mean that Jesus is, like all human beings, a full horror-participant (victim and perpetrator). Thus, Jesus is the *cause* of Herod's slaughter of the innocents (by being born) and the later destruction of Jerusalem in 70 CE under Emperor Titus. God in and through Christ's presence and ministry on earth indirectly contributes to the violence endemic in Roman-occupied Palestine. Thus, Christ is a horror-perpetrator. Jesus as the only begotten Son of God is *not* imbued with impeccability, but is rather possessed of a perfection of will in that he does not act with malign intent or apart from his divine purpose.[169] The divine purpose of Jesus is to enter into and defeat horror. Christ saves us by this horror-defeat.[170]

Stage-II horror-defeat involves the "healing and coaching" of our meaning-making capabilities so that we recognize what is already the case in stage I. This requires Christ to be our "inner teacher" who thereby draws human beings into friendship with God and one another. In Christ, the whole cosmos is united. Since Christ is the One "through whom all things were made,"[171] he is the architect of creation and the agent by which God created the cosmos, doing so out of the passion for unity and assimilation with this material creation. Thus, God desired "to be Christ for a material world such as this."[172]

In stage III, the "relation of embodied persons to our material environment is renegotiated so that we are no longer radically vulnerable to horrors."[173] Thus, we shall all be transformed (cf. 1 Cor 15:51). Both stages II and III require immortality because it is not possible to be invulnerable to horrors in this life. Until the eschaton, death is the one horror that no human being escapes. It is the dissolution of all meaning-making

---

168. CH, 47. Emphasis original.

169. Contradicting Heb 4:15: "For we do not have a high priest who is unable to sympathize with our weaknesses, but we have one who in every respect has been tested as we are, *yet without sin*."

170. CH, 71.

171. Nicene-Constantinopolitan Creed (381): δι' οὗ τὰ πάντα ἐγένετο. DS 150.

172. CH, 191.

173. CH, 48

capacities either by destroying the meaning-maker (*Ganztodtheorie*[174]) or by separating the soul from the body (*anima separata*) and thereby displaying the destructibility of human existence.[175] In order for God's purpose in creation to be fulfilled, the damaged or destroyed meaning-making capacities of human beings must be restored *in the flesh*.

A Sacrifice and Sacrament to Humanity

Adams additionally explores the role of sacrifice in its relation to horrors, in fact positing that the human-divine interaction is routed in sacrifice. In doing so, she equates human existence, which is horror-filled, with human sacrifice: "the horror-participant is the victim in a human sacrifice."[176] It is noteworthy that in her rejection of theodicy, Adams admits that this sacrificial aspect is built into human existence by God and yet, even though God indirectly perpetrates horrors, God "is the only good great enough to defeat horrors and restore us to positively meaningful lives." Yet, God is the One who sacrifices "human beings as holocausts insofar as death and horrors are known, if unintended, side effects of Divine creative policies."[177] Adams philosophical commitment to her christological project makes no excuses for God's "creative policies" and insists that this same God is entirely worthy of human love and worship. For Adams, the metaphysical gap between humanity and the Godhead is so great and God's remedy so perfect that the fact that God permits horrors and holocausts requires no justification, only explanation.

The divine sacrifice requires materiality—in the person of the God-Human. Thus, the sacrifice of Calvary is God's self-sacrifice to humanity *which propitiates our anger against God* for creating us in a world full of horrors. The crucifixion is indicative of God's sorrow for subjecting us to these horrors. The cross is eucharistic, but as a sacrifice of thanksgiving *to* humanity in "gratitude to us for living a human life in this horror-ridden world."[178] God's engagement in this 'gift-exchange' of reciprocal sacrifice "allows God to accept horror-participants as worthy offerings. . . . Their deaths and/or destruction of their meaning-making capacities return to God the very gift that God offered in the first place: the gift of being a

---

174. Cf. Jüngel, *Tod*; ET: *Death*, 115ff.
175. CH, 208–9.
176. CH, 271.
177. CH 274.
178. CH, 275–78.

personal animal, an enmattered spirit in a material world such as this. Horror for horrors!"[179]

It is here that Adams begins her treatment of the 'sacrament of the altar.' The Lord's Supper becomes a drama that re-enacts the sacrifice of Calvary, but in a way that is radically different from the inherited sacramental theology of the Western and Eastern churches. Here Adams makes some of her boldest assertions: we are invited to masticate the flesh of God. God "invites us to get even, horror for horror, urges us to fragment God's own Body in return for the way God has allowed horrors to shred the fabric of our lives."[180] The Eucharist therefore is a sacramental vehicle for us to bring our complaints to and rage at God for the evils we experience. God in Christ responds by expiating himself through the self-offering of his own body in the form of material bread and wine, food and drink, that we consume and by doing so we are sacramentally compensated for our sufferings.[181] This turns this sacrament upside down. It is neither a re-presentation of the expiatory sacrifice of Christ to the Father for the sins of the world nor a mere re-enactment of the Passover meal in the Upper Room. It is rather an outward and visible sign of divine *contrition* for the horrendous state of the world that we live. In effect, Adams has turned this sacrament into God's apology for the human condition—a bold reinterpretation.

(The Lack of) Divine Judgment

In *Horrendous Evils and the Goodness of God*, Adams develops a soteriological model of the "honor code" which she derives from social anthropology, particularly the categories of honor and shame in contemporary, rural Mediterranean society. In this context, honor centers "not on the evaluation of deeds, but on the sacred quality of persons."[182] She then changes the paradigm of human ascriptive honor to that of divine ascription with God as a cosmic *fons honorum*. Thus, God confers honor on persons and expects such persons to act honorably. However, persons honored by God do not always act in kind, such as when the sons of Jacob sell their brother Joseph into slavery (cf. Gen 37:27ff). However, Adams asserts that God too can be seen to violate this honor code, such as the

179. CH, 281.
180. CH, 294.
181. CH, 306.
182. HE, 107.

four hundred years of divine neglect of the Israelites resulting in their slavery in Egypt (Cf. Gen 15:13; Exod. 1:8).[183] However, just as Adams asserts that God has no obligations to creatures, she likewise claims that God owes honor to no one. Yet, God's divine honor code will overcome evil, human and otherwise, above all through the incarnation of Christ who honors "the suffering and humiliated with His presence and by identifying with them...." God does this because God is the greatest good—a good greater than which nothing can be conceived (Anselm). God also honors human beings in the same way as divine honors are given within the Trinity: "What else could lovers give each other in utopia, what can the Blessed Trinity offer one another, if not honor, mutual expressions of appreciation, praise, and thanksgiving for who the other is?"[184] In other words, God honors human beings like gods. (Cf. Ps 82:6).

Adams takes this concept of divine honor and applies it to the last judgment—and this is one of the rare occurrences of this topic within Adams' eschatological writings:

> ... the honor code allows even universalists to accommodate the Biblical threat that Judgment Day will put us to shame. For whatever else it means, Judgment symbolizes God's making plain and public the truth about Who God is, who we are, and the evaluative truth about what we have been and done. ... How could any created person not hide his/her face when confronted with the fact that s/he is not even the kind of thing that could respond to God appropriately ... ? [Nothing] will do anything to lessen that shame.[185]

Adams refers to this as "ontological shame." However, at this judgment with its inevitable, radical shame, God will use ascriptive honor to overcome it by convincing us that we are radically honored—made worthy—by God's full participation in and solidarity with incarnate humanity. Thus, the shame will be removed and human beings will enjoy God forever "in acts of mutual appreciation."[186]

As already noted, Adams' soteriology is overtly universalist so it is perhaps not surprising that divine judgment is not a major focus of her theology. In her later work, *Christ and Horrors,* her treatment of divine

---

183. HE, 113.
184. HE, 126
185. HE, 127. Emphasis original.
186. HE, 128.

judgment is briefer still. She does not refer to the honor-shame argument, but rather engages in an explanation of the medieval scholastic understanding of the last judgment with reference to Aquinas, Bonaventure, Quaracchi, and Parma:

> Medievals insist that that Divine justice requires that the *very same* agent who acted *ante mortem* be rewarded or punished *post mortem*. . . . Consequently, for Divine justice to be executed and manifested, the human dead must rise. . . . Inspired as they were by Scripture, medieval accounts posit a *juridical* connection between our earthly careers and our *post-mortem* status. . . . We rest on our laurels or sink into our depravity. Thus, death is the deadline for moral or religious achievement.[187]

Here Adams returns to her important posit that resurrection in the flesh is required. She rejects a juridical judgment and any insistence that death is a salvific deadline. In fact, death as a deadline is impossible because human persons are horror-participants and true "moral and religious achievement" is not possible *ante mortem*. She writes further:

> My own systematic assumptions take me away from the idea of a momentary final verdict pronounced from without. Rather, redemption from horrors involves the recovery and appropriation of positive personal meaning from the worse we can suffer, be, or do. Stage-II horror-defeat requires God to heal and enable our meaning-making capacities. Follow-through on the Divine design of human nature will involve God in enlisting the collaboration of the created person in reconstituting his/her fragmented self, and this suggests a *process*—*if* ante-mortem psychotherapy is an analogy, a long and arduous process—rather than a "twinkling-of-an-eye" declaration. Stage-II horror-defeat requires God to overcome our fear that God hates us. For Divine-human relations to become optimal, or even excellent, many radical misunderstandings of Divine intentions will have to be cleared up. If *ante-mortem* psycho-spiritual experience is an analogy, the cure might come through a dramatic "breakthrough" experience of the bigness of Divine Goodness followed by the labor of integrating of this datum into the rest of the horror-participant's life. This task of setting the "breakthrough" experience up against the experience of horror, and of questioning and disputing God for their meaning, is one that itself occurs

---

187. CH, 239. Emphasis original.

in the presence of the Goodness, of the Inner Teacher Who is increasingly recognized as God's own self.[188]

For Adams, divine judgment takes on a psychotherapeutic dimension with Christ as therapist. In this respect, there is in actuality no judgment and no verdict, but rather a type of eschatic *processus salutis* that heals human beings (horror-participants). The shame at the judgment is merely an unpleasant realization. Thus, divine judgment is more akin to divine diagnosis and treatment. This apparent lack of judgment is due to the fact that for Adams the world that God created is full of horrendous evils which prevent human beings from being fully accountable for their actions. Therefore, human accountability for sin is greatly reduced. The Christ who will "come again in glory to judge the living and the dead" will not actually pass any judgment. Even so, she does specifically refer to the "great judgment seat of Christ" (cf. 2 Cor 5:10):

> My own view is that Christ is judge according to His human nature. The manifestation of His resurrected and glorified wounds publishes the truth about our ante-mortem human condition, and the truth about God's everlasting ability, resourcefulness, and intentions to restore human beings thereby. Christ as God-man is judge, the One Who renders the final verdict on God's projects in material creation, because Christ is the One in Whom Stage-I, Stage-II, and Stage-III horror-defeats hold together.[189]

This is a striking assertion—that Christ is judge in his humanity and not in his divinity. This must be coupled with Adams' denial of the impeccability of Christ's humanity—Christ is sinless only in his deity. It will therefore be a one-time fallible yet still human judge, who was also a horror-participant and horror-perpetrator, like all other humans, who stands in judgment over creatures at the eschaton.

Human beings are part of God's project. The resurrected and glorified wounds of Christ are, for Adams, symbolic of the eventual restoration of humanity. In addition, the wounds also symbolize the self-judgment of God by God in the Son's incarnation wherein he suffers radical vulnerability to horrors with humanity. Christ joins us in horror-participation. To better illustrate this, it is worth reading what Adams says of her soteriology and the problem of human sin:

188. CH, 239–40. Emphasis original.
189. CH, 241.

> Naturally, I agree that Christ solves the sin-problem, but I do not identify this as the primary way of conceptualizing His soteriological job. I see the sin-problem in terms of dysfunction that is derivative from the metaphysical mismatches God has set up in creation: between the personal and the animal dimensions of human being, between human being and our material environment of scarcity, and between human being and Divine personal capacities. But *Divine* power working on the inside will be required to help us pull ourselves into functional coordination and *Divine* power will be required to renegotiate our relation to our material environment into something non-toxic. Consequently, I understand the sin-problem as something Christ deals with according to His *Divine* nature, which is sinless. Christ's human nature allows Christ to join us in horror-participation.[190]

Christ's salvific task is to restore human meaning-making capacity. Sin is a problem, but it is a by-product of other problems. She further writes:

> I take a page from Tillich and other neo-orthodox twentieth-century theologians to contend that *meaning* is the issue and *horrors* are the problem. I have defined horrors as evils participation which makes positive meaning *prima facie* impossible for the participant. Like Tillich, I have seen the meaning-problem as a fundamentally *ontological* problem, one that underlines and explains our propensity to inauthentic choices and living, and doing the kinds of things that medieval and reformed theology identified as sin.[191]

Sin is recognized, but the cause of sin is also recognized as horrors-participation. Therefore, there is no retributive, distributive or punitive function to divine judgment. There is only a *therapeutic* function:

Since the cure for horrors is the making of positive meaning, and the restoration to the horror participant of the capacity to make positive meanings; and since the process of letting go of the old and groping towards the new is and can be a painful process, all horror participants can expect to undergo painful rehabilitation. But whether one is a horror perpetrator or victim will make a big difference to the concrete steps and stages of rehabilitation, as well as to the particular shape of the positive meaning that can be made. Can we even begin to imagine the excruciating

---

190. CH, 79. Emphasis original.
191. CH, 205. Emphasis original.

process involved in Hitler's developing an empathetic capacity to suffer with those whom he tortured?[192]

In the judgment, Christ recognizes the human need to be rehabilitated from horror-participation. Continuing the psychotherapeutic model, Adams speculates that horror-perpetrators will be required to develop empathy by experiencing the suffering of their victims in a long, arduous process in order that their salvation may be achieved. This is certainly a novel eschatological model, but it also far removed from the harrowing accounts of the judgment in the Bible and later creedal formulae. The Christ who in the Gospels will divide the sheep from the goats will do no such thing at the judgment according to Adams. In this model, human beings are all sheep—the only "goat" is, in effect, God in Christ at Calvary.

Evaluation

The approach to soteriology and divine judgment in Adams is certainly unique. She changes the traditional understanding of the mission of Christ from one of saving human beings from sin and eternal death to one of restoring human meaning-making capacities. The world that human beings live in is dystopian and this dystopia is of God's own making. Indeed, the world for Adams is hellish—the tormented souls are the horror-victims and the devils are the horror-perpetrators. All are horror-participants, including Jesus Christ. As one sympathetic reviewer of *Christ and Horrors* wrote:

> It is bracing to encounter a contemporary commitment to the traditional account of God's attributes that does not seek to mitigate the consequences of divine foreknowledge, even though it may be impossible for those of us who are less philosophically astute to consider this a God worthy of worship, regardless of the awesomeness of God's works to mitigate the problems God decided to create.[193]

Yet, whether one is philosophically astute or not, it is perfectly plausible to accuse Adams of a type of dystheism. The God who willfully creates such a world with human beings so completely vulnerable to horrors does not seem like a God worthy of worship. The rejection of

---

192. Adams, "Horrors in Theological Context," 476.
193. Tonstad, "Review of *Christ and Horrors*," 32.

restricted-standard theism and bold assertion that "God has no obligation to creatures" has disturbing implications. However, Adams nonetheless presents a clear argument that affirms her belief in God as ontologically love and that the world, although indeed a form of dystopia, is the best of all possible worlds, especially due to the positive eschatological outcome that is divinely guaranteed.

The horrors of the world cannot be defeated until "the relation of embodied persons to our material environment is renegotiated so that we are no longer radically vulnerable to horrors."[194] This eschatic transformation of our existence constitutes the final defeat of horrors. Adams' incarnational theology is stated without apology: to be in true "solidarity with horror-participants, God must experience evils within the limits of a finite human consciousness, with a mind that can be 'blown' and at least *prima facie* unable to cope with horrors."[195] I find this radical approach to the incarnation to be a strength in her overall system.

However, I argue that Adams' reductionist approach to divine judgment creates severe challenges for the doctrine of God and human accountability. The judgment, which is a driving theme in Christianity, is reduced to an event where humans experience shame: "for the average person, at not trusting the One Who is completely trustworthy; for the wicked, of having hated Unsurpassable Love."[196] Shame, even if it is cosmic, ontological shame, is hardly a consequence for sin or evil actions, especially because God immediately removes this shame once it occurs. The purgatorial suffering required of "the wicked" is not a result of the judgment nor is it a punishment—it is simply a more intensive form of therapy.

The reason that the only verdict at the judgment is shame is that God created a dystopia full of horrors—so horrible that human beings are rendered into juveniles that cannot be held fully accountable in the divine court. Human sin, no matter how horrible or even genocidal, is reduced to a form of juvenile delinquency. As in human courts of law, youthful offenders are deemed to not have sufficient moral agency to be held accountable for their actions, even heinous acts. Such persons are normally released from detention when they reach adulthood. In effect,

---

194. CH, 48.
195. CH, 197–98.
196. HE, 127.

Christ is rendered into the magistrate of an eschatic court for young offenders. Human beings are thus divinely infantilized.

I take issue with Adams "psychotherapeutic" eschatology and her concept of the eschatic rehabilitation of horror-participants. While the idea of Christ as "Inner Teacher" has some resonance in tradition, it strikes me as highly reductionist: Christ in the last judgment is anthropomorphized into a therapist. It also seems too simple to deny human responsibility for evil actions due to human vulnerability to horrors.

The psychotherapeutic model also leads to another problem: for Adams, human beings are all, quite literally, mentally ill. The world is a madhouse. That said, considering the atrocities of the twentieth century alone, as eccentric as this claim may be in a theological text, it is arguably a valid claim. War and violence can indeed be said to be forms of insanity. Even so, another issue emerges: if God has created the world such that there is a metaphysical mismatch within human nature, between human nature and the material world, and between God and humanity, is not God both the author of human insanity and the eschatic therapist that cures the insanity at the eschaton? For Adams, this does not seem to be a problem. As she has emphasized, God has no obligation to humanity—which jettisons any sort of covenantal relationship. Even so, God in Christ has entered into the disordered material world which God created and God loves. The answer to the complaint that God has created (or at least permitted) a horror-filled world is the cross, the Eucharist, and the universal restoration—God is aware of what God has done; God has entered into our radical vulnerability and suffered its reality in Calvary; God gives us himself in the sacrament of the altar in material form as an *ante mortem* peace-offering; God will restore human beings *post mortem* to be invulnerable to horrors and to enjoy eternally the beatific vision. In short, God plays by God's own rules. For Adams, these acts by God in Christ more than compensate for the temporary and finite horrors of this world. She writes:

> For God to succeed, God has to defeat horrors for everyone. We have all been to hell by being tainted by horrors *ante-mortem*. We all will meet the horror of death at the end. For some, life has been one horror after another between the dawn of personhood and the grave. . . . To be good-to us, God will have to establish and fit us all for wholesome society, not establish institutions to guarantee that horrors last forever in the world to come![197]

---

197. CH, 230. Emphasis original.

While I appreciate what Adams is trying to do, I argue that her eschatological scheme negates divine judgment and also negates the possibility of salvific judgment—that salvation occurs within the act of judgment itself. Rather, the only thing that happens at the judgment is tantamount to the divine scolding of a brutalized, childish humanity that simply did not and could not know better. Actual salvation (reconciliation) happens after the judgment and not in it or even because of it. However, if human beings have any eschatic free will, why is it assumed that they would accept these post-resurrection therapeutic interventions from the God? This is the God who not only created a world full of horrendous evils, but also put human beings in that world knowing that they would be tortured to the point of non-accountability. Hence, I would argue that Adams' universalism fails because it is entirely reasonable that some human beings, now realizing what God has done to them, might freely *reject* this God as malign and choose exile in hell, which is, after all, the only reality they have ever known. Thus, Adams needs to explain whether human free will is eschatically operative and if so, whether it is also "healed" or whether it remains intact in spite of therapy with the ability to accept or reject the outcome. A healed human will that accords with the supreme freedom of God might yield a universalist outcome, but a sovereign will that is not amenable to eschatic transformation leaves the outcome in doubt.

6. Conclusion

In this chapter, I have assessed the soteriologies of four theologians noted for promoting overt or hopeful universal salvation. The question that I posed at the beginning is: do these theologians locate salvation (reconciliation) within the judgment? The secondary question was whether their salvific optimism is convincing.

Sergei Bulgakov clearly sees the eschatic judgment as the locus of salvation and retains much of the imagery associated with hell but transposes it into a purgatorial encounter with God's love. Bulgakov's eschatology is mystical, complex, but full of hope. The stumbling block is that while Bulgakov wants to assert that human free will is inviolate, his own ontological eschatology makes divine love not only irresistible, but inevitable because the very being of the human person is radically transformed. Thus, the preservation of earthly free will in the eschatic reality would be impossible. Yet, this is never clearly spelled out. The problem of evil is notably absent in this mystical work, perhaps because it was written *sub specie aeternitatis* towards the end of his life, a life that saw him an exile from Russia and a resident of Nazi-occupied Paris at the time his death. His sophiological commitments demand that he see the "big picture" that the humanization of the world as God's ordained project meant that despite the horrors of the world, God's salvific plan for the cosmos can never be thwarted. Thus, for Bulgakov, divine judgment is both the judgment of love and the event of salvation. It can be assumed that even unreformed eschatic human free will (which would seem to be impossible in his overall schema) cannot obstruct God's saving love. Bulgakov ends all his later books with the final words of the Book of Revelation: "Even so, come Lord Jesus!" (Rev 22:20). For Bulgakov, the parousia is an unstoppable force, always already happening, and it cannot be defeated.

Hans Urs von Balthasar provides the much more modest proposal of a hopeful universalism. Against his critics, he asserts that all should hope and pray that all will be reconciled with God. However, he is theologically restrained by his faithfulness to the teaching magisterium of the Catholic Church. This restraint means that Balthasar cannot assert the aphorism *iudicandus est salvandus*. Yet, he is silent on the problem of eschatic evil that remains if hell is populated. It would seem that for him revelation forbids going beyond universal hope, but he provides a useful corrective to the received tradition that asserts a salvific pessimism. One of his most striking and persuasive arguments is that human beings are always already under judgment. Indeed, the Christian tradition asserts this from its earliest creeds—the parousia of Christ is always the coming of the glorious Judge of the cosmos.

J. A. T. Robinson's early work on eschatology can be said to fully agree with Bulgakov. They both assert that judgment is salvific and that the judgment in grounded in divine love. The interesting things about Robinson is that his approach is entirely Western and his theological sources differ entirely from that of Bulgakov. In a very limited sense, one could argue that *In the End, God* . . . is a Western Protestant answer to the Eastern Orthodox *The Bride of the Lamb*. The two books are separated in time by a mere six years. Like Bulgakov, but more intensely, Robinson stumbles over the issue of human free will. It could be argued that if human will is deemed to be eternally inviolate, then Robinson is following this logic, which owes more to the Enlightenment than to earlier forms of Christianity. After all, for Luther, the human will is in bondage. Divine love for Robinson is irresistible and like "love at first sight" the human will shall freely yield to the Lover who cannot be refused. It might be called eschatic exhaustion. However, unless Robinson is willing to allow for the transformation of the human will at the judgment, it is questionable whether his project is plausible. It is fine to say that God's love cannot be scorned, but if that is true, then human will is not entirely sacrosanct.

Marilyn McCord Adams' christological project has fascinating soteriological implications. It breaks from received tradition freely while at the same time engaging in a free-wielding *ad fontes* exercise. Her high-low christology allows for an incarnational eschatology that brings creativity to the theologies of the cross and the Eucharist. Despite God's decision to create a material cosmos which leaves creatures vulnerable to horrors, the God who does this is still one of ontic love. And this love is made manifest in Christ, the God-Human, who incorporates earthly vulnerability into the triune Godhead. God plays by God's rules. The cross is part of divine experience and the gloriously transformed wounds of the Risen Christ, redolent of the resurrection panel of the Isenheim Altarpiece (1512–16), is a prolepsis of human futurity in the eschatic realm. Our wounds shall be as glorious as those of Christ.

However, Adams is strangely sparse in her comments on divine judgment, other than her striking assertion that we will be judged by Christ according to his human nature. Adams rejects that human beings in a world of horrors can make decisions of eternal import. Thus, one could say that human beings cannot be judged in the normal sense of this word in the same way that human courts cannot serve adult judgments on juveniles. Rather, the eschatic judgment is a therapeutic event, an event of healing. There is indeed consequence for sin, but this is solved by creating empathy in eschatic persons. Adams does not deal with human free will at the eschaton, perhaps because our status as horror-participants means that we do not have actual free will. However, by not discussing the eschatic transformation of human free will, she leaves herself open to the possibility that an eschatic person may reject the Divine Therapist and choose exile in what would be hell. Like Robinson, Adams assumes her project cannot fail, but likewise it is easily attacked by those for whom human freedom is a good that must remain "earthly" even in the eschaton. All the "optimistic" theologians explored understand divine judgment as a good thing, a place where divine mercy is fully operative. Balthasar is unwilling to say whether such mercy might permit some human being to suffer external separation in hell or how such a state squares with an eschatic reality that is wholly good. Bulgakov and Robinson are the theologians that can agree with the aphorism 'to be judged is to be saved' while Balthasar and Adams are silent, although for very different reasons. However, none of them state plainly that judgment is the event of eschatic reconciliation. It is in the next two chapters that this proposal will be further constructed and explored.

CHAPTER 4

The Purpose of Divine Judgment

1. Introduction

IN THIS CHAPTER, I shall explore the purpose of divine judgment. By purpose, I mean the rationale for the divine judgment of human beings: why is there any judgment at all; what is its goal; what is its outcome? One could question why an infinite God would exercise judgment on finite creatures. As Marilyn McCord Adams notes, the metaphysical gap between Creator and created is "enormous" and thus any such judgment could be understood as meaningless.[1] However, Christian tradition (and indeed the Abrahamic faiths collectively) asserts that God does indeed judge every person individually and all of humanity collectively. The received tradition has asserted that divine judgment is retributive, one of rewards and punishments. However, another way of looking at the judgment is *division*, as in the division of humanity between the sheep and the goats in Matthew 25:31–46. Interestingly, this Gospel passage refers to works of love rather than faith in Christ:

> Come, you that are blessed by my Father, inherit the kingdom prepared for you from the foundation of the world; for I was hungry and you gave me food, I was thirsty and you gave me something to drink, I was a stranger and you welcomed me, I was naked and you gave me clothing, I was sick and you took care of me, I was in prison and you visited me . . . .[2]

---

1. Cf. Adams, CH, 38. Adams herself does *not* argue that divine judgment of human beings is meaningless.

2. For a recent commentary on this parable, cf. Evans, *Matthew*, 421–424. Evans

Yet, the Christian tradition has generally presumed that salvation (reconciliation) is granted to those who confess Christ (cf. Rom 10:13). To this could be added certain ecclesiological requisites such as Cyprian's formula *nulla salus extra ecclesiam* (and by the fifth century CE there are competing *ecclesiae* in this matter); or that one must profess a certain formula of faith, such as the Apostles' Creed. In addition, some would add water baptism as a requisite to "salvation" (cf. Mark 16:16). So, even the requisite of confessing Christ as Lord and Savior is often qualified. That said, we could arrive at this division:

1. Those who confess Christ and die repentant and thus in a state of grace;

2. Those who confess Christ, but die with imperfect penitence ("venial" sin);

3. Those who confess Christ, but die totally impenitent ("mortal" sin);

4. Those who do not confess Christ.

The first two categories would usually be deemed to be among the "saved" with the second category perhaps undergoing some sort of purgation. The latter two categories would be deemed among the damned. It is noteworthy that good works or personal virtue play no role in these four categories. This is a "by faith alone" division, in spite of the Epistle of James that states "faith without works is dead" (Jas 2:17). However, a Pelagian salvation by good works alone has not been deemed part of the received salvific tradition; neither has salvation by character (e.g., living a virtuous life).[3] But even so, is it possible to divide humanity in these ways? This division becomes further complicated by the assumption of a dual outcome: the saved and the damned. Is this twofold division the purpose of judgment? The theologians discussed in chapter 3 would deny this, or at least hold this belief in doubt. While my own thesis insists that divine judgment is the judgment of love and is salvific, thus holding in doubt a dual outcome, it is necessary to explore the purpose of judgment from different angles before any proposals can be made.

---

names this parable "The Reward for the Merciful."

3. The British monk Pelagius (354–c.440 CE) denied original sin and claimed that human beings are capable of obeying the moral law without divine assistance. His ideas were condemned by the Council of Carthage (418) and this was affirmed by the Council of Ephesus (431). Cf. Lamberigts, "Pelagius and Pelagians."

2. Judgment's Purpose as Dualistically Retributive

The received tradition is that divine judgment is retributive dualism: it results in either eternal reward or eternal punishment. Even if one dispenses with the concept that the judgment is about rewarding those who confess a certain creed or have communion in a particular church, the belief in a retributive judgment is dominant in the Christian tradition.

The Received Tradition: Matthias Joseph Scheeben

> Opposed to the mystery of justification and grace is the mystery of sin. So, likewise, opposed to the shining mystery of heavenly glorification, whereby God crowns His grace and rewards the justice of man, there must open up an abyss of darkness and nothingness into which the justice of God thrusts those who have abused the grace offered them, and have turned its blessing into a curse.[4]

There are many sources within Christian tradition to explore the teaching that divine judgment is retributive. Scheeben (discussed previously in chapter 2, section 4) provides a succinct and creative summary of retributive judgment. In this schema, the purpose and outcome of judgment is positive or negative retribution; reward or punishment. For those who have responded positively to the operation of grace in their *ante mortem* lives, God will "reward" (*belohnen*) them with a positive transfiguration (*positive Verklärung*) into a state of everlasting glory. For those who have misused the grace God offered them on earth (i.e., rejected it), there will be the "curse" (*Fluch*) of a negative transfiguration (*negative Verklärung*) into an eternal state of damnation. However, in fairness to Scheeben and his most famous work cited above, *Die Mysterien des Christentums*, he only describes hell for a mere ten pages in a work that is almost eight

---

4. "Wie dem Mysterium der Gerechtigkeit und Gnade gegenüber das Mysterium der Sünde sich uns darstellte: so muß sich hier gegenüber dem Mysterium der Verklärung, womit Gott das Werk seiner Gnade krönt und die Gerechtigkeit des Menschen belohnt, ein Abgrund der Finsterniß öffnen, in welchen die Gerechtigkeit Gottes diejenigen hinabstürzt, welche die ihnen dargebotene Gnade mißbraucht und deren Segen in Fluch verwandelt haben." Cf. Scheeben, *Die Mysterien des Christentums*, 607. ET: Scheeben, *The Mysteries of Christianity*, 684. Note that English translator interprets "Mysterium der Verklärung" as "shining mystery of heavenly glorification," which is poetic rather than literal.

hundred pages long.⁵ For Scheeben, judgment's purpose is, above all, the glorification of humanity and the granting of the beatific vision. Scheeben explains at length that God's salvific will is universal. The divine desire is that all will be glorified, but this desire does not come to pass. This echoes Thomas Aquinas statement *"hoc ita non evenit"* ("It doesn't turn out this way"). Divine judgment is retributive in that it "pays back" the human response to God's grace *ante mortem* positively or negatively. Justifying grace renders human beings worthy of glorification while rejection of grace renders human beings worthy of damnation. This is the purpose and outcome in received tradition which *ex opere operato* would presumably exclude all non-Christians and those Christians who did not persevere in the faith until death.

The Received Tradition Revisited: Paul O'Callaghan

> [J]udgment may be considered as the definitive and universal revelation of the gift of salvation, whether received or rejected, that is consolidated in each human life lived historically, the very manifestation of the meaning of history. Salvation is offered to humans, but the offer will not last indefinitely. Judgment marks the end of God's concrete offer of mercy. After that, repentance will no longer be possible, for the just will remain perpetually separated from the unjust.⁶

For a modern conservative Catholic interpretation of the purpose of divine judgment, I turn to Paul O'Callaghan (b. 1956), Professor of Christian Anthropology at the Pontifical University of the Holy Cross, Rome, and a priest member of Opus Dei. In his book *Christ Our Hope: An Introduction to Eschatology*, he devotes a full chapter to the topic of the "final judgment."⁷ O'Callaghan maintains the distinction between the particular judgment and the final judgment, noting the problem of duplication, but maintaining it as something that finds "a sufficient basis in Scripture and in the Fathers of the Church."⁸ For O'Callaghan, judgment is retributive and the outcome eternal and dualistic—one of eternal life or eternal punishment. O'Callaghan sees judgment (in its final form) as the univer-

---

5. Other than the brief chapter on negative transfiguration, hell and damnation are not mentioned at all, except to mention that Christ has conquered hell. Cf. ET: 310.

6. O'Callaghan, *Christ Our Hope*, 136.

7. O'Callaghan, *Christ Our Hope*, 130–48.

8. O'Callaghan, *Christ Our Hope*, 281.

sal revelation of each person's historicity and the collective history of humanity. Each person's earthly biography is judged just as all of humanity is judged. Yet, this will result in the separation of the just and the unjust. Those human beings and their biographies who did not die in a state of grace cannot be redeemed at the judgment. For O'Callaghan, God's mercy is restricted to earthly life and neither *post mortem* repentance nor mercy are available to the "condemned": "The possibility of condemnation for the unrepentant sinner is a nonnegotiable [sic] element of the doctrinal patrimony of Christian faith."[9] However, O'Callaghan adds a seeming element of hope to this state of affairs:

This does not mean of course that Christians "believe" as such in hell. Much less are they obliged to believe that some specific individuals have actually been condemned, or that a certain percentage of believers have forfeited, or will have to forfeit, eternal life forever. Rather they believe in God who has created humans in such a way that they are capable of freely losing the reward of communion with the Trinity promised to those who are faithful, if they do so in a clear-minded, responsible, and irrevocable way, that their alienation from God becomes insuperable.[10]

The hope would lie in whether human beings, no matter their earthly wickedness, are capable of such an irrevocable decision. As was noted, Adams has said that the metaphysical gap between humans and God is such that human beings have no capacity to make decisions of eternal import. O'Callaghan's anthropology insists that human beings do possess this ability. In the end, O'Callaghan is pessimistic: "Even though it is possible at a hypothetical level that all will eventually be saved (if each one can be saved, one and all may be saved), it is clearly unwarranted to believe in the salvation of all . . . ."[11] In addition, *pace* Hans Urs von Balthasar, O'Callaghan does not believe that universal salvation can be "an object of Christian hope in the strict sense of the word."[12] Thus, for O'Callaghan, judgment itself is not salvific: "judgment is judgment and salvation is salvation."[13]

---

9. O'Callaghan, *Christ Our Hope*, 189.
10. O'Callaghan, *Christ Our Hope*, 189.
11. O'Callaghan, *Christ Our Hope*, 218.
12. O'Callaghan, *Christ Our Hope*, 221.
13. O'Callaghan, *Christ Our Hope*, 136.

Conclusion

Clearly, the proponents of the dual outcome of judgment, which is the received tradition of Christianity, do not see divine judgment as salvific in itself. O'Callaghan makes this very clear: judgment and salvation are distinct and should not be conflated. The purpose of judgment is the division of humanity into the saved and the damned, the sheep and the goats. It holds no possibility for eschatic repentance. Death closes the door to the human response to God. While universal salvation may be a noble hope, it is not justifiable. O'Callaghan is well aware of the hopeful eschatology of Hans Urs von Balthasar, but he does not consider it to be a valid expression of the received tradition. The *Catechism of the Catholic Church* is clear on the matter: "To die in mortal sin without repenting and accepting God's merciful love means remaining separated from him for ever by our own free choice. This state of definitive self-exclusion from communion with God and the blessed is called 'hell.'"[14]

Neither Marilyn McCord Adams' critique that human beings do not have the capacity to make such decisions nor the arguments of J. A. T. Robinson that God's love is omnipotent and thus cannot allow the damnation of any holds any weight. The only solution to a dual outcome of judgment would be that every person in the moment of death repents and accepts God's love. If human history is any guide, this is to be held in total doubt. Could God convict every person and make the offer of grace in the moment of death? This is certainly within the power of the divine omnipotence, but this would still require free choice on the part of each person. Thus, it would seem a dual outcome is inevitable in this type of eschatology. Scheeben, although inclined to God's mercy and cognizant of God's universal salvific will, cannot find a way for the misusers of grace to avoid a negative transfiguration. Thus, human free will, in the end, defeats the salvific will of God. This judgment's purpose can only be division and hell must remain an eternal part of the eschatic reality. To requote Paul Griffiths, "This is not a pleasing picture."[15] This may be why some theologians who desire to be faithful to the tradition have turned to a doctrine of annihilationism.

If the purpose of judgment is retribution in the form of a dual outcome, the end result is eternalization of evil in the eschaton. This presents enormous problems for the doctrine of God as has been already discussed.

14. CCC 1035.
15. Griffiths, *Decreation*, 247.

It also would imply that God is unable to defeat evil. It is only in moving away from salvific dualism that this problem can be potentially solved.

3. Judgment's Purpose as Salvific Retribution: Sergei Bulgakov

> *If what has been built on the foundation survives, the builder will receive a reward. If the work is burned, the builder will suffer loss; the builder will be saved, but only as through fire.*
> —1 Corinthians 3:14–15

Bulgakov's concept of divine judgment has already been discussed above in chapter 3, section 2. However, it is necessary to explore further his oeuvre here because of his unique understanding of retribution. Bulgakov is deeply critical of Christian theology's concept of judgment as retributive. However, this is not because he denies that there is a retributive element in judgment, but rather because he believes that the concept is misunderstood.

The Pre-Eschatic Judgment of Dormition

The concept that the dead live in an "afterlife" that Bulgakov refers to as dormition has been discussed in chapter 2, section 3. However, what is at issue here is not an intermediate state between death and resurrection, but the purpose of judgment. In the following passage, Bulgakov critiques the understanding that the "particular judgment" is retributive after the manner of human jurisprudence:

> Although the terms *retribution* and *reward* are found in Scripture and are even uttered by the Lord Himself, we must understand them not as an external juridical law (which would be contrary to the spirit of Christ's gospel) but as an ontological connection, an internal necessity, according to which an individual suffers to the end all that is inappropriate to his vocation but what was committed by him in earthly life: "he himself shall be saved; yet so as by fire" (1 Cor. 3:15).[16]

Additionally, Bulgakov doubts that retribution is applicable to anyone that is not a Christian at death: "the overwhelming majority of

---

16. NA, 368. Emphasis original.

humankind."[17] This is a radical concept within Christian orthodoxy (Western or Eastern) because it presumes that those who are outside Christ will *not* be subject to a particular judgment in the intermediate state. So, what is the purpose of the pre-eschatic judgment?

It is also necessary to recognize that this afterlife of an individual in communion with the spiritual world is not less important for his final state than early life and, in every case, is a necessary part of the path that leads to universal resurrection. Every individual must, in his own way, ripen spiritually to this resurrection and determine himself with finality both in good and in evil. One must therefore conclude that, even though in resurrection an individual remains identical to himself in everything he has acquired in earthly life, nevertheless, in the afterlife, he becomes other than he was even in relation to the state in which he found himself at the moment of death. The afterlife is not only "reward" and "punishment," and not only a "purgatory," but also a spiritual school, a new experience of life, which does not remain without consequence but enriches and changes each individual's spiritual image. We know nothing about the degree or manner of this process. But it is important to establish that, even in the afterlife, human souls experience and acquire something new, each in its own way, in its freedom.[18]

Thus, the judgment in the "dormition" is not static or passive. The psycho-spiritual human being, divorced from her earthly body, is in a dynamic state of "ripening." The processes (of which we know nothing) are preparatory for the resurrection and the final judgment. In some ways, this is analogous to persons who die in a state of "venial" sin and experience purgatory in anticipation of release into "heaven" in Catholic eschatology. However, the analogy is limited. For Bulgakov, all human beings are in this state of dormition and all are ripening. The Christian who dies may experience a type of purgatorial "fire" for failing in his vocation as a disciple of Christ (which is a type of judgment), but that Christian is in the company of all human beings who "live" in the mystery of the pre-eschatic dormition. In some sense, this "ripening" is reminiscent of Schleiermacher's *Zwischenzustand* as discussed in section 2.3.6, although Bulgakov's "dormition" is hardly the Elysian intermediate state that Schleiermacher implies.

---

17. NA, 369. The reference to 1 Cor 3:15 occurs frequently throughout Bulgakov's *The Bride of the Lamb*.

18. NA, 363.

Bulgakov explains that the cause of this ripening is rooted in the self- recognition of the person of her earthly life:

> In death and after death, an individual sees his past early life as a whole, in its synthesis. The latter is, in itself, already a judgment, for it clarifies the general connection, the content and meaning of the life that has passed. Here, there is a clear vision not only of the synthesis but of the truth itself, in the presence of the spiritual world, free of all carnal partiality, in the light of divine justice. This is the self-evidentness [sic] of the divine judgment.[19]

Death then provides a person with an immediate global vista of the self, of an entire autobiography, that is seen and recognized *nude, clare et aperte* to borrow the words of *Benedictus Deus*.[20] Rather than beholding the beatific vision (which Bulgakov does not imply is possible in this intermediate state), the person is given what might be called the *visio humana ipsius* (the human vision of herself). This results in self-judgment because it would be impossible to ignore this vision. In a sense, the pre-eschatic judgment is human judgment that anticipates divine judgment at the eschaton: "The afterlife state is a stage of the path leading to resurrection."[21]

Does this mean that it is possible to repent in the "dormition"? The answer is an emphatic *yes*. Bulgakov is fully aware that most theologians "consider death to be the limit that represents the end of the time of deeds and the beginning of the time of retribution, so that, after death, one can neither repent nor correct one's life" and that this is deemed, by them, to be a dogma of the Christian church.[22] However, for Bulgakov, those in the "dormition" are still *in life*, even if it is a "reduced form of life" due it its discarnate state.[23] For him, it is possible to assert that those in the pre-eschatic dormition are (in spite of horror film allusions) the "living dead" and thus they are capable of growth and change.[24] To restate this, persons in the "dormition" having undergone the self-judgment that is afforded them will not be the same persons who experience resurrection and the judgment of Christ.

19. NA, 360.
20. See chapter 2, section 3.
21. NA, 366.
22. NA, 368.
23. NA, 368.

24. I am aware that the term "living dead" is associated with a genre of horror films. Cf. *Night of the Living Dead*. Directed by George A Romero. Los Angeles: Image Ten, 1968.

The Purpose of the Eschatic Judgment

> Heaven and hell are, above all, a summation of life not only in its fullness and complexity but also in its diversity of forms. It is not by chance that the Lord speaks of *many* mansions in His Father's house which signifies first of all the diversity of their forms. And this diversity can be composed of different combinations of hell and heaven, life and death, incorruptibility and perdition in one and the same human destiny.[25]

The general scheme of Bulgakov's understanding of judgment has already been discussed. However, what is the purpose of this judgment, this intrapersonal separation in which the sheep-self is "saved" and the goat-self is annihilated? For Bulgakov, human beings are not sheep or goats, wheat or weeds (cf. Matt 13:24–30)—they are always *both*. Bulgakov only allows for two persons to be exempt: Jesus (cf. Heb 4:15) and his mother Mary: "But no one is perfectly sinless except the Sole Sinless One and the Most Pure Mother of God."[26] Christ is sinless because of his divinity and Mary is sinless because of her election to be the *theotokos*, the God-bearer. Yet, for Bulgakov, all human beings possess a sophiological anthropology: "the union in man of the Divine Sophia (the proto-image) and the creaturely Sophia (the "likeness"), divine creative power and creaturely freedom."[27] Using the passage from Genesis that human beings are created in the image and likeness of God (cf. Gen 1:26), Bulgakov interprets "image" and "likeness" in a unique way. Human beings possess divinity (as bearers of the image of the triune God manifest in Christ as Divine Sophia) and "creaturely freedom" (as bearers of the likeness of God; i.e., creaturely Sophia). For Bulgakov, Mary is the manifestation of creaturely Sophia.[28] The reason for his Mariological position relates to her assumption as the first human after Christ to be resurrected where "[s]he abides *at the boundary* of heaven and creation."[29] In other words, the proper destiny of all human beings is to become, as it were, like Mary.

Interestingly, in spite of Bulgakov's very high Mariology, Mary cannot enter the fullness of heavenly glory until the eschaton because she is a creature just like all human beings. For Bulgakov, as for many

25. NA, 465. Emphasis original.
26. NA, 462.
27. NA, 465–66.
28. NA, 414.
29. NA, 414. Emphasis original.

in Christianity, Mary represents the ideal human being who exercised her freedom without flaw. Thus, while Bulgakov would not suggest that Mary is subject to judgment, for the sake of argument, if Mary did pass before Christ at the judgment she would not be purged of the "goat-self" or the "weed-self." In other words, she would pass through the judgment unscathed and only glorified. This would be deemed orthodox belief for Eastern and Oriental Orthodoxy, as well as Catholicism. It would be held in doubt or denied by Protestantism. However, my point here is to not get side-tracked by Marian doctrine. The issue is Bulgakov's theological anthropology and its intersection with divine judgment.

Eschatic Anthropology: The Antinomic Judgment

For Bulgakov, human beings are antinomic. They are living paradoxes who are simultaneously saints and sinners (Luther's *simul iustus et peccator*). This state applies universally *intra et extra ecclesiam*. The reason for this has already been implied in terms of Bulgakov's admittedly controversial concept of the "sophianicity" of humanity. For Bulgakov, human beings are not simply made in the image of God, but also in the image of Christ (the Logos; a manifestation of the Divine Sophia). One could say that every human being is therefore a proto-Christian. This may seem to agree with Karl Rahner's concept of the "anonymous Christian," but it does not. For Rahner, to be an anonymous Christian is to be a person "who lives in the state of Christ's grace through faith, hope and love, yet who has no explicit knowledge of the fact that his life is orientated in grace-given salvation to Jesus Christ."[30] For Bulgakov, human beings are ontologically proto-Christians. But if this is true, how is it possible that human beings can be wicked?

Whatever may be the differences between different individuals as far as their personal sinfulness is concerned, this sinfulness always has an element of delusion and error, of acts of accomplishment in the name of an imaginary good. Pure evil for the sake of evil, satanic evil, is something not proper to man, who bears the principle of good. In individual cases, evil can decidedly predominate, but, in the final separation, evil itself is known only in conjunction with, even if in conflict with, good. In this sense, hell is a function of heaven, and evil is the shadow of the good, not only in the world in general but also in every human being in particular. It follows that the separation of the sheep and goats is accomplished (of

30. Rahner, *Theological Investigations*, vol. 14, 283.

course to different degrees) within every individual, and his right and left sides are bared in this separation. To a certain extent all are condemned and all are justified. A condemnation that would be the final casting into outer darkness (nonbeing) is metaphysical death. Even to be rejected, a person must have in himself the power of being; that is, he must find support in the image of God given to him. Thus, the *judgment* and its sentence introduce into the life of every person an antinomic separation that consists in participating in glory and incorruptibility, and, at the same time, burning in the fire of divine rejection.[31]

The first thing that is striking in this passage is the idea that no human being can be purely evil. Thus, there can be no Augustinian-Calvinist reprobation nor can the *imago Dei* be totally corrupted in a human being. No person is created for wrath and damnation. It also implies that the villains of history and persons that partake in despicable acts of evil are *salvageable*. They are able to be "saved" because the antinomic separation will quite literally split them in half. Such persons will be ontologically divided into two parts: sheep and goat. The "goat-self" will be subject to the loving hell of divine rejection—it will be burned away. And the person will experience this as the torment of divine love—which as Bulgakov says is the "most terrible judgment."[32] Heaven and hell exist in all human beings because every person has misused her creaturely freedom (i.e., has sinned). Thus, the purpose of judgment is to restore human beings to the "likeness" of God—which is theosis, the divinization of humanity. And this process will involve the seemingly impossible duality of glorification and damnation in each person:

> How can damnation and blessing go hand in hand? Or how can the one who was sent "into the world not to condemn the world; but that the world through him might be saved" (John 3:17) pronounced with love: "depart from me, ye cursed, into everlasting fire" (Matt. 25:41)? God's love, it must be said, is also His justice. God's love consumes in fire and rejects what is unworthy.... One must reject every pusillanimous, sentimental hope that evil committed by a human being and therefore present in him can simply be forgiven, as if ignored at the tribunal of justice. God does not tolerate sin, and its simple forgiveness is ontologically impossible. Acceptance of sin would not accord with God's holiness and justice. Once committed, a sin must be

---

31. NA, 462.
32. NA, 459.

lived through to the end, and the entire mercilessness of God's justice must pierce our being when we think of what defence we will offer at Christ's Dread Tribunal.[33]

This is a harrowing image of judgment and yet, in spite of the merciless piercing human beings will have to endure, it is done "with love." Sin can be forgiven, but the consequences (penance) cannot be avoided or absolved. There can be no earthly indulgences, works of charity, or even earthly penance that can cause a human being to avoid this fate. While this fate is personal, it is also collective: "Both man's life and his responsibility are conditioned by and linked with the destinies of the whole human race."[34] Thus, while human sins are unique to individuals and vary in degree, all will endure *together* this eschatic separation. No one endures the judgment alone. This is indeed retribution for sin, but it is *salvific retribution*. The end result of this process is that the "goat" or "weed" part of a human being, depending on his or her degree of earthly sins against love, will be annihilated: "It is precisely to this ontological condemnation, which is also metaphysical annihilation of what is condemned, its transformation into a phantom, into a nightmare vision, that the Scripture's pitiless words about death, perdition, annihilation, destruction, and disappearance refer."[35] While this is retributive, it is *not* punishment because divine judgment "is not the execution of any external laws and norms, whose violation entails punishment."[36] Bulgakov consistently refuses to allow human concepts of judicial rewards and punishments to be applied to divine judgment. But while it is not punishment, it is horrific. The "nonbeing" of evil (which is "antisophianicity") that is within every human being (except the *theanthropos* and *theotokos*) will be experienced as a

> ... metaphysical dying, a perishing, an eternal torment, a judgment of justice, a seeing of himself in the light of justice. Every human being experiences this in his own way, in conformity with his wrong state and to the degree that it is wrong.... But it is necessary to say again, with maximal force, that which constitutes the very essence of the judgment and immortal life: "Annihilation" is *not* spiritual death, and it does not extend to the entire being of a person. It is a separation or spiritual amputation,

33. NA, 475–76.
34. NA, 458.
35. NA, 463.
36. NA, 463.

so to speak, but not death by execution. In other words, the very possibility of this separation presupposes a person's participation in eternal life and therefore in its bliss, but also presupposes his burning in hell. Union in separation is an unfathomable (for the present moment) mystery of judgment and of the life of the future age. How can one life contain a union of joy and sorrow, of bliss and the torment of terrible remorse and late repentance, of a vision of the divine proto-image of creation and the dead form of one's own (even if only partial) nonbeing?[37]

It would seem in this passage that salvific retribution implies an eternal split within human persons in the eschaton so that we are experiencing heaven and hell, in varying degrees, simultaneously. This would *seem* to eternalize hell (strangely as a manifestation of God's love) with human beings in a state of perpetual agonies and ecstasies. This is hardly a welcome outcome. However, this is not what Bulgakov means. While this antinomic union occurs in the judgment, it is not part of eternal life—the life that is initiated from the judgment. If a hellish state of affairs was eternalized, it would mean that Christ is unable to conquer hell. It would also mean that the "sophianicity of the world has encountered a limit to itself in the antisophianicity of hell, in which the outer darkness in the absence of God's light, the dark antisophia, reigns."[38] This state of affairs is not possible because God is omnipotent and his Holy Wisdom cannot fail. "Antisophia" is effectively the antichrist—who will be defeated at the eschaton. The very suggestion that anything anti-Christian could endure is absurd to Bulgakov: "Such are the stupefying conclusions to which penitentiary theology leads."[39]

The Goal of the Antinomic Judgment as Universal Salvation

The question that then must be asked is what is the purpose of hell? As has been cited, Bulgakov claims that any sin has a consequence that must be "paid for" in full: "hell's torments of love necessarily contain the

---

37. NA, 463–64.
38. NA, 483.
39. NA, 483. "Penitentiary theology" is the term Bulgakov uses to refer to the idea that hell and eternal torment can be eternalized. This is also a subtle critique of Augustine of Hippo (whom he names) and he adds this comment: "To frighten theologically is a fruitless and inappropriate activity. It is unworthy of human beings, who are called to the free love for God." Cf. NA, 483.

regenerating power of the expiation of sin by the experiencing of it to the end."[40] But more interestingly, human beings willingly and fearlessly submit to this purgatory. Human beings in the judgment are not passive. They are active participants; they are irresistibly persuaded by the evidence of their earthly biography set before them with prefect clarity; and they are not cast into hell, but rather willingly welcome it as a means to heal their intrapersonal division. Thus, the purpose of the parousia of Christ and the judgment is a separation that leads to "the goal of universal salvation or the sophianization of creation."[41] If there is an eternity of torments, hell or antisophia, God's creation is a failure. But this cannot be:

> ... the judgment that separates the sheep from the goats and good from evil, both in humankind in its entirety and in individual hearts, is not the definitive conclusion of eschatology. It is only the first event of eschatology, the beginning, not the end. Both the judgment and the separation must be understood not as a static unchangeability but as a dynamic striving beyond their limits, on the pathways to universal deification or salvation. Only deification is capable of justifying creation. It is the only theodicy.[42]

In spite of what seems like a brutal purgatorial *processus salutis*, the purpose of judgment is, in the end not simply salvific retribution, but universal theosis. The retribution of the judgment is not imposed upon passive human beings by Christ, but rather willingly entered into by them. To *see* oneself clearly without any earthly limit or filter is to know how one has failed to act in love on earth. Christ is the proto-type of humanity and it is in the synergistic measuring of our own biography with its acts of non-love that we see our failings before Christ who is ontic love. We are thereby, without coercion, convicted of our sins and seek their purgation willingly by freely experiencing the hellish love that, with the sword of the Spirit, excises and puts to death all that is unloving in each of us. This non-love is nonbeing, antisophia, and antichrist and it is not proper to humanity nor the image that we reflect.

All human beings will be resurrected and glorious and within this glory there is also the fire of hell—it is in actuality part of our glorification.

---

40. NA, 498.
41. NA, 501.
42. NA, 501.

This does mean that those persons who have committed heinous acts of hatred (antisophianic actions) will share in this glorification, although the degree of their hellish intrapersonal division is beyond description and hidden in the mystery of the parousia. However, what can be said is that their sins will demand a "metaphysical dying" that fully expiates their terrible, but finite sins on earth. What remains will be saved, although it may be only a glimmer of glory that remains after the chaff is burned away. Bulgakov makes an allusion to 1 Corinthians 15:41 (AV) to explain this aesthetic difference: "one star differeth from another star in glory."[43]

Conclusion

For Bulgakov, judgment is in some way bipartite: one that happens in the bodily dormition and one that happens in the resurrection. However, the "afterlife" state that precedes the eschaton is more or less preparatory for resurrection. It is in this "dormition" that human beings are granted for the first time a perfect vision of their earthly biography. There they are able to ripen in a "spiritual school" (which for Bulgakov is an experience *in life*) and indeed they are capable of repentance. In the eschatic judgment, the fullness of human anthropology as "sophianic" is revealed. All that is antichrist is separated and cast away in the judgment and this process will be analogous to hell. Yet, humans enter this purgation of antinomic judgment willingly, compelled by their self-recognition and self-judgment, and allow all that is non-love to be excised. This process results in the purified lamb, the part of the person that is sophianic, to be glorified. Thus, all are "saved" by this process.

However, what is interesting is the end result. Making an allusion to 1 Corinthians 15:41, the implication is that each person will have a certain remainder of sophianicity (Christ-likeness). For some, it may be total (e.g., Mary), for others mostly intact, but for some it may be only a glimmer of the self that is salvageable by the spiritual surgery of the judgment. Thus, while all persons will be saved, it may only be a fraction of the earthly person that experiences deification. It would seem that the person (whose glory may shine dimly compared to others) has continuity with her earthly personhood (and memory of her earthly life), but that which is glorified may only be faintly recognizable in the eschatic community as the person that was known on earth. It would therefore seem that the "whole" person as constituted on earth who chose to be unloving

43. NA, 465.

in the majority of his being *is not* saved. Rather, for Bulgakov, such an eschatic "remnant person" would agree that his state is just and proper (and it would seem there is no choice in the matter). If such an eschatic person is of lesser glory, it is not a punishment. It is simply a fact of the eschatic reality where evil (nonbeing) has no place. Additionally, the *semper novum* aspect of the eschatic reality may mean that such glorified persons *may* continue to grow and in a sense "rebuild" what was separated at the judgment. This is because Bulgakov does not identify creaturely eternity with divine eternity. Rather, creaturely eternity in the eschatic reality is "ascent from glory to glory" (cf. 2 Cor 3:18).[44]

I find Bulgakov's concept of the purpose of judgment compelling. It is always referenced to divine love and thus the motivation of God in the judgment of human beings is grounded in this love. It implies a desire for *relationality* with all persons (even the most wicked) that have been created in the divine image. To enable loving relationality, all persons must be transfigured and made glorious, even if the purgative process to cause this transformation is one of "eschatic torment" that is beyond earthly human knowing. The one problem that arises is that of free will and the heinous earthly crimes that can occur with its misuse. As Paul Gavrilyuk noted, "Bulgakov's grasp of the problem of evil falls short of the profound insights of Dostoevsky . . . ."[45] This may be true, but the real question would be whether God's insistence on the sophianization of the cosmos (such that the universe reflects the image of Christ "through whom all things were made") overrides the creaturely free will of human beings. In other words, is God's grace irresistible? An answer from Bulgakov, however unsatisfying, might be that while grace is resistible, the Divine Sophia in Christ has created all human beings with its image as creaturely Sophia. This image must be restored because Christ cannot be defeated. This conquest would appear to defeat any "anti-sophianic" free will that human beings may try to retain, even at the eschatic judgment. This does not solve the problem if one holds that unreformed human free will must endure eternally. But for Bulgakov, human will is only truly "free" when it reflects the image of Christ. In other words, human beings only have "true" free will after their glorification.

The other aspect that I find challenging in Bulgakov's process of judgment is the extremity of its torments. Certainly, the finite character

---

44. NA, 478.

45. Gavrilyuk, "Universal Salvation in the Eschatology of Sergius Bulgakov," 132.

of these torments is hopeful. But the process seems horrendous—in effect, retaining the medieval concepts of purgatory and hell and translating them as the finite hellfire of love. It may be arguable that the villains of history "deserve" this fate, but this strikes me as a human desire for revenge. It would seem that divine correction could be achieved in a different way that did not use the symbols of earthly torture.

4. Judgment's Purpose as Non-retributive and Rectifying: Jürgen Moltmann

> The Christ with the two-edged sword in his mouth who exercises retributive justice towards human beings, with reward and punishments, is unrecognizable. He has nothing to do with Jesus of Nazareth, the preacher on the Mount, the healer of the sick, and the forgiver of sins. This retributive judge cannot be the Christ who was crucified for us and has risen ahead of us.[46]

It might be said that Jürgen Moltmann (b. 1926) is the theologian *par excellence* who insists that divine judgment is non-retributive.[47] Moltmann considers retributive divine judgment, in the form of a human criminal court, as atheistic. This is because he rejects the concept of God as a retributive judge because it contradicts God as the creator. In effect, for Moltmann to hold both beliefs about God is to believe in either a self-contradictory God or two Gods.[48] In addition, he believes that the received tradition of God as a wrathful judge is the cause of "much spiritual and psychological damage."[49] Due to this problematic eschatology, Moltmann posits that modern (liberal) theology has supplanted God as judge with human freedom: human beings determine whether they will go to heaven or hell: "So doesn't this make God superfluous? Belief in the freedom of the human will replaces belief in God."[50] Instead, Moltmann argues for an entirely different approach to divine judgment. He refers to divine justice as "God's creative justice."[51] In other words, divine judgment is the event that makes human persons and the entire created

---

46. Moltmann, *Sun of Righteousness, Arise!* 133–34.
47. Cf. Ansell, *The Annihilation of Hell*, 340ff.
48. Moltmann, *Sun of Righteousness, Arise!* 133.
49. Moltmann, *Sun of Righteousness, Arise!* 134,
50. Moltmann, *Sun of Righteousness, Arise!* 134.
51. Moltmann, *Sun of Righteousness, Arise!* 136.

order become righteous: "divine righteousness ... has nothing to do with rewards and punishments. It is a righteousness that creates justice and puts people right, so it is a redemptive righteousness (Is. 1.27)."[52]

Justitia justificans not *justitia retributiva*

> Jesus broke through the legalistic apocalyptic, because he proclaimed *justitia justificans* rather than *justitia retributiva* as the righteousness of the kingdom of God, and anticipated it in the law of grace among the unrighteous and those outside the law.[53]

The kingdom of God that will be established at the parousia will radically include the wicked and those outside the law (i.e., *extra ecclesiam*). Any human conception of the righteous or elect being rewarded with heaven and wicked or reprobate being damned are excluded. For Moltmann, the final judgment is strictly the consummation of Christ's reconciling project:

> This Judgment has to do with God and his creative justice, and is quite different from the forms our earthly justice takes. What we call the Last Judgment is nothing other than the universal revelation of Jesus Christ, and the consummation of his redemptive work. No expiatory penal code will be applied in the court of the crucified Christ. No punishments of eternal death will be imposed. The final spread of the divine righteousness that creates justice serves the eternal kingdom of God, not the final restoration of a divine world order that has been infringed. Judgment at the end is not the end at all; it is the beginning.[54]

The latter part of this statement is telling. For Moltmann, the eschaton is not about a final restoration of a fallen world—and it is not the "last thing" at all. Rather, it is the beginning of something entirely new. Part of the newness of the kingdom of God, now universalized, is that all things will be made righteous and redeemed. In effect, "justifying justice" is rectifying rather than retributive. The victims of evil will receive justice. God will "raise them up out of the dust, will heal their wounded lives, and put to right the lives that have been destroyed."[55]

52. Moltmann, *The Way of Jesus Christ*, 335.
53. Moltmann, *The Crucified God*, 177.
54. Moltmann, *The Coming of God*, 250.
55. Moltmann, *Sun of Righteousness, Arise!* 135.

But what about the wicked? At first glance, it seems that evildoers get off scot-free for their *ante mortem* sins. Nicholas Ansell asks this question in his exhaustive exploration of Moltmann's universalism:

> What exactly is the relationship between this judgment and this revelation that transforms God's enemies into the righteous? . . . Does this "creative" justice have anything to do with the justice for which those who have suffered from the horrendous injustices of history long for with all their hearts? Are their oppressors to be brought to justice or simply justified?[56]

Of course, Moltmann consistently disclaims divine retribution. So, it would seem that the oppressors of the victims of history will not be "punished" at the judgment. However, while Moltmann does not allow for retribution, he does allow for condemnation and annihilation:

> Judgment is the side of the eternal kingdom that is turned toward history. In that Judgment all sins, every wickedness and every act of violence, the whole injustice of this murderous world and suffering world, will be condemned and annihilated, because God's verdict effects what it pronounces. In the divine Judgment all sinners, the wicked and the violent, the murderers and the children of Satan, the Devil and the fallen angels will be liberated and saved from their deadly perdition through transformation into their true, created being, because God remains true to himself and does not give up on what he has once created and affirmed, or allow it to be lost.[57]

Thus, what is condemned and destroyed is not the perpetrator of wickedness, but the wickedness itself. It is sin itself that will be obliterated, not sinners. The wicked will be liberated from their "deadly perdition." However, if we consider the horrendous evils (to use a phrase favored by Marilyn McCord Adams) perpetrated by human beings that are part and parcel with earthly life, it does appear that the only eschatic consequence of evil actions is the triumph of grace: "Transforming grace is punishment for sinners . . . ."[58] The question that must be asked is what does this transformation entail? Is it the harrowing Bulgakovian fire of divine love that splits a person in half and burns away the chaff of sin? Is it the seemingly gentle eschatic "psychotherapy" of Marilyn McCord

---

56. Ansell, *The Annihilation of Hell*, 343.
57. Moltmann, *The Coming of God*, 255.
58. Moltmann, "The Logic of Hell," 47.

Adams that requires that perpetrators review the evils that they did and the consequences thereof as a means of eschatic repentance and healing? Moltmann does not give a succinct answer and Ansell considers this a *lacuna* in Moltmann's eschatology.[59]

However, this does not mean that Moltmann denies that the villains of history will not *answer* for their crimes at the judgment. He rejects conditional mortality as the fate of the wicked (i.e., that the wicked die and do not rise) because "it excludes God's judgment. Mass murderers might possibly welcome this solution, because they would not have to answer before God's judgment for what they have done."[60] Another aspect of the judgment is that it will be social:

> The judging of victims and perpetrators is a *social judgment*. We do not stand before the judge just on our own dependent on ourselves as we do in criminal courts, or in night time torments of conscience. In that other [divine] judgment the perpetrators stand together with the victims, Cain with Abel, Babylon with Israel, the violent with the helpless, the murderers with the murdered, the persecutors with the martyrs. . . . This means we ought to imagine the last judgment as a peaceful arbitration whose purpose is the furtherance of life, not as a criminal court which decides over life and death.[61]

This view of the judgment, which is more akin to a truth commission, may not be satisfying to the theological tradition that demands consequence for sin. It is however radical in its social element and the insistence that perpetrators must stand with their victims and answer for what they have done. It is perhaps in this exercise that the "punishment" of "transforming grace" occurs.

The Judgment of the Crucified God

A crucial way to understand Moltmann's rejection of any retribution in the divine judgment is through his *theologia crucis*. Christ alone is the bearer of the retribution for human sin. Thus, when Christ comes in judgment, the judgment he brings is *justitia justificans*: "If at the Last Judgment the crucified One himself is judge, the justice that will prevail

---

59. Ansell, *The Annihilation of Hell*, 345.
60. Moltmann, *The Coming of God*, 109.
61. Moltmann, *Sun of Righteousness, Arise!* 139–40.

is his merciful and justifying righteousness, and none other."[62] Thus, for Moltmann, the purpose of divine judgment is *rectification*: it makes that which is wrong right. God's enemies are "made right," but not according to any human concept of justice. For example, Moltmann writes: "It is a source of endless consoling joy to know, not just that the murderers will finally fail to triumph over their victims, but that they cannot in eternity even remain the murderers of their victims."[63] Thus, the murderers will be transformed.

However, Ansell questions whether Moltmann allows for any eschatic reparation on the part of the wicked.[64] While the victims of evil are healed and glorified, the very same thing also happens to their perpetrators. They are simply transformed into righteous people *ex gratia*. Is this then justice of any kind, human or divine? Ansell believes that Moltmann understands that there must be accountability for the perpetrators of evil, after all Moltmann did write (as cited above) that such persons will be made to answer for their crimes at the eschatic judgment. Yet, what Moltmann does not speculate about it is how such persons will be held to account.

For a possible answer, Ansell turns to Moltmann's student Miroslav Volf (b. 1956). Volf continues Moltmann's theme that the judgment is social and that the victims and perpetrators stand together before God.[65] In his essay "The Final Reconciliation: Reflections on a Social Dimension of the Eschatological Transition," Volf envisages the possibility of eschatic reconciliation between persons:

> The divine judgment will reach its goal when, by the power of the Spirit, all eschew attempts at self-justification, acknowledge their own sin in its full magnitude, experience liberation from guilt and the power of sin, and finally, when each recognises that all the others have done precisely that—given up on self-justification, acknowledged their sins, and experienced liberation. Having recognised that others have changed—that they have been given their true identity by being freed from sin—one will no longer condemn others but offer them the grace of

---

62. Moltmann, *The Way of Jesus Christ*, 225.
63. Moltmann, *The Coming of God*, 255.
64. Cf. Ansell, *The Annihilation of Hell*, 344.
65. It should be noted that Moltmann (like Marilyn McCord Adams) is aware that persons can be simultaneously victims and perpetrators. Cf. Moltmann, *Sun of Righteousness, Arise!* 138.

> forgiveness. When that happens, each will see himself or herself and all others in relation to himself or herself as does Christ, the judge who was judged in their place and suffered their fate.[66]

This quote from Volf's essay does seem to expand on Moltmann's theme of the social judgment. There is an eschatic confession of sins "in their full magnitude" before God, the self, and the others. One could speculate that this cosmic confession is in itself a kind of penance and, by the power of the Holy Spirit, the sinner is transformed. This enables interpersonal forgiveness to be offered and received. Former sinners are given their "true identity." There is no speculation in Volf's concept of a punitive character to this "penance of acknowledgment" which is in keeping with Moltmann's insistence that there is no retribution in judgment. So, one can agree with Ansell that Volf has provided a possible answer to where accountability for sin between persons as well as between the person and God plays a part in Moltmann's universalist eschatology.[67] The ecstatically reconciled are to see one another (no matter the magnitude of evil perpetrated and/or suffered on earth) as Christ sees them as the judge, who suffered judgment, retribution, and crucifixion, for their sake, and yet graciously forgives and loves without qualification.

Eschatic Rectification

> Purifying fire, transmigration of souls, the soul's journey, an expiatory passage through faults and omissions of this life are all images.... If we leave aside the external ecclesiastical and political motives that were often bound up with ideas of this kind, and look simply at what it meant, we could after all say: I shall again come back to my life, and in the light of God's grace and in the power of his mercy put right what has gone awry, finish what was begun, pick up what was neglected, forgive the trespasses, heal the hurts, and be permitted to gather up the moments of happiness and to transform mourning into joy.[68]

There is a radical gentleness to this understanding of how human persons will be able to right the wrongs of their earthly biographies at the judgment. The masterminds of genocide will be given this opportunity just as

---

66. Volf, "The Final Reconciliation," 103.
67. Ansell, *The Annihilation of Hell*, 349.
68. Moltmann, *The Coming of God*, 116–17.

those of saintly lives. However, the gentleness is perhaps mitigated by the fact that each one of us at the eschatic judgment will have to "put right" every sinful act we have ever committed in our earthly instantiation. For the ordinary person, this would be a purgatorial task, even if it is deemed a divine mercy rather than retribution. However, for the perpetrators of heinous crimes, this task—even as a mercy—would be "hellish." Ansell quotes Brian Walsh in his commentary on Isaiah 60:14 ("The descendants of those who oppressed you shall come bending low to you, and all who despised you shall bow down at your feet..."):

> Imagine that! Hitler on his knees before 6,000,000 Jews, Oliver North and Ronald Reagan on their knees before Nicaraguan peasants, Prime Minister Botha before Nelson Mandela and Steve Biko, various Prime Ministers and Ministers of Native Affairs kneeling before the Dene, Inuit, Lubicon, and Innu people of Canada, you and I before those we have oppressed.[69]

This political image of the eschaton is interesting because it accords with Moltmann's social and rectifying understanding of divine judgment. It implies accountability, yet also radical mercy. Hitler is not being tortured for crimes he committed (other than within his conscience) and those before whom he kneels are not demanding it. It would appear that for Moltmann the non-retributive judgment of the Crucified Judge will entail a type of profound remorse, so profound as to be impossible without sustaining aid of the Holy Spirit. This would then not be remorse as known to human beings on earth. It would be eschatic remorse, possible only for those transfigured by the resurrection.

Conclusion

> *What is the purpose of Christ's judgment?* When the victims are raised up and the perpetrators put right, the purpose is not the great reckoning, with reward and punishment; the intention is to bring about the victory of creative divine righteousness and justice over everything godless in heaven, on earth, and beneath the earth.[70]

---

69. Walsh, "Who Turned Out the Lights?" 18. Cited in Ansell, *The Annihilation of Hell*, 354.

70. Moltmann, *Sun of Righteousness, Arise!* 137. Emphasis original.

Moltmann presents a non-retributive eschatology of universal salvation. He denies salvific dualism and sees the "justifying justice" of God in Christ as rectifying the cosmos of all that is evil. Human beings will be "put right" whether they are the victims of evil, the perpetrators, or both. The vast Moltmannian oeuvre has no interest whatsoever in retributive judgment. This is not because he is unaware of it or ignores it. Rather, anthropomorphic concepts of justice have no place in the eschatic realm. Christ, the Crucified God, is the one who bears all retribution for the sins of the world. He is the one who dispenses, out of sheer grace, *justitia justificans*. For Moltmann, the Christ of the parousia is the one who says "Behold, I make all things new" (cf. Rev 21:5 AV). This is the eschatic decree and it is (it would seem) irresistible. Any suggestion that human beings can choose hell is rejected as atheistic. A God who reprobates some to damnation in double predestination is effectively dystheism and must also be rejected. The purpose of judgment is to establish cosmic joy in place of the vale of tears of our earthly instantiation. It is this divine power that annihilates evil in all things, including hell itself. There is no possibility of an immortalization of evil in Moltmann's eschaton. The wicked, the followers of the devil, will be put on the path of righteousness and they will have no choice in the matter. The choice for evil is not an option in eternal life because evil (nonbeing) has been destroyed. In effect, if human free will is operative in the world-to-come, it only has a choice of goods.

My critique of Moltmann's concept of judgment's purpose does not concern its aims. To put all things right at the eschaton is hopeful and accords with God's love. However, Moltmann offers a polar opposite approach to Bulgakov when it comes to the consequences of wrong actions. There is a public reckoning and a condemnation of evils—and these evils are destroyed. The "punishment" of the wicked is understood to mean that their evil schemes are destroyed and their victims are healed. Moltmann would agree with Volf's relational aspect as cited above: the purpose of the rectifying judgment is to create right relationships, to achieve reconciliation. However, what Moltmann cannot entertain is an additional possibility that Volf proposes:

> For those, however, for whom the judgment day does not become the giving and receiving of grace, it will be come a day of

wrath leading to a hellish world of indifference and hate. Seeking to justify themselves as Christ the judge reveals the truth about their lives, they will, in Matthean terms, seize their debtors "by the throat," demand payment, and, since it will not be not forthcoming, condemn them "into the prison" until they do pay (Matt. 18:30). They will have thereby showed themselves as not having received divine grace and will therefore be "handed over" by God "to be tortured" until they pay their "entire debt" (Matt. 18:34). To refuse to show grace to the offender and to receive grace from the offended, is to have rejected God's judgment of grace.[71]

The suggestion that the offender and the offended could refuse to give and receive divine grace, mediated by Christ, is not a possibility that Moltmann can entertain. It would mean that God's creative "justifying justice" could be thwarted. It is unclear if Volf's interpretation presupposes that the "entire debt" can be paid later (so a purgatory rather than a hell) or if it might be possible for persons "handed over" to resist eternally. It may be that the question is an open one: an open hell that some may choose to leave, but others may choose as their eternal state. Such a state would be impossible for Moltmann's universalism. It would represent the total defeat of putting everything to right in the new creation. Moltmann *might* allow for an "eschatic waiting room" that permits the recalcitrant to come to their senses and reconcile, but it seems unlikely because: "Nothingness will be annihilated, death will be slain, the power of evil dissolved. What will be dispelled from all created beings is sin, the misery of separation from the living God; hell will be destroyed."[72]

The possibility of non-reconciliation, as envisaged by Volf, would thus be impossible since sin itself will be removed from all beings. Thus, Moltmann's universalism is absolute and remarkably gentle, but human free will is overcome by *justitia justificans*. This leaves the problem between free will and grace unresolved if there is an assumption that free will always endures the judgment and is thus free to reject God's grace.

---

71. Volf, "The Final Reconciliation," 103-4.
72. Moltmann, *Sun of Righteousness, Arise!* 141-42.

5. Judgment's Purpose as the Transformation and Constitution of Personhood: Markus Mühling

Thus far, I have discussed the purpose of judgment as retributive dualism (Scheeben and O'Callaghan), as salvific retribution (Bulgakov), and as non-retributive rectifying universalism (Moltmann). Markus Mühling in his 2007 book *Grundinformation Eschatologie: Systematische Theologie aus der Perspektive der Hoffnung* proposes that the purpose of judgment is the "transformation and constitution of personal identity."[73] In order to explore this, it is necessary to explore how Mühling reaches this concept. Throughout his book, Mühling searches for a "third way" to avoid a dual outcome of salvation and damnation on the one hand and universal salvation on the other.[74] Mühling understands that the parousia of Christ which inaugurates the "eschatic reality" must be totally good.[75] He rejects the dual outcome of eternal reward and eternal punishment as not only compromising the total goodness of the eschatic reality, but because it makes God the author of this dual outcome with the "immortalization of evil."[76] He rejects the concept of an intermediate state ("the post-mortal but pre-eschatic action of God on some humans") because it would involve, to some degree, a "reduplication of the world" by means of a "second chance" that would nullify the eschatological relevance of actions that took place on earth.[77] He also rejects the concept of universal salvation as traditionally construed (*apokatastasis ton panton*) because this would imply that God would delay the eschaton until the damned in some sort of *refrigerium* would finally choose God (the assumption being that they all eventually would do so). Mühling cannot accept this because it implies salvific synergy on the part of human beings rather than the unilateral act of God's grace.[78] Mühling also does not find his third way in the doctrine of election in Christ of Karl Barth, which may or may not imply universal salvation. Lastly, he rejects the concept of "selective judgment" which implies that God can pass judgment on parts of a hu-

---

73. Mühling, *Grundinformation Eschatologie*; ET: *The T. & T. Handbook of Christian Eschatology*, 325ff. All citations marked Mühling with page number are from the English translation.

74. Mühling, *T. & T. Handbook*, 321.

75. Mühling, *T. & T. Handbook*, 326.

76. Mühling, *T. & T. Handbook*, 324-5.

77. Mühling, *T. & T. Handbook*, 321.

78. Mühling, *T. & T. Handbook*, 321.

man being (and excise them) while retaining those parts that are deemed salvageable. He finds this to violate the unity of human biographies and therefore their personhood.[79] He thus seeks for another solution.

Human Beings as Human "Becomings"

> The human being and becoming is a person in reciprocal but differentiated loving relations to God, to fellow humanity and to the non-personal environment. Since these relations can be understood as constitutive rules, they define the being and becoming of humans. Since human beings and becomings do not conform to this rule in the present, their personal being is eschatic, promised to them in the present, and thus remains an object of Christian hope.[80]

Mühling develops his "third way" by proposing a Christian anthropology that is based on the two-fold rule of love: love of God and love of neighbor (cf. Luke 10:27). He does not consider this rule to be deontic, but constitutive. In other words, human beings are constituted in their personhood by their loving relationships.[81] However, human beings do not in the present life conform to the two-fold rule of love because each human being is *simul iustus et peccator*. This means that: "Properly speaking, human beings *are not* yet persons but *will be* persons. In the present, human beings have their personal being and becoming and therefore their identities only in the mode of promise."[82]

Human beings are created in the image of God and for Mühling this implies relationality. It is in human loving *relata* that human personhood is constituted.[83] Since human beings are actually human becomings (they are in the process of becoming persons), their full personhood will only be realized at the eschaton. It is only then that we will be "complete" as persons. For Mühling, this completion of personhood is the purpose of judgment.

---

79. Mühling, *T. & T. Handbook*, 324–5.
80. Mühling, *T. & T. Handbook*, 211,
81. Mühling, *T. & T. Handbook*, 208ff.
82. Mühling, *T. & T. Handbook*, 211. Emphasis original.
83. Mühling, *T. & T. Handbook*, 208.

The Transformation of the World

The goal of judgement is the eschatical reality, which must be conceived as being exclusively good. At the same time, the present world, the world of the here and now, must be of eschatical relevance if the eschatical reality is to be the fulfilment of creation. But, this means that the negative events cannot simply fall out of the relational structure of the process of world events. On the contrary, they will be transformed into events with aesthetic differences.[84]

Mühling understands that the parousia of Christ inaugurates a new reality (an eschatic reality) that "can be only good and nothing but good."[85] He proposes that the

> ... judgement can be understood as God's final action on the world, which translates all remaining ethical differences—that is, variations consisting of more or less good—into goodness without remainder to the extent that ethical differences have no further influence on the eschatical identity since they have been transformed by divine action into aesthetic differences.[86]

This is crucial to understanding Mühling's project of finding a "third way." For him, this means:

> ... believing that the divine action of judgement is that evil will not only be eliminated, annihilated or immortalized through a form of eternal punishment, but that it can be transformed into the good to the extent that it is capable of making a contribution to the non-foreseeable aesthetic form of eschatic reality.[87]

Evil is transformed into a form of beauty that has an assumedly lesser aesthetic contribution to make to the eschatic reality established by God. In other words, all that is not "the good, the true and the beautiful" will be transformed in the judgment into the good.[88] This must be understood as Mühling's global view of the eschatic transformation of the cosmos: persons, non-personal creatures, and the earth, and all creation.

---

84. Mühling, *T. & T. Handbook*, 326.
85. Mühling, *T. & T. Handbook*, 325.
86. Mühling, *T. & T. Handbook*, 326.
87. Mühling, *T. & T. Handbook*, 326.
88. Mühling, *T. & T. Handbook*, 325. See all chapter 3, section 3.

The Transformation and Constitution of Persons

> The objects of the judgment as a transformative and constitutive process are nothing other than the relations of the unfulfilled world, from which persons and their actions and consequences are derived, because persons are the points of intersections of relations, and actions and consequences themselves are relations. The criterion of the judgement is the double surrender of God to humanity in the cross and resurrection of Christ through the Spirit.[89]

It would appear, at first glance, that Mühling argues that human beings are judged on their relationships with earthly *relata* and then constituted into true personhood with an eschatic variance as to that person's aesthetic quality—meaning some are "more beautiful" than others. This would be at least semi-Pelagian because it would appear that humans are judged by works. If so, there would be wrath against those in wrong relationships and reward for right relationships. However, human beings are sinners and no one follows the two-fold command perfectly on earth. Human beings are judged through the redeeming work of Christ and the Spirit (the "double surrender"). In effect, the judgment does not have a retributive component. Rather, because of the work of Christ, the judgment is "what God will make out of [human persons] eschatically."[90] There is no synergy here. This is the unilateral act of grace upon the human being. Thus, there is no judgment in terms of retribution. Rather, the human being's relations, actions, and claims are transformed by God in the eschatic transformation. God constitutes the eschatic person in the new creation. The human becoming becomes a "true" human being. The constituted eschatic person is no longer identified by his or her earthly biography. These aspects are but a part of the constitution of this "new" person. Thus, for Mühling, "*the final judgment is creation*, but not a new creation in the strict sense of the word."[91]

However, what about the truly wicked? The reason they cannot be annihilated or otherwise not "created" is because "they are only first created eschatically by the cross, resurrection, and judgement, and this verdict is retro-causally attributed to human persons."[92] In other words,

---

89. Mühling, *T. & T. Handbook*, 329.
90. Mühling, *T. & T. Handbook*, 328.
91. Mühling, *T. & T. Handbook*, 328. Emphasis original.
92. Mühling, *T. & T. Handbook*, 329.

all are saved by grace. Yet, this is not quite universal salvation—which Mühling wishes to avoid.

Since this judgment is itself constitutive for personal identity, there is to some extent something like a universal salvation in this perspective: if it is the eschatic confrontation between creaturely and divine action that first brings about the fulfillment of creaturely personhood, then God does not annihilate any created person. However, from a non-eschatical perspective at present, the judgment does not mean universal salvation for the individual human being: individual human persons do not know which of their identity claims will endure beyond the judgment, that is, in the actual process of the constitution of the person, and which elements in the relational structures in which they live will be translated into aesthetic differences. And, this process of transformation itself is to be understood as painful: for the person judged, for the persons who relate to them in one way or another and for God as judge as well.[93]

Thus, while no human becoming is ever "lost," the creative process of judgment means that the person living on earth today may be constituted differently in the eschatic reality. This does not mean that there is a loss of continuity between the earthly person and the eschatic person, but rather that certain identity attributes and relational structures may not endure the judgment.

Human Participation in the Eschatic Judgment

The judgment is the process of transformation in which the apparent contradiction between grace and freedom is resolved, in that those that are themselves judged also appear as judges next to Christ, the primary judge. The judgment would then be understood as the perfect revelation in such a way that it discloses the truth about the world and one's own life with certainty according to the twofold command as the criterion of judgment in that the one to be judged, with the help of the Holy Spirit, can do nothing other than pronounce the judgment as to its significance in relation to Christ, however it may turn out.[94]

Mühling makes use of scriptural texts that assign judgment not just to Christ but to the saints (cf. 1 Cor 6:2).[95] However, he makes use of this material to construct a concept of self-judgment. In this case, those

93. Mühling, *T. & T. Handbook*, 330.
94. Mühling, *T. & T. Handbook*, 333.
95. Mühling, *T. & T. Handbook*, 330ff.

who are judged also co-pronounce judgment on the cosmos and on themselves. The Spirit enables them to do this "however it may turn out." As was already discussed, in Mühling's scheme the reason salvation is not universal is because not "all of us" will necessarily be saved (what he refers to as "identity claims"). Thus, in the creative judgment that constitutes our full personhood as eschatic beings, it is actually the human person who judges what is to be constituted as our "heavenly" identity. However, while Mühling says we do this in freedom, it would seem that we do not have a free choice in the matter. One could argue that this is the eschatic freedom that enables us to "[s]tand fast therefore in the liberty wherewith Christ hath made us free, and be not entangled again with the yoke of bondage" (cf. Gal 5:1 AV). Thus, grace and freedom are united because the Spirit resolves the conflict between them. Our participation in judgment is not human synergy because everything is the unilateral act of God's grace.

Conclusion

Mühling's theology of divine judgment as the creative constitution of earthly "human becomings" into eschatic human beings is a fascinating exercise in eschatological exploration that contains a number of creative turns. It is a relational eschatology that sees human beings as "on the way" to true personhood which can only occur in the eschatic event. It has the simplicity of using the twofold dominical command to love God and the other as the overall criterion of judgment. Yet, it avoids dualistic outcomes in either the form of eternal damnation or annihilation. It also avoids the epistemically immodest proposition of unqualified universal salvation. In some respects, Mühling's eschatology could be termed *qualified universalism* with the "duality" being not between the saved and the damned, but rather between those identity claims of each person that will endure the judgment and those that will not. It is also noteworthy that Mühling retains the vexed term "identity." Since human identity is transitory and never static, Mühling prefers to use the term "identity claims." Human beings possess a number of such self-claims at any given time and these claims will be subject to judgment. Not all will be judged worthy. Rather, some will be excluded from constitutive and transformative judgment because they fail the twofold command. Reflecting on Bulgakov's idea of the sheep-self and the goat-self, it would seem that the "goat" identity claims are excluded in this constitution of full personhood.

Mühling's theology of judgment contains certain challenges. There seems to be an element of irresistible grace in the creative unilateral judgment. This puts to question whether human freedom can operate in the eschatic reality—and he shares this dilemma with Bulgakov and Moltmann. This would mean that human beings cannot resist their eschatic creation as "true" persons. Of course, Mühling does not accept the concept that hell can exist as eternal resistance to grace. The painful or purgative aspect that he presents, where the claims and actions that formed the "human becoming" on earth will be judged and may be condemned (the person judging them along with Christ as unworthy by the illumination of the Spirit) could be understood as quasi-retributive. However, it is never a punishment as all wrath for sin has been suffered by the Crucified. This resonates with Moltmann's idea, to a degree, of *justitia justificans.*

Mühling's eschatology would appear to agree with the position of this book: that the divine judgment is the judgment of love and is salvific. The missing element is his cursory treatment of eschatic repentance. Persons undergoing the creative judgment will agree with the verdict of Christ due to its irrefutable character. By the power of the Spirit, they are made able to cast away all unloving identity claims and actions. This seems to be a "lenient" sentence. All that remains of them is that which fulfilled the twofold command of love for God and neighbor. Yet, the act of casting away parts of one's identity must be a radical event, even though it dispenses with the fiery imagery used by Bulgakov.

Even if casting away bad identity claims is painful and a very small percentage of a person's claims and actions are constituted, there is still continuity. Thus, the former evildoer, now rendered perfect, would seem to be aware that he or she is a continuation of a certain "human becoming" on earth. Mühling proposes that all that is evil is radically transformed into the beautiful (albeit with aesthetic differences) at the judgment. So even a person who has been stripped of such "bad claims" is still beautiful. Indeed, all that is evil in the history of the world is overcome and transformed. This is how Mühling resolves the demands of justice: evil is vanquished and turned into its opposite. This has an analogue with the Moltmannian *justitia justificans* except it could be called *iustitia beatificans*—justice that beatifies. Thus, there is no evil in the eschatic reality of any kind.

Mühling's theology of divine judgment will not satisfy those who demand a stronger retributive aspect. However, it does seem to provide an interesting option to the problem of Moltmann's "gentle" universalism which would seem to demand almost no consequence for human acts of wickedness, other than eschatic accountability before God and the others sinned against. Volf's solution to Moltmann's *lacuna* adds a layer of eschatic socio-christological confrontation, but Volf is not a universalist in that he can conceive of a refusal to reconcile at the final judgment. Thus, Mühling creates a universalist soteriology that is not Origenistic nor so mild as to render human sin on earth as eschatically irrelevant, but avoids a dual outcome and the problem of eschatic evil.

6. Conclusion

In this chapter, I have explored four versions of the purpose of judgment: retributive with a dual outcome (Scheeben and O'Callaghan); retributive with a single, salvific outcome (Bulgakov); non-retributive, rectifying, and universalist (Moltmann); and non-retributive, personally transformative, and quasi-universalist (Mühling).

Relying on my thesis that divine judgment is the judgment of love and is salvific, the retributive judgment with a dual outcome as represented by Scheeben and O'Callaghan (although certainly not restricted to them) is deeply problematic. The idea that God's offer of mercy (and therefore love) ends at death and requires eternal punishment for the damned has been attenuated by some theologians, such as Paul Griffiths, as annihilation. Both options would seem to contradict God's ontic love and defeat the victory of Christ over evil. God would not be all in all if there is a place where hatred reigns.

Bulgakov's concept of judgment is ultimately salvific and is grounded in God's love, although the hellish fire of this love in its wrath against sin as it splits away the goat from the sheep in an intrapersonal separation has a seemingly barbarous element of metaphysical amputation. The other aspect that seems at odds with the synergistic system that Bulgakov advocates is that, in the end, God's grace is irresistible and the human will conforms to that of Christ. All will be purged and saved in order that the Divine Sophia permeates the cosmos. Yet, is this "sophianization" of human beings an event that results in true reciprocal love? It might be argued that to be made Christ-like is to love freely and without compulsion, but it seems that this would be an enforced freedom.

Moltmann's approach is to insist on a gracious universalism that heals the victims of evil and transforms the evildoers into saints. Volf's "corrective" that there must be a free will, mutual giving and receiving of grace between offenders and offended is not denied by Moltmann. Rather, Moltmann cannot allow that any human will would resist such an exchange. The judgment will rectify the human will just as it does everything else. Thus, Moltmann's universalism is achieved by irresistible grace. Moltmann does not consider human beings to be masters of their own fates, but rather it is God who is the master of destiny. To deny this is atheistic: "Belief in the freedom of the human will replaces belief in God."[96] Thus, irresistible, salvific grace presents no problem for Moltmann. However, if God desires relationality with human beings and that relationality is based on love, must it not be freely given by the creature to the Creator? For Moltmann, the natural state of human beings is to be freely loving and thus the eschatic event simply instantiates this by divine fiat.

Mühling tries to resolve this conflict between grace and freedom. Those who are judged will also be judges. Compelled by the truth set before them, they will agree with Christ as the chief Judge and demand a verdict upon themselves by the power of the Spirit. Thus, they accede to grace, but also give their free assent. However, this would imply that the truth set before them by Christ is irresistible: there can be no dissent. In this, the Johannine phrase is relevant: "truth will make you free" (cf. John 8:32)—it does not read the truth "might" make you free. It may be here that Mühling attempts to avoid the idea that human free will is thwarted. Rather, it is an irresistible truth that is presented. However, will the eschatically constituted persons, regardless of aesthetic differences, freely love the God who has re-created them? It would seem that the answer must be yes. But this raises the question of the authenticity of this love.

Reflecting on the purposes of judgment discussed above, it would thus seem that to find a purpose for judgment that accords with God's love, is salvific, avoids any dual outcome, and allows for total freedom in the giving and receiving of love in the eschaton requires further modification. This shall be the focus of the next chapter.

---

96. Moltmann, *Sun of Righteousness, Arise!*, 134.

CHAPTER 5

Towards a Christian Eschatology of Absolute Recognition

> *Oh yet we trust that somehow good*
> *Will be the final goal of ill,*
> *To pangs of nature, sins of will,*
> *Defects of doubt, and taints of blood;*
>
> *That nothing walks with aimless feet;*
> *That not one life shall be destroyed,*
> *Or cast as rubbish to the void,*
> *When God hath made the pile complete.*
> —Alfred, Lord Tennyson[1]

IN THIS CHAPTER, I shall explore the concept of salvific judgment as absolute recognition: the absolute and reciprocal recognition of the eschatic person of herself, of the other, and of God. I propose that it is in this recognition that both judgment and a threefold reconciliation to self, other, and God occur. The lines from the poem "In Memoriam AHH" (completed 1849) by Alfred, Lord Tennyson (1809–92), written as a memorial to his friend Arthur Henry Hallam (1811–33), express a universalist hope that "not one life shall be destroyed / Or cast as rubbish to the void." It is this hope that motivates my exploration.

As was discussed in the previous chapter on the purpose of judgment, in order to assert that judgment is one of divine love, is salvific,

---

1. Tennyson, "In Memoriam AHH," LIV, stanzas 1–2.

and avoids a dual outcome, yet allows the reciprocal giving and receiving of love between the person and God and between persons, another "third way" is needed between a dualistic soteriology and an absolute universalism that does not consider the need for reciprocal love. I am aware that it has been argued that human free will is "fallen" and thus must be healed in order to truly love. The question is whether this healing occurs in the eschatic judgment. The healed yet free will would then be "naturally" loving. I take it as a given that non-love is impossible in the eschatic kingdom of God. Yet, there is a longstanding counter-argument that it is essential that rational human beings must freely love God, the self, and the other *prior* (if not *ante mortem*) to eschatic judgment and reconciliation. Thus, there must be a choice in the matter according to the concept that libertarian free will (i.e., that human choices are free both from the constraints of human nature and from divine predetermination) is essential to human personhood. The prospect of a binding pre-eschatic choice leaves the door open to a dual outcome, thus defeating the victory of Christ.

1. Absolute Recognition: Eschatic Recognition Theory

Building on the theological foundation already explored in this book, divine judgment would seem to entail an absolute clarity of vision: a global vista of the person's earthly life and its effects on God, the self, and the other. Recognition theory is a broad philosophical topic, dominated by Axel Honneth (b. 1949) in his book *The Struggle for Recognition* and Paul Ricoeur (1913–2005) as contained in his last book, *The Course of Recognition*. However, I am not seeking to develop a new take on the philosophy of recognition for the basic reason that I am speaking about *eschatic* recognition. Honneth and Ricoeur are concerned with *ante mortem* human recognition, especially mutual recognition between persons. In effect, their quest is *political*. In addition, anything that can be called earthly absolute recognition is an impossibility for either philosopher. For example, Julie Connolly in her review essay on *The Course of Recognition* writes that:

> According to Ricoeur, the course of recognition, from recognizing things to recognizing one another, is one in which the individual who is recognizing becomes increasingly active and finally political. Moreover, this individual must chart a course through numerous obstacles: hesitation and doubt, forgetfulness and betrayal, and finally humiliation and futility. In each

of its manifestations—identification, attestation and acknowledgement—and each of its contexts—epistemology, ipseity and society—the course of recognition is not certain.[2]

Thus, recognition of any kind is never certain on earth and it cannot be described as absolute. What I shall seek to explore is the threefold absolute nature of eschatic recognition of God, self, and other. This does not exclude a reconciliation that also encompasses other creatures or the cosmos itself, but my focus is on human beings. It must be kept in mind that recognition is always *relational*. There is no recognition without relationality. Thus, absolute recognition also implies absolute relationality.

The Problem of Vocabulary

The word recognition is derived from the Latin word *recognitio*. This word itself takes its origin from the verb *recognoscere* ("to recall to mind"). It however has many meanings in its current English usage. It can mean the identification of a thing or person from a previous encounter or from knowledge; it can mean the bestowal of validity on something; it can mean that something is appreciated or valued or established. In fact, the *Oxford English Dictionary* lists eight meanings with numerous sub-meanings of this word.[3] The word "absolute" is derived from the past participle of the Latin word *absolvere*, the same word from which we derive the word "absolution." It literally means "to loosen away from." If one is absolved from her sins, she has been "loosened away from sin"—in other words, she is set free. The first definition in the *Oxford English Dictionary* for the word "absolute" is "Free from dependency, autonomous; not relative."[4] Therefore, *absolute recognition* is the event of unmediated, non-relative, and autonomous identification of the person or thing. This implies an ontological recognition: the recognition of the very being of the person or thing. To take a page from Bulgakov, the eschatic glorification of the body would render human persons capable of absolute recognition—it would resolve the dilemma of *finitum non capax infiniti*. Thus, this is recogni-

---

2. Connolly, "Charting a Course for Recognition," 135

3. "recognition, n." OED Online. December 2016. Oxford University Press. http://ezproxy-prd.bodleian.ox.ac.uk:2355/view/Entry/159646?redirectedFrom=recognition (accessed 10 January 2017).

4. "absolute, adj. (and adv.) and n." OED Online. December 2016. Oxford University Press. http://ezproxy-prd.bodleian.ox.ac.uk:2355/view/Entry/679?redirectedFrom=absolute& (accessed January 10, 2017).

tion without limitation. God always has this ability, but human beings in their finitude never do unless it is granted by some transformative means that exceeds the limits of human capacity.

This would mean that absolute recognition is an event that enables the human person to "see" God, the self, and the other. To put this in Rahnerian terms, it is the ability to recognize, through transforming grace, the absolute validity (authenticity) of the self and the others as constituted in temporal earthly freedom.[5] This validation does not mean approval, by God or the person, but rather the ontic seeing of the "being" as a whole as it existed on earth. As it relates to God, who is self-validating, it is the ability to see God without the limitations of finitude: to behold the *Shekinah*, the glory of the Lord, the Creator of all things.

El-roi: The Absolute Recognition of the Person by God

It is axiomatic that God always has the ability to recognize absolutely human beings. In addition, human beings as persons created by God are always in a state of relationship to God. However, human beings *ante mortem* cannot be said to have full awareness of their *ontological* recognition by God and many can be said to reject the concept of divine relationality. It is only in the eschatic encounter that human beings are made aware that God recognizes their total being. This encounter is piercing because it is a radical and cosmic exposure of the person. It is unprecedented because it occurs before the face of God in Christ. In other words, the person is made aware of this judgment and what it means. She is utterly transparent and there is no means to deflect the divine gaze. Thus, God's recognition of a person is unmediated and unconstrained. Yet, it is still relational. The dissecting gaze of God in Christ may be purgative, but it is not (as Tennyson hopes) destructive. Mühling makes this important remark:

> In faith and trust, Christians long for and experience the unmediated personal presence of Christ. This is because the judgement means nothing less than the definitive constitution of one's person and identity. Since at present humans also make sinful

---

5. "We must say: through death—not after it—there is (not: begins to take place) the achieved definitiveness of the freely matured existence of man. What has come to be is there as a hard-won and untrammelled validity of what was once temporal; it progressed as spirit and freedom, in order to be." Cf. Rahner, "The Life of the Dead," *Theological Investigations*, vol. 4, 348.

> identity claims, the judgement proves these to be provisional and incompatible with eschatical life.... It releases humanity from the notion that the identity claims that they inevitably have to make in the course of their [earthly] activity would also have to constitute their [eschatical] identities. Accordingly, the judgement becomes understood as consolation for the conflicting actions of both the offender and the victim.[6]

In other words, the identity claims human beings (not just Christians) have made about themselves will be tested by the judgment. Those that are not compatible will not endure the process of divine recognition. Yet, the consolation offered is that sin does not eternally constitute personhood. Thus, the judgment is salvific.

Hagar and the Rich Man: The Problem of Identification

> *Thou God seest me.*
> —Genesis 16:13a (AV)

> *Jesus, looking at him, loved him and said, "You lack one thing; go, sell what you own, and give the money to the poor, and you will have treasure in heaven; then come, follow me."*
> —Mark 10:21

The Hebrew Bible quotation above ("Thou God seest me") is from the story of the Egyptian slave-girl of Sarai (later Sarah), Hagar (cf. Genesis 16). As Sarai is childless, she consents to allow Abram (later Abraham) to father a child through Hagar. Once pregnant with Abram's child, Hagar shows contempt for her mistress. Sarai then treats her harshly and Hagar runs away. An angel intervenes and tells Hagar to return to Sarai, promising that her son will be the father of a great nation. Hagar then responds, "You are El-roi"; for she said, "Have I really seen God and remained alive after seeing him?" (cf. Gen 16:13). The Hebrew name "El-roi" (אל ראי) translates as "the God who sees." However, Hagar does not "see" God and it is unclear if she heard anything except an angel's voice. But Hagar is *seen* by God in her distress. In other words, the salvific moment for Hagar was *being seen and recognized by God*. It is noteworthy that this verse was frequently used in nineteenth-century Protestant Christianity as an expression of God's omniscience: that nothing done goes unnoticed, especially human sin. It was frequently accompanied by the all-seeing

---

6. Mühling, *T. & T. Clark Handbook*, 337.

eye. Yet, this is not the purpose of the verse in the story of Hagar. God is not looking for fault. Rather, the gaze of God is a salvific moment, albeit earthly.

In the New Testament account of Jesus's encounter with the Rich Man (cf. Mark 10:17–22), Jesus not only sees the man before him, but loves him. In his love, he tells the man what he must do to inherit eternal life: sell everything and follow Christ. The Rich Man departs with sadness because he has many possessions. The story continues:

> Then Jesus looked around and said to his disciples, "How hard it will be for those who have wealth to enter the kingdom of God!" And the disciples were perplexed at these words. But Jesus said to them again, "Children, how hard it is to enter the kingdom of God! It is easier for a camel to go through the eye of a needle than for someone who is rich to enter the kingdom of God." They were greatly astounded and said to one another, "Then who can be saved?" Jesus looked at them and said, "For mortals it is impossible, but not for God; for God all things are possible." (Mark 10:23:27)

In this passage, it would seem that the recognition of Christ of the Rich Man is not salvific. However, note the last phrase: "for God all things are possible." Christ's love for the Rich Man is not diminished by his seeming inability to sell all he has and become a disciple. In fact, we do not know what the Rich Man did after he departed. However, in the context suggested by Mühling, identity claims, such as that of being a wealthy person, are not barriers to the salvific recognition of God. In other words, while the identity claims of being a slave or being rich may not endure the judgment, Hagar and the Rich Man can be transformed through the loving gaze of Christ.

In these two passages, there is a limited (*ante mortem*) sense of what the process of absolute recognition entails. Hagar and the Rich Man are absolutely recognized; but are they recognized in a fixed state of identity? In other words, does God see Hagar solely as a slave-girl and a concubine? Does Christ see the Rich Man as simply a wealthy person? Both Hagar and the Rich Man are bearers of the divine image and are thus persons of sacred worth. The recognition by God of persons is thus always *more* than their earthly identity claims, be they assigned or self-assigned. They are seen by God in their ontology, in their very being, which exceeds even their own self-understanding. Hagar is told that her son will be the father of a great nation, hardly the self-assigned identity of an unmarried slave. The Rich Man is told that he can be a disciple of Christ, perhaps an apostle, if he gives away his possessions. This is not what he wanted to hear, but the offer to be in the fellowship of Christ was of infinitely more worth than his wealth. His own identity as a man with many possessions exceeded his desire to inherit eternal life (if he indeed did not decide otherwise). Yet, God recognized more in each biblical character because God recognizes the being of each person in totality.

In the encounter between the Rich Man with Christ, part of this recognition is expressed as love. God is Love (cf.1 John 4:8) and this means that God's absolute recognition of persons is always one of love. To further the definition: *eschatic absolute recognition is the unmediated, non-relative, autonomous, and loving identification and validation of the person or thing at an ontological level.* It is this recognition that is the judgment of God upon human beings and humanity as a whole. The eschatic encounter thus becomes our "El-roi" event. God sees us and thereby recognizes us to the depth of our being. We are seen ontologically and we are recognized absolutely. Keeping this in mind, the one who recognizes us is Love itself. This love is thus penetrating. We are changed by this gaze that knows everything about us, and yet loves us totally. Yet, this event is also the judgment. God is love precisely in this moment of judgment.

The Absolute Recognition of God by the Person: Visio Beata

To be seen by God is one thing, but to hear God's unmediated voice or to see God's face would mean immediate death to earthly human beings according to the Hebrew Bible. Moses asks to see God's glory, but God replies, "you cannot see my face; for no one shall see me and live" (Exod 33:20). One way to interpret this is that human finitude is incapable of looking upon the Infinite (*finitum non capax infiniti*). However, in the eschatic judgment, human finitude gives way to transformation: we are no longer bound by the limitation of earthly life. Thus, we are confronted with the fullness of God, face to face, and we are not destroyed. Rather, by the power of the Spirit, we too absolutely recognize God in Christ. This then would be the beatific vision. As Bulgakov notes, this recognition is loving and as perfect love casts out all fear (cf. 1 John 4:8), the encounter is fearless.[7] This would imply that absolute recognition could entail the element of irresistible love, which is (perhaps) not that same as irresistible grace. Thus, in the eschatic state, the option to not love God would

---

7. NA, 459.

seem to be impossible. However, this then puts the question of human free will in the eschatic encounter to the forefront.

Seeing God

> For I know that my redeemer liveth, and that he shall stand at the latter day upon the earth: And though after my skin worms destroy this body, yet in my flesh shall I see God: Whom I shall see for myself, and mine eyes shall behold, and not another.
> —Job 19:25–27 (AV)

> For now we see in a mirror, dimly, but then we will see face to face.
> —1 Corinthians 13:12

The verses from the Book of Job cited above, popular at Christian funerals, are much debated by biblical exegetes.[8] The modern exegetical consensus on this unique verse is that it does *not* refer to fleshly resurrection. Rather, Job will be healed of his afflictions by God and thus be vindicated. Thus, "seeing God" is not to be taken literally.[9] Of course, this verse was and sometimes still is deemed to allude to Christ and the resurrection of the dead by Christian commentators.[10] However, my interest in this verse is not in interpreting it through biblical criticism. Rather, I am looking at this passage in an eschatological context that is set apart from the fleshly resurrection of Job: what does it mean to "see God" in the eschatic reality? Moses asks God to show him God's glory, but God refused: to see God face to face would be to die. Hence, there is a contradiction between Job's pronouncement and the denial to Moses. However, if we add the Pauline verse from 1 Corinthians, there is a resolution: we cannot see God in God's fullness in this life. It is restricted to the eschaton; which means it is a *post mortem* event. It is only in the state of glorification (the imperishable body; cf. 1 Cor 15:42–44) that we may see God and live. The question then becomes not simply seeing God's glory but also loving God—loving the One we behold *nude, clare et aperte*. Will God's love be freely reciprocated by the creature? Since human beings do not possess the ontic love of God *ante mortem*, they are free not to love one another. However, since a state of pure hatred is not conceivable to a human being who is a bearer of the divine image (following Bulgakov), there must be

8. Cf. Pinker, "A New Interpretation of Job 19:26."
9. Pinker, "A New Interpretation of Job 19:26," 22–23.
10. Pinker, "A New Interpretation of Job 19:26," 5–6.

some part of that person capable of a loving response. In this sense, God elicits love from every human being in the eschatic encounter. However, the demands of love are tripartite: love of God, love of self, and love of the other. In my proposal, all three demands must be met. Thus far, all that has been discussed is the reciprocal love between God and persons in the eschatic encounter (which seems assured, even if only a pinpoint of a person can reciprocate this love). The other two parts of the demands of love have not been addressed.

The Absolute Recognition of the Self: The Problem of Identity

> *For now we see in a mirror, dimly, but then we will see face to face. Now I know only in part; then I will know fully, even as I have been fully known.*
> —1 Corinthians 13:12

> *Nor do I really know myself . . .*
> —Thomas Merton[11]

Here we are also confronted with the ontological vision of ourselves: the absolute recognition of ourselves—without filter. This is the flipside of the beatific vision: *visio humana*. Christ is the perfect mirror because, following Bulgakov, he is the prototype of humanity. This mirror image reflects our whole being and in this we recognize ourselves absolutely which has never occurred in our *ante mortem* lives. Here is the element of judgment's ferocity: to see oneself with all barriers stripped away. The challenge is not simply the repentance of wrongs brought about by this vision, but the question of whether we can still love the self (our ipseity) that we behold. Can a person confronted by every failure to love still love herself? Reconciliation is impossible with self-hate. Mark Corner does not believe that this self-recognition will of necessity be endurable (meaning we may fail to be able to love our ipseity): "We shall be where there are no more shadows, including the shadows we hide in to disguise ourselves. We shall know ourselves as we are known, overwhelmed by the unbearable self-knowledge that may or may not make it possible for us to survive."[12] In Corner's case, where he leaves the question open as to whether all or some will be able to survive this experience of self-knowl-

---

11. Thomas Merton, from his prayer "My Lord God," *Thoughts in Solitude*, 79.
12. Corner, *Death Be Not Proud*, 171.

edge, the assumption is that if we cannot bear the truth of our being, then annihilation is the only possibility. If we however reject annihilation as a possibility in the assumption that God will not destroy the creatures God has made, then we are left with the question on how we endure the unendurable. It may be that the Holy Spirit makes it possible for us to find a means to love what we see, even as all that is non-love is stripped away. This could be construed as the process that Mühling envisions as transformative judgment: that all our identity claims that fail the twofold command of love are rejected and destroyed. This then is the problem of ipseity and identity. Human identity is never static over the course of an earthly life. Yet, in the received tradition, there is an assumption that *post mortem* human identity is somehow frozen and it is this summation of biography that is subject to judgment resulting in a dual outcome. However, if in the moment of self-recognition our own desire, by the Spirit and by grace, is that God removes the horrors of non-love that are part of our biographies, what will this remnant be? If total evil (total non-love) is not proper to human beings, there must be *something* left of the person in this proposed purgative self-recognition. In other words, there must be a remnant that is worthy of self-love. I would suggest that ipseity gives a possible solution. Our unworthy identities may perish, but our ipseity (selfhood) is preserved: we do not lose our selfhood in the judgment.

I would further suggest that the *imago Dei* that a human being possesses is not a matter of identity, but (following Ricoeur) ipseity.[13] If the claim that God would be willing (or a human being would be able) to destroy the *imago Dei*, then our ipseity will not endure the judgment. However, if what is left of our earthly identity claims (for Ricoeur, the idem-identity) is only a pinpoint that can be salvaged at the self-judgment, can this be construed as universal salvation?[14] Mühling would suggest it cannot be construed as such. In this, I would agree. If after the separation of the "goat-self" (or perhaps the "goat-identity" modifying Bulgakov's concept) there is only a glimmer of the person that was once an earthly human being, even if there is memory of who that person was on earth, it cannot be said that the person reconciled ("saved") is the *same* person that lived on earth. It would still be a constituted person, as Mühling proposes, and it would possess selfhood, but there would be an element of radical discontinuity. This may not be something that Bulgakov, Ad-

---

13. Cf. Ricoeur, *Soi-même comme un autre*, 140ff.
14. Ricoeur, *Soi-même comme un autre*, 140ff.

ams, Robinson, or Moltmann could fully accept as their approaches seem to presume that personal identity is fully preserved, even though it is transformed or healed.

In chapter 2, section 2, I was critical of Antje Jackelén because her variant of the total death theory seemed to make continuity between the *ante mortem* person and the eschatic person almost impossible. However, her concept that the human self *post mortem* is not self-preserved, but rather *received* from God has resonance with Mühling's proposal that true human personhood is *given* at the judgment: in other words, the eschatic self is received from God. In my own understanding that death is neither total death nor intermediacy, but rather the immediate translation of the person to the eschatic judgment, the issue with personal continuity does not arise. However, this does not eliminate discontinuity between *ante mortem* and eschatic personhood. There is no fixity of identity, no Ricoeurian *mêmeté* ("sameness"). Rather, there is the glorified person, the imperishable, that is given an entirely new instantiation. The issue here is not then one of sameness (idem-identity).[15] Eternal sameness could be argued to be a form of hell: sameness is *not* life. Rather, I would argue that the linkage between the subjectivity of the earthly human being with the eschatic person is not dissolved. If anything, it is enhanced because the eschatic person now possesses the fullness of self-understanding that was never possible on earth. Thus, the goal of the eschatic transformation is not sameness or preserved earthly identity (following Jackelén), but rather an eschatic identity that surpasses individual biography, but does *not* negate it.

In effect, the eschatic person could claim that he *was* a certain person on earth, but that person "died" (at least in part) in the judgment. Only that remnant that was judged to be loving endured. Therefore, I would propose that universalism is only functionally true in this scenario in that no person can be annihilated totally, but the eschatic person that is constituted at the judgment may be radically different to the person known on earth. In this I am following Mühling's concept that there is "something like universal salvation" in the eschatic reality.[16] Thus, as far as human beings are instantiated on earth, universal salvation is *false* in that we do not know what part of our human self will endure the judgment (although we do know that all that is non-love will be purged).

---

15. Ricoeur, *Oneself as Another*, 2ff.
16. Mühling, *T. & T. Clark Handbook*, 330.

However, as far as the eschatic reality, universal salvation is *true* in that no one is "lost"—but we do not know the actual outcome of the judgment for ourselves or anyone else.[17] In other words, the continuity between the earthly human person and the eschatic person is unknowable until the judgment. All we can hope by faith is that result of the judgment will be entirely good.

The Eschatic Recognition of the Other: The Problem of Mutual Absolution

> *Jesus answered, "The first is, 'Hear, O Israel: the Lord our God, the Lord is one; you shall love the Lord your God with all your heart, and with all your soul, and with all your mind, and with all your strength.' The second is this, 'You shall love your neighbor as yourself.' There is no other commandment greater than these."*
> —Mark 12:29-31

The judgment is "public" and not an individualistic event (cf. Matt 25:31–46); we are judged with all the others just as the twofold command cited above is addressed to all human beings. Thus, the events of absolute recognition of and by God, and of the self, occur coterminously with mutual recognition between persons. Human beings are judged together, not like cattle as Kierkegaard says, but also not in solitude as if the experience of judgment is strictly an I-Thou event, utilizing a motif of Martin Buber (1878–1965).[18] It is a simultaneous I-Thou and We-Thou event. We are never judged alone nor are we reconciled alone.

Recognition theory in its focus on earthly human relations is restricted by the fact that there are numerous limitations to *ante mortem* interpersonal recognition. In the eschatic reality, these restrictions do not exist. This means that the absolute recognition of the other is possible. It is here that Miroslav Volf's idea comes into play: that we are confronted with all those whom we have offended by non-love and all those who have offended us.[19] This radical confrontation demands mutual reconciliation and mutual love. For Volf, this means recognizing that the offender has been freed from sin and given his true "identity" (or for Mühling, his true personhood). This will result in seeing that person as a new creation in

---

17. Mühling, *T. & T. Clark Handbook*, 330.
18. Cf. Buber, *I and Thou*; Original: *Ich und Du* (1923).
19. See chapter 4, section 4.

Christ. Rather than condemnation, the offended offers *absolution*, total forgiveness. The offender must in turn receive this grace of forgiveness. This is the eschatic reconciliation between persons. The result of this reconciliation is interpersonal love. This too is part of the trifold judgment. By the Spirit, we are given the opportunity to give and receive grace. But is this mutual reconciliation assured? It may be unbearable to recognize the other, other persons whom we have harmed or who have harmed us. And yet, this is what will be required. For Volf, this is *not* guaranteed. However, as we have seen, the absolute recognition entailed between God and persons is transformative. At minimum, the eschatic person in this encounter knows that he is absolutely loved by God and is able, after the dross is removed, to love the person that has been transformed. So, the persons that encounter each other are not the "human becomings" that they were on earth, to use Mühling's concept. They are now eschatic persons, some perhaps almost unrecognizable in comparison to their earthly personhood. Thus, it would seem that reconciliation with all the others is at least universally possible.

The process of such a reconciliation however is mindboggling for the villains of history, let alone for ordinary humans. If an earthly person was the architect of genocide, what would this reconciliation process be like? It would seem that it would be a type of hell because the process would entail an enormity of persons with the requisites of forgiveness, love, and grace. However, we are not dealing with earthly time-space in the eschatic reality. Thus, it is not conceivable to speak of "how much time" such a reconciliation would require. Yet, if we can see this as part of the purgative judgment, it could be likened to a type of non-fulfilment until the *processus salutis* is complete. In a way, the entrance of the person into the eschatic realm is difficult, even painful: it is *per crucem ad lucem*. After a fashion, it is the eschatic "Calvary" of every person before they enter the fullness of the *lumen gloriae*.

Conclusion

Thus far, I have proposed an eschatic judgment based on absolute recognition that requires reciprocal reconciliation and love in the eschatic judgment. The result of this judgment is very similar to the attenuated universalism proposed by Mühling. However, the thrust of my proposal seems to assume that universal reconciliation is guaranteed. This would seem to violate the concept that human free will endures the judgment unchanged. However, as Moltmann reminds us, human free will is also subject to transformation and it cannot be used as means to claim that humans alone choose salvation or damnation with God as merely the administrator. This returns us to the dilemma of reconciling divine grace and human freedom. If one holds that divine grace is irresistible in the end, then the dilemma is solved. If however, one holds that true love, even in the eschatic reality, demands unreformed free will, then the dilemma remains and even attenuated universalism is not possible.

2. The Problem of Eschatic Libertarian Free Will

> *A world containing creatures who are significantly free (and freely perform more good than evil actions) is more valuable, all else being equal, than a world containing no free creatures at all. Now God can create free creatures, but He can't cause or determine them to do only what is right. For if He does so, then they aren't significantly free after all; they do not do what is right freely. To create creatures capable of moral good, therefore, He must create creatures capable of moral evil; and He can't give these creatures the freedom to perform evil and at the same time prevent them from doing so. As it turned out, sadly enough, some of the free creatures God created went wrong in the exercise of their freedom; this is the source of moral evil. The fact that free creatures sometimes go wrong, however, counts neither against God's omnipotence nor against His goodness; for He could have forestalled the occurrence of moral evil only by removing the possibility of moral good.*
> —Alvin Plantinga[20]

Alvin Platinga's (b. 1932) classic free will defense is well-known. He seeks to preserve the omnibenevolence of God while allowing for the problem of evil. Indeed, it demands that a free creature be able to choose evil in order for them to be capable of choosing moral good. This dilemma means that the cost of moral goodness is the existence of moral evil since creatures that are incapable of evil are not free. It exonerates God as the cause of evil itself. The end result of this theodicy is the Edenic fall. The question would then be whether the eschatic judgment in its transformation of persons preserves libertarian free will so that an eschatic person could still choose moral evil in the eschaton.

---

20. Plantiga, *The Nature of Necessity*, 166–67. Emphasis original.

However, the eschatic reality is one where there is no evil. It is the event of *Christus Victor* over death, sin, and the devil, as proposed by Gustaf Aulén (1879–1977).[21] Thus, it would seem that in the world-to-come there can only be a choice of goods. What would it mean if an eschatic person exercised free will in not choosing a good, but has no opposite choice? My answer to this paradox is the thought experiment that an eschatic person makes no choice at all, i.e., eschatic indifference. In other words, there is no moral evil option, but of the goods that are options, the person chooses none. In such a situation, the following might be possible:

1. The person is absolutely recognized and loved by God;
2. The person absolutely recognizes God as ontic love;
3. The person absolutely recognizes himself and all that is non-loving in him;
4. The person absolutely recognizes the others and all that he did that was non-loving and that was done to him that was non-loving;
5. In one or all cases, the person remains indifferent to divine grace and love; and
6. The person is not reconciled, yet is not damned.

What state of affairs in the eschatic reality could this be? Since the eschatic reality cannot permit the eternalization of evil, hell as traditionally construed would not be an option for what amounts to neutrality.[22] Returning to Mühling's proposal that "human becomings" are not given their true personhood until the transforming judgment, such a neutral person is incomplete and not constituted. Echoing Volf's concept that the transformative judgment gives a person their true "identity" which is that of being freed from sin, would such an incomplete person be likewise free from her sins? Sin cannot have a place in the kingdom of God, thus we can presume that the eschatic confrontation did indeed burn away the dross of sin. But it is not enough to be cleansed. As Volf comments, receptivity of divine grace and the willingness to offer it to others is mandatory. The question then is whether such indifference is possible

---

21. Cf. Aulén, *Christus Victor*. First published in 1931.

22. Eschatic neutrality is an impossibility for Bulgakov and Moltmann. For others, such as Robinson and Adams, it would seem that it is possible, but that this neutrality would "eventually" be overcome.

within the concept of eschatic libertarian free will: the choice *not* to make a choice for or against God, the self, and the other; the choice not to love yet also not hate. It would seem that in this case, in spite of the goods offered, such an eschatic person would be incomplete and in effect self-exiles himself to a type of limbo that is neither eternal life nor hell, but a place of indifference; a place of incompletion through the free will that chooses *not* to choose.

The implication of this indifference implies that although Christ is victorious, this message must still be received by the indifferent—who are not damned, yet who seem to dwell "outside" the gates of the kingdom. This understanding is analogous to the concept discussed in chapter 2, section 4 about "hell" as an annex of "heaven." In other words, if evil has been defeated and Christ is Victor and the kingdom of God has been established as the eschatic reality, then those in the limbo of indifference are still denizens of eternal life. If such a state is possible, then they must simply exercise the free will to choose among the infinite goods that are possible. Yet, they will not be forced to do so. The "hell" that they undergo is not one of punishments or the absence of God, but rather God and the whole company of the eschatic kingdom are perpetually offering them love and grace. It may be that they will accept this or it may be that they will not, but there is no evil, sin, or hatred in their exile. In a sense, it is only a "hell" of divine love and grace—which is not the hell of tradition. However, this possibility seems to be incoherent if eschatic absolute recognition as transformation is true. There can be no antechambers to the eschatic reality. Thus, this thought experiment would seem to fail.

The Problem of Limiting God's Salvific Will

> ... *God our Savior, who desires everyone to be saved and to come to the knowledge of the truth.*
> —1 Timothy 3b–4

> *[Human] free will is a good thing, and for God to override it for whatever cause is to all appearances a bad thing.*
> —Richard Swinburne[23]

The problem with the possibility of eschatic indifference is that it would still be the thwarting of God's will in the eschatic reality. Swinburne's

---

23. Swinburne, "A Theodicy of Heaven and Hell," 43.

notion that it is always bad for God to override free will could be argued as mainstream philosophical theology. Yet, God hardened Pharaoh's heart (cf. Exod 9:12). It might be argued that God's overriding of Pharaoh's free will was a "bad thing" for the Israelites and the Egyptians, but in this case Pharaoh was denied libertarian free will. So, the idea that God does not override the human will, at least in the biblical record, seems to rest on dubious ground. That said, it is even more problematic when it comes to the eschatic judgment. If God is bound not to interfere with human free will, then absolute recognition would seem to be impossible because the human will could freely 'turn away' in an analogue to the pre-eschatic fall of some angelic beings.

In the Lord's Prayer, Jesus taught his disciples to include the petition "Thy will be done on earth as it is in heaven." It is obvious that God's will is not always done on earth. Stephen Davis writes that "God gave us the ability to say yes or no to God. One of the risks God ran in so doing was precisely that God's purposes would be frustrated, and this, sadly, is exactly what has happened. God's will is flaunted whenever anyone sins."[24] This may be true on earth, but can it possibly be true in the life of the world-to-come? The implication of "heaven" is that it is the realm where God's will is *always* done.

Marilyn McCord Adams opposes the concept that human beings have unfettered free will, be it earthly or eschatically, by labelling it the "idol of human agency."[25] This gets into the proposal that human beings do not have sufficient agency in a fallen material word (or as Adams refers to it, a world of "horrendous evils") to make decisions of eternal import. In other words, human free will is *impaired*. To invoke Paul Griffiths' favored word for the world as it is now, the "devastation," one could argue that human free will is devastated in its fallen condition. It would seem then that the only will that is truly free in the universe is that of the Will of God.

Jerry Walls argues that while God is the supreme good and it would seem impossible to choose evil knowing this to be the case, it may be possible for humans to avoid this knowledge through self-deception:

> If it is not within our power to avoid this knowledge [of God as the source of all goodness], neither is it within our power to choose damnation. And if this choice is not within our

---

24. Davis, "Universalism, Hell and the Fate of the Ignorant," 179.
25. Adams, "The Problem of Hell," 311–14.

power—as opposed to being psychologically possible for us—then we are not free with respect to it. Hence God cannot always remove our (self-imposed) deception without interfering with our freedom. If God allows us to retain libertarian freedom, some illusions will endure forever.[26]

However, this implies that at the eschatic event of absolute recognition, our self-deceptions and illusions endure because our libertarian free will is not subject to the Spirit's purging away of all falsehood. It would mean that human free will can defeat the salvific will of God. As Moltmann noted, such a concept is tantamount to atheism. It is even more problematic because it makes human free will superior to love. The apostle Paul reminds us that only three things endure forever: faith, hope, and love. Of these, the greatest is love (cf. 1 Cor. 13:13). Free will is not among these virtues. However, this does not mean human will is destroyed. Rather, it is *set free*. If to know Jesus Christ is to know the truth which sets us free (cf. John 8:32), then this freedom must apply to the human will. It is not that human will is forcibly rectified, but rather it is given its true freedom. It is axiomatic that while God is supremely free, God is not capable of sin or hatred. Thus, theosis must mean that human will corresponds to divine will. We are free—but divine freedom does not include the freedom to do evil.

In dualistic soteriology, those persons who make the right *ante mortem* choices are rewarded with glorification which presumably includes the gift of a divinely rectified will. Thus, the "saved" are rewarded for the good use of their free yet corrupted will and part of this reward is a "new" free will that chooses only the good. The damned are punished for their improper use of their corrupted free will and this corruption is eternalized. This is where the problem comes to an impasse. Solutions such as Augustinian predestination, Reformed supralapsarian double predestination, and others that either deny human free will entirely or Arminianism and its variants that demand libertarian free will via prevenient grace all result in a salvific dual outcome and the eternalization of evil.

The Eschatic Healing of the Human Will

> *Sin turns the human being's relationship to God upside down: correspondence becomes contradiction. With the human being's*

---

26. Walls, *Hell*, 133.

> *contradiction, his capacity for obedience (the* potentia oboedientalis) *ceases in his particular case, for his free will then becomes an "unfree will," as Luther rightly said. . . . Out of his relationship to the human being, and through an act of grace, God can restore the human being's* potentia oboedientalis, *and make what was for him impossible, once more possible: it becomes possible for him to correspond to the Creator and the source of his life. The* potentia oboedientalis *is a divine reality before it becomes a human possibility.*
>
> —Jürgen Moltmann [27]

Moltmann's understanding of human free will is that it is *not* free *ante mortem* due to sin. Referring to Luther's *On the Bondage of the Will*, human beings actually have "unfree will" which God alone can restore through divine grace. Thus, the *sola fide* formula "salvation by faith alone" is understood by Moltmann to mean "salvation creates faith for me."[28] In other words, salvation *precedes* faith. Paul Fiddes notes that, for Moltmann, "for human beings to have the power of choosing or declining their own salvation would be to make them into God themselves."[29] So we can see that for Moltmann, human free will cannot be decisive for or against salvation. There is no freedom to *not be saved* because the human will, at least *ante mortem*, is not free in the first place. Thus, it is God who bestows true freedom in grace—and this freedom "is a simple, undivided joy in the good."[30]

Returning to chapter 3, section 4, I questioned J. A. T. Robinson's insistence that love must be exercised in freedom but then comments that "May we not imagine a love so strong that ultimately no one will be able to restrain himself from free and grateful surrender?"[31] This is the conundrum of irresistible love. For Robinson, God's holy love is stronger than human freedom. Thus, human freedom freely yields to this love. The problem here is that Robinson does not make any claim that human freedom is transformed, as does Moltmann. It is rather drowned. In effect, rather than a transformation based on a reciprocal and absolute recognition between God and the person that results not simply in purgation, but an ontological change in the human being, Robinson seems to imply

---

27. Moltmann, *Experiences in Theology*, 158.
28. Moltmann, *The Coming of God*, 245.
29. Fiddes, *The Promised End*, 194.
30. Moltmann, *The Trinity and the Kingdom of God*, 55.
31. IEG, 106.

that earthy human will is the same things as eschatic human will. The effect of God's omnipotent love is simply to overwhelm the will so that it has no choice but to yield and reciprocate love. But such a love would in a sense be violent, if not rapacious. This must be avoided. Rather, an appeal to the Pauline assertion that "we will all be changed" (cf.1 Cor 15:51) might be a solution. The eschatic change is total—and one could argue that part of this change includes the restoration of a corrupted human will into one that shares God's supremely free will.

In chapter 3, section 5, I have been critical of Marilyn McCord Adams because I think her eschatology is too reductive towards human perpetrated evils and reduces human beings to a childlike state of responsibility. I also questioned whether humans, once healed from their status as both horror-perpetrators and horror-recipients due to their *ante mortem* vulnerable materiality, might not reject God for creating such a world in the first place. However, I do not reject her assertion of the finite human inability to make decisions of eternal import nor her concern that our own materiality and vulnerability render our *ante mortem* decision making processes deeply flawed. While I would prefer that a psychotherapeutic model of eschatic healing with Christ as "divine therapist" be avoided, I cannot deny that the eschatic process *is* one of healing. While my own concept requires a more robust self-judgment in the review of human biography in the form of absolute recognition, I also agree that the aim of the judgment as absolute recognition of God, the self, and the other must also be a radical process of healing. Part of this healing must include the human will. In Adams' eschatology as previously discussed, the eschatic rehabilitation for horror-perpetrators involves that they suffer and develop empathy for the victims of their evil actions through some divine process of rehabilitation:

> Since the cure for horrors is the making of positive meaning, and the restoration to the horror participant of the capacity to make positive meanings; and since the process of letting go of the old and groping towards the new is and can be a painful process, all horror participants can expect to undergo painful rehabilitation. But whether one is a horror perpetrator or victim will make a big difference to the concrete steps and stages of rehabilitation, as well as to the particular shape of the positive meaning that can be made. Can we even begin to imagine the excruciating process involved in Hitler's developing an empathetic capacity to suffer with those whom he tortured?[32]

32. Adams, 'Horrors in Theological Context," 476.

In this example, Adams speaks of pain in the context of eschatic rehabilitation and the need for the perpetrators of horror to develop empathy for the victims. Adams believes this will simply happen at some point—all will develop appropriate empathy (presumably resulting in love) and salvation will be universal. However, this implies a sort of duration of "time" in the eschaton for the therapeutic action of Christ to occur. It may be that this is an intermediate state, but it would seem to require an earthly time-space. This does not accord with the notion that eschatic "time" is not metronomic (as Griffiths claims). There is also the assumption that the divine psychotherapy will be universally effective. The missing aspect is the transformation of the will. If evil is the result of the misuse of human free will, then the human will must be transformed in order to be truly free. This would not satisfy Swinburne because anything that overrides human free will is "bad." Yet, we must remember that Adams is against the "idol" of human agency. Thus, she argues that God's unlimited resources will achieve a positive, salvific outcome:

> That love is, was, and always will be God's meaning; that beloved by God is who we are, have been, and always will be; that horrors never were or will be final; that God was never aloof from our horror-participation, neither was, is, nor ever shall be aloof to relation to us, because we are created for mutual indwelling; that God is powerful enough and resourceful enough to make the plots resolve, so that everything will be right.[33]

Thus, God in Christ will therapeutically transform the human will, although it is never put in these terms. Rather, it is divine power that achieves reconciliation by creating what might be called "irresistible meaning making." God will, in effect, transform each human being's life into one that is so eschatically meaningful that they will freely love and freely be reconciled. There is no contemplation of refusal to engage in this eschatic therapy. Thus, there *must* be a transformation of the human will to avoid a dual outcome at the judgment. This needs to be part of Adams' *processus salutis* and it needs to confront the free will defense that forms one of the chief arguments for salvific dualism.

---

33. Adams, *Christ and Horrors*, 240.

Conclusion

One of the main arguments that demands a dual outcome at the judgment is the sovereignty of human free choice, apart from those that entertain double predestination—which obviates human free will entirely. The Arminian concern, as Jerry Walls holds, is that if God eschatically transforms human will so that it is godly or divinized, God is forcing human beings to give up the "freedom" to choose evil.[34] It would seem that human autonomy, even in the eschatic encounter, is capable of thwarting God's salvific will if human libertarian freedom is deemed the highest good. Yet, is this stance theologically justifiable? It would suggest that the highest virtue, human or divine, is the will. Yet, God is defined not as will, but as *love*.

Returning to Mühling and his concern with the resolution between divine grace and human freedom, his answer to this quandary is this: at the transformative judgment, those that are judged are also judges, chiefly of themselves. By the Holy Spirit's assistance, those that are judged "can do nothing other than pronounce the judgement as to its significance in relation to Christ, however it turns out."[35] Thus, it would seem that in the dual role assigned to human beings as both judged and judges, the transformation of the human will occurs. In this moment, the human will is unilaterally sanctified yet without coercion. There is also no intermediate state or re-duplication of the world to enable sufficient "time" for human beings to amend their wills to that of God's. But is this a sort of divine brainwashing nonetheless? Mühling suggests it is not.

For Mühling, love on earth for human beings is only possible, alas, in a world where: "the imperfection of the cosmic regularities is a necessary condition for the deontic character of the double commandment of creaturely love."[36] In other words, a fallen world, with natural disasters, with suffering and death, and where the deontic rule of love can be violated is necessary for there to be any love at all. In a perfect world, without suffering or death, love cannot exist because in such a world "creatures could not develop who would be unable to love."[37] However, while a perfect world might sound ideal, the result is that: "The concept of choice or freedom would therefore be an empty concept if not self-

---

34. Cf. Walls, "A Hell of a Choice: Reply to Talbott."
35. Mühling, *T. & T. Clark Handbook*, 333.
36. Mühling, *T. & T. Clark Handbook*, 143.
37. Mühling, *T. & T. Clark Handbook*, 144.

contradictory—as would the understanding of love."[38] Thus, it would seem that for human beings to be able to love requires that they exist in the fallen world. In a way, Mühling is replacing Plantinga's necessity to choose evil for moral goodness to exist with a necessity to not love (hate) in order that love exists on earth. This conclusion resonates with Adams' understanding that God chose to create a material universe with beings vulnerable to horrors, knowing its high cost, yet also knowing that the resolution to this non-optimality would be achieved by the eschatic outcome. Mühling's solution, which also carries a high price for humanity's ability to love, is teleological and twofold: the eschatic reality will be "good and nothing but good" and "All human actions, including their good and evil deeds, will become ethically indifferent with respect to the *eschaton*, without damaging their pre-eschatic ethical value."[39]

As was discussed in the previous chapter, Mühling sees the judgment as transformative and the constitution of true personhood of "human becomings." Even evil actions will be transformed so as to contribute to the eschatic good. Thus, there will be *aesthetic* differences in persons in the eschatic reality but not ethical differences. Their transformation entails the resolution between grace and freedom where the human will is liberated so that it can freely choose only what God can choose: love, goodness, truth, and beauty. This then is the theosis of the human will, but it is also the giving of a human being's true free will because her personhood is not complete until the eschatic judgment of transformation.

If there is no transformation of the human will, then a dual outcome is not only possible at the eschaton, but also in the *semper novum* of eschatic life. This then would allow a repeat of the fall (perhaps cyclically in the Origenistic sense) which nullifies the victory of Christ. This would then mean that the eschatic reality is one where finitude is not overcome. Therefore, there must be a resolution between divine grace and human freedom that is entirely good.

---

38. Mühling, *T. & T. Clark Handbook*, 143–44.
39. Mühling, *T. & T. Clark Handbook*, 144–5.

3. Christ as the Recognizer of Human Beings: The Christological Dilemma

> *I have other sheep that do not belong to this fold. I must bring them also, and they will listen to my voice. So there will be one flock, one shepherd.*
> —John 10:16

The reason that there is a christological dilemma is because of the role of Christ as the eschatic Judge and its implications of christomonism. It is obvious from my argument thus far that I favor a high christology that takes seriously the *scandalous* claim that Jesus of Nazareth is God the Word Incarnate (cf. 1 Cor 1:23).[40] This also explains why Bulgakov, Adams, and Mühling are robust theological sources since their Trinitarianism is part and parcel of their respective Eastern Orthodox, Anglo-Catholic, and Lutheran provenances. My own Christian particularity may suggest that, regardless of my position that universal salvation is true in some way, I demand that the eschatic encounter of absolute recognition of the human person before Christ entail a rectification of their own religiosity (regardless of type) or lack thereof. However, this would be reductive. While my take on eschatology is christocentric, it is not christomonistic: I do not presume that Christ is the singular representation of God because my understanding of God is Trinitarian and because it is epistemically immodest to restrict how God may opt to manifest in the cosmos.

In addition, the eschatic encounter of the absolute recognition of God manifest in Christ will be as iconoclastic for "Chalcedonian Christians" as for all others. The reason is that no human definition can ever be said to be *homo capax Christi*. The demands of my high christological commitments mean that any attempt to define who Christ is *in se* will fail, especially at the judgment. This echoes Calvin's dictum that we can know God not as God is, but only as God is towards us.[41] It is beyond human capacity to know God's essence in this earthly instantiation. Karl Barth in his *The Epistle to the Romans* puts it in these words: "We are not saved by our knowledge of God. Our knowledge brings us under judgement. God is Alpha, and therefore Omega; He rejects, and therefore elects; He

---

40. By invoking the Pauline *scandalon* of preaching Christ crucified, I am not implying that Paul held to Chalcedonian definitions of christology.

41. Cf. "Non quis sit apud se, sed qualis erga nos." Calvin, *Institutes*, I.x.2.

condemns, and therefore is merciful. God conducts men down into Hell, and there releases them."[42] Thus, in the eschatic recognition and making use of this Barthian citation (who admittedly has been accused of christomonism), we are brought to the knowledge of God (in its fullness); we experience rejection and election, condemnation and mercy, hell and salvation. Thus, it is not nor has it ever been the assumption that eschatic absolute recognition is confined to those who identify themselves as Christians *ante mortem*. There is no concept within this thesis that can allow for an Augustinian *massa damnata* nor Calvin's *decretum horribile*. My eschatological hope is that humanity is rather a *massa salvata* because the eschatic judgment is salvific for all.

The concept of absolute recognition is admittedly christological. However, Christ as the Logos of God and God the Son is not constrained by human theological definitions. Christ is always *more* than what we can conceive. The absolute recognition of the eschatic Christ is not the same as the Petrine confession of faith: "Thou art the Christ, the Son of the living God" (cf. Matt 16:16 AV). The eschatic encounter with Christ is an encounter with the embodiment of divine love, the very ontology of the Trinity, loves within love. Thus, the human being is encountering God's ontic love in an unmediated way. It is a mystery as to what confession of faith this will entail for the human person, if such a confession is ever applicable. I propose that eschatic absolute recognition transcends Christian theological claims. It is also an event of radical iconoclasm because all of our images and concepts of God (or the lack of a God) will crumble in this encounter. Whatever confession of faith in Christ is uttered in the eschatic recognition by human beings, it is not something that can be uttered on earth. Thus, Christ the eschatic Judge transcends Christianity itself. This said, what then is the advantage in being a Christian? If all are judged in a similar manner, then why bother? Christianity is not a salvation game. The Christian salvific hope can never be restricted to Christians, nor even to humans because the eschaton is reconciliation of the cosmos. Paul Tillich, in one of his sermons, makes this point forcefully:

> We do not hope for us alone or for those who share our hope; we hope also for those who had and have no hope, for those whose hopes for this life remained unfulfilled, for those who are disappointed or indifferent, for those who despair of life or even for those who have hurt or destroyed life. Certainly, if we could only hope each for himself, it would be a poor and foolish hope.

---

42. Barth, *Epistle to the Romans*, 393.

Eternity is the ground and aim of every being for God shall be all in all.[43]

Tillich's argument is not christological, but it is a reminder that eschatological hope must be all-encompassing. Tillich is also not interested in eternal life for individuals but rather as a unity or collectivity within God that may or may not mean the dissolution of personhood. However, remembering the words of Christ to the "good thief" that he would be in paradise "today," it would seem that eternal life is both personal and collective, individuated and undivided. This could be seen as analogous to the understanding of the Trinity as social: God is love and also lovers. In other words, God is not "alone" in Godself because love requires alterity. Thus, human eschatic alterity (otherness) is requisite to the eschaton, just as the unity of humanity is also required. The glory of eternal life is that no one is ever alone—which is not true of material life on earth.

The Humanity of Christ as Eschatic Judge

> I, the creator of and redeemer of humanity, judge the flesh as one who became flesh and the hearts as one who is God.
> —Pantocrator mosaic, Cefalù Cathedral, Sicily (1148)[44]

In the twelfth century cathedral in Cefalù, Sicily, a project of the Norman king of Sicily, Roger II (reign 1130–54), there is a colossal mosaic of Christ the Pantocrator in the apse that was completed in 1148 by craftsmen from Constantinople. Christ holds an open Gospel book with the verse from John 8:12 in Greek and Latin: "I am the light of the world. Whoever follows me will never walk in darkness but will have the light of life." What is unusual about this mosaic from a soteriological viewpoint is the Latin inscription around the apse itself, as translated above. This inscription is neither biblical nor patristic. It is not from any known hymn or sacred text, and thus appears to be a unique composition for this mosaic. A more literal translation of the Latin yields a more striking statement: "Having become human, the Maker of humanity, and the Redeemer of what I have made: I—the embodied God (*corporeus*

---

43. Tillich, "The Right to Hope: A Sermon," 377.

44. My translation. The Latin original inscription on the upper part of the apse reads: "Factus Homo Factor Hominis Factique Redemptor Iudico Corporeus Corpora Corda Deus." Cf. Cilento, *Byzantine Mosaics in Norman Sicily*. See the cover illustration of the Mosaic of Christ Pantocrator, Cefalù Cathedral, Sicily (installed in 1148).

deus)—judge the bodies (*corpora*) and the hearts (*corda*) [of humanity]." The claim is that by virtue of Christ's incarnation as Son of Man he is able to judge human beings *kata sarka*, but as the *theanthropos* (the God-Human) he is also able to judge the human heart (*kata kardia*). This statement is christologically striking, but it implies that Christ will judge humanity at the eschaton according to both his human nature and his divine nature. The flesh is weak (cf. Mark 14:38 et al.) and Jesus Christ experienced this weakness inclusive of his crucifixion and death, but the human heart (which one could argue is inclusive of soul and spirit) is the locus of the divine image.

In John's Gospel, we read that the Father judges no one, but all judgment is given to the Son (John 5:22). Jesus, "in whom the whole fullness of deity dwells bodily" (Col 2:9), will be the judge of humanity because of his incarnation. Human beings are bodily beings. We recognize one another as beings *kata sarka*. Thus, for *absolute* recognition to occur between God and humanity, incarnation is necessary—to state this in another way, absolute recognition *requires* incarnation. For recognition to be absolute (not qualified or diminished in any way) the incarnation is required as a bridge between deity and humanity by the One who is both.

Returning to the question of whether human beings will recognize Christ as Jesus of Nazareth, I would suggest that this is not the key question. However, all will recognize the *embodied God* who is Jesus Christ. This does not mean that Christian particularity is wrong. It means that Christ is more than the One for Christians—he is the One *pro nobis hominibus* who is universally recognized and universally recognizes. He is thus the One who may judge—and this judgment is perfect. Through Christ, we are led absolutely into God. Rather than diminishing the Christian gospel, this understanding expands it. Christ is the One for others.

Adams makes a similar statement in her book *Christ and Horrors* as mentioned in chapter 3, section 5: "My own view is that Christ is judge according to His human nature. The manifestation of His resurrected and glorified wounds publishes the truth about our ante-mortem human condition, and the truth about God's everlasting ability, resourcefulness, and intentions to restore human beings thereby.[45] In other words, the resurrected Christ, his wounds turned into glorious form, represents the transformative capacities of God to do for human beings at the judgment what God did as a prolepsis for Christ at the resurrection. For Adams,

---

45. CH, 241.

Jesus is impeccable only in his deity and not in his humanity because he is both a passive horror-perpetrator and an active horror-recipient (e.g., Christ's birth results in the Slaughter of the Innocents). It is this horror-participant who is the God-Human and the Son of Man. Thus, Christ's judgment takes its validity by overcoming the metaphysical gap between deity and humanity. The eschatic Judge is judging us as One who took on flesh and its attendant vulnerabilities to evil. This tempers the ferocity of the judgment because it is implicit that Christ has experienced our plight—and thus so has God because the resurrection incorporates this experience within the Godhead. Yet, it also provides another solution to the christological problem of the eschatic judgment of the religious other and the non-religious other. Jesus is the Son of Man, the human manifestation of God.

Using Adams' bold assertion, I suggest that Christ, who is fully human, is both Judge and the divine representative of humanity. As I claimed before, the eschatic Christ is beyond what can be conceived by Christians. This does not mean that Christ is morphed to be another religious figure to accommodate world religions. That would be equally reductive. Rather, Christ exceeds all conceptuality. Assuming the transformation of the threefold absolute recognition occurs, would the denizens of eschatic life not come to see that the Son of Man is Jesus? My assumption is yes, but at this point there would no longer be any cognitive dissonance because of the radical transformation that eschatic life implies. If eschatic human freedom corresponds to divine freedom, the recognition of Christ as Christ Jesus is composite with this freedom.

Conclusion

In this section, I have argued that neither a pre-eschatic or eschatic confession of Jesus as Lord and Savior is required for the threefold absolute recognition of divine judgment and transformation. Rather, the process of reconciliation is christocentric without requiring a specific affirmation of the earthly instantiation of Jesus of Nazareth. I have also argued that all preconceptions about Jesus Christ, by Christians and non-Christians, will crumble before the eschatic Christ who is beyond human definitions. Yet, this does not denigrate the vocation of the Christian because being a disciple is its own reward: "For to this end we toil and struggle, because we have our hope set on the living God, who is the Savior of all people, especially of those who believe" (1 Tim 4:10).

I propose that the humanity of Christ is key to this judgment because the Judge is the Son of Man, the manifestation of humanity, who has experienced human vulnerability and has overcome it. Thus, in Christ we recognize both true humanity and true divinity. Assuming that all endure the process of judgment, the correspondence of human and divine wills would result in an understanding that the eschatic Judge is Jesus Christ, but this would no longer be an obstacle due to the transformation of personhood that occurs within the judgment.

4. The (Im)Possibility of Eschatic Non-Recognition

> But when the king came in to see the guests, he noticed a man there who was not wearing a wedding robe, and he said to him, "Friend, how did you get in here without a wedding robe?" And he was speechless. Then the king said to the attendants, "Bind him hand and foot, and throw him into the outer darkness, where there will be weeping and gnashing of teeth." For many are called, but few are chosen.
>
> —Matthew 22:11–14

In the Parable of the Wedding Banquet, Jesus tells the story about a king holding a wedding feast whose invited guests would not attend. So the king orders his slaves to invite anyone in the vicinity to attend and these include "both good and bad" (cf. Matt 22:10). Yet one person, among the random people invited, is not wearing a wedding robe. So he is cast into the "outer darkness" for his offence. This story is perplexing, but it is often understood to mean that the wedding robe is a robe of righteousness and that the unfortunate man did not meet this requirement and was cast out. Yet, Matthew's Gospel says that both the good and the bad were in attendance and somehow all had wedding robes—which would seem impossible if people are simply rounded up on the streets. Exegetical interpretations of this text run the gamut from associating the "man without the robe" as Judas, as a composite of all the bad invitees, such as the Jewish leaders who are opponents of Jesus; or unworthy Christians; or as a combination of all of these groups.[46] A dual outcome in the judgment presupposes that this is a division of persons with the damned being cast into outer darkness, which is often used as a synonym for hell. However, a commitment to a single outcome demands a different exegesis.

---

46. For an in depth exploration of this text, cf. Sim, "The Man without the Wedding Garment (Matthew 22:11–13)."

As was already suggested by Bulgakov in the Parable of the Sheep and the Goats, the "man without the wedding robe" at the eschatic banquet can also be interpreted as the "goat-self" or whatever is not clothed in the wedding garment at the eschatic judgment. In other words, that part of the self that is deemed unworthy is separated and cast into "outer darkness." This also accords with Mühling's concept of the destruction of identity claims that do not meet the requirements of the twofold commandment of love: such claims are bound and cast out.[47] The "weeping and gnashing of teeth" is the pain of the eschatic recognition of these unloving aspects that cannot endure the threefold process of absolute recognition. Thus, although the good and the bad are invited to the wedding feast (eschatic judgment), only the good clothed in their wedding garment (eschatic persons) will remain.

The question is whether non-recognition is possible for this would indeed be hell, the hell of non-reconciliation and eschatic exile. Is God in Christ the king who throws people into outer darkness, which would mean that this outer darkness is a permanent aspect of the eschatic reality? The thrust of the arguments in this book is that this is not possible. And that God is not the tyrannical king that invites the people on the street to the feast only to cast one or some of them out. Yet, the issue of hell is one that cannot be dismissed, but to entertain it as traditionally construed is a problem even for those who feel that they are bound by biblical authority to maintain it. The influential evangelical theologian John Stott (1921–2011) wrote this about the traditional understanding of hell: "I find the concept intolerable and do not understand how people can live with it without cauterizing their feelings or cracking under the strain."[48] Stott's solution, like the Catholic theologian Paul Griffiths, is to advocate the annihilation of the unrepentant and the non-believers.

Moltmann's remedy for hell is not to deny it, but to assert that it will be annihilated by God in Christ. Nicholas Ansell summarizes Moltmann's rejection of hell: "Do not tell me that some people may or must go to Hell on the basis of some theological system (indeed some theological 'necessity'); say that (if you can) in light of the cross, in the face of the crucified God."[49] This is an interesting take on Luther's *crux probat omnia*. Moltmann's eschatology asserts that hell does not pass the test

---

47. Mühling, *T. & T. Clark Handbook*, 330–31.

48. Edwards with Stott, *Essentials*, 314.

49. Ansell, *Annihilation of Hell*, 206. NB: Ansell is writing as if Moltmann is speaking these words, but it is not a quotation.

of the cross. In other words, the Crucified God destroys hell, but "saves" humanity.

If non-recognition can be deemed the analogue of hell, then it would seem that hell is impossible because God's salvific and absolute recognition which is demanded in a threefold manner (God, self, other) cannot be thwarted. However, if hell is rather that some or most of our identity claims that constitute our sense of the earthly selfhood do not endure the judgment, then hell can be said to be a real possibility—because we shall see our biographies penetrated and purged of everything that is incompatible with the kingdom of God. Mühling does not call this aspect of judgment hell, but it would seem that this would be its best definition since it is our unloving *ante mortem* aspects that will be cast out into outer darkness and thereby annihilated.

The form of unqualified universalism that simply states all is forgiven and nothing of the earthly person is lost in the judgment would effectively mean that nothing we do matters and there is no God that will judge our biographies. This would be as atheistic, *pace* Moltmann, as the concept of an eternal hell. However, in the model of qualified universal salvation, human biography is not only accountable but there is no guarantee as to the nature of outcome as to the eschatic person constituted in the judgment, but rather asserts that the person will not be entirely lost. I go beyond Mühling in proposing that "hell" is (im)possible for every person, because we shall be judged, we shall be absolutely recognized, but if there is hell in this process it is not a destination, rather it is a creative process. Hell is, therefore, eschatically functional rather than a fixed state of being.

4. *Semper Novum*: The Outcome of the Judgment of Absolute Recognition

> *For since by man came death,*
> *By man came also the resurrection of the dead.*
> *For as in Adam all die,*
> *Even so in Christ shall all be made alive.*
> —1 Corinthians 15:21–22 (AV)

There has been little mention of "heaven" in this dissertation because the promise in Christianity is not "heaven" but resurrection and eternal life. Human speculation about what "heaven" is like often resemble an earthly paradise. However, this cannot be what eternal life entails because it is simply a repetition of a perfected earth. It is not the eschatic New Jerusalem, but rather a decidedly earthly renovation of the old Jerusalem. This earthly, temporo-spatial imagery of the "afterlife" and "heaven" has a long history.[50]

However, since ideas about what eternal life is like are speculative, it is hardly surprising that human beings simply project onto an "afterlife" the imagery that they know from lived experience. Yet, as Corner notes, death as the "gateway" to eternal life cannot be understood as natural or beneficial. The Christian tradition deems death to be unnatural and evil. Corner notes that Jean-Paul Sartre's (1905–80) understanding of death as an absurdity in his *Being and Nothingness* "prevents any facile identification with mortality with 'beneficial learning experiences.'"[51] Thus, the irony of writing about eternal life is that it demands the horror of human death. In many ways, talk concerning the joys of "heaven" is often a means to ameliorate the tragedy and sadness that death entails for the dying person as well as the bereaved.

The Problem with Earthly Concepts about Eternal Life

One of the problems of thinking that eternal life is a reduplication of earthly life, but one where there is no death or evil, is that it is analogous to the Hegelian "bad infinity" (*die schlechte Unendlichkeit*) of an Edenic world where our lives have infinite duration.[52] This would be perpetual stasis as presumably we would not age and we would be confined to the limits of human intellect. And this "heaven" would be hell: human beings are not static. A perpetual sameness, with infinite time to pursue leisure activities or hobbies, would be a horror of eternal boredom. This earth, even if perfected, would grow ever smaller. The end result would be the desire for death among those who are deathless.

One analogy to this "bad infinity" could be the elves of J. R. R. Tolkien's legendarium. They are naturally immortal, although they can be killed. Yet, even if killed, their spirits will go to Valinor (the Undying Lands) and they will reincarnate in the same bodies. Eventually, they will become bodiless immortals who will last as long as the world lasts or

---

50. For an overall study, cf. McDannell and Lang, *Heaven: A History*.
51. Corner, *Death Be Not Proud*, 49. Cf. Sartre, *Being and Nothingness*.
52. Cf. Hartnack, *An Introduction to Hegel's Logic*, 21–22.

perhaps forever.⁵³ Thus, the elves are immortal, but in a temporo-spatial realm, a place of great beauty, yet everlasting sameness. Tolkien captures, at least for the elves, what some may think of as a paradisiacal existence worthy of the name "heaven." Yet, there cannot be any novelty in such a place and human life without novelty is unthinkable. Yet, "heaven" as an idyllic garden-world has very strong appeal in Christianity.

The popular Swedish hymn *En vänlig grönskas rika dräkt* ("A friendly green, richly dressed") was composed by the poet Carl David af Wirsén (1842–1912) whose Lutheran piety fills the verses of the hymn. However, only the first three are normally sung in Sweden today.⁵⁴ The hymn reflects the ephemeral beauty of summer, but the last two verses insist that this will all fade and only paradise is eternal. A literal translation of the three select verses of the hymn reads:

> 1. A friendly green, richly dressed,
> Has adorned valley and meadows.
> Now the caress of the warm wind fans
> The fair herb-meadows.
> And the sun's light
> And the rustling in the grove
> And the murmur of the wave in the willows
> Proclaim summertime.
>
> 3. But you, O God, who makes our earth
> So beautiful in the summer's moments:
> Grant that I may receive your word above all
> And your wondrous grace.
> All flesh is grass,
> And the flowers die,
> And time banishes everything,
> Only the Word of the Lord endures.
>
> 5. Then let summer's glory fade
> And let all vanity wither;
> My beloved is mine and I am his,

---

53. Cf. Tolkien, "The Laws and Customs of the Eldar."

54. Hymn 201, *Den svenska psalmboken*. For commentary, cf. Hans Holmberg, "Från lovsång till förgängelse," *Kristianstadsbladet*, 9 June 2004, http://www.kristianstadsbladet.se/kultur/fran-lovsang-till-forgangelse/ (accessed 29 January 2017).

Our bond is imperishable.
In paradise
He, kind and wise,
Shall at last replant me
There nothing withers ever.[55]

Wirsén's fourth and final verses allude to the view that summer's glory will fade away, but only paradise, the garden of the Lord, is imperishable. Thus, his allegory that Christ will "replant" the possessors of eternal life in paradise. This may also explain why only the first three verses remain popular in the context of Swedish secularism, even though the third verse is theological and contains words favored by the Magisterial Reformers: *verbum Dei manet in aeternum*. The hymn is, of course, poetry not eschatology, but is resonant with Tolkien's earthly (usually non-human) idyllic landscapes as described in his legendarium.

Yet, is this remotely applicable to eternal life? The answer must be no for the simple reason that it is anthropomorphically restricted and can hardly do justice to the infinite resources of God. Flowers that do not whither may be an attractive concept, but human beings confined to the enchanted and "enclosed garden" (*pairidaēza*, the Persian route meaning of "paradise") is hardly the place where novelty can occur. It rather implies the same stasis implied by Tolkien's Undying Lands. If the eschatic reality is a place that "no eye has seen, nor ear heard, nor the human heart conceived, what God has prepared for those who love him" (cf. 1 Cor 2:9), then it cannot resemble the things of earthly life—all of which we can easily conceive.

The Problem of Eternal Life as a Perpetual Reunion

One of the main themes concerning "heaven" is that we will meet our loved ones again and be reunited with them forever. The Caroline Divine Jeremy Taylor was also looking forward to conversing "with Homer and Plato, with Socrates and Cicero, with Plutarch and Fabricius."[56] What is interesting about Taylor's desire is that his table talk in "heaven" would be with non-Christians who evidently were "saved" in Taylor's soteriology. However, while eschatic sociality could indeed mean that we meet

---

55. My translation.
56. Cf. Taylor, *The Rule and Exercise of Holy Living and Holy Dying*, 88. Cited in Corner, *Death Be Not Proud*, 51.

our loved ones and others who may have been famous in earthly life, we should be mindful of a comment attributed to Karl Barth. He was reported to respond when asked this very question ("will we meet our loved ones in heaven?"): "Not only the loved ones!"[57] Volf comments further that: "The not-loved-ones will have to be transformed into the loved ones and those who do not love will have to begin to do so; enemies will have to become friends."[58] To put this another way, eternal life is not a realm of social cliques where we are able to have eternal fellowship with people we loved or admired *ante mortem*. Rather, and radically, it is the state of being where love is not hierarchically based on earthly kinship or affection. Indeed, we love the loved ones of our earthly instantiation, but we will also love *equally* all the others. In other words, if the process of the transformative judgment of absolute recognition results in a realm of mutual love, then no one will be loved more and others loved less: not God, the self, or the other. Eschatic love is the freedom to love and be loved equally by all.

The creates a problem for the bereaved who understandably want to be reunited with deceased spouses, daughters, sons, other family, and friends. However, it is a given that not all marriages or families are loving on earth. In fact, the modern concept of marriage as a free will choice between lovers hardly accords with marriage as it was once known in the Western countries of the nineteenth century and earlier (and still is elsewhere) as arranged, based on economic, customary or obligatory factors. Not all desire to be reunited with family. However, the problem is not eschatic reunion, but rather eschatic love.

Yet, the model of perfect love is to be found in God and the social Trinity in which God is understood as a mutual loving of three persons in which no person is loved less or more—in other words the Trinity is co-amorous. This model of divine life implies that our eschatic lovers will be "Trinitarian" in the sense that we love God and all persons (indeed all things) equally. All eschatic beings are lovers and friends, none is superior or inferior. This is hardly the reality of earthly loves. This may also seem undesirable to *ante mortem* human beings who think of love as exclusive and often binary affairs. The suggestion that you would love the person who was your beloved spouse on earth as much as anyone else in the eschatic reality might seem offensive. Yet, we are not offended by the

---

57. Cited in Volf, "The Final Reconciliation," 91.
58. Volf, "The Final Reconciliation," 91.

belief that God loves all equally. Thus, theosis entails that eschatic love mirrors divine love and this implies a radical discontinuity from the way human beings order their loving relationships on earth.

The Problem of Eternal Life as Beholding the Beatific Vision

It would seem that seeing God face to face would be its own reward. Thus, there is a tradition that the eschatic contemplation of the beatific vision is the extent of what eternal life offers. To see God is so all-fulfilling that there would be no desire for anything else. Pope Emeritus Benedict XVI comments indirectly on this issue in his encyclical *Spe salvi*:

> Do we really want this—to live eternally? Perhaps many people reject the faith today because they do not find the prospect of eternal life attractive. What they desire is not eternal life at all, but this present life, for which faith in eternal life seems something of an impediment. To continue living for ever—endlessly—appears more like a curse than a gift. . . . To live always, without end—this, all things considered, can only be monotonous and ultimately unbearable.[59]

While the dilemma of the "bad infinity" noted by the Pope Emeritus is a problem, there is also the problem of eternal life, even if outside earthly time-space, that seems to have no activity or novelty. Even sociality seems to be lost in an infinite contemplation of the Divine Being. The Spanish existentialist philosopher Miguel de Unamuno (1864–1936) writes about how such a life could be interpreted:

> A beatific vision, a loving contemplation in which the soul is absorbed in God, and lost, as it were, in him, seems to be either self-annihilation or a prolonged tedium, according to our natural way of feeling. This feeling causes the sentiment, frequently expressed, with satire, irreverence, or perhaps impiety, that the heaven of eternal glory is an abode of eternal boredom. It is of no use to scorn these feelings, so spontaneous and natural as they are, or to denigrate them.[60]

Unamuno certainly captures the concern with this hyper-Thomistic idea of eternal life. O'Callaghan sees the solution to eternal boredom by proposing that eternal life is a life of "divine praise, activity, and repose"

---

59. Cf. Benedict XVI, *Spe salvi*, 10.
60. Unamuno, *Del sentimiento trágico de la vida*, 226. My translation.

citing Ephraim the Syrian and Augustine, among others. He posits that the activity of eternal life will be one of delights and the fulfillment of all (presumably virtuous) desires.[61] Yet, these delights do not imply novelty because the eschaton is the "last thing" and thus it is the *novissimum* of human life and divine life. Nothing can possibly be "new" and there cannot be anything like the *semper novum* in eschatic life. Thus, even the delights of "heaven" have a static aspect.

The metaphors of eternal life as the New Jerusalem, the perfect garden, the wedding banquet, have limits if there is nothing else besides a perfect city, garden, or feast. Corner comments that "no one wants a meal with unlimited courses or to spend too long admiring even the nicest azaleas."[62] In a sense, even the beatific vision of God is anthropomorphic because it implies a beholding of something that is the most beautiful and human beings can only measure beauty by what they know on earth. Thus, God, *pace* Anselm, as that which nothing more beautiful can be conceived, tends to evoke images that humans associate with beauty, such as art or flowers or attractive persons. However, this does not seem to accord with the concept of a radical transformation at the judgment if it is meant to re-create human being as static cherubim who sing God's praises without end.

The Proposal That the Eternal Life Is Not the Last Thing

The very concept of the eschaton ("the last thing") implies, for some, that it precludes anything new because there is neither an "after" nor linear time. Griffiths' approach to eschatology is to see it as an event that heals damaged time. But he also states that "a creature with an endlessly novel future lacks a *novissimum*."[63] However, Barth takes a different view. Rather than "healed time" God's time is "real time" and God's space is "real space": "Eternity is the negation of time only because and to the extent that it is first and foremost God's time and therefore real time, in a way that God's omnipresence is not simply the negation of our space, but first and foremost is positively God's space and therefore real space."[64] In other words, earthly time-space is "unreal" and God is not bound by it, but also is not outside it. In this way, the incarnation of Christ was the

---

61. O'Callaghan, *Christ our Hope*, 157–59.
62. Corner, *Death Be Not Proud*, 63.
63. Griffiths, *Decreation*, 25. See also chapter 2, section 3.
64. Barth, *Church Dogmatics* 2/1, 610ff.

breaking in of divine reality into earthly non-reality and the resurrection was a breaking away from non-reality back into divine reality. As Corner notes, the message to the good thief on the cross that "today you will be with me in paradise" is to be taken literally—that at his death, the thief was transported immediately to the eschaton before God in Christ in divine (real) time-space. For Barth, there is no sense that earthly time-space has any similarity to divine time-space: ours is broken and subjects everything to decay. This explains why Barth cites Boethius (c. 480–524) in his *De consolatione philosophiae* 5 that *aeternitas est interminabilis vitae tota simul et perfecta possessio* ("eternity is the total, simultaneous, and complete possession of unlimited life").[65] God has this possession ontologically. This gives an idea of how Barth conceives of God's time (eternity). In my own understanding, the unlimited life that God possesses is what is given to human beings at the transformative judgment—we share in God's eternity of unlimited life.

The possession of unlimited life would seem to contradict the understanding that the eschaton is the Last Thing, but rather it is simply the last thing of earthly time-space which gives way to the new creation of persons and things that share in the unlimited life of God, no longer bound by the limits and linearity of "unreal" time. Thus, it cannot be thought of as perpetual stasis, but a new creation that allows *novelty*. Mühling proposes this definition of eternal life:

> First, eternal life is a synonym for divine life. Second, it is a synonym for successful life especially in the Johannine writings. Third, eternal life is a designation for the eschatical incorporation of creaturely life into the inner-Trinitarian divine life by grace and therefore means unmediated vision and enjoyment of God. The concept of life does go beyond the previously mentioned imagery used to depict the eschatical reality to the extent that it includes permanency of choice, even in the eschatical reality, and therefore actually novelty (newness) of both God and creation.[66]

What Mühling means by divine life as it applies to creatures is that the eschatic transformation resolves the dilemma of *simul iustus et peccator* and grants creaturely life a share of this divinity which is always rightly ordered and loving. The successful life is the life that is *iustus sed non*

---

65. Barth, *Church Dogmatics* 2/1, 610ff.
66. Mühling, *T. & T. Clark Handbook*, 365.

peccator through justification by grace and is not measured by worldly achievements, riches, or pleasures (what might be called the "good life"). Thus, the successful life *apud Deum* does not correspond to what human beings deem worthy achievements or celebrity. To "succeed" with God is solely to be a recipient of grace. Thus, *ante mortem* human success is of no account in the eschaton. Since a choice of infinite goods is part of eternal life, the *semper novum* ("always new") is maintained, even though it does not correspond to pre-eschatic earthly time-space. Thus, the eschaton is only the last thing of this age (aeon; *saeculum*). By way of illustration, Mühling cites a passage from C. S. Lewis's book *The Last Battle*:

> "There *was* a real railway accident," said Aslan softly. "Your father and mother and all of you are—as you used to call it in the Shadowlands—dead. The term is over: the holidays have begun. The dream is ended: this is the morning."
>
> And as He spoke, He no longer looked to them like a lion; but the things that began to happen after that were so great and beautiful that I cannot write them. And for us this is the end of all stories, and we can most truly say that we loved happily ever after. But for them it was only the beginning of the real story. All their life in this world and their adventures in Narnia had only been the cover and title page: now they were beginning Chapter One of the Great Story which no one on earth has read: which goes on for ever: in which every chapter is better than the one before.[67]

Mühling considers this passage to be (possibly) a sort of Christian Platonism with its assumptions of ever-higher "ascensions" in the successive chapters of eternal life. Be that as it may, it captures the idea of eschatic novelty in poetic fashion.[68]

The passage from C. S. Lewis resonates with Corner's own concept of eschatic life. I interpret Corner as suggesting that earthly life is on the edge of reality and thus we see things "as through a mirror dimly." Thus, our life on earth is more akin to a dream because God alone possesses real life, real time, and real space. Human beings, however, possess only these things as a shadow (hence Lewis's understanding of this world as the "Shadowlands"). In effect, the earth (and indeed all worlds in creation) is the "valley of the shadow of death" and humans and all created

---

67. Lewis, *The Last Battle*, 224. Emphasis original.
68. Mühling, *T. & T. Clark Handbook*, 367.

things occupy this shadow realm.⁶⁹ In effect, our life as we know it is a dream:

> At death the players leave the stage and act no more. Death is the "final curtain," the end of the play, and it is absurd to believe the players go on acting off-stage. This is the folly of the "intermediate state," that attempts to perpetuate the dream. There is nothing beyond death that we can possibly imagine. But insofar as we have the ability to recognise from within the dream itself that the reality it depicts is an incomplete one, then we have something—the possibility (and no more) of a reality as unimaginable to us now as the waking moment is to the sleeper:
>
> One short sleepe past, wee wake eternally,
> And death shall be no more: death thou shalt die.⁷⁰

Here Corner cites John Donne's (1573–1631) poem *Death Be Not Proud* to drive home the point that death is not "survived," it is *overcome* (which is a concept already proposed by Antje Jackelén)—and the overcoming of death is a waking from the dream that is our earthly life.⁷¹ Thus, the Pauline trumpet that shall sound to raise the dead incorruptible (cf. 1 Cor 15:52) is the wake-up call that rouses us from the dream of unreal life into the eschatic real life:

> If, as 1 Corinthians promises, the trumpet sound, then it will sound in a world that we cannot yet know. No afterlife, no life after death, for "after" is a word which we recognise only in terms of our own understanding of time.... We shall recognise our lives as a dream from which we have awakened, and St Peter not as the gatekeeper of the heavenly city, but as the herald of all things new, the piper as the gates of dawn.⁷²

The suggestion that human beings and indeed all creation exists in a dream world (which, by definition, is not "real") and that we awaken to eternal life, to the reality of God's realm, is not easily accepted and it also calls into questions how our unreal actions can possibly be judged. It is a challenging idea that dispenses with an intermediate state and a general resurrection at the end of earth's time-space. It is, in effect, very similar to Gisbert Greshake's "resurrection-in-death" concept: that the moment of

---

69. Cf. Corner, *Death Be Not Proud*, 258ff.
70. Corner, *Death Be Not Proud*, 270–71.
71. Jackelén, *Time and Eternity*, 112.
72. Corner, *Death Be Not Proud*, 271.

death is the moment of resurrection.[73] For Corner, eschatic awakening is the same thing as resurrection. This has christological implications: the incarnation, life, death, and resurrection of Christ was an event where the divine reality was clothed in a dream (*kata sarka*) and at the resurrection, the dream-clothing (*sarx*) was transfigured and awakened into the reality of God. Thus, the Word made flesh was a breaking in of God's reality into the dream of humanity. The reason earthly life is a dream is because "[r]eality is located with God, and we have carried but the faintest traces of divinity into our exile on earth."[74] Thus, this fallen mortal life is truly a life in the "Shadowlands" and thus is not "true life" because this is possessed by God alone. It is only by awakening (i.e., dying) that we are transfigured and transferred into God's reality which presumably includes a "real" corporeality (perhaps going beyond the Pauline *soma pneumatikon*). Therefore, for Corner, the eschaton is not the Last Thing, but is actually the *first* thing for human beings within the reality of the realm of God.

However, this sort of logic that "life is but a dream," although it has certain advantages, seems to be a form of Docetism. While I do not think that Corner is implying that we live in a dream world, his concept has implications that come too close to implying human beings and the universe are illusions, i.e., merely the dream of God. Rather, I would propose that eternal life is the *semper novum*. The eschaton is not the first thing for human beings, but rather the New Thing that possesses infinite novelty.

Implications for the Communion of Saints

It is the proposal of this book that the dead neither wait in an intermediate state nor are totally dead awaiting the last day, but rather are immediately present before God in Christ at the eschatic judgment. Through a threefold process of absolute recognition, they are transformed and participate in eternal life which is the realization of the kingdom of God. They therefore enter divine time-space, which is the possession of unlimited life, no longer bound by the limitations of their earthly instantiation. Eschatic life is to be understood as corporeal, not according to corruptible flesh, but rather according to the transubstantiation into glorious form after the manner of the resurrection of Christ. Thus, the dead have overcome death, experienced resurrection, and dwell in the eschatic reality in an

---

73. Cf. Greshake, *Auferstehung der Toten*, 360–414
74. Corner, *Death Be Not Proud*, 100.

instant from the perspective of earthly time-space. The dead are always already alive to God.

The implication for the communion of saints is that the saints on earth are still connected to the those who are in eternal life. In Rahner's essay "The Life of the Dead," he writes about the connection between the living and the dead:

> ... we meet the living dead, even when they are those who are loved by us, in faith, hope and love, that is, when we open our hearts to the silent calm of God, in which they live; not by calling them back to where we are, but by descending into the silent eternity of our own hearts, and through faith in the risen Lord, creating in time the eternity which they have brought forth for ever.[75]

Rahner's comment, despite claiming it as "Catholic," has an almost Protestant tone. He does not mention the intercession of the saints even though at least some of the "living dead" are not in an "intermediate state" (purgatory), but enjoy the beatific vision (granted without benefit of the reunited body), except for those, perhaps, who have been taken up "body and soul" into "heavenly glory" by God according to Scripture or tradition (e.g., Enoch, Elijah, and Mary). Yet, Rahner's text is useful in the context of the concept that the eschatic reality is an immediate event at the moment of death. Mühling makes the following claim:

> The judgement takes place in the present in so far as the presence of Christ is given but remains disputed. The judgement as final judgement means the process of transformation and constitution that created person's experience when they are transferred from the spatio-temporally individuating framework into the eschatically individuating framework that is God. This dispenses with the need to determine the location of the judgement either temporally or spatially.[76]

Mühling understands the parousia as simultaneously ahistorical, supra-historical, and historical. For the dead, the parousia is one of "universal immediacy." By this he means that the resurrection occurs at the moment of death regardless of the spatio-temporal location of persons. Yet, it is historical in an earthward and metaphoric sense.[77] It is in

---

75. Rahner, "The Life of the Dead," in *Theological Investigations*, vol. 4, 353–54.
76. Mühling, *T. & T. Clark Handbook*, 336.
77. Mühling, *T. & T. Clark Handbook*, 272–73.

this context that Mühling mentions Gisbert Greshake, but only once in a footnote.[78] Combining the concepts of Rahner, Corner, and Mühling, the dead are always already sharing in the eschatic reality and thus have been transformed and glorified. They share in God's simultaneous unlimited life. Thus, the "dead" are with us and aware of us in the same manner as God. However, this communion is asymmetrical because we are bound by earthly, fallen time-space and they are not. Thus, as Rahner says, the "dead" cannot manifest in their transformed state to the "living" on earth—unless, as Rahner claims, by a special revelation granted by God. The communion of saints includes all who live and all who have died, but this does not mean that the saints in glory can grant us favors, even if they do continuously intercede for us, just as Christ does within the Godhead.

I would thus propose that an outcome of the transformative and absolute recognition of divine judgment is the positive connection that endures between the denizens of earthly time-space and the denizens of eternal life. Thus, to love the "dead" is not unilateral in the sense of the communion of saints, but it is unilateral in that the "dead" cannot reciprocate our love or do our bidding because they are like the eschatic Christ, whom we cannot see in mortal life "face to face," but we can know by faith, in hope, and through love.

Conclusion

In this section, I explored the concept of eternal life as one where the *semper novum* ("always new") is part of the eschatic reality avoiding the problems of an anthropomorphizing of "heaven" that restricts eternal life to fit within human finite expectations, but also contains the potential for eschatic boredom creating a "bad infinity" of static being for the denizens of the life to come. Rather than proposing that "heaven" is a perfected yet duplicate earthly realm or a state of simply pondering the delights of the beatific vision in a state of blissful stasis, I agree with Lewis, Corner, and Mühling: novelty must be part of the eschatic reality. Mühling proposes a solution to the linear time that newness seems to demand in the eschaton by opting to describe eschatic novelty as "event-like" to avoid the concept of duration. Corner takes a page from Karl Barth by asserting that God's time-space is "real" while earthly (fallen) time-space is shadow of this reality, a dream from which we must awaken in order to enter the perfect

---

78. Mühling, *T. & T. Clark Handbook*, 273n42.

time-space of God. The formula of Boethius that the possession of eternity is unlimited life in simultaneity also seems to avoid the problem of what Griffiths' refers to as metronomic time (devastated time). Thus, the eschatic reality can be said to have no clocks because time does not pass. Thus, eschatic beings are not subject to the limitations of earthly time-space. Thus, they share in divine time-space which is beyond categories such as "outside space and time" or supra-temporality. What we can say about divine time is that it exceeds the capacities of human intellect in this mortal life.

The example suggested by C. S. Lewis that this life is a title page, but eternal life contains the chapters with every succeeding chapter better than the one before it is attractive, even if it suggests a Neoplatonism with its attendant baggage. Yet, I think Lewis, well aware of Christian Platonism, is suggesting that eternal life can only be a place of infinite goods where not only novelty is present, but that the goods on offer are of such a nature that to the eschatic person they would have qualities that would always exceed the joys of previously chosen goods due to the infinite resources of God. Thus, eschatic humanity becomes part of God's creativity as the eternal *fons bonorum*.

Lastly, the proposal that death is the moment of resurrection has an implication for the communion of saints in that it can be said that those in eternal life are aware of the denizens of those who remain in earthly time-space. The inference (or feeling) that the "dead" are a living presence that could in part explain the cultus of the veneration of saints and ancestors within and without Christianity could be said to be an earthly awareness that the "dead" share in divine life. This is not a justification or endorsement of saintly veneration or intercession, but more a possible explanation of a near universal phenomenon in human religiosity.

6. Conclusion: *Ut sit Deus omnia in omnibus*

> *This life, therefore, is not godliness but the process of becoming godly, not health but getting well, not being but becoming, not rest but exercise. We are not now what we shall be, but we are on the way. The process is not yet finished, but it is actively going on. This is not the goal but it is the right road. At present, everything does not gleam and sparkle, but everything is being cleansed.*
> —Martin Luther[79]

79. Cf. Luther, Article 2 in "Defence and Explanation of All the Articles," in *Luther's*

In this chapter, I have explored the concept that divine judgment is the event of absolute recognition in a threefold manner of God, self, and other. The proposal is that absolute recognition is the process of transformation and glorification that happens at the moment of death and is not bound by any temporo-spatial location. This concept of "absolute" recognition goes beyond recognition theory and therefore I did not seek to use Ricoeur or Honneth (or others) as models for this eschatological concept.

I have attempted to explore what such an unmediated recognition would entail for the person as to God in Christ, the self, and all others. Throughout this exploration, there has been an awareness of the problem of universal salvation as well as the problem of a dual outcome of salvation and damnation (recognition and non-recognition). While the eschatology proposed is one of hope, it is also one that has attenuated traditional universalism by making use of Markus Mühling's proposal that not all identity claims will endure the judgment, thus a discontinuity between the earthly person and the eschatic person is perhaps universal. Therefore, universal salvation as usually construed is *false* because the eschatic person will "be changed" and only that which was loving on earth will be "saved" while all non-loving identity claims will be rejected. In this, there is both continuity and discontinuity between earthly and eschatic instantiations, but no total loss of the person as a bearer of God's image.

The problem of free will was addressed, but the concept that human libertarian free will as experienced on earth (which is a "fallen" will) would not be subject to transformation at the judgment was deemed incoherent. If the divine judgment is an event of the creation and constitution of real personhood (per Mühling), then this process must include a transformation of the will that accords with the eschatic reality as totally good. The will is thereby freed in the judgment and not restricted.

The issue of christology was addressed in terms of the requirements of absolute recognition of the Judge who is Jesus Christ. My argument is that the recognition of Christ as the God-Human who alone can judge human beings takes precedent over earthly statements about the nature of Jesus Christ. Yet, I maintain that Christ the Judge is also the human being known as Jesus of Nazareth on earth. Yet, the judgment is neither a process that demands human beings confess Christ as Jesus of Nazareth

---

Works, vol. 32, 24.

nor it is a process that seeks to rectify other religious or non-religious earthly claims. Even so, absolute recognition would mean that every person will recognize Jesus of Nazareth as the Christ, but this is neither punitive nor triumphal.

The possibility that eschatic indifference could result in non-recognition which would be a type of hell was rejected since this would mean that the eschatic reality still would contain a dual outcome. However, the process of judgment can be said to contain "hell" in that the stripping away of all that is non-love can be understood as seeing our unworthy self-claims annihilated and not knowing what the outcome of this process will be, other than it will be entirely good.

The problems with earthly and anthropomorphic concepts of eternal life were explored. All images of gardens, reunions, the beatific vision are inadequate and equate to a human desire to extend earthly life indefinitely through different "bad infinities" that restrict the infinite goods of the kingdom of God. Rather, as a corrective to what amounts to an alternate hell of eternal boredom, it was proposed that the new creation of the eschaton is not the Last Thing, but the New Thing that comprises the *semper novum* of eschatic novelty that allows for an infinite and creative participation in God's goodness. The speculation of C. S. Lewis that the eschatic life is a series of chapters where each one is better than the one before, while suggesting a Neoplatonism, is attractive since an infinite choice of goods would allow for this infinite event-like (as Mühling would suggest) happening since each good encountered would be entirely novel. Eschatic boredom is thus impossible. Within the concept of *semper novum*, I explored the concept of Boethius that eternal life is the possession of simultaneous, unlimited life. This led to a discussion of the problem of the "timing" of the judgment. Agreeing with Mühling, I affirmed Greshake's proposal of immediate resurrection-in-death (which Mühling only referred to in passing). Thus, the eschaton happens at the moment of death for every person and all humanity within a divine time-space that is not bound by linearity: we are judged individually and collectively at once.

I explored what the implications of this type of eschatology means for the communion of saints. I suggest that there is a connection (communion) between those in earthly time-space and eternal life, but this connection is, as Rahner asserts, based in faith, hope, and love. The denizens of eternal life are not lesser divinities that can grant requests, but rather their participation in divine life may cause us to be aware of them as alive with God. This variant of the *sensus divinitatis* could explain the almost universal human practice of the veneration of saints and ancestors, but I do not suggest that such veneration is to be commended. Rather, I would commend that we love the "dead" as we do the living, just as the "dead" love us.

Above, I cited the Pauline "all in all" and a quotation from Luther in his 1521 rejection of the papal bull *Exurge Domine* of Pope Leo X (1475–1521) that excommunicated him. In terms of earthly life, Luther's quote is apt and echoes Mühling's understanding that we are "human becomings" that are *in via*. The outcome of the eschaton is the All in All (cf. 1 Cor 15:28) in that God, who is wholly good, will transfigure all things so that there is only the good "for the former things have passed away" (Rev 21:4 AV).

CHAPTER 6

Conclusion

O give thanks to the Eternal One who is good;
whose loving-kindness and mercy endures forever.
—Psalm 136:1[1]

I have nothing to say at the finish except that if one wants a permanent rock in life and goes deep enough for it, it is difficult for historical events to shake it. There are times when we can never meet the future with sufficient elasticity of mind, especially if we are locked in the contemporary systems of thought. We can do worse than remember a principle which both gives us a firm Rock and leaves us the maximum elasticity for our minds: the principle: "Hold to Christ and for the rest be totally uncommitted."
—Herbert Butterfield (1900–1979)[2]

Epistemologically, human beings cannot know what lies beyond death. Within our limited nature, it is possible to reflect on the divine-human relationship revealed to us by God and, on this basis, propose certain eschatological possibilities rooted in hope. Keeping this principle in mind, I have argued that the constructed aphorism *iudicandus est salvandus* ("to be judged is to be saved") is a convincing Christian eschatological claim. Within this claim, I have proposed that divine judgment is creative, hopeful, and non-dualistic. To wit, the act of divine judgment is the event of salvation and reconciliation for human beings. The basis of this argument is the understanding that God is love and is love precisely

1. My translation of the Masoretic text.
2. Butterfield, *Christianity and History*, 130.

in judgment. I have posited that the act of judgment is one of absolute recognition in which human persons "see" in an unfiltered and unlimited way the reality of their own earthly lives, the reality of God, and the reality of the impact of their lives on all other persons. It is this recognition that enables not only reconciliation, but also the full constitution of human personhood. This creative act of God in the judgment is analogous to theosis, the incorporation of human beings into the divine life; which is an unlimited life in relationality *between persons*: between divine persons (using the metaphor of the Trinity) and human persons made divine. Rather than an eternal stasis of beatitude, I have argued that the eschatic realm of God is the *semper novum*, one of perpetual "novelty," of glory to glory. My contribution to Christian theology is therefore the claim that *salvific judgment* is a viable concept and an alternative to the largely dominant soteriological dualism of the Christian tradition.

To recall what I have argued in this book: in the first chapter, I explored the subject of Christian eschatology and a dualistic soteriology that divides human beings into two camps, the elect and the reprobate. I then argued that this dualism must be rejected on the ground that it endangers the coherence of the doctrine of God. I also rejected this dualism as a problem of theodicy that leads to the ultimate defeat of Christ and the eternalization of evil within the eschatic kingdom. I have decided against traditional understandings of universal salvation. Instead, I have argued that universalism is both true and false. It is true because no person is "lost." It is false because no person knows which self-claims will endure the judgment. Death is therefore the event of a simultaneous and radical continuity and discontinuity between earthly and eschatic human lives. To this can be added that no person knows the outcome of the judgment or what aspects of the self will be "saved."

In chapter 2, I investigated three symbols and problems of judgment: death, the intermediate state, and hell. The problem of death was explored in its materialist and theological interpretations. Death is a universal problem for human beings irrespective of religiosity. It represents an end to earthly relationality notwithstanding if an "afterlife" is presumed or denied. For the materialist, it is negation because the life lived is annihilated. For the believer in an "afterlife," it is still a radical separation from an earthly instantiation into an unknown realm. For both, as Marilyn McCord Adams asserts, it is a horror. This led to an exploration of death in the Stoic sense, as Martin Heidegger commends, by simply facing our thrownness-towards-death and living authentically in spite of it. Kierkegaard provided an existentialist Christian framework that views death as both the fearsome event of immortality and judgment. Karl Rahner, Eberhard Jüngel, and Antje Jackelén modify the Heiddegerian position through a Christian lens. Unlike Jüngel and Jackelén, Rahner cannot affirm "total death" but all three understand death in the christological sense that just as Christ suffered, died, and overcame death, so must human beings. However, "total death theory" without an intermediate state or an immediate translation to the eschaton raises a question about the continuity of individual personhood between death and resurrection.

I then turned to a discussion of the intermediate state of discarnation or soul separation. This remains the popular understanding of death within and outside Christianity. Whether this is a borrowing from Hellenistic thanatology or not, the intermediate state represents a deep challenge to human personhood because it presumes that the dead are psychosomatically bifurcated, resulting in a sub-human discarnate entity that wanders in some sort of time-space that is either harrowing, as in the interpretations of Thomas Aquinas, Paul Griffiths, and to some extent Sergei Bulgakov; or Platonist and seemingly "gentle," as in the thought of Friedrich Schleiermacher. I proposed a recovery of the concept of Gisbert Greshake that departs from discarnation in favor of resurrection-in-death. This avoids body-soul dualism by positing that the dead are transphysical—meaning that for the dead, the eschaton has always already occurred and they have already been transubstantiated into glorious form. This implies that from our earthbound perspective, the dead are indeed *ganz tot* (entirely dead), but from the eschatic perspective they are already sharing in unlimited divine life. Thus, the dead do not wander or wait, but for them the eschaton, inclusive of the judgment, is immediate.

In my exploration of the concept of hell as a symbol and problem of judgment, I find it to be the most profound challenge to Christian theology because it devastates the doctrine of God and turns the triumph of Christ into a pyrrhic victory. Joseph Ratzinger notes that "no quibbling helps us here" and he is indeed right, but the choice is stark: either defend the traditional doctrine of hell and its eternalized binary implications for human beings or reject it. As I have claimed, to defend this doctrine is to embrace dystheism. To avoid this, various modifications of the doctrine have been attempted. I discussed those of William Lane Craig (transworld damnation); Paul Griffiths (annihilationism);

C. S. Lewis (hell as self-imposed); Jonathan Kvanvig (a hell issuant from God's love); and Eleonore Stump (hell as quarantine). A more radical solution to this problem is proposed by Andrei Buckareff and Allen Plug in their "escapist" hell, a hell that one can leave freely. In my own attempt to find a solution, I was left with an "annex" in the eschaton that proved unsatisfactory.

In chapter 3, I engaged with the optimistic eschatology of four theologians who are normally deemed universalists or, in the case of Hans Urs von Balthasar, an almost-universalist. I researched these theologians not only to seek a solution to the problem of hell, but also to query whether they implicitly agreed with my thesis that divine judgment is salvific.

Sergei Bulgakov clearly sees the eschatic judgment as the locus of salvation and retains much of the imagery associate with hell, but transposes it into a purgatorial encounter with God's love. Bulgakov never overtly claims that the judgment is salvific, but his writings lead inexorably to that conclusion. However, Bulgakov wants to assert that human free will is inviolate yet he also asserts that divine love is irresistible. The transposition of an earthly free will in the eschatic reality would be impossible. Yet, this is never clearly spelled out. Theodicy is notably absent in his mystical theology, but creative sophiological commitments demand a diminution of earthly sufferings in favor of a cosmic approach that sees the "humanization" of the world as God's preordained project. This divine determinism grounded in God's love demands universal salvation. For Bulgakov, the second coming of Christ is not only an unstoppable, salvific force, but it is always already happening and it cannot be defeated.

Hans Urs von Balthasar refuses to affirm universalism, but urges that we hope that universal salvation is true. Thus, the aphorism *iudicandus est salvandus* cannot be asserted. A populated hell as an eschatic problem of evil is not addressed. My own understanding of Balthasar's eschatology is that it is magisterially constrained. He will only go so far as the boundaries of orthodoxy will permit. However, his hopeful universalism provides a counterpoint to the salvific pessimism of the received Augustinian and Thomistic inheritances. However, where I find Balthasar's thought most striking is in his assertion that human beings are always already under judgment. For Balthasar, this is reflected in the *sensus fidelium*. However, I would expand Balthasar's concept anthropologically to be a human *sensus iudicii*. By this, I mean that all human beings have some sort of understanding that their actions matter, even if no earthly authority will ever hold them to account.

J. A. T. Robinson's early work on eschatology seems to suggest that human beings are indeed "saved" at the judgment. In a very limited sense, his book *In the End, God* is a Western Protestant answer to Bulgakov's *The Bride of the Lamb*. The two books are separated in time by a mere six years. Robinson, however, stumbles over the issue of human free will. He seems to argue that human free will, in its earthly form, is eternally inviolate, but that somehow divine love overwhelms this will without any violation. Thus, irresistible love overrides human free will because God as Lover cannot be refused—free will shall yield.

Marilyn McCord Adams' high christology produces a case for universal salvation that is grounded in the incarnation and the cross. She has no interest in theodicy in defence of God who created a universe where human beings are vulnerable to horrors. Rather, Adams constructs an eschatology that results in universal salvation based upon the Creator's entrance into and owning of the vulnerability of material creation. Earthly vulnerability to horrors is incorporated into the Godhead. Our wounds, de facto caused by God because God created us vulnerable, shall be as glorious as those of the Risen Christ. In other words, God will make good on our plight in the glory of the eschaton. Yet, perhaps because Adams asserts that human beings, ravaged by horrors, are not fully accountable for their actions, she is sparse in her treatment of divine judgment. Yet, her most important contribution within her scheme is her assertion that human beings will be judged by a human Christ, who through incarnation shared our exact plight as both a horror-perpetrator and a horror-recipient. This partially denies the impeccability of Christ. Jesus, at least passively, causes sin to occur. While I did not find her therapeutic approach to eschatic transformation compelling, I find her overall approach both radical and refreshing. Adams does not deal with eschatic human free will, but this seems to accord with her concept that humans as horror-participants have attenuated agency. For Adams, the *ante mortem* human will is limited and cannot be said to be truly free. However, her eschatological understandings have a weakness in that she does not consider the possibility that an eschatic person who is finally gifted with true free agency in the eschaton might reject the God who created a horrendous earthly world.

In chapter 4, I explored four conceptions of the purpose of judgment: (1) retributive with a dual outcome (Matthias Scheeben and Paul

O'Callaghan); (2) retributive with a single, salvific outcome (Sergei Bulgakov); (3) non-retributive, rectifying, and universalist (Jürgen Moltmann); and (4) non-retributive, constitutive of human personhood, and quasi-universalist (Markus Mühling).

Using my thesis that divine judgment is the judgment of divine love and is salvific, the retributive judgment with a dual outcome as represented by Scheeben and O'Callaghan must be rejected. Their understanding of judgment is that God's offer of mercy ends at death and therefore those who remain impenitent will be subject to eternal punishment. Paul Griffiths proposes a softening of this in the form of annihilation. Both options for the damned would seem to contradict God's ontic love and defeat the victory of Christ over evil. If Christ in the resurrection and the parousia is unable to defeat all evils (i.e., non-loving relationalities), God would not be "all in all" if there is a place where hatred reigns.

For Bulgakov, divine judgment is ultimately salvific and is grounded in God's love. The hellish fire of divine love in its "wrath" against sin effects an eschatic division between the "goat-self" and the "sheep-self" in every person. This intrapersonal separation has a seemingly barbarous element of metaphysical amputation. Although Bulgakov advocates an eschatic synergism, in the end God's grace is irresistible. Human will, though free, conforms to that of Christ's *ex opere operato*. The demands of Bulgakov's sophiology and its unstoppable divinization of the cosmos obviate questions of whether human beings are forced to accede to God's love or rather are set free to do so.

Moltmann insists on a gracious universalism that heals the victims of evil and transforms the evildoers into saints. Demands for recompense or justice are rejected as functionally idolatrous because human justice is never the equivalent of divine justice. Miroslav Volf's "corrective" that there must be a mutual giving and receiving of grace between offenders and offended in freedom is not denied by Moltmann. Rather, Moltmann cannot allow that any human will would resist such an exchange. The justifying judgment will rectify the human will, freeing it from its earthly bondage. Thus, his universalism is achieved through irresistible and rectifying grace. Moltmann denies that human beings are masters of their own destinies and consider such a belief tantamount to atheism. However, if God desires relationality with human beings and that relationality is based on love, must it not be freely given by the creature to the Creator? For Moltmann, human beings are meant to be freely loving, but this is not realizable on earth. The eschatic judgment is the event that instantiates this love in freedom by divine fiat.

Mühling tries to resolve this conflict between grace and freedom. Those who are judged will also be self-judges. By the illumination of the Spirit, human beings in the judgment will be compelled by the truth set before them. They will not only accept any divine verdict, but will plead that the "sentence" be carried out upon them. Instead of irresistible grace, Mühling posits irresistible truth: "truth will make you free" (cf. John 8:32). However, will the eschatically constituted person, regardless of aesthetic differences, freely love the God who has re-created them? Mühling would answer yes because it is only in the eschaton that human beings attain the fullness of personhood which entails an orthonomous agency that is freely loving.

In chapter 5, I proposed that divine judgment can be understood as the event of absolute recognition of God, the self, and the other. It is the act of absolute recognition, which may be harrowing, that initiates the process of transformation and glorification. This event is not bound by earthward time-space or concepts of locality. I explored what such an unmediated recognition would entail for the person in relation to God, the self, and all others. The outcome of this process would not be a verdict on persons, but on their earthly identity claims and actions. Identity claims and the actions that proceed from them may or may not endure the judgment. It can thus be presumed that there is a universal discontinuity between the earthly person and the eschatic person constituted by the judgment. The eschatic person will "be changed" and only that which was loving will be "saved" while all non-loving identity claims will be rejected and destroyed. Thus, there is both continuity and discontinuity between earthly and eschatic instantiations. This renders traditional ideas about universal salvation false, but maintains that no person is ever totally lost in the life to come.

The problem of eschatic free will was considered, but the concept that human libertarian free will as experienced on earth (and is thus a "bound" will) would not be subject to transformation at the judgment was deemed incoherent. Thus, if the divine judgment is an event of the creation and constitution of real personhood through the event of absolute recognition, then this must include a transformation of the will that accords with the eschatic reality as totally good. The human will only becomes truly free through divine judgment.

I investigated the issue of christology as an aspect of the absolute recognition of the Judge who is Jesus Christ. My argument is that the recognition of Christ as the God-Human who alone can judge human beings takes precedence over earthly claims about the nature of Jesus Christ. In this recognition, Christ is revealed as the incarnation of the Son of God in Jesus of Nazareth, but this revelation is neither punitive nor triumphal.

The possibility that eschatic indifference could result in non-recognition, which would be a type of hell, was rejected as this allows for an eschatic dual outcome. However, I do retain "hell" within the context of judgment. "Hell" is not a place, but a *process*. It is the stripping away of all that is non-loving. The outcome of this purgation is not known for any one person or humanity as a whole, but we can *trust* that whatever it is, it will be entirely good.

I explored the problems with earthly and anthropomorphic concepts of eternal life ("heaven"). I concluded that human concepts of "heaven" as gardens, reunions, cities, and beatific visions are inadequate. I argued against the understanding of "heaven" as some sort of perfected, earth-like paradise with immortal denizens as representing a "bad infinity." Rather, I propose that the new creation of the eschaton is not the Last Thing, but the New Thing that comprises the *semper novum* of eschatic "novelty" that allows for an infinite and creative participation in God's goodness. I find the proposal of C. S. Lewis that the eschatic life is a series of chapters where each one is better than the one before it attractive because an infinite choice of goods would allow for this an event-like typology of eternal life. Eschatic boredom, which would also be hell, would thereby be avoided.

Within the concept of *semper novum*, I explored the concept of Boethius that eternal life is the possession of simultaneous, unlimited life. This led to a discussion of the problem of the "timing" of the judgment. I recovered and affirmed Gisbert Greshake's concept of immediate resurrection-in-death. Thus, the eschaton happens *in hora mortis* for every person and all of humanity in a divine time-space that is not bound by linearity.

I explored the implications of this type of eschatology for the communion of saints. I suggested that there is a connection (communion) between those in earthly time-space and eternal life, but this connection is, as Rahner asserts, based in faith, hope, and love. The denizens of eternal life are not lesser divinities that can grant requests, but rather their participation in divine life may cause us to sense their love for us. This variant of the *sensus divinitatis* could explain the almost universal human practice of the veneration of saints and ancestors, but I do not suggest that such veneration is to be commended.

In conclusion, I have argued that divine judgment is the judgment of love: salvific, non-dualistic, in which nothing is lost except that which is non-love. The process of judgment is the event of absolute recognition where everything is revealed, the chaff is burned away, the will is freed, and that which remains is glorified and experiences the *semper novum* of the realm of God to which, in human understanding, no limits can be ascribed. As to the relationship between an eschatic humanity and God's material creation, both animate and inanimate creatures and their eternal vocation (e.g., Pope Francis's 2015 encyclical *Laudato Si'*), that is an investigation for another time.

I believe that my contribution to Christian eschatology is one that enables us as human beings to approach death and judgment with faith, hope, and love—not only for ourselves, but for the whole human race—past, present, and future—and humanity's interrelationship with God's creative and reconciling project:

> For I am convinced that neither death, nor life, nor angels, nor rulers, nor things present, nor things to come, nor powers, nor height, nor depth, nor anything else in all creation, will be able to separate us from the love of God in Christ Jesus our Lord. (Rom 8:38–39)

Bibliography

Abbaye Saint-Pierre de Solesmes. *Graduale Romanum*. Paris: Desclée & Co., 1922.
Abbott, Walter M, ed. *The Documents of Vatican II*. New York: Guild, 1966.
Adams, Marilyn McCord. *Christ and Horrors: The Coherence of Christology*. Cambridge: Cambridge University Press, 2006.
———. *Horrendous Evils and the Goodness of God*. Ithaca, NY: Cornell University Press, 1999.
———. "Horrors in Theological Context." *Scottish Journal of Theology* 55.4 (2002) 468–79.
———. "The Problem of Hell: A Problem of Evil for Christians." In *Reasoned Faith: Essays in Philosophical Theology in Honor of Norman Kretzman*, edited by Eleonore Stump, 301–27. Ithaca, NY: Cornell University Press, 1993.
Alfeyev, Hilarion. *Christ the Conqueror of Hell: The Descent into Hades from an Orthodox Perspective*. Crestwood, NY: St Vladimir's Seminary Press, 2009.
Alper, Becka A. "Millennials are less religious than older Americans, but just as spiritual." *Pew Research Center*. Online: http://www.pewresearch.org/fact-tank/2015/11/23/millennials-are-less-religious-than-older-americans-but-just-as-spiritual. Accessed 18 June 2016.
Ambrose of Milan. "De excessu fratris sui Satyri." In *Corpus Scriptorum Ecclesiasticorum Latinorum* 73. Edited by Otto Faller. Vienna: Hoelder-Pichler-Tempsky, 1955.
Ansell, Nicholas. *The Annihilation of Hell: Universal Salvation and the Redemption of Time in the Eschatology of Jürgen Moltmann*. Eugene, OR: Cascade, 2013.
Aquinas, Thomas. *Summa Theologiae*. Edited and translated by Timothy Suttor. Cambridge: Cambridge University Press, 2006.
Armstrong, Regis J., and Ignatius C. Brady, eds. *Francis and Clare: The Complete Works*. Classics of Western Spirituality. Mahwah, NJ: Paulist, 1982.
Augustine of Hippo. *City of God*. Translated by Henry Bettenson. 1972. Rev. ed. Edited by G. R. Evans. London: Penguin Classics, 2003.
———. *The Enchiridion of Faith, Hope and Love*. Edited and translated by Albert O. Outler. Philadelphia: Westminster, 1955.
———. *S. Aurelii Augustini Opera Omnia: Patrologiae Latinae Elenchus*. Rome: Città Nuova. Online: http://www.augustinus.it. (Accessed 4 April 2017).
Aulén, Gustaf. *Christus Victor: An Historical Study of the Three Main Types of the Idea of the Atonement*. Translated by A. G. Hebert. 1931. Reprint. New York: Macmillan, 1969.

Balthasar, Hans Urs von. *Dare We Hope "That all Men be Saved"?* with *A Short Discourse on Hell*. Translated by David Kipp and Lothar Krauth. San Francisco: Ignatius Press, 1988.

———. *Du krönst das Jahr mit deinem Huld*. Einsiedeln: Johannes Verlag, 1982.

———. *Glaubhaft ist nur Liebe*. Einsiedeln: Johannes Verlag, 1963.

———. *The Glory of the Lord: A Theology of Aesthetics I: Seeing the Form*. Translated by Erasmo Leiva-Merikakis. Edinburgh: T. & T. Clark, 1982.

———. *Kleiner Diskurs über die Hölle*. Ostfildern: Schwabenverlag, 1987.

———. *Love Alone Is Credible*. Translated by D. C. Schindler. San Francisco: Ignatius Press, 2004.

———. *Mysterium Paschale: Die Theologie der Drei Tage*. Einsiedeln: Benziger Verlag, 1970.

———. *Mysterium Paschale: The Mystery of Easter*. Translated by Aidan Nichols OP. Edinburgh: T. & T. Clark, 1990.

———. *Theo-drama: Theological Dramatic Theory*. Translated by Graham Harrison. 5 vols. San Francisco: Ignatius, 1988–98.

———. *Theodramatik*. 5 vols. Einsiedeln: Johannes Verlag, 1973–83.

———. *Theologie der Geschichte*. Einsiedeln: Johannes Verlag, 1959.

———. *A Theology of History*. Translator unknown. New York: Sheed and Ward, 1963.

———. *Was dürfen wir hoffen?* Einsiedeln: Johannes Verlag, 1986.

———. *You Crown the Year with Your Goodness: Sermons through the Liturgical Year*. Translated by Graham Harrison. San Francisco: Ignatius, 1989.

Barth, Karl. *Church Dogmatics, II.1: The Doctrine of God*. Edited and translated by G. W. Bromiley and T. F. Torrance. Edinburgh: T. & T. Clark, 1957.

———. *Church Dogmatics II.2: The Doctrine of the Word of God*. Translated by G. T. Thompson. New York: Scribners, 1936.

———. *Church Dogmatics III.2: The Doctrine of Creation*. Edited and translated by G. W. Bromiley and T. F. Torrance. 1960. Reprint. London: T. & T. Clark, 2009.

———. *The Epistle to the Romans*. Translated by Edwyn C. Hoskins. Oxford: Oxford University Press, 1933.

———. *The Faith of the Church: A Commentary on the Apostle's Creed according to Calvin's Catechism*. Edited by Jean-Louis Leuba and translated by Gabriel Vahanian. New York: Meridian, 1963.

———. *Die Römerbrief*. 2nd ed. 1922. Reprint. Zürich: Theologischer Verlag Zürich, 2010.

———. "Witness to an Ancient Truth." *TIME* magazine, 20 April 1962. Cover story.

Becker, Ernest. *Denial of Death*. New York: Free, 1973.

Berdyaev, Nikolai. *The Meaning of the Creative Act*. Translated by Donald Lowry. London: Gollancz, 1955.

———. *Smysl Tvorchestva* [Смысл Творчества]. Moscow: Leman and Sakharov, 1916.

Bettis, Joseph D. "Is Karl Barth a Universalist?" *Scottish Journal of Theology* 20 (1967) 423–36.

Bird-David, Nurit. "Animism Revisited: Personhood, Environment, and Relational Epistemology." *Current Anthropology* 40.S1 (February 1999) 67–91.

Blondel, Maurice. *L'Action*. 1893. Reprint. Paris: Presses Universitaires de France, 1950.

Brecht, Bertolt. *Bertolt Brechts Hauspostille*. 1927. 4th ed. Frankfurt: Suhrkamp Verlag, 1997.

Brown, Claire, and Jerry Walls. "Annihilationism: A Philosophical Dead End?" In *The Problem of Hell: A Philosophical Anthology*, edited by Joel Buenting, 45–64. London: Routledge, 2016.

Browning, Don S., ed. *Universalism vs. Relativism: Making Moral Judgments in a Changing, Pluralistic, and Threatening World*. Lanham, MD: Rowman and Littlefield, 2006.

Brunner, Emil. *The Christian Doctrine of God. Dogmatics Vol. 1*. Translated by Olive Wyon. London: Lutterworth, 1949.

———. *Dogmatik I: Die christliche Lehre von Gott*. Zürich: Zwingli-Verlag, 1946.

———. *Eternal Hope*. Translated by Harold Knight. London: Lutterworth, 1954.

———. *The Mediator: A Study of the Central Doctrine of the Christian Faith*. Translated by Olive Wyon. London: Lutterworth, 1934.

———. *Der Mittler: Zur Besinnung über den Christusglauben*. Tübingen: Mohr (Paul Siebeck), 1927.

———. *Die Mystik und das Wort*. 2nd ed. Tübingen: Mohr (Siebeck), 1928.

Buber, Martin. *I and Thou*. Translated by. Ronald Gregor Smith. Edinburgh: T. & T. Clark, 1942.

Buckareff, Andrei A. and Allen Plug. "Escaping Hell: Divine Motivation and the Problem of Hell." *Religious Studies* 41.1 (2005) 29–54

———. "Escaping Hell But Not Heaven." *International Journal of Philosophy and Religion* 77 (2015) 247–53.

Bulgakov, Sergei. *Agnets Bozhiy* [Агнец Божий]. Paris: YMCA, 1933.

———. *The Bride of the Lamb*. Translated by Boris Jakim. Grand Rapids: Eerdmans, 2002.

———. *The Lamb of God*. Translated by Boris Jakim. Grand Rapids: Eerdmans, 2008.

———. *Neviesta Agntsa* [Невеста Агнца]. Paris: YMCA, 1945.

———. *The Orthodox Church*. Translated by Lydia Kesich. Crestwood, NY: St. Vladimir's Seminary Press, 1988.

———. *Pravoslaviye* [Православие]. Paris: YMCA, 1935.

———. *Sophia: The Wisdom of God. An Outline of Sophiology*. Translated by Patrick Thompson, O. Fielding Clarke, and Xenia Braikevitc. 1937. Reprint. Hudson, NY: Lindisfarne, 1993.

Bultmann, Rudolf, *Kerygma and Myth: A Theological Debate*. Edited by Hans Werner Bartsch and translated by Reginald H. Fuller. New York: Harper & Row, 1961.

Butera, Giuseppe. "Incomplete Persons: Thomas Aquinas on Separated Souls and the Identity of the Human Person." In *Distinctions of Being: Philosophical Approaches to Reality*, edited by Nikolaj Zunic, 61–82. Washington, DC: Catholic University of America Press, 2013.

Butterfield, Herbert. *Christianity and History*. London: Bell, 1949.

Calvin, John. *Institutes of the Christian Religion*. Edited and translated by John T. McNeil and Ford Lewis Battles. The Library of Christian Classics. Vol. 21. Philadelphia: Westminster, 1960.

———. *Ioannis Calvini Opera Supersunt Omnia*. Edited by G. Baum, E. Cunitz, and E. Reuss. Vol. 5. Brunswick: Schwetschke, 1866.

Catechism of the Catholic Church: Revised in Accordance with the Official Latin Text Promulgated by Pope John Paul II. London: Chapman, 1999.

Chignell, Andrew. *What May I Hope? (Kant's Questions)*. London: Routledge, 2017.

Cilento, Adele. *Byzantine Mosaics in Norman Sicily: Palermo, Monreale, Cefalù.* Translated by Brian Eskenazi. Udine: Magnus, 2009.

Commissio Theologica Internationalis. "De quibusdam quaestionibus actualibus circa eschatologiam." *Gregorianum* 73 (1992) 395–435.

Connolly, Julie. "Charting a Course for Recognition: A Review Essay." *History of Human Sciences* 20.1 (2007) 133–44.

Cooper, John M., ed. *Plato: Complete Works.* Translated by G. M. A. Grube. Indianapolis: Hackett, 1997.

Corner, Mark. *Death Be Not Proud: The Problem with the Afterlife.* Bern: Lang, 2011.

Craig, William Lane. "'No Other Name': A Middle Knowledge Perspective on the Exclusivity of Salvation through Christ." *Faith and Philosophy* 6.2 (1989) 172–88.

———. *Reasonable Faith: Christian Truth and Apologetics.* Wheaton, IL: Crossway, 1994.

———. "Talbott's Universalism." *Religious Studies* 27.3 (1991) 297–308.

Cross, F. L., and E. A. Livingstone, eds. *The Oxford Dictionary of the Christian Church.* 3rd ed. Oxford: Oxford University Press, 1997.

Cullmann, Oscar. *Immortality of the Soul or Resurrection of the Dead? The Witness of the New Testament.* The Ingersoll Lecture on Human Immortality, Harvard University. 1955. Reprint. London: Epworth, 1958.

———. "Unsterblichkeit der Seele und Auferstehung der Toten. Das Zeugnis des Neuen Testaments." Festschrift für Karl Barth zum 70. Geburtstag, Teil I. *Theologische Zeitschrift* 12.2 (1956) 126–56.

Cunningham, Lawrence S., ed. *John Henry Newman: Heart Speaks to Heart. Selected Spiritual Writings.* Hyde Park, NY: New City, 2004.

Darbishire, Helen, ed. *The Poetical Works of John Milton.* Vol.1. Oxford: Oxford University Press, 1963.

Davies, Brian, and G. R. Evans, eds. *Anselm of Canterbury: The Major Works.* Oxford: Oxford University Press, 1998.

Davis, Stephen. "Universalism, Hell and the Fate of the Ignorant." *Modern Theology* 6 (1990) 173–86.

Dawkins, Richard. *The God Delusion.* London: Bantam, 2006.

De Grey, Aubrey. *Ending Aging: The Rejuvenation Breakthroughs That Could Reverse Human Aging in our Lifetime.* New York: St Martin's Press, 2007.

Den svenska psalmboken: antagen av 1986 års kyrkomöte. Stockholm: Verbum, 1986.

Denzinger, Heinrich and Adolf Schönmetzer, eds., *Enchiridion Symbolorum Definitionum et Declarationum de Rebus Fidei et Morum.* Freiburg: Herder, 1965.

Dieb, Nathan D. "The Precarious Status of Resurrection in Friedrich Schleiermacher's Glaubenslehre." *International Journal of Systematic Theology* 9.4 (2007) 398–414.

Dodd, C. H. *Interpretation of the Fourth Gospel.* Rev. ed. Cambridge: Cambridge University Press, 1968.

Donne, John. Devotions XVII "Nunc lento sonitu dicunt, morieris." In *The Works of John Donne,* vol. III, edited by Henry Alford, 574. London: John W Parker, 1839.

Eberl, Jason T. "Do Human Persons Persist between Death and Resurrection?" In *Metaphysics and God: Essays in Honor of Eleonore Stump,* edited by Kevin Tripe, 188–205. New York: Routledge, 2009.

Edwards, David L., with John Stott. *Essentials: A Liberal-Evangelical Dialogue.* London: Hodder and Stoughton, 1988.

Epicurus. "Letter to Menoeceus." In *The Epicurus Reader: Selected Writings and Testimonia*, translated and edited by Brad Inwood and L. P. Gerson, 28–31. Indianapolis: Hackett, 1994.

Evans, Craig A. *Matthew*. New Cambridge Bible Commentary. Cambridge: Cambridge University Press, 2012.

Feuerbach, Ludwig. *The Essence of Christianity*. Translated by George Elio. Mineola, NY: Dover, 2012.

———. *Das Wesens des Christentums*. Leipzig: Verlag von Otto Wigand, 1841.

Fergusson, David, and Marcel Sarot, eds. *The Future as God's Gift: Explorations in Christian Eschatology*. Edinburgh: T. & T. Clark, 2000

Fiddes, Paul. *Past Event and Present Salvation: The Christian Idea of Atonement*. London: Darton, Longman and Todd, 1989.

———. *The Promised End*. Oxford: Blackwell, 2000.

Frede, Michael. "On Aristotle's Conception of the Soul." In *Essays on Aristotle's De Anima*, edited by Martha C. Nussbaum and Amelie O. Rorty, 93–107. Oxford: Clarendon, 1992.

Gallaher, Brandon. "Antinomism, Trinity and the Challenge of Solov'ĕvan Pantheism in the Theology of Sergij Bulgakov." *Studies in Eastern European Thought* 64 (2012) 205–55.

Gavrilyuk, Paul. "Universal Salvation in the Eschatology of Sergius Bulgakov." *Journal of Theological Studies*, NS, 57.1 (2006) 110–32.

Geach, Peter T. *Providence and Evil*. Cambridge: Cambridge University Press, 1977.

Gerrish, B. A. *Tradition in the Modern World: Reformed Theology in the Nineteenth Century*. Chicago: University of Chicago Press, 1978.

Green, Clifford, ed. *Karl Barth: Theologian of Freedom*. London: Collins, 1989.

Gow, A. S. F., ed. and trans. *Theocritus*. 2 vols. Cambridge: Cambridge University Press, 1950.

Greggs, Tom. *Barth, Origen, and Universal Salvation: Restoring Particularity*. Oxford: Oxford University Press, 2009.

———. "'Jesus is Victor': Passing the Impasse of Barth on Universalism." *Scottish Journal of Theology* 60.2 (2007) 196–212.

———. "Pessimistic Universalism: Rethinking the Wider Hope with Bonhoeffer and Barth." *Modern Theology* 26.4 (2010) 495–510.

Greshake, Gisbert. *Auferstehung der Toten: Ein Beitrag zur gegenwärtigen theologischen Diskussion über die Zukunft der Geschichte*. Koinonia 10. Essen: Ludgerus, 1969.

———. "Die Leib-Seele-Problematik und die Vollendung der Welt." In *Naherwartung-Auferstehung-Unsterblichkeit: Untersuchungen zur christlichen Eschatologie*, edited by Gisbert Greshake and Gerhard Lohfink, 154–84. 4th ed. Freiburg: Herder, 1982.

———. "'Seele' in der Geschichte der christlichen Eschatologie: Ein Durchblick." In *Seele: Problembegriff christlicher Eschatologie*, edited by Wilhelm Breuning, 107–58. Quaestiones Disputatae 106. Freiburg: Herder, 1986.

Greshake, Gisbert, and Jacob Kremer. *Resurrectio mortuorum: Zum theologischen Verständnis der leiblichen Auferstehung*. 1986. Reprint. Darmstadt: Wissenschaftliche Buchgesellschaft, 1992.

Griffiths, Paul. *Decreation: The Last Things of All Creatures*. Waco, TX: Baylor University Press, 2014.

Hammond, Guy B. "Tillich on the Personal God." *The Journal of Religion* 44.4 (1964) 289–93.

Harder, Johannes, ed. *Blumhardt: Ansprachen, Predigten, Reden, Briefe: 1865–1917*. Neukirchen: Neukirchener Verlag, 1978.

Hebblethwaite, Brian. *The Christian Hope*. Rev. ed. Oxford: Oxford University Press, 2010.

———. *Philosophical Theology and Christian Doctrine*. Oxford: Blackwell, 2005.

Heidegger, Martin. *Being and Time*. Translated by John Macquarrie and Edward Robinson. Oxford: Blackwell, 1962.

———. "Letter on Humanism." In *Martin Heidegger: Basic Writings*, edited by David Farrell Krell, 253–54. New York: HarperCollins, 1993.

———. *Sein und Zeit. Gesamtausgabe*. Vol. 2. Edited by Friedrich-Wilhelm von Herrmann. Frankfurt: Klostermann, 1977.

Hampson, Daphne. *Kierkegaard: Exposition and Critique*. Oxford: Oxford University Press, 2013.

Hannay, Alastair, and Gordon D. Marino, eds. *The Cambridge Companion to Kierkegaard*. Cambridge: Cambridge University Press, 1998.

Härle, Wilfried. *Dogmatik*. Berlin: de Gruyter, 1995.

Hartnack, Justus. *An Introduction to Hegel's Logic*. Translated by Lars Aagaard-Mogensen and edited by Kenneth R. Westphal. Indianapolis, IN: Hackett, 1998.

Hick, John. *Death and Eternal Life*. Rev. ed. Louisville: Westminster/John Knox, 1994.

———. *Evil and the Love of God*. London: Macmillan, 1966.

———. "Jesus and the World Religions." In *The Myth of God Incarnate*, edited by John Hick, 167–85. London: SCM, 1977.

———. "A Pluralist View." In *More Than One Way? Four Views of Salvation in a Pluralist World*, edited by Dannis L. Okholm and Timothy R. Phillips, 29–59. Grand Rapids: Zondervan, 1995.

———. "Religious Pluralism and Salvation." *Faith and Philosophy* 5.4 (1988) 365–77.

Honneth, Axel. *The Struggle for Recognition*. Translated by Joel Anderson. Cambridge, MA: MIT, 1995.

Hoye, William J. *The Emergence of Eternal Life*. Cambridge: Cambridge University Press, 2013.

Howe, Charles A. *The Larger Faith: A Short History of American Universalism*. Boston: Skinner Book House, 1992.

International Theological Commission. "Some Current Questions in Eschatology." *The Irish Theological Quarterly* 58 (1992) 209–243.

Inwagen, Peter van, ed. *The Possibility of Resurrection and Other Essays in Christian Apologetics*. Boulder, CO: Westview, 1998.

Inwood, M. J. "Dasein." In *The Oxford Companion to Philosophy*, edited by Ted Honderich, 189. Rev. ed. Oxford: Oxford University Press, 2005.

———. "Martin Heidegger." In *The Oxford Companion to Philosophy*, edited by Ted Honderich, 371–75. Rev. ed. Oxford: Oxford University Press, 2005.

Isidor of Seville. *Isidori Hispalensis Episcopi Etymologiarum sive Originum libri XX*. Edited by W. M. Lindsay. Oxford: Oxford University Press, 1911.

Jackelén, Antje. *Time and Eternity: The Question of Time in Church, Science, and Theology*. Translated by Barbara Harshaw. West Conshohocken, PA: Templeton Foundation, 2005.

———. *Zeit und Ewigkeit*. Neukirchen-Vluyn: Neukirchener Verlag, 2002.

Jeanrond, Werner G. *Call and Response: The Challenge of Christian Life*. Dublin: Gill and Macmillan, 1995.

---. *Theological Hermeneutics: Development and Significance*. New York: Macmillan, 1991.

---. *A Theology of Love*. Edinburgh: T. & T. Clark, 2010.

Johnston, Mark. *Surviving Death*. Princeton: Princeton University Press, 2011.

Jüngel, Eberhard. *Death: The Riddle and the Mystery*. Translated by Iain and Ute Nicol. Edinburgh: St Andrew Press, 1975.

---. *Entsprechungen: Gott-Wahrheit-Mensch. Theologische Erörterungen*. Munich: Christian Kaiser, 1980.

---. "The Last Judgment as an Act of Grace." *Louvain Studies* 14 (1990) 389–405.

---. *Tod*. Stuttgart: Kreuz-Verlag, 1971.

Kant, Immanuel. *Critique of Pure Reason*. 1781/1787. Translated by Paul Guyer and Allen Wood. Cambridge: Cambridge University Press, 1998.

Kierkegaard, Søren. "At the Graveside." 1845. In *Three Discourses on Imagined Occasions*. Translated and edited Howard H. Hong and Edna H. Hong. Kierkegaard's Writings, vol. 10. Princeton: Princeton University Press, 1993.

---. *Samlede Værker*. Edited by A. B. Drachmann, J. L. Heiberg, and H. O. Lange. Copenhagen: Gyldendal, 1962.

---. *Søren Kierkegaard's Journals and Papers*. Translated and edited by Howard H. Hong and Edna H. Hong. Bloomington, IN: Indiana University Press, 1978.

---. "There will be a Resurrection of the Dead, of the Righteous—and of the Unrighteous." 1848. In *Christian Discourses: The Crisis and a Crisis in the Life of an Actress*. Translated and edited by Howard H. Hong and Edna H. Hong. Kierkegaard's Writings, vol. 17. Princeton: Princeton University Press, 1997.

Klein, Terrance W. "Karl Rahner on the Soul." *The Saint Anselm Journal* 6.1 (2008) 1–10.

Kornblatt, Judith Deutsch. *Divine Sophia: The Wisdom Writings of Vladimir Solovyov*. Ithaca, NY: Cornell, 2009.

Kronen, John, and Eric Reitan. *God's Final Victory: A Comparative Philosophical Case for Universalism*. London: Bloomsbury, 2011.

Kübler-Ross, Elizabeth. *On Death and Dying*. New York: Macmillan, 1969.

Küng, Hans. *Eternal Life?* Translated by Edward Quinn. London: SCM, 1984.

Kvanvig, Jonathan. *The Problem of Hell*. Oxford: Oxford University Press, 1993.

Lamberigts, Mathijs. "Pelagius and Pelagians." In *The Oxford Handbook on Early Christian Studies*, edited by Susan Ashbrook Harvey and David G. Hunter, 258–79. Oxford: Oxford University Press, 2008.

Le Goff, Jacques. *The Birth of Purgatory*. Translated by Arthur Goldhammer. Chicago: University of Chicago Press, 1984.

Lenehan, Kevin A. "*Etsi deus non daretur*: Bonhoeffer's Useful Misuse of Grotius' Maxim and Its Implications for Evangelization in the World Come of Age." In *The Bonhoeffer Legacy: Australasian Journal of Bonhoeffer Studies* 1 (2003) 34–60.

Lenin, Vladimir Ilyich. "Socialism and Religion." 1905. In *Lenin: Collected Works*, Vol. 10, edited and translated by Andrew Rothstein, 83–86. Moscow: Progress, 1962.

Levertov, Denise. "The Avowal." In *Denise Levertov: The Poetry of Engagement*, edited by Audrey T. Rogers, 184. London: Associated University Presses, 1993.

Lewis, C. S. *The Great Divorce*. 1945. Reprint. San Francisco: HarperSanFrancisco, 2001.

---. *The Last Battle*. 1956. Reprint. London: Collins, 2001.

Ludlow, Morwenna. *Universal Salvation: Eschatology in the Thought of Gregory of Nyssa and Karl Rahner*. Oxford: Oxford University Press, 2000.

Luther, Martin. *Luther's Works*. Edited by Jaroslav Pelikan and translated by George V. Schick. St. Louis: Concordia, 1968.

———. *Luther's Works: Career of the Reformer II*. Vol. 32. Edited by George W. Forell and translated by Charles M. Jacobs. Philadelphia: Fortress, 1958.

MacDonald, Gregory, ed. *All Shall be Well: Explorations in Universal Salvation and Christian Theology from Origen to Moltmann*. Eugene, OR: Cascade, 2011.

———. *The Evangelical Universalist*. Eugene, OR: Cascade, 2006.

MacGregor, Kirk. *Luis de Molina: The Life and Theology of the Founder of Middle Knowledge*. Grand Rapids: Zondervan, 2015.

Mandelbaum, Allen, trans. *The Divine Comedy of Dante Alighieri: Inferno*. Berkeley: University of California Press, 1980.

Matheson, Benjamin. "Escaping Heaven." *International Journal of Philosophy and Religion* 75 (2014) 197–206.

Martelet, Gustave SJ. *L'au-delà retrouvé. Christologie des fins dernières*. Paris: Desclée, 1974.

Martin, Michael, and Keith Augustine, eds. *The Myth of the Afterlife: The Case against Life after Death*. Lanham, MD: Rowan and Littlefield, 2015.

McCulloh, Gerald O., ed. *Man's Faith and Freedom: The Theological Influence of Jacobus Arminius*. Eugene, OR: Wipf and Stock, 2007.

McDannell, Colleen, and Bernard Lang. *Heaven: A History*. New Haven, CT: Yale University Press, 1988.

Merton, Thomas. *Thoughts in Solitude*. 1958. Reprint. New York: Farrar, Straus and Giroux, 1999.

Milton, John. *The Poetical Works of John Milton*, vol. 1. Edited by Helen Darbishire. Oxford: Oxford University Press, 1963.

Moltmann, Jürgen. *The Coming of God: Christian Eschatology*. Translated by Margaret Kohl. London: SCM, 1996.

———. *The Crucified God: The Cross of Christ as the Foundation and Criticism of Christian Theology*. Translated by R. A. Wilson and John Bowden. London: SCM, 1974.

———. *Experiences in Theology: Ways and Forms of Christian Theology*. Translated by Margaret Kohl. London: SCM, 2000.

———. *In the End—The Beginning: The Life of Hope*. Translated by Margaret Kohl. Minneapolis: Fortress, 2004.

———. "The Logic of Hell." In *God Will Be All in All: The Eschatology of Jürgen Moltmann*, edited by Richard Bauckham, 43–47. Edinburgh: T. & T. Clark, 1999.

———. *Sun of Righteousness, Arise! God's Future for Humanity and the World*. Translated by Margaret Kohl. Minneapolis: Fortress, 2010.

———. *Theology of Hope: On the Ground and Implications of a Christian Eschatology*. Translated by J. W. Leitch. London: SCM, 1967.

———. *The Trinity and the Kingdom of God: The Doctrine of God*. Translated by Margaret Kohl. London: SCM, 1981.

———. *The Way of Jesus Christ: Christology in Messianic Dimensions*. Translated by Margaret Kohl. London: SCM, 1990.

Morris, Paul. "Exiled from Eden: Jewish Interpretations of Genesis." In *A Walk in the Garden: Biblical, Iconographical and Literary Images of Eden*, edited by Paul Morris and Deborah Sawyer, 21–38. Sheffield, UK: Sheffield Academic Press, 1992.

Mühling, Markus. *Grundinformation Eschatologie: Systematische Theologie aus der Perspektive der Hoffnung*. Göttingen: Vandenhoeck & Ruprecht, 2007.

———. *The T. & T. Clark Handbook of Christian Eschatology*. Translated by Jennifer Adams-Maßmann and David Andrew Gilland. London: Bloomsbury, 2015.

Myers, David B. "Exclusivism, Eternal Damnation, and the Problem of Evil: A Critique of Craig's Molinist Soteriological Theodicy." *Religious Studies* 39.4 (2003) 407–19

———. "Rejoinder to William Lane Craig." *Religious Studies* 39.4 (2003) 427–30.

Neuner, Josef, and Jacques Dupuis, eds. *The Christian Faith in the Doctrinal Documents of the Catholic Church*. Rev. ed. London: Collins, 1983.

The New England Primer: Improved for the More Easy Attaining the True Reading of English: To Which Is Added the Assembly of Divines, and Mr. Cotton's Catechism.1777. Accessed 18 June 2016. Online: http://www.sacred-texts.com/chr/nep/1777/index.htm.

Nickelsburg, George W. E. *Resurrection, Immortality, and Eternal Life in Intertestamental Judaism*. Cambridge: Harvard University Press, 1972.

Nietzsche, Friedrich. *Also Sprach Zarathustra: Ein Buch für Alle und Keinen*. Leipzig: Verlag von E.W. Fritsch, 1885.

———. *Thus Spoke Zarathustra: A Book for All and None*. Edited and translated by Adrian del Caro. Cambridge: Cambridge University Press, 2006.

Oakes, Edward SJ. "Christ's Descent into Hell: The Hopeful Universalism of Hans Urs von Balthasar (1905–1988)." In *"All Shall Be Well": Explorations in Universal Salvation and Christian Theology. From Origen to Moltmann*, edited by Gregory MacDonald, 382–99. Eugene, OR: Cascade, 2011.

Oakes, Edward SJ, and David Moss, eds. *The Cambridge Companion to Hans Urs von Balthasar*. Cambridge: Cambridge University Press, 2004.

O'Callaghan, Paul. *Christ our Hope: An Introduction to Eschatology*. Washington, DC: Catholic University of America Press, 2011.

O'Donnell, John SJ. *Hans Urs von Balthasar*. London: Continuum, 1991.

Parry, Robin A., and Christopher H. Partridge, eds. *Universal Salvation? The Current Debate*. Carlisle, UK: Paternoster, 2003.

Pattison, George. *Heidegger on Death: A Critical Theological Essay*. Farnham, UK: Ashgate, 2013.

Peacocke, Arthur. "The Cost of New Life." In *The Work of Love: Creation as Kenosis*, edited by John Polkinghorne, 21–42. London: SPCK, 2001.

Petzet, Heinrich Wiegand. *Auf einen Stern zugehen. Begegnungen und Gespräche mit Martin Heidegger 1929–1976*. Frankfurt: Societäts Verlag, 1983.

Phan, Peter C. "Eschatology." In *The Cambridge Companion to Karl Rahner*, edited by Declan Marmion and Mary E. Hines, 179–81. Cambridge: Cambridge University Press, 2005.

Phillips, D. Z. *Death and Immortality*. London: Macmillan, 1970.

Pieper, Joseph. *On Hope*. Translated by Mary Frances McCarthy. San Francisco: Ignatius, 1986.

———. *Über die Hoffnung*. Leipzig: Hegner, 1935.

Pinker, Aron. "A New Interpretation of Job 19:26." *Journal of Hebrew Scriptures* 15.2 (2015) 1–23.

Pinnock, Clark. "The Destruction of the Finally Impenitent." *Criswell Theological Review* 4 (1990) 243–59.

Pitstick, Alyssa Lyra, and Edward T. Oakes. "Balthasar, Hell, and Heresy: An Exchange." *First Things*, December 2006, 25–32.

Plantinga, Alvin. *The Nature of Necessity*. Oxford: Clarendon, 1974.

Plath, Sylvia. *The Unabridged Journals of Sylvia Plath, 1950–1962*. Edited by Karen V. Kukil. New York: Anchor, 2000.

Polkinghorne, John. *The God of Hope and the End of the World*. New Haven, CT: Yale University Press, 2002.

Polkinghorne, John, and Michael Welker, eds. *The End of the World and the Ends of God*. Harrisburg, PA: Trinity, 2000.

Prusak, Bernard P. "Bodily Resurrection in Catholic Perspective." *Theological Studies* 61 (2000) 64–105.

Quenstedt, Johannes Andreas. *Theologia Didacto-Polemica*. Wittenberg: Quenstedt & Schumacher, 1685.

Rahner, Karl. *Foundations of the Christian Faith*. Translated by William Dych. New York: Crossroads, 1986.

———. *Geist in Welt: Zur Metaphysik der endlichen Erkenntnis bei Thomas von Aquin*. Innsbruck: Rauch, 1939.

———. "Das Leben der Toten." In *Schriften zur Theologie*, Vol. 4, 429–37. Einsiedeln: Benziger, 1960.

———. *On the Theology of Death*. Translated by Charles Henkley. New York: Herder and Herder, 1961.

———. *Spirit in the World*. Translated by William Dych. New York: Herder and Herder, 1968.

———. *Theological Investigations*. Vol. 4. Translated by Kevin Smyth. London: Darton, Longman and Todd, 1966.

———. *Theological Investigations*. Vol. 14. Translated by David Bourke. London: Darton, Longman and Todd, 1976.

———. *Theological Investigations*. Vol. 17. Translated by Margaret Kohl. New York: Crossroad, 1981.

———. *Zur Theologie des Todes*. Freiburg: Herder, 1958.

Raphael, Simcha Paull. *Jewish Views of the Afterlife*. 2nd ed. Lanham, MD: Rowman and Littlefield, 2009.

Ratzinger, Joseph. *Eschatology: Death and Eternal Life*. Translated by Michael Waldstein. Washington, DC: Catholic University of America Press, 1988.

Reitan, Eric. "Eternal Damnation and Blessed Ignorance: Is the Damnation of Some Incompatible with the Salvation of Any?" *Religious Studies* 38 (2002) 429–50.

———. "A Guarantee of Salvation?" *Faith and Philosophy* 24.4 (2007) 413–32.

Ricoeur, Paul. *Oneself as Another*. Translated by Kathleen Blarney. Chicago: University of Chicago Press, 1990.

———. *Parcours de la Reconnaissance*. Paris: Éditions Stock, 2004.

———. *The Path of Recognition*. Translated by David Pellauer. Cambridge: Harvard University Press, 2005.

———. *Soi-même comme un autre : L'ordre philosophique*. Paris: Éditions du Seuil, 1990.

Robinson, John A. T. *Honest to God*. London: SCM, 1963.

———. *In the End, God . . . The Christian Doctrine of the Last Things*. 1950. Reissued as a special edition and edited by Robin Parry. Eugene, OR: Pickwick, 2011.

———. "Universalism – A Reply." *Scottish Journal of Theology* 2 (1949) 378–80.
———. "Universalism – Is it Heretical?" *Scottish Journal of Theology* 2 (1949) 139–55.
Rolston, Holmes III, "Kenosis and Nature." In *The Work of Love: Creation as Kenosis*, edited by John Polkinghorne, 43–65. London: SPCK, 2001.
Rossetti, Christina. "A Better Resurrection." In *Selected Poems of Christina Rossetti*, edited by Katherine McGowran, 164. Ware, UK: Wordsworth, 2001.
Russell, Bertrand. "What I Believe." 1925. In *The Basic Writings of Bertrand Russell*, edited by Robert E. Egner and Lester E. Denonn, 344–67. London: Routledge, 2006.
Sakharov, Sophrony. *Saint Silouan the Athonite*. Translated by Rosemary Edmunds. Tolleshunt Knights: Stavropegic Monastery of St. John the Baptist, 1991.
———. *We Shall See Him as He Is*. Tolleshunt Knights: Stavropegic Monastery of St John the Baptist, 2004.
Sartre, Jean-Paul. *Being and Nothingness*. Translated by Hazel E. Barnes. London: Routledge, 2003.
Sayers, Dorothy, ed. and trans. With Barbara Reynolds. *The "Comedy" of Dante Alighieri the Florentine. Cantica II: Purgatory*. Harmondsworth, UK: Penguin, 1955.
Scanlon, James P. "Bulgakov, Sergei Nikolaevich (1871–1944)." In *Encyclopedia of Philosophy*, Vol. 1, edited by Paul Edwards. London: Macmillan, 1967.
Schaff, Philip. *Creeds of Christendom*. 1877. 3 vols. Reprint. Grand Rapids: Baker, 1984.
Schärtl, Thomas. "Bodily Resurrection: When Metaphysics Needs Phenomenology." In *Personal Identity and Resurrection: How Do We Survive Our Own Death?* edited by Georg Gasser, 103–25. Farnham, UK: Ashgate, 2010.
Scheeben, Matthias J. *Die Mysterien des Christentums*. 2nd ed. Freiburg: Herder, 1898.
———. *The Mysteries of Christianity*. Translated by Cyril Vollert. St Louis: Herder, 1946.
Schillebeeckx, Edward. *Church: The Human Story of God*. Translated by John Bowden. New York: Crossroad, 1990.
Schleiermacher, Friedrich. *The Christian Faith*. Translated and edited by H. R. Mackintosh and J. S. Stewart. 1928. Reprint. Edinburgh: T. & T. Clark, 1989.
———. *Der christliche Glaube*. 2nd ed. 1830–31. Reprint. Berlin: de Gruyter, 2008.
Schmid, Heinrich. *The Doctrinal Theology of the Evangelical Lutheran Church*. 1843. Translated by Charles Hay and Henry Jacobs. 4th ed. Philadelphia: Lutheran Publication Society, 1889.
Schopenhauer, Arthur. *Essays and Aphorisms*. Edited and translated by R. J. Hollingdale London: Penguin, 1970.
Seymour, Charles. *A Theodicy of Hell*. Studies in Philosophy and Religion, Vol. 20. Dordrecht: Kluwer Academic, 2000.
Sider, Robert D. "Credo Quia Absurdum?." *The Classical World* 73.7 (1980) 417–19.
Sider, Theodore. "Hell and Vagueness." *Faith and Philosophy* 19 (2002) 58–68.
Sim, David C. "The Man without the Wedding Garment (Matthew 22:11–13)." *The Heythrop Journal* 31 (1990) 165–78.
Spiegel, James S. "Annihilation, Everlasting Torment and Divine Justice." *International Journal of Philosophy and Theology* 76.3 (2015) 241–48.
Staume, David. *The Atheist Afterlife*. Victoria, BC: Agio Publishing House, 2009.
Stump, Eleonore. "Dante's Hell, Aquinas's Moral Theory, and the Love of God." *Canadian Journal of Philosophy* 6 (1986) 181–98.

———. "Resurrection and the Separated Soul." *The Oxford Handbook of Aquinas*, edited by David Davies and Eleonore Stump, 458–66. Oxford: Oxford University Press, 2012.

———. "Resurrection, Reassembly, and Reconstitution: Aquinas on the Soul." In *Die menschlishe Seele: Brauchen wir den Dualismus?* edited by Bruno Niederbacher and Edmund Runggaldier, 151–72. Frankfurt: Ontos Verlag, 2006.

Swinburne, Richard. *The Evolution of the Soul*. Rev. ed. Oxford: Oxford University Press, 1997.

———. "A Theodicy of Heaven and Hell." In *The Existence and Nature of God*, edited by A. Fredosso, 37–54. Notre Dame, IN: University of Notre Dame Press, 1983.

Talbott, Thomas. "The Doctrine of Everlasting Punishment." *Faith and Philosophy* 7 (1990) 19–42.

———. "Providence, Freedom, and Human Destiny." *Religious Studies* 26 (1990) 227–45.

———. *The Inescapable Love of God*. 2nd ed. Eugene, OR: Cascade Books, 2014.

Tanner, Katheryn. "God's Umpire." *First Things*, October 2015, 55–58.

———. "Incarnation, Cross, and Sacrifice: A Feminist-Inspired Reappraisal." *Anglican Theological Review* 86.1 (Winter 2004) 35–56.

Tanner, Norman P., ed. *Decrees of the Ecumenical Councils 1: Nicaea I to Lateran V*. Washington, DC: Georgetown University Press, 1990.

Tappert, Theodore G., ed. and trans. *The Book of Concord: The Confessions of the Evangelical Lutheran Church*. Philadelphia: Fortress, 1959.

Taylor, Jeremy. *The Rules and Exercises for Holy Dying*. 1651. London: George Bell and Sons, 1883.

Teilhard de Chardin, Pierre. *Le Milieu Divin*. Translated by Bernard Wall. London: Collins, 1960.

Tennyson, Alfred, Lord. "In Memoriam A. H. H." In *In Memoriam: Authoritative Text, Criticism*. Edited by Erik Gray. London: Norton, 2004.

Terry, Justyn. *The Justifying Judgement of God*. Paternoster Theological Monographs. Milton Keynes, UK: Paternoster, 2007.

Thielecke, Helmut. *Der evangelische Glaube*. 3 vols. Tübingen: Mohr (Siebeck), 1968–78.

Thiselton, Anthony. *Life and Death: A New Approach to the Last Things*. Grand Rapids: Eerdmans, 2012.

Tillich, Paul. *The Courage to Be*. 1952. Reprint. New Haven, CT: Yale University Press, 2000.

———. *Religiöse Verwirklichung*. Berlin: Furche-Verlag, 1930.

———. "The Right to Hope: A Sermon." *Neue Zeitschrift für Systematische Theologie und Religionsphilosophie* 7 (January 1965) 371–77.

Tipler, Frank. *The Physics of Immortality: Modern Cosmology, God and the Resurrection of the Dead*. New York: Doubleday, 1994.

Tolkien, J. R. R. "The Laws and Customs of the Eldar." In *Morgoth's Ring*. History of Middle Earth, Vol. 10, edited by Christopher Tolkien, 207–53. Boston: Houghton Mifflin, 1993.

Toner, Patrick. "St Thomas Aquinas on Death and the Separated Soul." *Pacific Philosophical Quarterly* 91.4 (2010) 587–99.

Tonstad, Linn Marie. "Review of *Christ and Horrors: The Coherence of Christology* by Marilyn McCord Adams." *Conversations in Religion and Theology* 8:1 (2010) 27–34.
Torrance, T. F. "Universalism or Election?" *Scottish Journal of Theology* 2 (1949) 310–18.
Travis, Stephen. *Christ and the Judgement of God.* 2nd ed. Milton Keynes, UK: Paternoster, 2008.
Trawny, Peter, ed. *Martin Heidegger: Überlegungen II-VI (Schwarze Hefte 1931–1938).* In *Gesamtausgabe.* Vol. 94. Frankfurt: Klostermann, 2014.
Troeltsch, Ernst. *The Christian Faith.* Edited by Gertrud von Le Fort and translated by Garrett E. Paul. Minneapolis: Fortress, 1991.
Troeltsch, Ernst, Marta Troeltsch, and Gertrud von Le Fort, *Glaubenslehre: Nach Heidelberger Vorlesungen aus den Jahren 1911 und 1912.* Munich: Duncker und Humboldt, 1925.
Tyacke, Nicholas. "The Rise of Arminianism Reconsidered." *Past & Present* 115 (May 1987) 201–16.
Unamuno, Miguel de. "Cartas inéditas de Miguel de Unamuno y Pedro Jiménez Ilundain." Edited by Hernán Benítez. *Revista de la Universidad de Buenos Aires* 3.9 (1949) 135–50.
———. *Del sentimiento trágico de la vida.* Madrid: Renacimiento, 1930.
United Methodist Church. *The Book of Discipline of the United Methodist Church.* Nashville, TN: United Methodist Publishing House, 2016.
Vattimo, Gianni. *Belief.* Translated by Luca D'Isandro and David Webb. Stanford, CA: Stanford University Press, 1999.
Verweyen, Hans-Jürgen. *Christologische Brennpunkte.* Essen: Ludgerus, 1977.
Volf, Miroslav. "The Final Reconciliation: Reflections on a Social Dimension of the Eschatological Transition." *Modern Theology* 16.1 (2000) 91–113.
Walker, D. P. *The Decline of Hell: Seventeenth-Century Discussions of Eternal Torment.* Chicago: University of Chicago Press, 1964.
Walls, Jerry. *Heaven, Hell, and Purgatory: A Protestant View of the Cosmic Drama.* Grand Rapids, MI: Brazos, 2015.
———. "A Hell of a Choice: Reply to Talbott." *Religious Studies* 40.2 (2004) 203–16.
———. *Hell: The Logic of Damnation.* Notre Dame, IN: University of Notre Dame Press, 1992.
———. *Purgatory: The Logic of Total Transformation.* Oxford: Oxford University Press, 2012.
Walls, Jerry, ed. *The Oxford Handbook of Eschatology.* Oxford: Oxford University Press, 2008.
Walsh, Brian. "Who Turned Out the Lights? The Light of the Gospel in a Post-Enlightenment Culture: An Inaugural Lecture." Toronto: Institute for Christian Studies, 1989.
Ward, Graham. "Postmodern Theology." In *Modern Theologians*, edited by David Ford and Rachel Muers, 322–38. 3rd ed. Oxford: Blackwell, 2005.
Ware, Kallistos. *How Are We Saved? The Understanding of Salvation in the Orthodox Tradition.* Minneapolis: Light and Life, 1996
———. *The Orthodox Way.* Crestwood, NY: St Vladimir's Press, 1995.
Watkin, Julia. "Kierkegaard's View of Death." *History of European Ideas* 12 (1990) 65–78.

Watson, John Richard. *An Annotated Anthology of Hymns.* Oxford: Oxford University Press, 2003.
Weil, Simone. *Gravity and Grace.* Translated by Emma Crawford and Mario von der Ruhr. London: Routledge, 2002.
———. *La pesanteur et la grâce.* Paris: Librairie Plon, 1947.
West, Thomas G., and Grace Starry West, eds. *Four Texts on Socrates: Plato's Euthyphro, Apology, and Crito, and Aristophanes' Clouds.* Rev. ed. Ithaca, NY: Cornell University Press, 1998.
Wilkinson, Robert J. *Tetragrammaton: Western Christians and the Hebrew Name of God.* Leiden: Brill, 2015.
Williams. Oscar, ed. *Modern Verse.* Rev. ed. New York: Pocket Books, 1958.
Wittgenstein, Ludwig. *Lectures and Conversations on Aesthetics, Psychology and Religious Belief.* Edited by Cyril Barrett. 1967. Reprint. Berkeley: University of California Press, 2007.
———. "Logisch-philosophische Abhandlung." *Annalen der Naturphilosophie* 14 (1921): 185–262.
———. *Tractatus Logico-Philosophicus.* Translated by Charles K. Ogden. London: Kegan Paul, 1922.
Wollheim, Richard, ed. *Hume on Religion.* London: Fontana, 1963.
Zucal, Silvano. *La teologia della morte in Karl Rahner.* Bologna: EDB, 1982.

www.ingramcontent.com/pod-product-compliance
Lightning Source LLC
Chambersburg PA
CBHW050618300426
44112CB00012B/1552